"*Sacred Reading* offers a superb introduction to Ignatian prayer that anyone can use. Too often Ignatian prayer is seen as something reserved only for Jesuits, for people trained in the Spiritual Exercises, or for those who have time for a directed retreat. But this book, created by experts in the traditions of Ignatian prayer, helps the reader to encounter Jesus through short scripture passages, inviting questions and accessible reflections. It's an innovative way to be invited, with gentle wisdom, into meeting Jesus in your prayer."

Rev. James Martin, S.J.
Author of *Jesus: A Pilgrimage*

"*Sacred Reading* has become a friend in prayer. I find the format particularly engaging as it inspires me to reflect on the Word of God in a prayerful, practical, and personal way."

Hilda Walter
Administrative Assistant at Gesu Parish
University Heights, Ohio

"*Sacred Reading* is an indispensable resource in deepening your prayer and devotional life. Lectio divina will change how you see your relationships—with the Lord, with others, and with yourself. Highly recommended!"

Most Rev. David L. Ricken
Bishop of Green Bay

"Communion with God increases dramatically as we grow in knowledge of God's Word. For most people the problem is simply getting started: determining where to begin. A most ancient and venerable practice is *lectio divina*, scripture reading that is meditation and contemplation but also application. *Sacred Reading* is an uncommonly useful tool in really getting into scripture in just this way."

Rev. Michael White and **Tom Corcoran**
Authors of *Rebuilt*

"In just six simple steps, *Sacred Reading* opens our minds and hearts to scripture in refreshing and profound ways. The daily meditations are clear and concise and yet filled with wisdom and promise. Reading scripture daily is good; reading scripture daily with *Sacred Reading* as your guide is awesome."

Marge Fenelon
Author of *Imitating Mary*

"This guide through the gospel texts of the daily lectionary offers a fully-embodied experience that includes the mind, heart, imagination, desire, and behavior. This way of prayerfully reading the gospels as the Spirit-empowered Word of God shows us how to open our lives to be continually formed in Christ."

Stephen J. Binz
Speaker and author of *Transformed by God's Word*

"In his apostolic exhortation 'The Joy of the Gospel,' Pope Francis invites us to be people of prayer. *Sacred Reading* is an excellent aid in responding to that invitation. This book offers a clear, helpful, and inspirational guide to deepen our love for scripture as we ponder God's Word and live it out in our daily lives."

Most Rev. Robert F. Morneau
Auxiliary Bishop Emeritus of Green Bay

"I am thankful for the ministry of the Apostleship of Prayer and their many ways of drawing people to active lives of encounter with a living God. I encourage anyone looking to deepen their prayer life to spend time learning this ancient practice and coming to know a God who dances freely in our imaginations if we will but go there with him."

Tim Muldoon
Author of *Six Sacred Rules for Families*

"*Sacred Reading* is the perfect companion for the lectio journey."

Sonja Corbitt
Author of *Unleashed*

SACRED READING

The 2017 Guide to Daily Prayer

Apostleship of Prayer

Douglas Leonard, Executive Director

AVE MARIA PRESS AVE Notre Dame, Indiana

Founded in 1865, Ave Maria Press is a ministry of the United States Province of Holy Cross.

www.avemariapress.com

Paperback: ISBN-13 978-1-59471-695-9

E-book: ISBN-13 978-1-59471-696-6

Cover image © Thinkstock.

Cover and text design by David Scholtes.

Printed and bound in the United States of America.

CONTENTS

INTRODUCTION

Christians throughout the world are rediscovering a powerful, ancient form of prayer known as sacred reading (*lectio divina*) that invites communion with God through scripture reading and contemplation. What better way to deepen one's friendship with Jesus Christ, the Word of God, than by prayerfully encountering him in the daily gospel reading? This book will set you on a personal prayer journey with Jesus from the start of Advent in November 2016 through the end of Ordinary Time in December 2017: the entire Church year.

Sacred reading is a spiritual practice that, guided by the Holy Spirit, invites you to interact with the words of the daily gospel. As you read and pray this way, you may find—as many others have—that the Lord speaks to you in intimate and surprising ways. The reason for this is simple: as we open our hearts to Jesus, he opens his heart to us.

St. Paul prays beautifully for his readers:

> For this reason I kneel before the Father, from whom every family in heaven and on earth is named, that he may grant you in accord with the riches of his glory to be strengthened with power through his Spirit in the inner self, and that Christ may dwell in your hearts through faith; that you, rooted and grounded in love, may have strength to comprehend with all the holy ones what is the breadth and length and height and depth, and to know the love of Christ that surpasses knowledge, so that you may be filled with all the fullness of God. (Eph 3:14–19)

This book moves you through each day's gospel by prompting you at each step of lectio divina, getting you started with reading, observing, praying, listening, and resolving to act. But most important is your own response to the Word and the Spirit for that is how you will grow in your relationship with Jesus. If you are sincerely seeking God, the Holy Spirit will lead you in this process.

How to Use This Book

The *Sacred Reading* prayer book is intended to guide your prayerful reading during the entire Church year. (Small booklets, suitable for use in parish groups, are also available for Advent and Lent.) Each weekday reflection begins with the date, and some include a reference to the solemnity, feast, or sometimes a memorial on that day for which there is a special lectionary gospel reading. When these are indicated, the regular lectionary gospel reading for that day has been replaced with the gospel reading used to celebrate the solemnity or feast. Sunday reflections include both the date and its place in the liturgical calendar; any Sunday reading that includes a reference to a feast day rather than its place in the liturgical calendar uses the gospel reading for the feast day. For the sake of simplicity, other feast days are not cited when their gospel reading has not been used. Due to the length of the gospel readings during Lent, some have been shortened. The citation for shortened readings will first show the reading that is included in the book and will then show the citation for the day's complete reading in parentheses.

In prayerful reading of the daily gospels throughout the year—including feast days, days during the high seasons, and days in Ordinary Time—you join your prayers with those of believers all over the world. In addition to reading the gospel for each season of the liturgical calendar, each day you will be invited to reflect on the gospel text for the day in six simple but profound steps:

1. Know that God is present with you and ready to converse.

At all times God is everywhere, including where you are in this very moment. The human mind is incapable of fully grasping the mystery of God, but we do know some things about God from scripture. God is the transcendent ground of all being, invisible, eternal, and infinite in power. God is Love, with infinite love for you and me. God is one with and revealed through the Word, Jesus Christ, who became flesh. Through him all things were made, and by him and for him all things subsist. Jesus is the Way, the Truth, and the Life. He says that those who know him also know his Father. Through the passion, death, and resurrection of Jesus, we are reconciled with God. If we believe in Jesus Christ, we become the sons and daughters of Almighty God.

God gives us the Holy Spirit to lead us to truth and understanding. The Holy Spirit also gives us power to live obedient to the teachings of Jesus. The Holy Spirit draws us to prayer and works in us as we pray. No wonder we come into God's presence with gladness! All God's ways are good and beautiful. We can get to know God better by encountering God in the Word, which is Jesus himself.

The prayer prompt at the beginning of each day's reading is just that: a prompt, something to get you started. In fact, all the elements in the process of sacred reading are meant to prompt you to your own conversations with God. After reading the prompt, feel free to continue to pray in your own words: respond in your own way, pray in your own way, and hear God speaking to you personally. Your goal is to make sacred reading your own prayer time each day.

2. Read the gospel.

The entire Bible is the Word of God, but the gospels (Matthew, Mark, Luke, and John) contain the story of Jesus' life, his teachings, his works, his passion and death on the cross, his resurrection on the third day, and his ascension into heaven. Because of this, the Sacred Reading series (the prayer books as well as the seasonal booklets for Advent/Christmas and Lent/Easter) concentrates on praying with the daily gospel readings.

The gospels interpret Jesus' ministry for us. Much more, by the Holy Spirit, we can find in the gospels the very person of Jesus Christ. Prayerful reading of the daily gospel is an opportunity to draw close to the Lord: Father, Son, and Holy Spirit. As we pray with the gospels, we can be transformed by the grace of God, enlightened, strengthened, and moved. Seek to read each day's gospel passage with a complete openness to what God is saying to you. Many who pray with the daily gospel recommend rereading the gospel passage several times.

3. Notice what you think and feel as you read the gospel.

Sacred reading can involve every faculty—mind, heart, emotions, soul, spirit, sensations, imagination, and much more—though usually not all at once. Different passages touch different keys in us. Sometimes we may laugh. Sometimes we may need to stop and worship before we continue. Sometimes we will be puzzled, amazed, stung, abashed, reminded of something lovely, or reminded of something we had wanted to forget.

Seek to feel all of your emotions as you read. Apply your intellect, too. You will confront problems of context and exegesis on a daily basis. That's okay. Sometimes you may experience very little. That's okay, too. God is always at work. Give yourself to the gospel reading and take from it what is there for you each day.

Most important, notice what in particular jumps out at you, whatever it may be. It may be a word, a phrase, a character, an image, a pattern, an emotion, a sensation—some arrow to your heart. Whatever it is, pay attention to it because the Holy Spirit is using it to accomplish something in you.

Sometimes a particular gospel passage repeats during the liturgical year of the Church. To pray through the same gospel passage even on successive days presents no problem whatsoever to your sacred reading. St. Ignatius of Loyola, founder of the Jesuits and author of *The Spiritual Exercises*, actually recommends repeated meditation on passages of scripture. Read in the Spirit, gospel passages have unlimited potential to reveal to us the truths we are ready to receive. For the receptive soul, the Word of God has boundless power to illuminate and transform the prayerful believer.

4. *Pray as you are led for yourself and others.*

Praying is simply talking with God. Believe God hears you. Believe God will answer you. Believe God knows what you need even before you ask. Jesus says so in Matthew 6:8. Your conversation with God can go far beyond asking for things, though. You may thank, praise, worship, rejoice, mourn, explain, or question, revealing your fears, seeking understanding, or asking forgiveness. Your conversation with God has no limits. God is the ideal conversationalist, and God wants to spend time with you.

Being human, we can't help being self-absorbed, but praying is not just about our own needs. We are often moved by the gospel to pray for others. We will regularly remember our loved ones in prayer. Sometimes we will be led to pray for someone who has hurt us. At other times we will be moved to pray for a class of people in need wherever they are in the world, such as persecuted Christians, refugees, the mentally ill, teachers, the unborn, or the lonely.

We may also pray with the universal Church by praying for the pope's prayer intentions. Those intentions are entrusted to the Apostleship of Prayer and are available through its website and its annual and monthly leaflets. You may get your own copy of this year's papal prayer intentions by contacting the Apostleship of Prayer. The Apostleship is the pope's prayer group and has more than fifty million members worldwide. Jesus asked us to unite in prayer, promising that the Father would grant us whatever we ask in his name, and it is during this time of sacred reading that we take advantage of this invitation to speak with God for ourselves and others.

5. *Listen to Jesus.*

Jesus the Good Shepherd speaks to his own sheep, who hear his voice (see Jn 10:27). This listening is a most wonderful time in your prayer experience. The italicized words in this passage are the words I felt impressed upon my heart as I prayed with these readings. I included them in order to help you listen more actively for whatever it is the Lord might be saying to you.

Jesus speaks to all in the gospels, but in *Sacred Reading*, he can now speak exclusively to you. If you wish, write down what he says to you and reread his words during the day. Put all of Jesus' words to you in a folder or keep a spiritual notebook. Believers through the ages have recorded the words of Jesus to them, holy mystics and ordinary believers alike.

It takes faith to hear the voice of Jesus. This faith will grow as you practice listening. Ideally, we will learn to hear what Jesus is saying to us all day long, as we face difficult situations perhaps. Listening to the voice of Jesus is practicing the presence of God. As St. Paul said, "In him we live and move and have our being" (Acts 17:28).

St. Ignatius of Loyola called this conversation with Jesus *colloquy.* That word simply means that two or more people are talking. St. Ignatius even urges us to include the saints in our prayer conversations. We believe in the Communion of Saints. If you have a patron saint, don't be afraid to talk to him or her. In her autobiography, St. Thérèse of Lisieux, a member of the Apostleship of Prayer, describes how she spoke often with Mary and Joseph, as well as Jesus.

6. Ask God to show you how to live today.

Pope Benedict XVI commented that sacred reading is not complete without a call to action; something in our praying leads us to do something in our day. Perhaps we find an opportunity to serve, to love, to give, to lead, or to do something good for someone else. Perhaps we find occasion to repent, to forgive, to ask forgiveness, to make amends. Open your heart to anything God might want you to do. Try to keep the conversation with God going all day long.

Asking God to show you how to live is the last step of the *Sacred Reading* prayer time, but that doesn't mean you need to end it here. Keep it going. You may drift off in the presence of God, lose attention, or even fall asleep, but you can come back. God is always present, seeking to love you and to be loved. God is always seeking to lead us to the green pastures. God is our strength, our rock, our ever-present help in time of trouble. God is full of mercy, ready to forgive us again and again. God sees us through very difficult times. God heals us. God gives his life to us constantly. God is our Maker, Father, Mother, Lover, Servant, Savior, and Friend. We know that from the Gospel. He is an inexhaustible spring of blessing and holiness in our innermost selves. The sanctification of our souls is God's work, not our own.

As you read, ask the Holy Spirit to lead you in this process. With genuine faith, open yourself to respond to the Word and the Spirit, and your relationship with Jesus will continue to deepen and grow just as the infant Jesus grew within the womb of the Blessed Mother. This in turn will lead you to share the love of Christ with all those you encounter just as the Blessed Mother draws all those who encounter her directly to her Son.

Other Resources to Help You

These Sacred Reading resources, both the seasonal books and this annual prayer book, are enriched by the spirituality of the Apostleship of Prayer. Since 1844 our mission has been to encourage Catholics to pray each day for the good of the world, the Church, and the prayer intentions of the Holy Father. In particular, we encourage Christians to respond to the loving gift of Jesus Christ by making a daily offering of themselves. As we give the Lord our hearts, we ask him to make them like his own heart, full of love, mercy, and peace.

These prayer books are intended to guide you to a prayer experience that you will find personally helpful and spiritually enriching. In addition to the daily prayers in the book, you can also adapt your prayer time in ways that are best suited to your particular needs. For example, some choose to continue to reflect upon each day's reading in writing, either in the book or in a separate journal or notebook, to create a record of their spiritual journey for the entire year. Others supplement their daily reading from the book with online resources, such as those available through the Apostleship of Prayer website.

For more information about the Apostleship of Prayer (the "pope's worldwide prayer network") and about the other resources we have developed to help men and women cultivate habits of daily prayer, visit our website at apostleshipofprayer.org.

I pray that this experience may help you walk closely with God every day.

Douglas Leonard, PhD
Executive Director
Apostleship of Prayer

We Need Your Feedback!
Ave Maria Press and the Apostleship of Prayer would like to hear from you. After you've finished reading, please go to avemariapress. com/feedback to take a brief survey about your experience with *Sacred Reading: The 2017 Guide to Daily Prayer.* We'll use your input to make next year's book even better.

The Advent and Christmas Seasons

INTRODUCTION

A dvent is all about waiting for Jesus Christ. The gospel readings of Advent make us mindful of three ways we await Jesus: past, present, and future. First, we remember and accompany Mary, Joseph, and the newborn Jesus. Second, we prepare for the celebration of his birth this Christmas so that the day doesn't pass us by with just meaningless words and worthless presents. Third, we anticipate the second coming of Jesus Christ, who will come in power and glory for everyone to see and establish his kingdom of peace and justice upon the earth.

Christ is born, and we follow him in exile and in those joyful early years with the Holy Family. We are blessed, but we are challenged, too, to understand the ways of God and how we personally may understand and respond to them now.

Sunday, November 27, 2016
First Sunday of Advent

Know that God is present with you and ready to converse.

Many of us learned as children that God is everywhere. St. Augustine in his *Confessions* details his slow realization that God is wholly and infinitely present in every place at once, for God is not impersonal substance distributed through the created universe. St. Ignatius taught his followers to seek God in all things. So we turn to God's Word, knowing God is present and ready to speak to us.

When you are ready, lift your heart to God and receive God in the Word.

Read the gospel: Matthew 24:37–44.

Jesus said, "For as the days of Noah were, so will be the coming of the Son of Man. For as in those days before the flood they were eating and drinking, marrying and giving in marriage, until the day Noah entered the ark, and they knew nothing until the flood came and swept them all away, so too will be the coming of the Son of Man. Then two will be in the field; one will be taken and one will be left. Two women will be grinding meal together; one will be taken and one will be left. Keep awake therefore, for you do not know on what day your Lord is coming. But understand this: if the owner of the house had known in what part of the night the thief was coming, he would have stayed awake and would not have let his house be broken into. Therefore you also must be ready, for the Son of Man is coming at an unexpected hour."

Notice what you think and feel as you read the gospel.

Jesus warns us to be ready for his return. We are preparing to celebrate his birth in Bethlehem, preparing to receive him fully into our hearts as our redeemer, the one who makes us God's own children by his birth, death, and resurrection. We are preparing to see him in heaven, when we will know him as he knows us. We are also preparing to see him at the Second Coming at the end of time, when he shall judge all people. God help us to prepare well.

Pray as you are led for yourself and others.

"Jesus, come to me. I want to walk with you today and every day. I pray for all those souls you have given me to pray for, including those I love, those who need you and your saving power . . ." (Continue in your own words.)

Listen to Jesus.

My heart aches for souls who have strayed from me, who cannot believe and love. Love is long. Pray for them in my love; unite with me, beloved. What else is Jesus saying to you?

Ask God to show you how to live today.

"Lord, make it easy for me to mention your holy name and to give you the glory for your saving love for me. I praise you and thank you, marvelous Lord. Amen."

Monday, November 28, 2016

Know that God is present with you and ready to converse.

"Jesus offers salvation to all. He is with me now, ready to do his work in my soul if I let him."

Read the gospel: Matthew 8:5–11.

When Jesus entered Capernaum, a centurion came to him, appealing to him and saying, "Lord, my servant is lying at home paralyzed, in terrible distress." And he said to him, "I will come and cure him." The centurion answered, "Lord, I am not worthy to have you come under my roof; but only speak the word, and my servant will be healed. For I also am a man under authority, with soldiers under me; and I say to one, 'Go,' and he goes, and to another, 'Come,' and he comes, and to my slave, 'Do this,' and the slave does it." When Jesus heard him, he was amazed and said to those who followed him, "Truly I tell you, in no one in Israel have I found such faith. I tell you, many will come from east and west and will eat with Abraham and Isaac and Jacob in the kingdom of heaven."

Notice what you think and feel as you read the gospel.

The good centurion has great faith. He also loves his servant who lies at home paralyzed and suffering. He understands the authority of the Lord to heal. Most touching, the centurion understands his own unworthiness. Jesus is moved by this man and holds him up as an example to us.

Pray as you are led for yourself and others.

"God, you welcome strangers and sinners into your kingdom. You welcome me. I love you and pray now for people I know who need your healing . . ." (Continue in your own words.)

Listen to Jesus.

You have faith, child. Apply it in prayer for those who come to your mind. This is how you may join with me every day to spread the kingdom of God to those in need. What else is Jesus saying to you?

Ask God to show you how to live today.

"Lord, you are great, and I am so small. But if you are with me nothing shall be impossible. Let God's holy will be done on earth as it is in heaven. Amen."

Tuesday, November 29, 2016

Know that God is present with you and ready to converse.

"Your disciples were blessed to see you, Lord. I am your disciple, too. Let me see you here and now."

Read the gospel: Luke 10:21–24.

At that same hour Jesus rejoiced in the Holy Spirit and said, "I thank you, Father, Lord of heaven and earth, because you have hidden these things from the wise and the intelligent and have revealed them to infants; yes, Father, for such was your gracious will. All things have been handed over to me by my Father; and no one knows who the Son is except the Father, or who the Father is except the Son and anyone to whom the Son chooses to reveal him."

Then turning to the disciples, Jesus said to them privately, "Blessed are the eyes that see what you see! For I tell you that many prophets and kings desired to see what you see, but did not see it, and to hear what you hear, but did not hear it."

Notice what you think and feel as you read the gospel.

Jesus prays aloud, rejoicing in the Spirit, blessing his Father for the ways God chooses to reveal the Son to people. He tells his disciples how blessed they are to have seen him, for they are not prophets and kings, nor the wise and the intelligent.

Pray as you are led for yourself and others.

"Lord, my election to your kingdom is your election. I depend entirely upon you . . ." (Continue in your own words.)

Listen to Jesus.

My child, pray too for others who do not yet know me. God wills that all may come. What else is Jesus saying to you?

Ask God to show you how to live today.

"Lord, give me humility to trust your working in my life and the lives of those I pray for. Give me awareness of my blessedness in knowing you. Amen."

Wednesday, November 30, 2016
Saint Andrew, Apostle

Know that God is present with you and ready to converse.

"Lord, you call me to follow you. Let me immediately obey your call."

Read the gospel: Matthew 4:18–22.

As Jesus walked by the Sea of Galilee, he saw two brothers, Simon, who is called Peter, and Andrew his brother, casting a net into the lake—for they were fishermen. And he said to them, "Follow me, and I will make you fish for people." Immediately they left their nets and followed him. As he went from there, he saw two other brothers, James son of Zebedee and his brother John, in the boat with their father Zebedee, mending their nets, and he called them. Immediately they left the boat and their father, and followed him.

Notice what you think and feel as you read the gospel.

Jesus doesn't spend time getting to know those whom he calls to be his followers because he already knows them. Besides, he knows they will be changed men by the power of his blood on Calvary, his resurrection, and the coming of the Holy Spirit upon them.

Pray as you are led for yourself and others.

"I will to follow you, Jesus, in every area of my life, for I believe your teaching and your words of salvation . . ." (Continue in your own words.)

Listen to Jesus.

I give you grace to live for me today, dear disciple, for you come to me with your heart. What else is Jesus saying to you?

Ask God to show you how to live today.

"Reveal to me, Lord, the parts of me and my life that I try to hide or withhold from you so with your help I can turn them over to you. Amen."

Thursday, December 1, 2016

Know that God is present with you and ready to converse.

"Lord, give me grace to hear your words and act on them."

Read the gospel: Matthew 7:21, 24–27.

Jesus said to his disciples, "Not everyone who says to me, 'Lord, Lord,' will enter the kingdom of heaven, but only one who does the will of my Father in heaven. . . .

"Everyone then who hears these words of mine and acts on them will be like a wise man who built his house on rock. The rain fell, the floods came, and the winds blew and beat on that house, but it did not fall, because it had been founded on rock. And everyone who hears these words of mine and does not act on them will be like a foolish man who built his house on sand. The rain fell, and the floods came, and the winds blew and beat against that house, and it fell—and great was its fall!"

Notice what you think and feel as you read the gospel.

Jesus says that not what we say but what we do in response to the Word of God is the ticket into the kingdom of heaven. If we do the will of the Father, we have wisely built our house on a rock.

Pray as you are led for yourself and others.

"Jesus, be my rock. I offer myself to do the Father's will. I offer myself in the service of you and others . . ." (Continue in your own words.)

Listen to Jesus.

My Father's will is all around you, beloved. Find God in all your circumstances; look for God in all your choices. What else is Jesus saying to you?

Ask God to show you how to live today.

"Lord, give me eyes to see today. I seek you. I seek to do your will. Amen."

Friday, December 2, 2016

Know that God is present with you and ready to converse.

"Lord, let me see and believe in your power in my life. Teach me by your Word today."

Read the gospel: Matthew 9:27–31.

As Jesus went on from there, two blind men followed him, crying loudly, "Have mercy on us, Son of David!" When he entered the house, the blind men came to him; and Jesus said to them, "Do you believe that I am able to do this?" They said to him, "Yes, Lord." Then he touched their eyes and said, "According to your faith let it be done to you." And their eyes were opened. Then Jesus sternly ordered them, "See that no one knows of this." But they went away and spread the news about him throughout that district.

Notice what you think and feel as you read the gospel.

The blind men want to be healed, but Jesus questions their faith. When he touches them, he says "according to your faith let it be done to you." They are healed.

Pray as you are led for yourself and others.

"Lord, I ask for faith to be healed in my own body, mind, and soul. Give me faith that pleases you . . ." (Continue in your own words.)

Listen to Jesus.

Faith is action obeying God, dear servant. I grant you what you ask. I love you. What else is Jesus saying to you?

Ask God to show you how to live today.

"Open my eyes to every little way I may obey God and serve my neighbor. Let me act in the power of the faith, hope, and love you give me. Thank you, Lord. Amen."

Saturday, December 3, 2016

Know that God is present with you and ready to converse.

You are here to command me, Lord, for I am your servant. Let your servant listen to your Word now.

Read the gospel: Matthew 9:35–10:1, 5a, 6–8.

Then Jesus went about all the cities and villages, teaching in their synagogues, and proclaiming the good news of the kingdom, and curing every disease and every sickness. When he saw the crowds, he had compassion for them, because they were harassed and helpless, like sheep without a shepherd. Then he said to his disciples, "The harvest is plentiful, but the laborers are few; therefore ask the Lord of the harvest to send out laborers into his harvest."

Then Jesus summoned his twelve disciples and gave them authority over unclean spirits, to cast them out, and to cure every disease and every sickness. . . .

These twelve Jesus sent out with the following instructions: "Go . . . to the lost sheep of the house of Israel. As you go, proclaim the good news, 'The kingdom of heaven has come near.' Cure the sick, raise the dead, cleanse the lepers, cast out demons. You received without payment; give without payment."

Notice what you think and feel as you read the gospel.

Jesus says God seeks laborers for the great harvest of souls. We are to pray for more laborers. To those who do labor for the harvest, Jesus gives power to serve in every way he wills. We received without payment and so should we give, knowing that Jesus will give us what we need for this work.

Pray as you are led for yourself and others.

"I pray for laborers to go into God's harvest, Lord. Give them and me a great and generous spirit to serve others . . ." (Continue in your own words.)

Listen to Jesus.

Your prayers are answered. I give you power to serve. What else is Jesus saying to you?

Ask God to show you how to live today.

"Give me discernment, dear Jesus, to recognize the little actions I can make to serve you as well as guidance to act upon opportunities to serve you in larger ways. Amen."

Sunday, December 4, 2016
Second Sunday of Advent

Know that God is present with you and ready to converse.

The Word of God is Truth, but we must hear that truth in the Spirit of the ones who wrote the scriptures as St. Peter says in his epistles. We should know, Peter continues, that no scripture is of purely private interpretation. The Church has the final word in interpretation of the Word. Today the images in the gospels are both beautiful and frightening.

"Lord, sometimes your Word is gentle, sometimes it is harsh. Let me be open to all and come to true understanding and repentance."

Read the gospel: Matthew 3:1–12.

In those days John the Baptist appeared in the wilderness of Judea, proclaiming, "Repent, for the kingdom of heaven has come near." This is the one of whom the prophet Isaiah spoke when he said,

"The voice of one crying out in the wilderness:
'Prepare the way of the Lord,
    make his paths straight.'"

Now John wore clothing of camel's hair with a leather belt around his waist, and his food was locusts and wild honey. Then the people of Jerusalem and all Judea were going out to him, and all the region along the Jordan, and they were baptized by him in the river Jordan, confessing their sins.

But when he saw many Pharisees and Sadducees coming for baptism, he said to them, "You brood of vipers! Who warned you to flee from the wrath to come? Bear fruit worthy of repentance. Do not presume to say to yourselves, 'We have Abraham as our ancestor'; for I tell you, God is able from these stones to raise up children to Abraham. Even now the axe is lying at the root of the trees; every tree therefore that does not bear good fruit is cut down and thrown into the fire.

"I baptize you with water for repentance, but one who is more powerful than I is coming after me; I am not worthy to carry his sandals. He will baptize you with the Holy Spirit and fire. His winnowing-fork is in his hand, and he will clear his threshing-floor and will gather his wheat into the granary; but the chaff he will burn with unquenchable fire."

Notice what you think and feel as you read the gospel.

John the Baptist, a man of rough appearance, preaches to the people in the wilderness, baptizing those who repent in the Jordan. But he calls the professed religious of his day "vipers," warning them of destruction because they do not bear good fruit. Then he prophesizes about the coming Messiah, who will baptize with the Holy Spirit and fire, as Isaiah had said.

Pray as you are led for yourself and others.

"John had a mission. He spoke your truth. He spoke of you, my Jesus. Let me be as committed and as true as John in your service . . ." (Continue in your own words.)

Listen to Jesus.

I am gathering you into the granary. I wash away your sins so you may bear good fruit. Stay close to me, beloved servant. What else is Jesus saying to you?

Ask God to show you how to live today.

"I praise and adore you, my Lord, my Savior. Baptize me with your Holy Spirit that I may have power to serve. Amen."

Monday, December 5, 2016

Know that God is present with you and ready to converse.

"Lord, I bow to your authority. By your Word you have power to forgive sins and to heal."

Read the gospel: Luke 5:17–26.

One day, while Jesus was teaching, Pharisees and teachers of the law were sitting nearby (they had come from every village of Galilee and Judea and from Jerusalem); and the power of the Lord was with him to heal. Just then some men came, carrying a paralyzed man on a bed. They were trying to bring him in and lay him before Jesus; but finding no way to bring him in because of the crowd, they went up on the roof and let him down with his bed through the tiles into the middle of the crowd in front of Jesus. When he saw their faith, he said, "Friend, your sins are forgiven you." Then the scribes and the Pharisees began to question, "Who is this who is speaking blasphemies? Who can forgive sins but God alone?" When Jesus perceived their questionings, he answered them, "Why do you raise such questions in your hearts? Which is easier, to say, 'Your sins are forgiven you,' or to say, 'Stand up and walk'? But so that you may know that the Son of Man has authority on earth to forgive sins"—he said to the one who was paralyzed—"I say to you, stand up and take your bed and go to your home." Immediately he stood up before them, took what he had been lying on, and went to his home, glorifying God. Amazement seized all of them, and they glorified God and were filled with awe, saying, "We have seen strange things today."

Notice what you think and feel as you read the gospel.

That day the people see great things—the paralyzed man on a bed; the crowd; the letting him down, bed and all, through the roof right in front of Jesus; Jesus forgiving him; the scribes and Pharisees questioning his authority; Jesus asserting his authority; and the healing of the paralytic, who takes up his bed and goes home, glorifying God. Then all of them, filled with awe, glorify God.

Pray as you are led for yourself and others.

"Lord, let me appear before you now, for I need your forgiveness and healing. You can make me well and make me whole . . ." (Continue in your own words.)

Listen to Jesus.

I do as you ask, my child. Strive to sin no more. What else is Jesus saying to you?

Ask God to show you how to live today.

"Jesus, I know that you are still working wonders today. Let me recognize them and glorify you. Amen."

Tuesday, December 6, 2016

Know that God is present with you and ready to converse.

"Word of God, Jesus, let any part of me that has gone astray return to you."

Read the gospel: Matthew 18:12–14.

Jesus asked his disciples, "What do you think? If a shepherd has a hundred sheep, and one of them has gone astray, does he not leave the ninety-nine on the mountains and go in search of the one that went astray? And if he finds it, truly I tell you, he rejoices over it more than over the ninety-nine that never went astray. So it is not the will of your Father in heaven that one of these little ones should be lost."

Notice what you think and feel as you read the gospel.

This little parable speaks of the love of the shepherd for his sheep, emphasizing his concern for the lost sheep and his joy in finding and returning the lost sheep to the fold. So the Father wills that not one of the sheep, "these little ones," be lost.

Pray as you are led for yourself and others.

"Loving Shepherd, find me. I long to make you happy by being found, redeemed, and returned to the fold. I pray for all the lost sheep . . ." (Continue in your own words.)

Listen to Jesus.

The love of God is endless, little one. God seeks the lost, night and day until the end of the age. What else is Jesus saying to you?

Ask God to show you how to live today.

"What can I do to help find your sheep, Lord? I offer myself to do whatever you have for me. Amen."

Wednesday, December 7, 2016

Know that God is present with you and ready to converse.

"Make my heart like your own, Jesus, so that I can glorify you with my life."

Read the gospel: Matthew 11:28–30.

Jesus said, "Come to me, all you that are weary and are carrying heavy burdens, and I will give you rest. Take my yoke upon you, and learn from me; for I am gentle and humble in heart, and you will find rest for your souls. For my yoke is easy, and my burden is light."

Notice what you think and feel as you read the gospel.

Jesus asks for a great commitment from those who would follow him. As we learn from the one who is gentle and humble of heart, he promises rest for our souls. He declares his yoke easy, his burden light.

Pray as you are led for yourself and others.

"Jesus, you ask us to take up our cross daily, lose our lives, and follow you. Yet you offer unimaginable rewards, even eternal life . . ." (Continue in your own words.)

Listen to Jesus.

All my promises to you are true, beloved. Join your heart to mine. What else is Jesus saying to you?

Ask God to show you how to live today.

"I give myself to you, Jesus. Let me learn from you the way of love.
Amen."

Thursday, December 8, 2016
Immaculate Conception of the Blessed Virgin Mary

Know that God is present with you and ready to converse.

"Open my heart to the Blessed Virgin Mary, the Mother of God."

Read the gospel: Luke 1:26–38.

In the sixth month the angel Gabriel was sent by God to a town in Galilee
called Nazareth, to a virgin engaged to a man whose name was Joseph, of
the house of David. The virgin's name was Mary. And he came to her and
said, "Greetings, favored one! The Lord is with you." But she was much
perplexed by his words and pondered what sort of greeting this might
be. The angel said to her, "Do not be afraid, Mary, for you have found
favor with God. And now, you will conceive in your womb and bear a
son, and you will name him Jesus. He will be great, and will be called
the Son of the Most High, and the Lord God will give to him the throne
of his ancestor David. He will reign over the house of Jacob for ever,
and of his kingdom there will be no end." Mary said to the angel, "How
can this be, since I am a virgin?" The angel said to her, "The Holy Spirit
will come upon you, and the power of the Most High will overshadow
you; therefore the child to be born will be holy; he will be called Son of
God. And now, your relative Elizabeth in her old age has also conceived
a son; and this is the sixth month for her who was said to be barren. For
nothing will be impossible with God." Then Mary said, "Here am I, the
servant of the Lord; let it be with me according to your word." Then the
angel departed from her.

Notice what you think and feel as you read the gospel.

Mary is perplexed by the angel's greeting; she wonders how she, a virgin,
can bear a son, yet she gives herself fully to serve the Lord as the angel
has announced to her. How she must have wondered at the glorious
ways of God!

Pray as you are led for yourself and others.

"I honor your mother, Jesus. I, too, resolve to serve you as you will, no
matter how I may struggle sometimes to understand your ways . . ."
(Continue in your own words.)

Listen to Jesus.
I am being born in you, too, my servant. I am your hope, your salvation. What
else is Jesus saying to you?

Ask God to show you how to live today.
"Be with me today, Jesus, washing me, helping me to love others and
glorify you. Blessed Virgin Mary, pray for me now and at the hour of
my death. Amen."

Friday, December 9, 2016

Know that God is present with you and ready to converse.
"Loving God Almighty, you are strong to save, yet the human heart
resists you. Let me hear you now in your Word."

Read the gospel: Matthew 11:16–19.
Jesus said, "But to what will I compare this generation? It is like children
sitting in the market-places and calling to one another,

> 'We played the flute for you, and you did not dance;
> we wailed, and you did not mourn.'

For John came neither eating nor drinking, and they say, 'He has a
demon'; the Son of Man came eating and drinking, and they say, 'Look,
a glutton and a drunkard, a friend of tax-collectors and sinners!' Yet
wisdom is vindicated by her deeds."

Notice what you think and feel as you read the gospel.
God seeks people in many, many ways that they may come to him and
inherit eternal life. However, Jesus says that nothing seems to work
with some people for they resist the love of God and God's servants no
matter what.

Pray as you are led for yourself and others.
"Lord, break down resistance to you in me and in those you have given
me to care for. We need you . . ." (Continue in your own words.)

Listen to Jesus.
*My child, I am always ready to receive the seeker or the penitent. I do not stop
reaching out to them.* What else is Jesus saying to you?

Ask God to show you how to live today.

"Dear Trinity of Love and Power, I give myself to you and to your service today. Show me ways to love and give me power to do it in your name. Amen."

Saturday, December 10, 2016

Know that God is present with you and ready to converse.

"Lord, thank you for being with me here and now. Teach me by your Word."

Read the gospel: Matthew 17:9–13.

As they were coming down the mountain, Jesus ordered them, "Tell no one about the vision until after the Son of Man has been raised from the dead." And the disciples asked him, "Why, then, do the scribes say that Elijah must come first?" He replied, "Elijah is indeed coming and will restore all things; but I tell you that Elijah has already come, and they did not recognize him, but they did to him whatever they pleased. So also the Son of Man is about to suffer at their hands." Then the disciples understood that he was speaking to them about John the Baptist.

Notice what you think and feel as you read the gospel.

It's almost funny that the disciples seem not to hear Jesus say that he will be raised from the dead. Nor do they react when he predicts that he, too, is to suffer at the hands of men. They do finally understand that when he explained to them about Elijah he was speaking to them about John the Baptist.

Pray as you are led for yourself and others.

"Human understanding can be so dark, Lord. Your ways are not our ways, and you are so infinitely great and good. Give us your Spirit to understand and do as you will . . ." (Continue in your own words.)

Listen to Jesus.

You need only me, beloved servant, for I am the Truth and the Way to Life. Let us be lovers. What else is Jesus saying to you?

Ask God to show you how to live today.

"Lord, help me to love you with all my heart, all my soul, all my mind, and all my strength today. Amen."

Sunday, December 11, 2016
Third Sunday of Advent

Know that God is present with you and ready to converse.

The Word of God came by the words of the prophets, the many who wrote under the influence of God's Spirit, as St. Peter puts it in his epistle. The prophets speak of the coming of the Messiah. They also speak of the one who would come before the Messiah to make straight the way of the Lord. That's John the Baptist, greater than the prophets before him.

"Teacher, Son of God and son of man, open my eyes and heart to your Word."

Read the gospel: Matthew 11:2–11.

When John heard in prison what the Messiah was doing, he sent word by his disciples and said to Jesus, "Are you the one who is to come, or are we to wait for another?" Jesus answered them, "Go and tell John what you hear and see: the blind receive their sight, the lame walk, the lepers are cleansed, the deaf hear, the dead are raised, and the poor have good news brought to them. And blessed is anyone who takes no offence at me." As they went away, Jesus began to speak to the crowds about John: "What did you go out into the wilderness to look at? A reed shaken by the wind? What then did you go out to see? Someone dressed in soft robes? Look, those who wear soft robes are in royal palaces. What then did you go out to see? A prophet? Yes, I tell you, and more than a prophet. This is the one about whom it is written,

> 'See, I am sending my messenger ahead of you,
>   who will prepare your way before you.'

Truly I tell you, among those born of women no one has arisen greater than John the Baptist; yet the least in the kingdom of heaven is greater than he."

Notice what you think and feel as you read the gospel.

Jesus speaks like a poet about John the Baptist, the one with the great calling to prepare the way of the Lord. Yet he ends this passage with the assertion that the least in the kingdom of heaven is greater than John. Jesus' way is riddled with paradox.

Pray as you are led for yourself and others.

"Lord, teach me how to embrace your paradoxes and trust you alone . . ."
(Continue in your own words.)

Listen to Jesus.

The wisdom of God is beyond you, my dear. Seek God's glory today. What else is Jesus saying to you?

Ask God to show you how to live today.

"You take dust and ashes and raise them to eternal life in your kingdom. Glory be to the Father, the Son, and the Holy Spirit forever. Amen."

Monday, December 12, 2016

Know that God is present with you and ready to converse.

"All power in heaven and earth is yours, Lord. I bow to your glory."

Read the gospel: Matthew 21:23–27.

When he entered the temple, the chief priests and the elders of the people came to him as he was teaching, and said, "By what authority are you doing these things, and who gave you this authority?" Jesus said to them, "I will also ask you one question; if you tell me the answer, then I will also tell you by what authority I do these things. Did the baptism of John come from heaven, or was it of human origin?" And they argued with one another, "If we say, 'From heaven,' he will say to us, 'Why then did you not believe him?' But if we say, 'Of human origin,' we are afraid of the crowd; for all regard John as a prophet." So they answered Jesus, "We do not know." And he said to them, "Neither will I tell you by what authority I am doing these things."

Notice what you think and feel as you read the gospel.

Jesus faced constant opposition from the religious people of his day. They try to trap him with a question about his authority, but he turns the tables on them. They are not interested in the truth, and their fear of the crowd means they will not answer Jesus' question, so Jesus does not answer theirs.

Pray as you are led for yourself and others.

"Lord, I know you are the Holy One of God. I give you all authority over my life—and the lives of those you have given me to care for . . ." (Continue in your own words.)

Listen to Jesus.

Losing your life to abide in my life—that is your journey. I receive you with joy, beloved servant. What else is Jesus saying to you?

Ask God to show you how to live today.

"I need you every hour, Lord. Let me be aware of you in my life very often. Thank you! Amen."

Tuesday, December 13, 2016

Know that God is present with you and ready to converse.

"The Word of God is sometimes blunt against those who resist its truth. I open myself to all it has for me."

Read the gospel: Matthew 21:28–32.

Jesus asked, "What do you think? A man had two sons; he went to the first and said, 'Son, go and work in the vineyard today.' He answered, 'I will not'; but later he changed his mind and went. The father went to the second and said the same; and he answered, 'I go, sir'; but he did not go. Which of the two did the will of his father?" The chief priests and elders of the people said, "The first." Jesus said to them, "Truly I tell you, the tax-collectors and the prostitutes are going into the kingdom of God ahead of you. For John came to you in the way of righteousness and you did not believe him, but the tax-collectors and the prostitutes believed him; and even after you saw it, you did not change your minds and believe him."

Notice what you think and feel as you read the gospel.

Jesus' parable of the two sons illustrates that it is not what we say but what we do that counts before God. Those who repent go into the kingdom of God ahead of those who cling to their own righteousness.

Pray as you are led for yourself and others.

"Teach me obedience like yours, Jesus, even to the end. I long to go into your kingdom with those I love and those I pray for . . ." (Continue in your own words.)

Listen to Jesus.

Your journey shall be short, my beloved, and the kingdom of heaven stretches out before you forever. Rejoice today. What else is Jesus saying to you?

Ask God to show you how to live today.

"Let me count my blessings all day long. Let me rejoice in my blessed hope of glory. Alleluia. Amen."

Wednesday, December 14, 2016

Know that God is present with you and ready to converse.
"Jesus, you manifested that you are the Christ by many works of mercy. Let your power also work in me."

Read the gospel: Luke 7:18b–23.
John summoned two of his disciples and sent them to the Lord to ask, "Are you the one who is to come, or are we to wait for another?" When the men had come to him, they said, "John the Baptist has sent us to you to ask, 'Are you the one who is to come, or are we to wait for another?'" Jesus had just then cured many people of diseases, plagues, and evil spirits, and had given sight to many who were blind. And he answered them, "Go and tell John what you have seen and heard: the blind receive their sight, the lame walk, the lepers are cleansed, the deaf hear, the dead are raised, the poor have good news brought to them. And blessed is anyone who takes no offence at me."

Notice what you think and feel as you read the gospel.
Without saying so directly, Jesus lets it be known that he is the Christ, the Messiah from God. His works prove it. What he says at the end is intriguing: blessed is the person who takes no offense at him.

Pray as you are led for yourself and others.
"Are you saying that blessed is the one who is not ashamed of you, Lord? Forgive me for the times I have denied you or acted as if I did not know you for fear of what others might think, say, or do . . ." (Continue in your own words.)

Listen to Jesus.
You need not be afraid to own me, beloved, for we are close friends. What else is Jesus saying to you?

Ask God to show you how to live today.
"How may I acknowledge our close friendship before others, Lord? Make me bold by the power of your Spirit. Amen."

Thursday, December 15, 2016

Know that God is present with you and ready to converse.
"God, you will that I follow Jesus, learning from the Word of God. Illuminate me."

Read the gospel: Luke 7:24–30.
When John's messengers had gone, Jesus began to speak to the crowds about John: "What did you go out into the wilderness to look at? A reed shaken by the wind? What then did you go out to see? Someone dressed in soft robes? Look, those who put on fine clothing and live in luxury are in royal palaces. What then did you go out to see? A prophet? Yes, I tell you, and more than a prophet. This is the one about whom it is written,

> 'See, I am sending my messenger ahead of you,
> who will prepare your way before you.'

I tell you, among those born of women no one is greater than John; yet the least in the kingdom of God is greater than he." (And all the people who heard this, including the tax-collectors, acknowledged the justice of God, because they had been baptized with John's baptism. But by refusing to be baptized by him, the Pharisees and the lawyers rejected God's purpose for themselves.)

Notice what you think and feel as you read the gospel.
Those who believe that John was a prophet and more than a prophet acknowledge the justice of God for they had been baptized by him. Those who refused to be baptized by John rejected God's purpose for themselves.

Pray as you are led for yourself and others.
"God, I do not wish to reject but to accept fully your purpose for me. Soften my heart to obey you. Open my eyes to see your way . . ." (Continue in your own words.)

Listen to Jesus.
Stay with me, dear child, for without me you are in danger. With me you are safe. What else is Jesus saying to you?

Ask God to show you how to live today.
"Great Shepherd, if I am tempted to stray from your path, draw me to yourself. I place my trust in you, my God. Amen."

Friday, December 16, 2016

Know that God is present with you and ready to converse.

"Jesus, you came from the Father. You are coming again at the end of the age. Come to me now."

Read the gospel: John 5:33–36.

Jesus said, "You sent messengers to John, and he testified to the truth. Not that I accept such human testimony, but I say these things so that you may be saved. He was a burning and shining lamp, and you were willing to rejoice for a while in his light. But I have a testimony greater than John's. The works that the Father has given me to complete, the very works that I am doing, testify on my behalf that the Father has sent me."

Notice what you think and feel as you read the gospel.

Jesus praises John but affirms that he has a testimony greater than John's for he does the very works of the Father who sent him.

Pray as you are led for yourself and others.

"Jesus seems never to doubt his authority, his testimony, his works, or his destiny. He knows who he is, the Son of God sent by the Father. Help me, Lord, to know with certainty who you are and what work you want me to do in your world . . ." (Continue in your own words.)

Listen to Jesus.

By abiding in me, dear disciple, you strengthen the authentic person God made you to be. What else is Jesus saying to you?

Ask God to show you how to live today.

"I want to be the person God wants me to be. Help me stay true to you in everything, today, tomorrow, and always. Thank you, Savior. Amen."

Saturday, December 17, 2016

Know that God is present with you and ready to converse.

"God is your Father, Lord, yet you took human flesh as a man. I rejoice in your mystery, Son of God and of son of man."

Read the gospel: Matthew 1:1–17.

An account of the genealogy of Jesus the Messiah, the son of David, the son of Abraham.

Abraham was the father of Isaac, and Isaac the father of Jacob, and Jacob the father of Judah and his brothers, and Judah the father of Perez and Zerah by Tamar, and Perez the father of Hezron, and Hezron the father of Aram, and Aram the father of Aminadab, and Aminadab the father of Nahshon, and Nahshon the father of Salmon, and Salmon the father of Boaz by Rahab, and Boaz the father of Obed by Ruth, and Obed the father of Jesse, and Jesse the father of King David.

And David was the father of Solomon by the wife of Uriah, and Solomon the father of Rehoboam, and Rehoboam the father of Abijah, and Abijah the father of Asaph, and Asaph the father of Jehoshaphat, and Jehoshaphat the father of Joram, and Joram the father of Uzziah, and Uzziah the father of Jotham, and Jotham the father of Ahaz, and Ahaz the father of Hezekiah, and Hezekiah the father of Manasseh, and Manasseh the father of Amos, and Amos the father of Josiah, and Josiah the father of Jechoniah and his brothers, at the time of the deportation to Babylon.

And after the deportation to Babylon: Jechoniah was the father of Salathiel, and Salathiel the father of Zerubbabel, and Zerubbabel the father of Abiud, and Abiud the father of Eliakim, and Eliakim the father of Azor, and Azor the father of Zadok, and Zadok the father of Achim, and Achim the father of Eliud, and Eliud the father of Eleazar, and Eleazar the father of Matthan, and Matthan the father of Jacob, and Jacob the father of Joseph the husband of Mary, of whom Jesus was born, who is called the Messiah.

So all the generations from Abraham to David are fourteen generations; and from David to the deportation to Babylon, fourteen generations; and from the deportation to Babylon to the Messiah, fourteen generations.

Notice what you think and feel as you read the gospel.

The Messiah is truly man, a son of Abraham and part of a long line of men both good and evil, powerful and humble. God's plan in human affairs is inscrutable and wonderful.

Pray as you are led for yourself and others.

"Your plan for me is also wonderful, Lord. Let me abandon myself to it. I ask you to lead all those you have given me along your way . . ." (Continue in your own words.)

Listen to Jesus.

Do not be wise in your own eyes, my child. Look to God in all things. What else is Jesus saying to you?

Ask God to show you how to live today.

"As I face choices today, Lord, let me discern by your grace what your way is. Let trust in you grow in my heart. Amen."

Sunday, December 18, 2016
Fourth Sunday of Advent

Know that God is present with you and ready to converse.

Almighty God has always been active in human history for God made us in God's image and, though we sinned, seeks to redeem us. God sent the Spirit upon Mary that she might bear God's Son, the Savior. God sent an angel to instruct Joseph, announcing to him that the child shall be named Emmanuel, meaning "God is with us."

"How wonderful are your ways, God. You are with me now."

Read the gospel: Matthew 1:18–24.

Now the birth of Jesus the Messiah took place in this way. When his mother Mary had been engaged to Joseph, but before they lived together, she was found to be with child from the Holy Spirit. Her husband Joseph, being a righteous man and unwilling to expose her to public disgrace, planned to dismiss her quietly. But just when he had resolved to do this, an angel of the Lord appeared to him in a dream and said, "Joseph, son of David, do not be afraid to take Mary as your wife, for the child conceived in her is from the Holy Spirit. She will bear a son, and you are to name him Jesus, for he will save his people from their sins." All this took place to fulfill what had been spoken by the Lord through the prophet:

"Look, the virgin shall conceive and bear a son,
and they shall name him Emmanuel,"

which means, "God is with us." When Joseph awoke from sleep, he did as the angel of the Lord commanded him; he took her as his wife.

Notice what you think and feel as you read the gospel.

This passage focuses on Joseph's response to the pregnancy of Mary. He is a just and reasonable man, and he wants to do what is right so he plans to dismiss her quietly. But God sends him an angel in a dream to let him know that the pregnancy is of God and that Joseph has a role to play in the coming of the Messiah. Joseph obeys.

Pray as you are led for yourself and others.

"Help me to obey as Joseph obeyed. Make your will clear to me, and give me the grace to do it . . ." (Continue in your own words.)

Listen to Jesus.

I love you. You delight me with your love for me. Ask of me whatever you wish, and I will give you the desires of your heart. What else is Jesus saying to you?

Ask God to show you how to live today.

"You are good to me, Lord. Strengthen my faith, my hope, and especially my love for you and others. Amen."

Monday, December 19, 2016

Know that God is present with you and ready to converse.

"Constant God of infinite holiness, you work in time and in the hearts of your people. Prepare me for your coming, Lord."

Read the gospel: Luke 1:5–25.

In the days of King Herod of Judea, there was a priest named Zechariah, who belonged to the priestly order of Abijah. His wife was a descendant of Aaron, and her name was Elizabeth. Both of them were righteous before God, living blamelessly according to all the commandments and regulations of the Lord. But they had no children, because Elizabeth was barren, and both were getting on in years.

Once when he was serving as priest before God and his section was on duty, he was chosen by lot, according to the custom of the priesthood, to enter the sanctuary of the Lord and offer incense. Now at the time of the incense-offering, the whole assembly of the people was praying outside. Then there appeared to him an angel of the Lord, standing at the right side of the altar of incense. When Zechariah saw him, he was terrified; and fear overwhelmed him. But the angel said to him, "Do not be afraid, Zechariah, for your prayer has been heard. Your wife Elizabeth will bear you a son, and you will name him John. You will have joy and gladness, and many will rejoice at his birth, for he will be great in the sight of the Lord. He must never drink wine or strong drink; even before his birth he will be filled with the Holy Spirit. He will turn many of the people of Israel to the Lord their God. With the spirit and power of Elijah he will go before him, to turn the hearts of parents to their children, and the disobedient to the wisdom of the righteous, to make ready a people prepared for the Lord." Zechariah said to the angel, "How will I know that this is so? For I am an old man, and my wife is getting on in years." The angel replied, "I am Gabriel. I stand in the presence of God, and I have been sent to speak to you and to bring you this good news. But now, because you did not believe my words, which will be fulfilled in their time, you will become mute, unable to speak, until the day these things occur."

Meanwhile, the people were waiting for Zechariah, and wondered at his delay in the sanctuary. When he did come out, he could not speak to them, and they realized that he had seen a vision in the sanctuary. He kept motioning to them and remained unable to speak. When his time of service was ended, he went to his home.

After those days his wife Elizabeth conceived, and for five months she remained in seclusion. She said, "This is what the Lord has done for me when he looked favorably on me and took away the disgrace I have endured among my people."

Notice what you think and feel as you read the gospel.

Because Zechariah cannot believe the announcement of the angel, he is struck mute. Nevertheless, Elizabeth conceives the great prophet John who would come before the Messiah, turning parents toward their children and the disobedient toward the righteous, preparing them for the Lord.

Pray as you are led for yourself and others.

"Lord, turn me in love toward all those you have given me, that I may be ready for you. I long to have you be born in my heart this Advent and Christmas season that I may please you. Dispel my disbelief . . ." (Continue in your own words.)

Listen to Jesus.

As you come to me in prayer, my beloved, I work to prepare you for the kingdom of God. What else is Jesus saying to you?

Ask God to show you how to live today.

"Lord, turn me toward you often. Inspire me to pray. Glory to you, Holy Spirit. Amen."

Tuesday, December 20, 2016

Know that God is present with you and ready to converse.

"You know my heart, Lord. Let it be open now to your Word."

Read the gospel: Luke 1:26–38.

In the sixth month the angel Gabriel was sent by God to a town in Galilee called Nazareth, to a virgin engaged to a man whose name was Joseph, of the house of David. The virgin's name was Mary. And he came to her and said, "Greetings, favored one! The Lord is with you." But she was much perplexed by his words and pondered what sort of greeting this might be. The angel said to her, "Do not be afraid, Mary, for you have found favor with God. And now, you will conceive in your womb and bear a son, and you will name him Jesus. He will be great, and will be called the Son of the Most High, and the Lord God will give to him the throne of his ancestor David. He will reign over the house of Jacob for ever, and of his kingdom there will be no end." Mary said to the angel, "How can this be, since I am a virgin?" The angel said to her, "The Holy Spirit will come upon you, and the power of the Most High will overshadow you; therefore the child to be born will be holy; he will be called Son of God. And now, your relative Elizabeth in her old age has also conceived a son; and this is the sixth month for her who was said to be barren. For nothing will be impossible with God." Then Mary said, "Here am I, the servant of the Lord; let it be with me according to your word." Then the angel departed from her.

Notice what you think and feel as you read the gospel.

Like Zechariah, Mary doesn't understand how a child can be conceived. Zechariah thought his wife was too old to conceive. Mary is a virgin. But with God all things are possible. Why is Zechariah struck mute for unbelief but Mary suffers nothing? She does say, "let it be with me." Also, God knows her immaculate heart.

Pray as you are led for yourself and others.

"Lord, let me be open to all things that befall me, knowing they come from you. I am your servant, Lord . . ." (Continue in your own words.)

Listen to Jesus.

Hear my voice, servant. I speak to you for your good and the good of those you love. What else is Jesus saying to you?

Ask God to show you how to live today.

"Jesus, let me always hear your voice speaking in my heart. Let me hear you more and more. Amen."

Wednesday, December 21, 2016

Know that God is present with you and ready to converse.
"Lord, your Word is true. Let me believe it in my heart, my soul, my mind. Your Spirit is present with me now."

Read the gospel: Luke 1:39–45.
In those days Mary set out and went with haste to a Judean town in the hill country, where she entered the house of Zechariah and greeted Elizabeth. When Elizabeth heard Mary's greeting, the child leapt in her womb. And Elizabeth was filled with the Holy Spirit and exclaimed with a loud cry, "Blessed are you among women, and blessed is the fruit of your womb. And why has this happened to me, that the mother of my Lord comes to me? For as soon as I heard the sound of your greeting, the child in my womb leapt for joy. And blessed is she who believed that there would be a fulfillment of what was spoken to her by the Lord."

Notice what you think and feel as you read the gospel.
Elizabeth receives her cousin Mary with joy, and the child leaps in her womb. She blesses Mary for her faith, for her great role as the Mother of the Lord. She exclaims at her own good fortune that the Mother of her Lord has come to her.

Pray as you are led for yourself and others.
"Lord, fill me with the expectation of your coming. Fill me with hope. Let me share hope with others . . ." (Continue in your own words.)

Listen to Jesus.
I love you and love to be with you, beloved disciple. Let us walk together in love. What else is Jesus saying to you?

Ask God to show you how to live today.
"Lord, let me turn away from anything in my life that displeases you. Help me to turn fully toward you and your holy will. Thank you. Amen."

Thursday, December 22, 2016

Know that God is present with you and ready to converse.
"Let me magnify you, my Lord, in the same Spirit as your servant Mary."

Read the gospel: Luke 1:46–56.

And Mary said,

> "My soul magnifies the Lord,
>> and my spirit rejoices in God my Savior,
> for he has looked with favor on the lowliness of his servant.
>> Surely, from now on all generations will call me blessed;
> for the Mighty One has done great things for me,
>> and holy is his name.
> His mercy is for those who fear him
>> from generation to generation.
> He has shown strength with his arm;
>> he has scattered the proud in the thoughts of their hearts.
> He has brought down the powerful from their thrones,
>> and lifted up the lowly;
> he has filled the hungry with good things,
>> and sent the rich away empty.
> He has helped his servant Israel,
>> in remembrance of his mercy,
> according to the promise he made to our ancestors,
>> to Abraham and to his descendants forever."

And Mary remained with her for about three months and then returned to her home.

Notice what you think and feel as you read the gospel.

God scatters the proud and lifts up the lowly, and Mary rejoices because the Lord has looked with favor upon her lowliness.. God sends the rich away empty but fills the hungry with good things. God helps his servants and keeps his promises forever.

Pray as you are led for yourself and others.

"Lord, lower me; teach me true humility that I may understand that all I have from you is blessing. I rejoice in you. I pray for those you have given me . . ." (Continue in your own words.)

Listen to Jesus.

You see how it is, my child. Take off all pretense of worthiness and power. Seek God from your lowliness, and you will find God. What else is Jesus saying to you?

Ask God to show you how to live today.
"I live too much in my ego, Lord. Too much is about me. Let me step out of myself today and find you. Let me find you in others. Amen."

Friday, December 23, 2016

Know that God is present with you and ready to converse.
"Open my ears to hear your Word, Lord. Free my tongue to praise you."

Read the gospel: Luke 1:57–66.
Now the time came for Elizabeth to give birth, and she bore a son. Her neighbors and relatives heard that the Lord had shown his great mercy to her, and they rejoiced with her.

On the eighth day they came to circumcise the child, and they were going to name him Zechariah after his father. But his mother said, "No; he is to be called John." They said to her, "None of your relatives has this name." Then they began motioning to his father to find out what name he wanted to give him. He asked for a writing-tablet and wrote, "His name is John." And all of them were amazed. Immediately his mouth was opened and his tongue freed, and he began to speak, praising God. Fear came over all their neighbors, and all these things were talked about throughout the entire hill country of Judea. All who heard them pondered them and said, "What then will this child become?" For, indeed, the hand of the Lord was with him.

Notice what you think and feel as you read the gospel.
Elizabeth bears a son, and all rejoice. They are skeptical of the name John, however, until mute Zechariah confirms it by writing that name on a tablet. After doing so, his tongue is freed and he praises God. People throughout the hill country of Judea marvel, and they wonder what this child would become.

Pray as you are led for yourself and others.
"Lord, work your purposes in my life and fill me with praise for you. Do great things with me for the glory of your name and the good of others . . ." (Continue in your own words.)

Listen to Jesus.
You are important, beloved disciple. I have work for you. You will serve me in love. What else is Jesus saying to you?

Ask God to show you how to live today.

"I can do only what you give me to do, Lord. I offer all that I am and all that I have to you. Let God be glorified. Amen."

Saturday, December 24, 2016

Know that God is present with you and ready to converse.

"God, you keep all your promises to your people. I am ready to hear your Word."

Read the gospel: Luke 1:67–79.

Then John's father Zechariah was filled with the Holy Spirit and spoke this prophecy:

> "Blessed be the Lord God of Israel,
>> for he has looked favorably on his people and redeemed them.
> He has raised up a mighty savior for us
>> in the house of his servant David,
> as he spoke through the mouth of his holy prophets from of old,
>> that we would be saved from our enemies and from the hand of all who hate us.
> Thus he has shown the mercy promised to our ancestors,
>> and has remembered his holy covenant,
> the oath that he swore to our ancestor Abraham,
>> to grant us that we, being rescued from the hands of our enemies,
> might serve him without fear, in holiness and righteousness
>> before him all our days.
> And you, child, will be called the prophet of the Most High;
>> for you will go before the Lord to prepare his ways,
> to give knowledge of salvation to his people
>> by the forgiveness of their sins.
> By the tender mercy of our God,
>> the dawn from on high will break upon us,
> to give light to those who sit in darkness and in the shadow of death,
>> to guide our feet into the way of peace."

Notice what you think and feel as you read the gospel.

Zechariah glorifies God for keeping promises made to his people. Full of the Spirit, he addresses the infant and declares that John will be the prophet of the Most High who prepares the people for the Messiah. The people will have forgiveness of sins, and the dawn shall give light to those who sit in darkness and in the shadow of death.

Pray as you are led for yourself and others.

"Praise to you, O Lord, for you have done what Zechariah prophesied. Guide my feet into the way of your peace . . ." (Continue in your own words.)

Listen to Jesus.

Find your peace in me, beloved. The things that swirl outside and inside need not take away our peace. Share my peace. Love me. What else is Jesus saying to you?

Ask God to show you how to live today.

"Your peace is like no other, Lord. Let me truly be a peaceful person by the power of your Spirit. Let me share that peace with others. Amen."

Sunday, December 25, 2016
Nativity of the Lord

Know that God is present with you and ready to converse.

Despite the many distractions of the holiday, Christmas is the holy day of the Nativity of our Lord, Jesus Christ. God has come to live with people in the flesh, fully human, yet fully divine. What simplicity and humility to be laid in a manger! What glory did the angels sing!

"Word of God, you became flesh and dwelt among us. Dwell in my heart as I love you."

Read the gospel: John 1:1–18.

In the beginning was the Word, and the Word was with God, and the Word was God. He was in the beginning with God. All things came into being through him, and without him not one thing came into being. What has come into being in him was life, and the life was the light of all people. The light shines in the darkness, and the darkness did not overcome it.

There was a man sent from God, whose name was John. He came as a witness to testify to the light, so that all might believe through him. He himself was not the light, but he came to testify to the light. The true light, which enlightens everyone, was coming into the world.

He was in the world, and the world came into being through him; yet the world did not know him. He came to what was his own, and his own people did not accept him. But to all who received him, who believed in his name, he gave power to become children of God, who were born, not of blood or of the will of the flesh or of the will of man, but of God.

And the Word became flesh and lived among us, and we have seen his glory, the glory as of a father's only son, full of grace and truth. (John testified to him and cried out, "This was he of whom I said, 'He who comes after me ranks ahead of me because he was before me.'") From his fullness we have all received, grace upon grace. The law indeed was given through Moses; grace and truth came through Jesus Christ. No one has ever seen God. It is God the only Son, who is close to the Father's heart, who has made him known.

Notice what you think and feel as you read the gospel.

The eternal Word of God, Jesus Christ, is Life, Light, and God's glory and power to those who accept him as Son of God to become children of God. We are born now not of blood or flesh or the will of humans but of God. All things in the world came into being through this Word, matter, life, and Spirit.

Pray as you are led for yourself and others.

"Most High Triune God, I worship you. I thank you for making me your child. I praise you for . . ." (Continue in your own words.)

Listen to Jesus.

I knew you before you were born, child, and loved you. I will for you to be transformed and come into my kingdom. What else is Jesus saying to you?

Ask God to show you how to live today.

"In the majesty of this mystery, Lord, show me how to live my moments in ways that glorify you and serve others. Walk with me today, my Jesus. Amen."

Monday, December 26, 2016
Saint Stephen, First Martyr

Know that God is present with you and ready to converse.

"You invite me to follow you even to persecution. I need your grace, Lord."

Read the gospel: Matthew 10:17-22.

Jesus taught his disciples, "Beware of them, for they will hand you over to councils and flog you in their synagogues; and you will be dragged before governors and kings because of me, as a testimony to them and the Gentiles. When they hand you over, do not worry about how you are to speak or what you are to say; for what you are to say will be given to you at that time; for it is not you who speak, but the Spirit of your Father speaking through you. Brother will betray brother to death, and a father his child, and children will rise against parents and have them put to death; and you will be hated by all because of my name. But the one who endures to the end will be saved."

Notice what you think and feel as you read the gospel.

Jesus wants his disciples to endure betrayals and persecutions to the end so he warns them of some of the terrible things that will befall them— floggings, trials, accusations, betrayals, hatred—because of his name. We see how it worked out for the first martyr of the Church, St. Stephen, and legions of martyrs through history and many even in our day. When persecuted, we can rely on Jesus' promise of the Spirit with us. We can rest in the Spirit.

Pray as you are led for yourself and others.

"This warning is frightening, but why should a follower of the Crucified have a different path than the sinless Lord? Let me accept persecution for your name and rely on the Spirit. I pray for the persecuted today . . . " (Continue in your own words.)

Listen to Jesus.

I am with you always, beloved disciple. Rely on me and on my Spirit for words, for grace, and for endurance. What else is Jesus saying to you?

Ask God to show you how to live today.

"Remind me to forgive and to pray for anyone who opposes me, even in the smallest way. Help me follow you, Jesus. Amen."

Tuesday, December 27, 2016
Saint John, Apostle and Evangelist

Know that God is present with you and ready to converse.

"Risen Lord, I run to you now. Let me see and believe your Word."

Read the gospel: John 20:1–8.

Early on the first day of the week, while it was still dark, Mary Magdalene came to the tomb and saw that the stone had been removed from the tomb. So she ran and went to Simon Peter and the other disciple, the one whom Jesus loved, and said to them, "They have taken the Lord out of the tomb, and we do not know where they have laid him." Then Peter and the other disciple set out and went towards the tomb. The two were running together, but the other disciple outran Peter and reached the tomb first. He bent down to look in and saw the linen wrappings lying there, but he did not go in. Then Simon Peter came, following him, and went into the tomb. He saw the linen wrappings lying there, and the cloth that had been on Jesus' head, not lying with the linen wrappings but rolled up in a place by itself. Then the other disciple, who reached the tomb first, also went in, and he saw and believed.

Notice what you think and feel as you read the gospel.

After Jesus' resurrection, the story turns to how the disciples came to know of it and understand it. St. John's gospel begins with a woman who in the dark sees that the stone has been removed from the tomb. She runs to tell Peter and John who themselves run to the tomb. John arrives first and hesitates, but Peter rushes in. He sees the linen wrappings lying there and the head cloth rolled up separately. Then John goes in, sees what Peter sees, and believes. The story will continue from here.

Pray as you are led for yourself and others.

"What did Peter and John believe, Lord? I ask for that faith that I, too, may serve you as they did in my life and in my death . . ." (Continue in your own words.)

Listen to Jesus.

You are my beloved disciple, for you love me only as you can. What else is Jesus saying to you?

Ask God to show you how to live today.

"I do love you, Lord. Magnify this love in me so that I may please you more and more. Let me show our love to others. Amen."

Wednesday, December 28, 2016
Holy Innocents, Martyrs

Know that God is present with you and ready to converse.
"Lord, I cling to you. You are my light and my salvation."

Read the gospel: Matthew 2:13–18.
Now after the magi had left, an angel of the Lord appeared to Joseph in a dream and said, "Get up, take the child and his mother, and flee to Egypt, and remain there until I tell you; for Herod is about to search for the child, to destroy him." Then Joseph got up, took the child and his mother by night, and went to Egypt, and remained there until the death of Herod. This was to fulfill what had been spoken by the Lord through the prophet, "Out of Egypt I have called my son."

When Herod saw that he had been tricked by the wise men, he was infuriated, and he sent and killed all the children in and around Bethlehem who were two years old or under, according to the time that he had learned from the wise men. Then was fulfilled what had been spoken through the prophet Jeremiah:

> "A voice was heard in Ramah,
>   wailing and loud lamentation,
> Rachel weeping for her children;
>   she refused to be consoled, because they are no more."

Notice what you think and feel as you read the gospel.
The angel warns Joseph to escape the cruelty of Herod, so the Holy Family flees to Egypt. Meanwhile, Herod is furious to have been tricked by the wise men. He kills all the children less than two years of age in and around Bethlehem, fulfilling Jeremiah's doleful prophesy of wailing and loud lamentation for the children are no more.

Pray as you are led for yourself and others.
"As I grieve for the atrocities committed in my own time, Lord, let me trust that somehow your will will be done, even in the aftermath of evil . . ." (Continue in your own words.)

Listen to Jesus.
In this age, God allows evil to continue. But justice will prevail. I have overcome the world. Child, apply yourself to doing good. What else is Jesus saying to you?

Ask God to show you how to live today.
"By your grace, Lord, I will persevere in doing good, seeking peace, and working for justice for all. Amen."

Thursday, December 29, 2016

Know that God is present with you and ready to converse.
"Let your Word be a light of revelation in my heart, mind, and soul, mighty God."

Read the gospel: Luke 2:22–35.
When the time came for their purification according to the law of Moses, they brought him up to Jerusalem to present him to the Lord (as it is written in the law of the Lord, "Every firstborn male shall be designated as holy to the Lord"), and they offered a sacrifice according to what is stated in the law of the Lord, "a pair of turtle-doves or two young pigeons."

Now there was a man in Jerusalem whose name was Simeon; this man was righteous and devout, looking forward to the consolation of Israel, and the Holy Spirit rested on him. It had been revealed to him by the Holy Spirit that he would not see death before he had seen the Lord's Messiah. Guided by the Spirit, Simeon came into the temple; and when the parents brought in the child Jesus, to do for him what was customary under the law, Simeon took him in his arms and praised God, saying,

> "Master, now you are dismissing your servant in peace,
>   according to your word;
> for my eyes have seen your salvation,
>   which you have prepared in the presence of all peoples,
> a light for revelation to the Gentiles
>   and for glory to your people Israel."

And the child's father and mother were amazed at what was being said about him. Then Simeon blessed them and said to his mother Mary, "This child is destined for the falling and the rising of many in Israel, and to be a sign that will be opposed so that the inner thoughts of many will be revealed—and a sword will pierce your own soul too."

Notice what you think and feel as you read the gospel.
Obedient to the law, Joseph and Mary present the infant Jesus to aged Simeon in the temple. God had revealed to Simeon that he would not die before he had seen the Messiah. When Simeon saw Jesus he praised God for he knew he was holding in his arms the salvation of the world. After

blessing them, Simeon spoke of the opposition the child would evoke in Israel, saying a sword would pierce Mary's soul, too.

Pray as you are led for yourself and others.

"I share the amazement of Joseph and Mary, Lord. Let all things happen as you have ordained, for you are great and good . . ." (Continue in your own words.)

Listen to Jesus.

There is a sword and a cross for all who follow me, dear one. Find comfort in my Holy Spirit. What else is Jesus saying to you?

Ask God to show you how to live today.

"With you, Lord, I can do anything, suffer anything. Let your glory be revealed. I praise you. Amen."

Friday, December 30, 2016
Holy Family of Jesus, Mary, and Joseph

Know that God is present with you and ready to converse.

"As you guided the Holy Family, Lord, guide me in my life by your Word."

Read the gospel: Matthew 2:13–15, 19–23.

Now after they had left, an angel of the Lord appeared to Joseph in a dream and said, "Get up, take the child and his mother, and flee to Egypt, and remain there until I tell you; for Herod is about to search for the child, to destroy him." Then Joseph got up, took the child and his mother by night, and went to Egypt, and remained there until the death of Herod. This was to fulfill what had been spoken by the Lord through the prophet, "Out of Egypt I have called my son." . . .

When Herod died, an angel of the Lord suddenly appeared in a dream to Joseph in Egypt and said, "Get up, take the child and his mother, and go to the land of Israel, for those who were seeking the child's life are dead." Then Joseph got up, took the child and his mother, and went to the land of Israel. But when he heard that Archelaus was ruling over Judea in place of his father Herod, he was afraid to go there. And after being warned in a dream, he went away to the district of Galilee. There he made his home in a town called Nazareth, so that what had been spoken through the prophets might be fulfilled, "He will be called a Nazorean."

Notice what you think and feel as you read the gospel.

Joseph was an active dreamer in those days. In his sleep angels speak to him, directing him to Egypt to escape Herod and then back to Israel but to another place there, the town Nazareth in Galilee—all this in fulfillment of the words of the prophets.

Pray as you are led for yourself and others.

"Let me trust you are also guiding me, Lord. Let your Word be fulfilled in me and in those I pray for . . ." (Continue in your own words.)

Listen to Jesus.

I do guide you for you are a child in this Holy Family. Have no fear. What else is Jesus saying to you?

Ask God to show you how to live today.

"I wish to grow in wisdom and in grace that I may be an honor to this holy family of God. You will grant me what I ask, Lord. Amen."

Saturday, December 31, 2016

Know that God is present with you and ready to converse.

"Most High Lord of Hosts, your Word is infinite. Let it swell my mind to grasp it and my heart to love and obey it."

Read the gospel: John 1:1–18.

In the beginning was the Word, and the Word was with God, and the Word was God. He was in the beginning with God. All things came into being through him, and without him not one thing came into being. What has come into being in him was life, and the life was the light of all people. The light shines in the darkness, and the darkness did not overcome it.

There was a man sent from God, whose name was John. He came as a witness to testify to the light, so that all might believe through him. He himself was not the light, but he came to testify to the light. The true light, which enlightens everyone, was coming into the world.

He was in the world, and the world came into being through him; yet the world did not know him. He came to what was his own, and his own people did not accept him. But to all who received him, who believed in his name, he gave power to become children of God, who were born, not of blood or of the will of the flesh or of the will of man, but of God.

And the Word became flesh and lived among us, and we have seen his glory, the glory as of a father's only son, full of grace and truth. (John testified to him and cried out, "This was he of whom I said, 'He who comes after me ranks ahead of me because he was before me.'") From his fullness we have all received, grace upon grace. The law indeed was given through Moses; grace and truth came through Jesus Christ. No one has ever seen God. It is God the only Son, who is close to the Father's heart, who has made him known.

Notice what you think and feel as you read the gospel.

Although God created all things, the world is shrouded in darkness because of sin. God, out of love for sinners, sends the Light into the world, and the darkness does not overcome it. The Light shines on the whole world, but the world does not know it, does not accept him, the Word of God, the Son of God. But those who do accept him receive grace upon grace.

Pray as you are led for yourself and others

"Lord, I, too, walk among the darkness—even darkness within me. Be my light. Be a light unto others, especially those you have given me . . . " (Continue in your own words.)

Listen to Jesus.

The glory of God is being revealed in you, beloved. Enter into the love between us. What else is Jesus saying to you?

Ask God to show you how to live today.

"I have the treasure of your grace in an earthen vessel, Lord. Make me more and more a temple of your Spirit. Amen."

Sunday, January 1, 2017
Blessed Virgin Mary, Mother of God

Know that God is present with you and ready to converse.

Mary has given birth to her child and named him Jesus as instructed by the angel. Now they remain in that humble place outside of Bethlehem, a stable. The child lies in a manger. Now come the shepherds with amazing news Mary would ponder all her life.

"Sweet Child of God, I come with the shepherds to adore you and praise you."

Read the gospel: Luke 2:16–21.

So the shepherds went with haste and found Mary and Joseph, and the child lying in the manger. When they saw this, they made known what had been told them about this child; and all who heard it were amazed at what the shepherds told them. But Mary treasured all these words and pondered them in her heart. The shepherds returned, glorifying and praising God for all they had heard and seen, as it had been told them.

After eight days had passed, it was time to circumcise the child; and he was called Jesus, the name given by the angel before he was conceived in the womb.

Notice what you think and feel as you read the gospel.

After being directed by an angel and having witnessed the heavenly host praising God, the shepherds find Mary, Joseph, and the infant in the manger. The shepherds tell Mary and Joseph what they had heard from the angel about this child, and Mary treasures their words and ponders them in her heart. The shepherds return to their fields, rejoicing in God.

Pray as you are led for yourself and others.

"I rejoice in the trustworthiness of the Word of God. I praise the works of God in history and in my life . . ." (Continue in your own words.)

Listen to Jesus.

I am the same yesterday, today, and forever, dear one. Ask me for whatever you want today. What else is Jesus saying to you?

Ask God to show you how to live today.

"Help me stay very close to you every moment of this day. Let me practice your presence in all I think, do, and say. Amen."

Monday, January 2, 2017

Know that God is present with you and ready to converse.

"You are with me now, Lord. Let me know you in your Word."

Read the gospel: John 1:19–28.

This is the testimony given by John when the Jews sent priests and Levites from Jerusalem to ask him, "Who are you?" He confessed and did not deny it, but confessed, "I am not the Messiah." And they asked him, "What then? Are you Elijah?" He said, "I am not." "Are you the prophet?" He answered, "No." Then they said to him, "Who are you?

Let us have an answer for those who sent us. What do you say about yourself?" He said,

> "I am the voice of one crying out in the wilderness,
> 'Make straight the way of the Lord,'"

as the prophet Isaiah said.

Now they had been sent from the Pharisees. They asked him, "Why then are you baptizing if you are neither the Messiah, nor Elijah, nor the prophet?" John answered them, "I baptize with water. Among you stands one whom you do not know, the one who is coming after me; I am not worthy to untie the thong of his sandal." This took place in Bethany across the Jordan where John was baptizing.

Notice what you think and feel as you read the gospel.

John the Baptist is interrogated by the priests and Levites. They want to know just who he is. He answers them with scripture from Isaiah that he is the voice crying in the wilderness to make straight the way of the Lord. He goes on to tell them that one stands among them who they do not know, the one who is coming after him whose sandal he is not worthy to untie. Were they happy, puzzled, or dismayed to hear this?

Pray as you are led for yourself and others.

"God, I do not want to miss my moment to know you and love you. Baptize me with your Spirit and . . ." (Continue in your own words.)

Listen to Jesus.

I rejoice in your love, child of God. Follow me and all will be well with you. What else is Jesus saying to you?

Ask God to show you how to live today.

"You are good to me, Lord. Show me how to be good to others today. Glory to God in the highest. Amen."

Tuesday, January 3, 2017

Know that God is present with you and ready to converse.

"Let me receive the testimony of the prophets, Lord, for they speak what they know."

Read the gospel: John 1:29–34.

The next day John saw Jesus coming towards him and declared, "Here is the Lamb of God who takes away the sin of the world! This is he of whom

I said, 'After me comes a man who ranks ahead of me because he was before me.' I myself did not know him; but I came baptizing with water for this reason, that he might be revealed to Israel." And John testified, "I saw the Spirit descending from heaven like a dove, and it remained on him. I myself did not know him, but the one who sent me to baptize with water said to me, 'He on whom you see the Spirit descend and remain is the one who baptizes with the Holy Spirit.' And I myself have seen and have testified that this is the Son of God."

Notice what you think and feel as you read the gospel.

John recognizes Jesus as the Lamb of God who takes away the sins of the world. Does he know that Jesus is destined to be a sacrificial lamb? He certainly knows Jesus ranks ahead of him and existed before him. Does he know that Jesus is one with God? He testifies that Jesus is the Son of God because he saw the Spirit descend and remain on him.

Pray as you are led for yourself and others.

"Lamb of God, take away my sins and baptize me with the Holy Spirit that I may please you always . . ." (Continue in your own words.)

Listen to Jesus.

I take away your sins and baptize you, dear disciple. Give my gifts to others. What else is Jesus saying to you?

Ask God to show you how to live today.

"Guide me in my giving, doing, and praying today, Lord. Let me give as generously as I have received. Thank you for taking away my sins, Lamb of God. Amen."

Wednesday, January 4, 2017

Know that God is present with you and ready to converse.

"I come into your presence with awe, Lord, for you are the living God who sustains the whole universe by your Word."

Read the gospel: John 1:35–42.

The next day John again was standing with two of his disciples, and as he watched Jesus walk by, he exclaimed, "Look, here is the Lamb of God!" The two disciples heard him say this, and they followed Jesus. When Jesus turned and saw them following, he said to them, "What are you looking for?" They said to him, "Rabbi" (which translated means

Teacher), "where are you staying?" He said to them, "Come and see." They came and saw where he was staying, and they remained with him that day. It was about four o'clock in the afternoon. One of the two who heard John speak and followed him was Andrew, Simon Peter's brother. He first found his brother Simon and said to him, "We have found the Messiah" (which is translated Anointed). He brought Simon to Jesus, who looked at him and said, "You are Simon son of John. You are to be called Cephas" (which is translated Peter).

Notice what you think and feel as you read the gospel.

Jesus' first disciples are drawn to him by the words of John the Baptist. He does not recruit them, but he invites them to come and see where he is staying. Andrew tells his brother Simon that they have found the Messiah. When Simon comes to see him, Jesus identifies him as Cephas, Peter.

Pray as you are led for yourself and others.

"Lord, let me come and see you. Please know me as your own and let me be a true disciple that others may also come to you . . ." (Continue in your own words.)

Listen to Jesus.

Those who follow me must forsake worldly desires. They must set their hearts on God. Are you ready for that? What else is Jesus saying to you?

Ask God to show you how to live today.

"Only by your grace can I aspire to and do your will, Lord. Fill me and make me new. Amen."

Thursday, January 5, 2017

Know that God is present with you and ready to converse.

"I desire to see you in all things, Lord, but especially in your Word here and now."

Read the gospel: John 1:43–51.

The next day Jesus decided to go to Galilee. He found Philip and said to him, "Follow me." Now Philip was from Bethsaida, the city of Andrew and Peter. Philip found Nathanael and said to him, "We have found him about whom Moses in the law and also the prophets wrote, Jesus son of Joseph from Nazareth." Nathanael said to him, "Can anything good come out of Nazareth?" Philip said to him, "Come and see." When Jesus saw Nathanael coming towards him, he said of him, "Here is truly an Israelite in whom there is no deceit!" Nathanael asked him, "Where did you come to know me?" Jesus answered, "I saw you under the fig tree before Philip called you." Nathanael replied, "Rabbi, you are the Son of God! You are the King of Israel!" Jesus answered, "Do you believe because I told you that I saw you under the fig tree? You will see greater things than these." And he said to him, "Very truly, I tell you, you will see heaven opened and the angels of God ascending and descending upon the Son of Man."

Notice what you think and feel as you read the gospel.

Jesus knows Nathanael inside and out, amazing Nathanael and prompting him to believe that Jesus is the Son of God. Jesus tells him he hasn't seen anything yet. Nathanael will see heaven open one day and the angels ascending and descending upon Jesus.

Pray as you are led for yourself and others.

"Lord, let me be a person in whom there is no deceit. Let me be honest with you and with all whom I encounter. Let me be honest with myself. . . ." (Continue in your own words.)

Listen to Jesus.

I am the Truth, beloved disciple. Cling to me, and you will be part of the great truth of God. What else is Jesus saying to you?

Ask God to show you how to live today.

"Open my eyes to your presence, Lord, especially in those people, situations, and things I might otherwise not see. Thank you. Amen."

Friday, January 6, 2017

Know that God is present with you and ready to converse.

"Lord, you are Spirit and Father of the Word, your beloved Son."

Read the gospel: Mark 1:7–11.

John proclaimed, "The one who is more powerful than I is coming after me; I am not worthy to stoop down and untie the thong of his sandals. I have baptized you with water; but he will baptize you with the Holy Spirit."

In those days Jesus came from Nazareth of Galilee and was baptized by John in the Jordan. And just as he was coming up out of the water, he saw the heavens torn apart and the Spirit descending like a dove on him. And a voice came from heaven, "You are my Son, the Beloved; with you I am well pleased."

Notice what you think and feel as you read the gospel.

John the Baptist proclaims that the great one who is coming after him will baptize not with water but with the Holy Spirit. The Spirit descends from above on Jesus when he is baptized by John, and the voice from heaven calls Jesus "my Son, the Beloved."

Pray as you are led for yourself and others.

"What a moment that must have been, Lord! God was present as Jesus began his earthly ministry. Be present with me, Spirit of God . . ." (Continue in your own words.)

Listen to Jesus.

Allow me to lead you, dear follower. Give yourself to me. I care for you. What else is Jesus saying to you?

Ask God to show you how to live today.

"I want to love you better, Jesus, and walk more closely with you. How may I please you today? Amen."

Saturday, January 7, 2017

Know that God is present with you and ready to converse.

"Lord, reveal your glory to me. I turn to your Word for light and life."

Read the gospel: John 2:1–11.

On the third day there was a wedding in Cana of Galilee, and the mother of Jesus was there. Jesus and his disciples had also been invited to the wedding. When the wine gave out, the mother of Jesus said to him, "They have no wine." And Jesus said to her, "Woman, what concern is that to you and to me? My hour has not yet come." His mother said to the servants, "Do whatever he tells you." Now standing there were six stone water-jars for the Jewish rites of purification, each holding twenty or thirty gallons. Jesus said to them, "Fill the jars with water." And they filled them up to the brim. He said to them, "Now draw some out, and take it to the chief steward." So they took it. When the steward tasted the water that had become wine, and did not know where it came from (though the servants who had drawn the water knew), the steward called the bridegroom and said to him, "Everyone serves the good wine first, and then the inferior wine after the guests have become drunk. But you have kept the good wine until now." Jesus did this, the first of his signs, in Cana of Galilee, and revealed his glory; and his disciples believed in him.

Notice what you think and feel as you read the gospel.

Jesus performs his first sign at a wedding. It is a simple, practical, yet extravagant sign for he changes much water into good wine. He refers to himself as the Bridegroom throughout his ministry. He loves his bride and lays down his life for her, for us.

Pray as you are led for yourself and others.

"Redeemer, you have power to transform elements. Transform me. Let me drink the wine of your Blood that I may be one with you . . ." (Continue in your own words.)

Listen to Jesus.

Come and drink my cup, beloved. It is eternal life. What else is Jesus saying to you?

Ask God to show you how to live today.

"Let me be full of awe at the mysteries of your words, your life, your death, and your resurrection. Lord, I glorify you and give you thanks for your great glory. Amen."

Sunday, January 8, 2017
Epiphany of the Lord

Know that God is present with you and ready to converse.

Mary has her baby. Born of God and Mary, he is Emmanuel, "God with us." Immediately, God begins to reveal the Son who is destined to become king, a ruler to shepherd God's people. Overjoyed, the wise men find him in Bethlehem and kneel before the baby.

"Let me come and worship, too, Lord. Here is my heart."

Read the gospel: Matthew 2:1–12.

In the time of King Herod, after Jesus was born in Bethlehem of Judea, wise men from the East came to Jerusalem, asking, "Where is the child who has been born king of the Jews? For we observed his star at its rising, and have come to pay him homage." When King Herod heard this, he was frightened, and all Jerusalem with him; and calling together all the chief priests and scribes of the people, he inquired of them where the Messiah was to be born. They told him, "In Bethlehem of Judea; for so it has been written by the prophet:

'And you, Bethlehem, in the land of Judah,
    are by no means least among the rulers of Judah;
for from you shall come a ruler
    who is to shepherd my people Israel.'"

Then Herod secretly called for the wise men and learned from them the exact time when the star had appeared. Then he sent them to Bethlehem, saying, "Go and search diligently for the child; and when you have found him, bring me word so that I may also go and pay him homage." When they had heard the king, they set out; and there, ahead of them, went the star that they had seen at its rising, until it stopped over the place where the child was. When they saw that the star had stopped, they were overwhelmed with joy. On entering the house, they saw the child with Mary his mother; and they knelt down and paid him homage. Then, opening their treasure-chests, they offered him gifts of gold, frankincense, and myrrh. And having been warned in a dream not to return to Herod, they left for their own country by another road.

Notice what you think and feel as you read the gospel.

Ironically, the mysterious wise men learn the infant Messiah's location from Herod, the chief priests, and the scribes—all of whom would sooner or later seek to kill Jesus. God also guides them by the star to the place and later by a dream so they do not return to Herod.

Pray as you are led for yourself and others.

"Guide me to you, Lord, and guide those I love to you. Guide all those you have given me to you . . ." (Continue in your own words.)

Listen to Jesus.

I came to shepherd my people, and I will always do so. You have entrusted yourself to me, beloved, and I am trustworthy. What else is Jesus saying to you?

Ask God to show you how to live today.

"I would like others to recognize you as the Great Shepherd. Open the eyes and hearts of those who are closed to you. Let me know what I may do to help. Amen."

Ordinary Time

INTRODUCTION

Ordinary Time is the time of the year in which Christ walks among us, calling us, teaching us, transforming us. Advent, Lent, and the Christmas and Easter seasons are special periods excluded from Ordinary Time. Ordinary Time begins on the Monday following the first Sunday after the Feast of the Epiphany and runs until Ash Wednesday; it then continues on the Monday after Pentecost Sunday and runs until the First Sunday of Advent, which is when the new liturgical year begins.

Ordinary Time is called "ordinary" simply because the weeks are numbered. Like the word *ordinal*, the word *ordinary* comes from a Latin word for numbers. Ordinary Time refers to the ordered life of the Church; the gospels of Ordinary Time treat all aspects of Jesus' ministry and sayings more or less in sequence.

Monday, January 9, 2017
Baptism of the Lord

Know that God is present with you and ready to converse.
"Ever-present Lord, God of heaven and earth, let me hear your voice today and be converted."

Read the gospel: Matthew 3:13–17.
Then Jesus came from Galilee to John at the Jordan, to be baptized by him. John would have prevented him, saying, "I need to be baptized by you, and do you come to me?" But Jesus answered him, "Let it be so now; for it is proper for us in this way to fulfill all righteousness." Then he consented. And when Jesus had been baptized, just as he came up from the water, suddenly the heavens were opened to him and he saw the Spirit of God descending like a dove and alighting on him. And a voice from heaven said, "This is my Son, the Beloved, with whom I am well pleased."

Notice what you think and feel as you read the gospel.
John the Baptist knows his place before Jesus. He is a sinful man needing conversion, but humble Jesus wishes to be baptized by John for, though sinless, he is fully man as well as fully divine. What mystery is here! The Spirit descends, and the Father speaks: "This is my Son."

Pray as you are led for yourself and others.
"I aspire to fulfill all righteousness, Lord, to repent and be conformed to your image. Lead me, Jesus . . ." (Continue in your own words.)

Listen to Jesus.
As you gaze upon me, beloved follower, you will assume my holiness. What else is Jesus saying to you?

Ask God to show you how to live today.
"Let me hear your voice in my heart all day long, Lord. Let me see your face and praise your name. Amen."

Tuesday, January 10, 2017

Know that God is present with you and ready to converse.
"You are with me, Lord. Let me hear your good news."

Read the gospel: Mark 1:21–28.

They went to Capernaum; and when the sabbath came, Jesus entered the synagogue and taught. They were astounded at his teaching, for he taught them as one having authority, and not as the scribes. Just then there was in their synagogue a man with an unclean spirit, and he cried out, "What have you to do with us, Jesus of Nazareth? Have you come to destroy us? I know who you are, the Holy One of God." But Jesus rebuked him, saying, "Be silent, and come out of him!" And the unclean spirit, throwing him into convulsions and crying with a loud voice, came out of him. They were all amazed, and they kept on asking one another, "What is this? A new teaching—with authority! He commands even the unclean spirits, and they obey him." At once his fame began to spread throughout the surrounding region of Galilee.

Notice what you think and feel as you read the gospel.

Jesus begins his ministry by teaching and doing mighty works with authority. Even the unclean spirit recognizes him as the "Holy One of God" before Jesus rebukes him and casts him out. All are amazed and Jesus' fame spreads.

Pray as you are led for yourself and others.

"Lord, cast out of me all uncleanness that my whole being may be obedient to you. Let me serve all those you have given me . . ." (Continue in your own words.)

Listen to Jesus.

I grant you what you ask, my child. Follow me today. What else is Jesus saying to you?

Ask God to show you how to live today.

"Amid distractions and confusions today, Lord, let me follow you steadily. I praise you and glorify you, blessed Savior. Amen."

Wednesday, January 11, 2017

Know that God is present with you and ready to converse.

"You have all power in heaven and in earth, Jesus, for you are the Lord. I bow to your authority."

Read the gospel: Mark 1:29–39.

As soon as Jesus and his disciples left the synagogue, they entered the house of Simon and Andrew, with James and John. Now Simon's mother-in-law was in bed with a fever, and they told him about her at once. He came and took her by the hand and lifted her up. Then the fever left her, and she began to serve them.

That evening, at sunset, they brought to him all who were sick or possessed with demons. And the whole city was gathered around the door. And he cured many who were sick with various diseases, and cast out many demons; and he would not permit the demons to speak, because they knew him.

In the morning, while it was still very dark, he got up and went out to a deserted place, and there he prayed. And Simon and his companions hunted for him. When they found him, they said to him, "Everyone is searching for you." He answered, "Let us go on to the neighboring towns, so that I may proclaim the message there also; for that is what I came out to do." And he went throughout Galilee, proclaiming the message in their synagogues and casting out demons.

Notice what you think and feel as you read the gospel.

Jesus is beginning his ministry of healing and preaching. He rises early to pray. When his disciples find him, he informs them that they must leave to proclaim the message in the neighboring towns because that is what he came to do.

Pray as you are led for yourself and others.

"Jesus, what am I here to do? Let me be your companion in my work and in my prayer. I pray especially for . . ." (Continue in your own words.)

Listen to Jesus.

You are right, beloved. As you draw nearer to me, you will have more power to do good among those I have given you to love and serve. What else is Jesus saying to you?

Ask God to show you how to live today.

"I am willing to do your work, Lord. I long to serve others as you direct me. Thank you for your goodness to me. Amen."

Thursday, January 12, 2017

Know that God is present with you and ready to converse.

"Stretch out your hand, Lord, and touch me, for I know you choose to make me clean."

Read the gospel: Mark 1:40–45.

A leper came to Jesus begging him, and kneeling he said to him, "If you choose, you can make me clean." Moved with pity, Jesus stretched out his hand and touched him, and said to him, "I do choose. Be made clean!" Immediately the leprosy left him, and he was made clean. After sternly warning him he sent him away at once, saying to him, "See that you say nothing to anyone; but go, show yourself to the priest, and offer for your cleansing what Moses commanded, as a testimony to them." But he went out and began to proclaim it freely, and to spread the word, so that Jesus could no longer go into a town openly, but stayed out in the country; and people came to him from every quarter.

Notice what you think and feel as you read the gospel.

Jesus is moved with pity for the leper. The leper has faith that Jesus can heal him if he chooses to. Of course, Jesus chooses to and heals him on the spot. The leper spreads the word, and soon Jesus can no longer go into a town openly. Now people have to come to him in the country.

Pray as you are led for yourself and others.

"Lord, I pray for people to come to you. People who have resisted, people with great needs, people who have turned away from God . . ." (Continue in your own words.)

Listen to Jesus.

I long to gather them all to me. Continue to pray for them, beloved. What else is Jesus saying to you?

Ask God to show you how to live today.

"Thank you for choosing me, Lord, and for letting me follow you. Lead me where you will today and tomorrow. Amen."

Friday, January 13, 2017

Know that God is present with you and ready to converse.

"I come into your presence, Lord, needing your healing Word."

Read the gospel: Mark 2:1–12.

When Jesus returned to Capernaum after some days, it was reported that he was at home. So many gathered around that there was no longer room for them, not even in front of the door; and he was speaking the word to them. Then some people came, bringing to him a paralyzed man, carried by four of them. And when they could not bring him to Jesus because of the crowd, they removed the roof above him; and after having dug through it, they let down the mat on which the paralytic lay. When Jesus saw their faith, he said to the paralytic, "Son, your sins are forgiven." Now some of the scribes were sitting there, questioning in their hearts, "Why does this fellow speak in this way? It is blasphemy! Who can forgive sins but God alone?" At once Jesus perceived in his spirit that they were discussing these questions among themselves; and he said to them, "Why do you raise such questions in your hearts? Which is easier, to say to the paralytic, 'Your sins are forgiven,' or to say, 'Stand up and take your mat and walk'? But so that you may know that the Son of Man has authority on earth to forgive sins"—he said to the paralytic—"I say to you, stand up, take your mat and go to your home." And he stood up, and immediately took the mat and went out before all of them; so that they were all amazed and glorified God, saying, "We have never seen anything like this!"

Notice what you think and feel as you read the gospel.

Jesus' fame has spread, making it hard to get close to him. He is moved by the faith of those who lower the paralyzed man from the roof. Shocking some of the scribes, he absolves the man of his sins before he heals him. Who can forgive sins but God alone? All are amazed.

Pray as you are led for yourself and others.

"Forgive me, Lord, and I shall be healed. I forgive those who have sinned against me . . ." (Continue in your own words.)

Listen to Jesus.

I am the same today as I ever was, dear one. I am. If you follow me, I will faithfully lead you. What else is Jesus saying to you?

Ask God to show you how to live today.

"So I follow you, Lord. Let me glorify you by my life. Amen."

Saturday, January 14, 2017

Know that God is present with you and ready to converse.

"Lord, though I am a sinner, you come to me and call me by your Word. Teach me, Jesus."

Read the gospel: Mark 2:13–17.

Jesus went out again beside the lake; the whole crowd gathered around him, and he taught them. As he was walking along, he saw Levi son of Alphaeus sitting at the tax booth, and he said to him, "Follow me." And he got up and followed him.

And as he sat at dinner in Levi's house, many tax-collectors and sinners were also sitting with Jesus and his disciples—for there were many who followed him. When the scribes of the Pharisees saw that he was eating with sinners and tax-collectors, they said to his disciples, "Why does he eat with tax-collectors and sinners?" When Jesus heard this, he said to them, "Those who are well have no need of a physician, but those who are sick; I have come to call not the righteous but sinners."

Notice what you think and feel as you read the gospel.

Jesus is all about saving sinners. He gathers them and teaches them. He calls sinners, even the hated tax collectors, to follow him, and he eats with them in Levi's house. When the scribes and Pharisees complain, Jesus declares his mission is to call not the righteous but sinners. Do his critics think he means that they are righteous?

Pray as you are led for yourself and others.

"Lord, I, too, am in need of you in my life. Have mercy on me . . ." (Continue in your own words.)

Listen to Jesus.

I love the holy soul in every person. If you put yourself in my company, I will wash you and bring you to the glory of my kingdom. What else is Jesus saying to you?

Ask God to show you how to live today.

"Give me your Spirit that I may not judge others in my heart or with my words. Help me to turn to you continuously for mercy. Amen."

Sunday, January 15, 2017
Second Sunday in Ordinary Time

Know that God is present with you and ready to converse.

John the Baptist understood that God sent him to call people to repentance and to baptize with water for the forgiveness of sins. He also understood that he was the advance-man for the greater One who would come after. Jesus would not repeal or replace John's baptism but raise it to another level: baptism with the Holy Spirit.

"Holy Spirit, testify to my heart about the Son of God. Let me learn and worship God in the reading of the Word."

Read the gospel: John 1:29–34.

The next day John saw Jesus coming towards him and declared, "Here is the Lamb of God who takes away the sin of the world! This is he of whom I said, 'After me comes a man who ranks ahead of me because he was before me.' I myself did not know him; but I came baptizing with water for this reason, that he might be revealed to Israel." And John testified, "I saw the Spirit descending from heaven like a dove, and it remained on him. I myself did not know him, but the one who sent me to baptize with water said to me, 'He on whom you see the Spirit descend and remain is the one who baptizes with the Holy Spirit.' And I myself have seen and have testified that this is the Son of God."

Notice what you think and feel as you read the gospel.

When John sees Jesus coming, he calls him the Lamb of God. He understands already that Jesus' ultimate mission is to be sacrificed for the sins of the world. John says that the one who sent him to baptize with water told him that he would see the Spirit descend upon the one who baptizes with the Holy Spirit. Clearly, God had spoken with John.

Pray as you are led for yourself and others.

"Lord, speak to me, too. Let me be guided today by your Holy Spirit. Let all I think, say, and do give you glory . . ." (Continue in your own world.)

Listen to Jesus.

I do speak with you, beloved disciple. You have me. Many do not. Love and pray for them. What else is Jesus saying to you?

Ask God to show you how to live today.

"I am deeply privileged to be a child of God, Lord. I did nothing to deserve your mercy and sustaining love. Let me share you with others. Amen."

Monday, January 16, 2017

Know that God is present with you and ready to converse.

"I rejoice that you are here with me, Jesus. You will lift me by your Word."

Read the gospel: Mark 2:18–22.

Now John's disciples and the Pharisees were fasting; and people came and said to him, "Why do John's disciples and the disciples of the Pharisees fast, but your disciples do not fast?" Jesus said to them, "The wedding-guests cannot fast while the bridegroom is with them, can they? As long as they have the bridegroom with them, they cannot fast. The days will come when the bridegroom is taken away from them, and then they will fast on that day.

"No one sews a piece of unshrunk cloth on an old cloak; otherwise, the patch pulls away from it, the new from the old, and a worse tear is made. And no one puts new wine into old wineskins; otherwise, the wine will burst the skins, and the wine is lost, and so are the skins; but one puts new wine into fresh wineskins."

Notice what you think and feel as you read the gospel.

Jesus calls himself the bridegroom, and his presence is reason for joy and feasting. His disciples are the wedding guests, and they will fast only after he is taken away from them. Jesus speaks practically of patching an old cloak and putting up new wine. Something new is happening, and those who hear must adjust their understanding to receive it.

Pray as you are led for yourself and others.

"Lord, you grant me your freedom. I choose to follow you. Give me grace to understand, speak, and honor you in the presence of others . . . " (Continue in your own words.)

Listen to Jesus.

You are my ambassador, dear friend. You will not always know how your prayers, words, and actions glorify me before others. What else is Jesus saying to you?

Ask God to show you how to live today.

"Let me live each moment in your presence, Jesus, that my choices may be led by your Spirit. Amen."

Tuesday, January 17, 2017

Know that God is present with you and ready to converse.

"Almighty God, your ways are high and inscrutable. I stand before you in awe."

Read the gospel: Mark 2:23–28.

One sabbath Jesus was going through the cornfields; and as they made their way his disciples began to pluck heads of grain. The Pharisees said to him, "Look, why are they doing what is not lawful on the sabbath?" And he said to them, "Have you never read what David did when he and his companions were hungry and in need of food? He entered the house of God, when Abiathar was high priest, and ate the bread of the Presence, which it is not lawful for any but the priests to eat, and he gave some to his companions." Then he said to them, "The sabbath was made for humankind, and not humankind for the sabbath; so the Son of Man is lord even of the sabbath."

Notice what you think and feel as you read the gospel.

The Pharisees are critical of Jesus' disciples plucking and eating heads of grain on the Sabbath. Jesus refutes them with scripture. While they are all about keeping religious rules, he is all about God, for the Son of Man is Lord even of the Sabbath.

Pray as you are led for yourself and others.

"Jesus, let me always choose you above rules, grace above laws, mercy above judgment. Give me wisdom to discern these things . . ." (Continue in your own words.)

Listen to Jesus.

I fulfill the law. Keep my commandments first and last—love God and all people. What else is Jesus saying to you?

Ask God to show you how to live today.

"I have far to go in keeping your commandments, Lord. Will you help me today? Amen."

Wednesday, January 18, 2017

Know that God is present with you and ready to converse.
"Lord, break down my hardness of heart that I may receive your Word of grace and truth."

Read the gospel: Mark 3:1–6.
Again Jesus entered the synagogue, and a man was there who had a withered hand. They watched him to see whether he would cure him on the sabbath, so that they might accuse him. And he said to the man who had the withered hand, "Come forward." Then he said to them, "Is it lawful to do good or to do harm on the sabbath, to save life or to kill?" But they were silent. He looked around at them with anger; he was grieved at their hardness of heart and said to the man, "Stretch out your hand." He stretched it out, and his hand was restored. The Pharisees went out and immediately conspired with the Herodians against him, how to destroy him.

Notice what you think and feel as you read the gospel.
Jesus looks upon the Pharisees with anger for they are intent upon gathering evidence that he is a law-breaker. Jesus knows their hearts and their thoughts. He silences them with common sense: How can it be unlawful to do good on the Sabbath? They are silent, and Jesus heals the man's hand. The Pharisees have seen it and immediately go off to conspire with the Herodians as to how they might destroy him.

Pray as you are led for yourself and others.
"Lord, do not be angry with me. Heal me by your mercy . . ." (Continue in your own words.)

Listen to Jesus.
Present your wounded and broken parts to me, dear servant, and I will heal you.
What else is Jesus saying to you?

Ask God to show you how to live today.
"You are good to me, Lord. What good may I do today? Amen."

Thursday, January 19, 2017

Know that God is present with you and ready to converse.
"Lord, Master of the Universe, you are present everywhere. I thank you for being with me now as I read your Word."

Read the gospel: Mark 3:7–12.
Jesus departed with his disciples to the lake, and a great multitude from Galilee followed him; hearing all that he was doing, they came to him in great numbers from Judea, Jerusalem, Idumea, beyond the Jordan, and the region around Tyre and Sidon. He told his disciples to have a boat ready for him because of the crowd, so that they would not crush him; for he had cured many, so that all who had diseases pressed upon him to touch him. Whenever the unclean spirits saw him, they fell down before him and shouted, "You are the Son of God!" But he sternly ordered them not to make him known.

Notice what you think and feel as you read the gospel.
Everyone wants something from Jesus. The crowd might crush him, so he asks his disciples to ready a boat by which he may need to escape. All who have diseases press upon him to touch him. Unclean spirits shout, "You are the Son of God!"

Pray as you are led for yourself and others.
"Son of God, I, too, wish to touch you. Let me do so today not for my good but for the good of someone else . . ." (Continue in your own words.)

Listen to Jesus.
I bless you for putting others first, my friend. I grant your prayer. What else is Jesus saying to you?

Ask God to show you how to live today.
"Make me strong in prayer, Lord, for by it I know you and love you. By prayer I cooperate with you to serve others. Amen."

Friday, January 20, 2017

Know that God is present with you and ready to converse.
"Glory to you, Father, Son, and Holy Spirit. You are the mystery of One. You are Love."

Read the gospel: Mark 3:13-19.

Jesus went up the mountain and called to him those whom he wanted, and they came to him. And he appointed twelve, whom he also named apostles, to be with him, and to be sent out to proclaim the message, and to have authority to cast out demons. So he appointed the twelve: Simon (to whom he gave the name Peter); James son of Zebedee and John the brother of James (to whom he gave the name Boanerges, that is, Sons of Thunder); and Andrew, and Philip, and Bartholomew, and Matthew, and Thomas, and James son of Alphaeus, and Thaddaeus, and Simon the Cananaean, and Judas Iscariot, who betrayed him.

Notice what you think and feel as you read the gospel.

Jesus appoints the twelve apostles. He intends them to be with him and to be sent out from him with power. Among them is Judas Iscariot, whom Jesus knew would betray him.

Pray as you are led for yourself and others.

"Thank you for your wisdom, Jesus. You know me, and you have your purposes for me . . ." (Continue in your own words.)

Listen to Jesus.

If you want me to use you, beloved servant, stay close to me. Seek me every day. What else is Jesus saying to you?

Ask God to show you how to live today.

"I come to you, Jesus. I want to know you well. I surrender to your will. Amen."

Saturday, January 21, 2017

Know that God is present with you and ready to converse.

"Jesus, you desire to save and heal all who come to you. I stand before you now."

Read the gospel: Mark 3:20-21.

Jesus went home, and the crowd came together again, so that they could not even eat. When his family heard it, they went out to restrain him, for people were saying, "He has gone out of his mind."

Notice what you think and feel as you read the gospel.

Jesus is so focused on his mission to preach and heal all those who come to him he is in danger from the crowds. Yet he allows them to come to him. His family tries to restrain him for his own sake. Some people think he may be out of his mind.

Pray as you are led for yourself and others.

"Jesus, help me to be fearless in following you. Who can harm me when I am with you?" (Continue in your own words.)

Listen to Jesus.

I am with you always, my beloved. Ask me for whatever you desire. What else is Jesus saying to you?

Ask God to show you how to live today.

"I pray for the mentally ill. Let them be comforted and healed, not persecuted or neglected. How may I help? Amen."

Sunday, January 22, 2017
Third Sunday in Ordinary Time

Know that God is present with you and ready to converse.

After his baptism by John, Jesus begins his earthly ministry. It will be a brief and stressful journey. He will announce the coming of the kingdom of God, heal all who ask him, multiply food to feed thousands, quiet the storm, cast out devils, dispute with scribes and Pharisees, and be betrayed, arrested, tortured, and crucified. What courage he showed! What love motivated God to take flesh for a hard life like that?

"Be my Light, Jesus. Dispel all my darkness by your Word."

Read the gospel: Matthew 4:12–23.

Now when Jesus heard that John had been arrested, he withdrew to Galilee. He left Nazareth and made his home in Capernaum by the lake, in the territory of Zebulun and Naphtali, so that what had been spoken through the prophet Isaiah might be fulfilled:

> "Land of Zebulun, land of Naphtali,
>> on the road by the sea, across the Jordan, Galilee of the Gentiles—
> the people who sat in darkness
>> have seen a great light,

and for those who sat in the region and shadow of death
light has dawned."

From that time Jesus began to proclaim, "Repent, for the kingdom of heaven has come near."

As he walked by the Sea of Galilee, he saw two brothers, Simon, who is called Peter, and Andrew his brother, casting a net into the lake—for they were fishermen. And he said to them, "Follow me, and I will make you fish for people." Immediately they left their nets and followed him. As he went from there, he saw two other brothers, James son of Zebedee and his brother John, in the boat with their father Zebedee, mending their nets, and he called them. Immediately they left the boat and their father, and followed him.

Jesus went throughout Galilee, teaching in their synagogues and proclaiming the good news of the kingdom and curing every disease and every sickness among the people.

Notice what you think and feel as you read the gospel.

Jesus knows what the arrest of John means: Herod will kill John. He, Jesus, will now be singled out by the authorities, both civil and religious. Yet he picks up where John left off, proclaiming "Repent, for the kingdom of heaven has come near." He calls his disciples and travels throughout the region teaching, announcing the good news, and healing every disease.

Pray as you are led for yourself and others.

"Jesus, this world is still in darkness. Let your light dawn everywhere . . . " (Continue in your own words.)

Listen to Jesus.

You are my light, beloved. Be truth and goodness before others. They will know me through you. What else is Jesus saying to you?

Ask God to show you how to live today.

"Lead me to opportunities to be true and good today, Lord. Open my eyes to possibilities. Thank you. Amen."

Monday, January 23, 2017

Know that God is present with you and ready to converse.

"Almighty God, no one can stand against you. I choose you and embrace your will."

Read the gospel: Mark 3:22–30.

And the scribes who came down from Jerusalem said, "He has Beelzebul, and by the ruler of the demons he casts out demons." And Jesus called them to him, and spoke to them in parables, "How can Satan cast out Satan? If a kingdom is divided against itself, that kingdom cannot stand. And if a house is divided against itself, that house will not be able to stand. And if Satan has risen up against himself and is divided, he cannot stand, but his end has come. But no one can enter a strong man's house and plunder his property without first tying up the strong man; then indeed the house can be plundered.

"Truly I tell you, people will be forgiven for their sins and whatever blasphemies they utter; but whoever blasphemes against the Holy Spirit can never have forgiveness, but is guilty of an eternal sin"—for they had said, "He has an unclean spirit."

Notice what you think and feel as you read the gospel.

The big-city scribes accuse Jesus of casting out demons by the power of the devil. Jesus points out that what they say makes no sense. His analogy of tying up the strong man to plunder his house implies Jesus' power over Satan. His power comes from the Holy Spirit, not from evil spirits. The scribes will hold this against him until one day they get their revenge.

Pray as you are led for yourself and others.

"Lord, vanquish all evil in me. Give me your Holy Spirit so that I can know and do what is right and good . . ." (Continue in your own words.)

Listen to Jesus.

I breathe my Spirit upon you, dear child, dear friend. Walk with me and do what I do. What else is Jesus saying to you?

Ask God to show you how to live today.

"Let my sights be set exclusively on you, Lord. Help me turn away from all that is not you. Amen."

Tuesday, January 24, 2017

Know that God is present with you and ready to converse.

"Jesus, you invite me into your Holy Family. I come to do your will, Lord."

Read the gospel: Mark 3:31–35.

Then Jesus' mother and his brothers came; and standing outside, they sent to him and called him. A crowd was sitting around him; and they said to him, "Your mother and your brothers and sisters are outside, asking for you." And he replied, "Who are my mother and my brothers?" And looking at those who sat around him, he said, "Here are my mother and my brothers! Whoever does the will of God is my brother and sister and mother."

Notice what you think and feel as you read the gospel.

When his mother and his other kin come to see him, they cannot enter the house for the crowd present, so they send Jesus a message that they are there. Jesus uses that moment as an opportunity to show that family relationships are not as important as relationship with God. Those who do God's will, he says, belong to the family of God.

Pray as you are led for yourself and others.

"Jesus, you are generous to me. Let me be a true child of God. Give me love for all in God's family . . ." (Continue in your own words.)

Listen to Jesus.

Those who love are of God, beloved. Practice loving, especially when it is hard. What else is Jesus saying to you?

Ask God to show you how to live today.

"By your grace, Lord, I will love even those I have never loved. Reveal to me my hardness of heart toward others so that you may soften it. Make my heart like yours, Jesus. Amen."

Wednesday, January 25, 2017
Conversion of Saint Paul, Apostle

Know that God is present with you and ready to converse.

"Lord, let your power cover me, protecting me and helping me do your work well."

Read the gospel: Mark 16:15–18.

And Jesus said to the disciples, "Go into all the world and proclaim the good news to the whole creation. The one who believes and is baptized will be saved; but the one who does not believe will be condemned. And these signs will accompany those who believe: by using my name they will cast out demons; they will speak in new tongues; they will pick up snakes in their hands, and if they drink any deadly thing, it will not hurt them; they will lay their hands on the sick, and they will recover."

Notice what you think and feel as you read the gospel.

Jesus commands his followers to preach the Good News to everyone. They will receive from God power and protection as they do God's work. Those who believe the Good News will be saved; those who do not will be condemned.

Pray as you are led for yourself and others.

"These are hard words, Lord, for you will that no one be condemned. I pray now for all those who do not believe, that their eyes will be opened to the Good News and they will believe . . ." (Continue in your own words.)

Listen to Jesus.

You are right to pray for unbelievers. But do not be afraid. All shall be well. What else is Jesus saying to you?

Ask God to show you how to live today.

"How shall I proclaim your Good News today, Lord? Show me opportunities. Amen."

Thursday, January 26, 2017

Know that God is present with you and ready to converse.

"Light of the world, illuminate me by your Word."

Read the gospel: Mark 4:21–25.

Jesus said to them, "Is a lamp brought in to be put under the bushel basket, or under the bed, and not on the lampstand? For there is nothing hidden, except to be disclosed; nor is anything secret, except to come to light. Let anyone with ears to hear listen!" And he said to them, "Pay attention to what you hear; the measure you give will be the measure you get, and still more will be given you. For to those who have, more will be given; and from those who have nothing, even what they have will be taken away."

Notice what you think and feel as you read the gospel.

Jesus discloses what seem to be two spiritual laws. The first is that light reveals things, even all hidden or secret things. Does that mean God's light in general or God's light in us? Probably both. The second spiritual law has to do with how we give ourselves away. The paradox is that the more we give, the more we receive. The stingy will lose everything.

Pray as you are led for yourself and others.

"Lord, banish the darkness within me. Give me your light and let me shine before others. Let me give selflessly to others, that I may be rich in your love . . ." (Continue in your own words.)

Listen to Jesus.

You understand, dear servant. You make me joyful. I grant your prayers. What else is Jesus saying to you?

Ask God to show you how to live today.

"I do not like to stray from you, Lord. Teach me how to stay close to you all day long. I praise you, Lord. Amen."

Friday, January 27, 2017

Know that God is present with you and ready to converse.

"Creator of all life, be life in me and let it grow as I receive your Word."

Read the gospel: Mark 4:26–34.

Jesus also said, "The kingdom of God is as if someone would scatter seed on the ground, and would sleep and rise night and day, and the seed would sprout and grow, he does not know how. The earth produces of itself, first the stalk, then the head, then the full grain in the head. But when the grain is ripe, at once he goes in with his sickle, because the harvest has come."

He also said, "With what can we compare the kingdom of God, or what parable will we use for it? It is like a mustard seed, which, when sown upon the ground, is the smallest of all the seeds on earth; yet when it is sown it grows up and becomes the greatest of all shrubs, and puts forth large branches, so that the birds of the air can make nests in its shade."

With many such parables he spoke the word to them, as they were able to hear it; he did not speak to them except in parables, but he explained everything in private to his disciples.

Notice what you think and feel as you read the gospel.

Jesus' parables are about the mystery of spiritual life explained by familiar things. Seeds are scattered, sprout, and grow—even that common event is mysterious. Eventually, the seed yields ripe grain and is harvested. So we will grow and be harvested by God when God is ready. The kingdom of God in us starts out small but grows very large.

Pray as you are led for yourself and others

"I open my soul to your seeds, Lord. Let them grow and bear good fruit to your glory . . ." (Continue in your own words.)

Listen to Jesus.

You are mine, beloved, and I am making you beautiful. What else is Jesus saying to you?

Ask God to show you how to live today.

"I long for the birds of the air to make nests in the shade of the faith, hope, and love you have planted in me, Lord. Amen."

Saturday, January 28, 2017

Know that God is present with you and ready to converse.

"God, you are with me in storm and in calm. You are with me now. Glory to you, Lord."

Read the gospel: Mark 4:35–41.

On that day, when evening had come, Jesus said to his disciples, "Let us go across to the other side." And leaving the crowd behind, they took him with them in the boat, just as he was. Other boats were with him. A great gale arose, and the waves beat into the boat, so that the boat was already being swamped. But he was in the stern, asleep on the cushion; and they woke him up and said to him, "Teacher, do you not care that we are perishing?" He woke up and rebuked the wind, and said to the sea, "Peace! Be still!" Then the wind ceased, and there was a dead calm. He said to them, "Why are you afraid? Have you still no faith?" And they were filled with great awe and said to one another, "Who then is this, that even the wind and the sea obey him?"

Notice what you think and feel as you read the gospel.

During the storm, the disciples awaken Jesus and ask him whether he cares that the boat is beginning to sink. He does not rebuke them but rebukes the wind and commands the sea to be still. Then he asks them why they are afraid. They must have been more afraid of his great power over nature than of the forces of nature itself. Jesus wants them to know him and believe in him.

Pray as you are led for yourself and others.

"Lord, I, too, am afraid at times. Perhaps I am always afraid. Fill me with faith that I may trust you completely, please you, and serve others . . ." (Continue in your own words.)

Listen to Jesus.

When storms come, my friend, look to me. Do not forget how I save you. Have faith in me. What else is Jesus saying to you?

Ask God to show you how to live today.

"Bring to my mind the many times you have rescued me from perils, Lord, and let me glorify you. Let me go on my journey trusting you more and more. Amen."

Sunday, January 29, 2017
Fourth Sunday in Ordinary Time

Know that God is present with you and ready to converse.

To be blessed is to be happy. Our Blessed Lord Jesus Christ was happy, as was his mother, the Blessed Virgin Mary. Happiness is doing God's will, even when our human nature resists it. Perhaps especially then. Jesus taught the crowd the secrets of happiness.

"Jesus, I am among that crowd you are speaking to. Teach me now."

Read the gospel: Matthew 5:1–12.

When Jesus saw the crowds, he went up the mountain; and after he sat down, his disciples came to him. Then he began to speak, and taught them, saying:

"Blessed are the poor in spirit, for theirs is the kingdom of heaven.

"Blessed are those who mourn, for they will be comforted.

"Blessed are the meek, for they will inherit the earth.

"Blessed are those who hunger and thirst for righteousness, for they will be filled.

"Blessed are the merciful, for they will receive mercy.

"Blessed are the pure in heart, for they will see God.

"Blessed are the peacemakers, for they will be called children of God.

"Blessed are those who are persecuted for righteousness' sake, for theirs is the kingdom of heaven.

"Blessed are you when people revile you and persecute you and utter all kinds of evil against you falsely on my account. Rejoice and be glad, for your reward is great in heaven, for in the same way they persecuted the prophets who were before you."

Notice what you think and feel as you read the gospel.

The poor, the hurting, the just, the pure—victims and idealists of all kinds—will inherit the kingdom of God. We may rejoice in our sufferings in this world, especially if we suffer innocently or in doing good. Our reward is great in heaven.

Pray as you are led for yourself and others.

"Lord, make me poor in spirit, truly humble, for that is your first beatitude. Let me know that I am nothing, have nothing without your grace . . ." (Continue in your own words.)

Listen to Jesus.

I love you, dear friend, and I always have. You make me happy that you come to me for life. I grant you all you ask. What else is Jesus saying to you?

Ask God to show you how to live today.

"Jesus, where there is discord let me sow peace. Guide me by your Spirit. Amen."

Monday, January 30, 2017

Know that God is present with you and ready to converse.

"What have you to do with me, Son of the Most High God?"

Read the gospel: Mark 5:1-20.

They came to the other side of the lake, to the country of the Gerasenes. And when Jesus had stepped out of the boat, immediately a man out of the tombs with an unclean spirit met him. He lived among the tombs; and no one could restrain him anymore, even with a chain; for he had often been restrained with shackles and chains, but the chains he wrenched apart, and the shackles he broke in pieces; and no one had the strength to subdue him. Night and day among the tombs and on the mountains he was always howling and bruising himself with stones. When he saw Jesus from a distance, he ran and bowed down before him; and he shouted at the top of his voice, "What have you to do with me, Jesus, Son of the Most High God? I adjure you by God, do not torment me." For he had said to him, "Come out of the man, you unclean spirit!" Then Jesus asked him, "What is your name?" He replied, "My name is Legion; for we are many." He begged him earnestly not to send them out of the country. Now there on the hillside a great herd of swine was feeding; and the unclean spirits begged him, "Send us into the swine; let us enter them." So he gave them permission. And the unclean spirits came out and entered the swine; and the herd, numbering about two thousand, rushed down the steep bank into the lake, and were drowned in the lake.

The swineherds ran off and told it in the city and in the country. Then people came to see what it was that had happened. They came to Jesus and saw the demoniac sitting there, clothed and in his right mind, the very man who had had the legion; and they were afraid. Those who had seen what had happened to the demoniac and to the swine reported it. Then they began to beg Jesus to leave their neighborhood. As he was getting into the boat, the man who had been possessed by demons begged him that he might be with him. But Jesus refused, and said to him, "Go home to your friends, and tell them how much the Lord has done for you, and what mercy he has shown you." And he went away and began to proclaim in the Decapolis how much Jesus had done for him; and everyone was amazed.

Notice what you think and feel as you read the gospel.

Jesus casts many demons out of a tormented man in a country of the Gentiles. Afterward, the man wishes to follow Jesus, but Jesus directs him to return to his own people and speak to them of the mercy God has shown to him.

Pray as you are led for yourself and others.

"Lord, I gladly obey you in whatever you will for me to be or do, just let me be truly your own. I love you with all my heart . . ." (Continue in your own words.)

Listen to Jesus.

God has only good things for you, beloved. As you detach yourself from earthly things, you will enjoy the graces of heaven. What else is Jesus saying to you?

Ask God to show you how to live today.

"I offer myself to you today, Lord, for the sake of others in need. Let my whole day—my thoughts, words, deeds, joys, and sufferings—be a prayer for others. Amen."

Tuesday, January 31, 2017

Know that God is present with you and ready to converse.
"Jesus, I need to touch you as you pass by today."

Read the gospel: Mark 5:21–43.

When Jesus had crossed again in the boat to the other side, a great crowd gathered round him; and he was by the lake. Then one of the leaders of the synagogue named Jairus came and, when he saw him, fell at his feet and begged him repeatedly, "My little daughter is at the point of death. Come and lay your hands on her, so that she may be made well, and live." So he went with him.

And a large crowd followed him and pressed in on him. Now there was a woman who had been suffering from hemorrhages for twelve years. She had endured much under many physicians, and had spent all that she had; and she was no better, but rather grew worse. She had heard about Jesus, and came up behind him in the crowd and touched his cloak, for she said, "If I but touch his clothes, I will be made well." Immediately her hemorrhage stopped; and she felt in her body that she was healed of her disease. Immediately aware that power had gone forth from him, Jesus turned about in the crowd and said, "Who touched my clothes?" And his disciples said to him, "You see the crowd pressing in on you; how can you say, 'Who touched me'?" He looked all round to see who had done it. But the woman, knowing what had happened to her, came in fear and trembling, fell down before him, and told him the whole truth. He said to her, "Daughter, your faith has made you well; go in peace, and be healed of your disease."

While he was still speaking, some people came from the leader's house to say, "Your daughter is dead. Why trouble the teacher any further?" But overhearing what they said, Jesus said to the leader of the synagogue, "Do not fear, only believe." He allowed no one to follow him except Peter, James, and John, the brother of James. When they came to the house of the leader of the synagogue, he saw a commotion, people weeping and wailing loudly. When he had entered, he said to them, "Why do you make a commotion and weep? The child is not dead but sleeping." And they laughed at him. Then he put them all outside, and took the child's father and mother and those who were with him, and went in where the child was. He took her by the hand and said to her, "Talitha cum," which means, "Little girl, get up!" And immediately the girl got up and began to walk about (she was twelve years of age). At this they were overcome with amazement. He strictly ordered them that no one should know this, and told them to give her something to eat.

Notice what you think and feel as you read the gospel.

The narrative of the raising of Jairus's daughter from the dead is interrupted by the healing of the woman with hemorrhages. In faith, she touches the hem of Jesus' garment and immediately the hemorrhage stops. Jesus does not seem to be aware of it until it happens. Then she comes to him and he blesses her for her faith. This "little" miracle feels as great as the raising of Jairus's daughter from the dead.

Pray as you are led for yourself and others.

"Lord, nothing is too small for you, nothing too great. Heal me and raise me up to your service . . ." (Continue in your own words.)

Listen to Jesus.

When you speak to me, beloved, you reveal your faith. Pray often, and I will reward your faith with fruitfulness. What else is Jesus saying to you?

Ask God to show you how to live today.

"Forgive me for lapses in prayer and faithfulness, Lord. Let me walk more closely with you today. Amen."

Wednesday, February 1, 2017

Know that God is present with you and ready to converse.

"Lord, let me hear your holy Word afresh and respond with faith."

Read the gospel: Mark 6:1–6.

Jesus left that place and came to his home town, and his disciples followed him. On the sabbath he began to teach in the synagogue, and many who heard him were astounded. They said, "Where did this man get all this? What is this wisdom that has been given to him? What deeds of power are being done by his hands! Is not this the carpenter, the son of Mary and brother of James and Joses and Judas and Simon, and are not his sisters here with us?" And they took offence at him. Then Jesus said to them, "Prophets are not without honor, except in their home town, and among their own kin, and in their own house." And he could do no deed of power there, except that he laid his hands on a few sick people and cured them. And he was amazed at their unbelief. Then he went about among the villages teaching.

Notice what you think and feel as you read the gospel.

The people of Jesus' hometown are aware of his wisdom and miracles, but they cannot believe in him because they know his background and his relatives. They actually take offense at him. Jesus is amazed at their unbelief and moves on.

Pray as you are led for yourself and others.

"Jesus, let me not take you for granted. Let your mercy be new every morning upon me and upon those I pray for . . ." (Continue in your own words.)

Listen to Jesus.

The more we are together, beloved, the more you will love me and serve me. What else is Jesus saying to you?

Ask God to show you how to live today.

"I give myself to you today, Lord. Let me rejoice all day in your presence. Amen."

Thursday, February 2, 2017
Presentation of the Lord

Know that God is present with you and ready to converse.

"Let your Word be light in my heart and soul and mind, O Lord."

Read the gospel: Luke 2:22–40.

When the time came for their purification according to the law of Moses, Mary and Joseph brought Jesus up to Jerusalem to present him to the Lord (as it is written in the law of the Lord, "Every firstborn male shall be designated as holy to the Lord"), and they offered a sacrifice according to what is stated in the law of the Lord, "a pair of turtle-doves or two young pigeons."

Now there was a man in Jerusalem whose name was Simeon; this man was righteous and devout, looking forward to the consolation of Israel, and the Holy Spirit rested on him. It had been revealed to him by the Holy Spirit that he would not see death before he had seen the Lord's Messiah. Guided by the Spirit, Simeon came into the temple; and when the parents brought in the child Jesus, to do for him what was customary under the law, Simeon took him in his arms and praised God, saying,

"Master, now you are dismissing your servant in peace,
according to your word;

for my eyes have seen your salvation,
    which you have prepared in the presence of all peoples,
a light for revelation to the Gentiles
    and for glory to your people Israel."

And the child's father and mother were amazed at what was being said about him. Then Simeon blessed them and said to his mother Mary, "This child is destined for the falling and the rising of many in Israel, and to be a sign that will be opposed so that the inner thoughts of many will be revealed—and a sword will pierce your own soul too."

There was also a prophet, Anna the daughter of Phanuel, of the tribe of Asher. She was of a great age, having lived with her husband for seven years after her marriage, then as a widow to the age of eighty-four. She never left the temple but worshipped there with fasting and prayer night and day. At that moment she came, and began to praise God and to speak about the child to all who were looking for the redemption of Jerusalem. When they had finished everything required by the law of the Lord, they returned to Galilee, to their own town of Nazareth. The child grew and became strong, filled with wisdom; and the favor of God was upon him.

Notice what you think and feel as you read the gospel.

Simeon is overjoyed to lay eyes on the child Jesus, who was destined to be God's means of salvation for Israel and the whole world. Simeon understands that Jesus' coming will raise conflicts and opposition and that Mary will suffer, too.

Pray as you are led for yourself and others.

"I experience conflicts, too, Lord, outside and inside. Help me to do my best and trust that all things are for my good and the good of those you have given me . . ." (Continue in your own words.)

Listen to Jesus.

I go before you as you follow me, my child, my friend. I give you strength and grace to endure all things and to embrace all things. What else is Jesus saying to you?

Ask God to show you how to live today.

"I trust in your grace, Lord, and not in my own strength. Help me to walk in your way perfectly. Amen."

Friday, February 3, 2017

Know that God is present with you and ready to converse.
"Worldliness blinds a person's eyes to the presence of God in all things.
Let me turn away from worldliness and see you in your Word, Lord."

Read the gospel: Mark 6:14–29.

King Herod heard of it, for Jesus' name had become known. Some were
saying, "John the baptizer has been raised from the dead; and for this reason these powers are at work in him." But others said, "It is Elijah." And
others said, "It is a prophet, like one of the prophets of old." But when
Herod heard of it, he said, "John, whom I beheaded, has been raised."

For Herod himself had sent men who arrested John, bound him,
and put him in prison on account of Herodias, his brother Philip's wife,
because Herod had married her. For John had been telling Herod, "It
is not lawful for you to have your brother's wife." And Herodias had
a grudge against him, and wanted to kill him. But she could not, for
Herod feared John, knowing that he was a righteous and holy man, and
he protected him. When he heard him, he was greatly perplexed; and
yet he liked to listen to him. But an opportunity came when Herod on
his birthday gave a banquet for his courtiers and officers and for the
leaders of Galilee. When his daughter Herodias came in and danced, she
pleased Herod and his guests; and the king said to the girl, "Ask me for
whatever you wish, and I will give it." And he solemnly swore to her,
"Whatever you ask me, I will give you, even half of my kingdom." She
went out and said to her mother, "What should I ask for?" She replied,
"The head of John the baptizer." Immediately she rushed back to the
king and requested, "I want you to give me at once the head of John the
Baptist on a platter." The king was deeply grieved; yet out of regard for
his oaths and for the guests, he did not want to refuse her. Immediately
the king sent a soldier of the guard with orders to bring John's head. He
went and beheaded him in the prison, brought his head on a platter, and
gave it to the girl. Then the girl gave it to her mother. When his disciples
heard about it, they came and took his body, and laid it in a tomb.

Notice what you think and feel as you read the gospel.

Herod is a confused man. While drunk with friends at his birthday party,
Herod makes a rash promise to his daughter; her mother uses the opportunity to demand John's death. Herod, though he fears John, has him
beheaded.

Pray as you are led for yourself and others.

"Lord, take away from me all darkness of mind. Let my eye look toward you, loving God and my neighbor . . ." (Continue in your own words.)

Listen to Jesus.

Do not be afraid of what others think and say about you because of your devotion to me. I will defend you. What else is Jesus saying to you?

Ask God to show you how to live today.

"Teach me simplicity, Lord, and humility as I walk behind you today. Amen."

Saturday, February 4, 2017

Know that God is present with you and ready to converse.

"You are my Shepherd, Lord, and you teach me by your Word."

Read the gospel: Mark 6:30–34.

The apostles gathered around Jesus, and told him all that they had done and taught. He said to them, "Come away to a deserted place all by yourselves and rest a while." For many were coming and going, and they had no leisure even to eat. And they went away in the boat to a deserted place by themselves. Now many saw them going and recognized them, and they hurried there on foot from all the towns and arrived ahead of them. As he went ashore, he saw a great crowd; and he had compassion for them, because they were like sheep without a shepherd; and he began to teach them many things.

Notice what you think and feel as you read the gospel.

Jesus seems thwarted in his own purposes. As he seeks to escape the crowd by boat, the people anticipate his destination and arrive there before him by land. Is Jesus frustrated? Not at all. He has compassion on them and begins to teach them. He is the Great Shepherd.

Pray as you are led for yourself and others.

"Let me be as you are, Lord, in the midst of events that might frustrate me. Let me operate with your patience and compassion . . ." (Continue in your own words.)

Listen to Jesus.

Accept all things as God's will to work good in your life. I love you and have much to teach you. What else is Jesus saying to you?

Ask God to show you how to live today.

"Thank you, Lord. Thank you for all the things in my life. May I learn from you today, Shepherd. Amen."

Sunday February 5, 2017
Fifth Sunday in Ordinary Time

Know that God is present with you and ready to converse.

Jesus said that his Father still works and he does, too. We see him at this time of the Church year healing the sick, teaching the people about the ways of God, challenging the religionists of his day, and making enemies, actions that would eventually lead to his crucifixion.

"Lord, you came in love to do your Father's will. Continue your work in me."

Read the gospel: Matthew 5:13–16.

Jesus said, "You are the salt of the earth; but if salt has lost its taste, how can its saltiness be restored? It is no longer good for anything, but is thrown out and trampled underfoot.

"You are the light of the world. A city built on a hill cannot be hidden. No one after lighting a lamp puts it under the bushel basket, but on the lampstand, and it gives light to all in the house. In the same way, let your light shine before others, so that they may see your good works and give glory to your Father in heaven."

Notice what you think and feel as you read the gospel.

Jesus affirms the people who have come out to learn from him. He calls them salt of the earth and light of the world, two essential elements for life. The salt should be tasted and the light should shine so that God may be glorified.

Pray as you are led for yourself and others.

"Let me do good works, Lord, for I want God to give glory to your and my Father in heaven . . ." (Continue in your own words.)

Listen to Jesus.
You know what to do, for I have placed you here. Follow me in doing the will of our Father. What else is Jesus saying to you?

Ask God to show you how to live today.
"I do not want to live my life mechanically, Lord. Show me how to live intentionally in close friendship with you. Let me begin again today. Thank you, Savior. Amen."

Monday, February 6, 2017

Know that God is present with you and ready to converse.
"I come into your presence in all my weakness, Lord. Let me touch the fringe of your cloak."

Read the gospel: Mark 6:53–56.
When Jesus and his disciples had crossed over, they came to land at Gennesaret and moored the boat. When they got out of the boat, people at once recognized him, and rushed about that whole region and began to bring the sick on mats to wherever they heard he was. And wherever he went, into villages or cities or farms, they laid the sick in the market-places, and begged him that they might touch even the fringe of his cloak; and all who touched it were healed.

Notice what you think and feel as you read the gospel.
What a picture of people rushing around to lay their sick before Jesus. Coming to him from villages, cities, or farms, all who touch the fringe of his cloak are healed.

Pray as you are led for yourself and others.
"Jesus, I lay before you now those who need your healing touch, myself included. I give you . . ." (Continue in your own words.)

Listen to Jesus.
I hear your prayers, beloved disciple. I know your love for me and for others. What else is Jesus saying to you?

Ask God to show you how to live today.
"Help me become stronger in prayer for those in need, Lord. Get me out of myself so that I can see others with your compassion. Amen."

Tuesday, February 7, 2017

Know that God is present with you and ready to converse.

"Lord, I exult in your presence now. By your Word turn me away from vain and hypocritical practices and let me do instead acts of love."

Read the gospel: Mark 7:1–13.

Now when the Pharisees and some of the scribes who had come from Jerusalem gathered around Jesus, they noticed that some of his disciples were eating with defiled hands, that is, without washing them. (For the Pharisees, and all the Jews, do not eat unless they thoroughly wash their hands, thus observing the tradition of the elders; and they do not eat anything from the market unless they wash it; and there are also many other traditions that they observe, the washing of cups, pots, and bronze kettles.) So the Pharisees and the scribes asked him, "Why do your disciples not live according to the tradition of the elders, but eat with defiled hands?" He said to them, "Isaiah prophesied rightly about you hypocrites, as it is written,

> 'This people honors me with their lips,
>> but their hearts are far from me;
> in vain do they worship me,
>> teaching human precepts as doctrines.'

You abandon the commandment of God and hold to human tradition."

Then he said to them, "You have a fine way of rejecting the commandment of God in order to keep your tradition! For Moses said, 'Honor your father and your mother'; and, 'Whoever speaks evil of father or mother must surely die.' But you say that if anyone tells father or mother, 'Whatever support you might have had from me is Corban' (that is, an offering to God)—then you no longer permit doing anything for a father or mother, thus making void the word of God through your tradition that you have handed on. And you do many things like this."

Notice what you think and feel as you read the gospel.

The Pharisees are sticklers for their ritual traditions and expect Jesus and his disciples to observe them, too. But Jesus calls them hypocrites, teaching human precepts as doctrines but not honoring God or God's commandments.

Pray as you are led for yourself and others.

"Lord, I pray for my father and mother today . . ." (Continue in your own words.)

Listen to Jesus.
Be grateful to God for all you have, beloved servant. What else is Jesus saying to you?

Ask God to show you how to live today.
"Let me live an entire day of thanksgiving, Lord, as I recognize the many blessings you give me. It is right to give you thanks and praise. Amen."

Wednesday, February 8, 2017

Know that God is present with you and ready to converse.
"Almighty Trinity, Father, Son, and Holy Spirit, I place myself here before you and ask for your mercy and grace. I will read your Word."

Read the gospel: Mark 7:14–23.
Then Jesus called the crowd again and said to them, "Listen to me, all of you, and understand: there is nothing outside a person that by going in can defile, but the things that come out are what defile."

When he had left the crowd and entered the house, his disciples asked him about the parable. He said to them, "Then do you also fail to understand? Do you not see that whatever goes into a person from outside cannot defile, since it enters, not the heart but the stomach, and goes out into the sewer?" (Thus he declared all foods clean.) And he said, "It is what comes out of a person that defiles. For it is from within, from the human heart, that evil intentions come: fornication, theft, murder, adultery, avarice, wickedness, deceit, licentiousness, envy, slander, pride, folly. All these evil things come from within, and they defile a person."

Notice what you think and feel as you read the gospel.
Speaking against rules about food and food preparation, Jesus asserts that foods do not defile a person but what comes out of the human heart defiles a person. He says that sins begin in and proceed from the heart, and he lists many.

Pray as you are led for yourself and others.
"Lord, I am not clean. I submit my heart to you for mercy and cleansing. After you cast out the evil in me, fill me with love. Make my heart like yours, Jesus . . ." (Continue in your own words.)

Listen to Jesus.

God asks you to be holy, beloved disciple. Long for it, pray for it, work for it in your life, and you will have joy and bear fruit to the glory of God. What else is Jesus saying to you?

Ask God to show you how to live today.

"I resolve to amend my life, Lord, from the inside of my heart. Pour out your grace upon me so that I may please God with my life. Thank you. Amen."

Thursday, February 9, 2017

Know that God is present with you and ready to converse.

"Your name is mercy, Lord. You love us and care for us every day."

Read the gospel: Mark 7: 24–30.

From there Jesus set out and went away to the region of Tyre. He entered a house and did not want anyone to know he was there. Yet he could not escape notice, but a woman whose little daughter had an unclean spirit immediately heard about him, and she came and bowed down at his feet. Now the woman was a Gentile, of Syrophoenician origin. She begged him to cast the demon out of her daughter. He said to her, "Let the children be fed first, for it is not fair to take the children's food and throw it to the dogs." But she answered him, "Sir, even the dogs under the table eat the children's crumbs." Then he said to her, "For saying that, you may go—the demon has left your daughter." So she went home, found the child lying on the bed, and the demon gone.

Notice what you think and feel as you read the gospel.

Jesus surprises us with his response to the woman's request. He might have been annoyed to have been discovered in the house, but more likely he was testing her and making the point that he came to save all of us, not just the Jews. She answers him cleverly, assertively, and for that answer he casts the demon out of her daughter.

Pray as you are led for yourself and others.

"Jesus, I, too, persevere in asking from you what I need. I am concerned about the needs of others and bring these petitions to you now . . ." (Continue in your own words.)

Listen to Jesus.
When you persevere in prayer, my child, you show your faith. Step out in faith, and I will reward you. What else is Jesus saying to you?

Ask God to show you how to live today.
"Lord, give me wisdom to know your will and then the strength to do it. Thank you. Amen."

Friday, February 10, 2017

Know that God is present with you and ready to converse.
"Lord, let my ears be open to your Word and let me sing your praises."

Read the gospel: Mark 7:31–37.
Then Jesus returned from the region of Tyre, and went by way of Sidon towards the Sea of Galilee, in the region of the Decapolis. They brought to him a deaf man who had an impediment in his speech; and they begged him to lay his hand on him. He took him aside in private, away from the crowd, and put his fingers into his ears, and he spat and touched his tongue. Then looking up to heaven, he sighed and said to him, "Ephphatha," that is, "Be opened." And immediately his ears were opened, his tongue was released, and he spoke plainly. Then Jesus ordered them to tell no one; but the more he ordered them, the more zealously they proclaimed it. They were astounded beyond measure, saying, "He has done everything well; he even makes the deaf to hear and the mute to speak."

Notice what you think and feel as you read the gospel.
Jesus takes the deaf man away from the crowd. He seems burdened by all the demands for healing. He sighs, but he heals the man of all his infirmities. He does everything well. Of course, he cannot escape the crowds.

Pray as you are led for yourself and others.
"Lord, I give you all I am and all I have. You know what I need before I ask it. You do all things well . . ." (Continue in your own words.)

Listen to Jesus.
I wish to do things through you, beloved. Be open to opportunities for loving service. What else is Jesus saying to you?

Ask God to show you how to live today.
"Make me very sensitive to your bidding, Lord. Give me grace to serve.
I praise your holy name. Amen."

Saturday, February 11, 2017

Know that God is present with you and ready to converse.
"Master of the Universe, you condescend to be with me, a sinner. Let me
grow in love for you by the reading of your Word."

Read the gospel: Mark 8:1–10.
In those days when there was again a great crowd without anything
to eat, Jesus called his disciples and said to them, "I have compassion
for the crowd, because they have been with me now for three days and
have nothing to eat. If I send them away hungry to their homes, they will
faint on the way—and some of them have come from a great distance."
His disciples replied, "How can one feed these people with bread here
in the desert?" He asked them, "How many loaves do you have?" They
said, "Seven." Then he ordered the crowd to sit down on the ground;
and he took the seven loaves, and after giving thanks he broke them
and gave them to his disciples to distribute; and they distributed them
to the crowd. They had also a few small fish; and after blessing them, he
ordered that these too should be distributed. They ate and were filled;
and they took up the broken pieces left over, seven baskets full. Now
there were about four thousand people. And he sent them away. And
immediately he got into the boat with his disciples and went to the district of Dalmanutha.

Notice what you think and feel as you read the gospel.
Jesus has compassion for the crowd. He knows they are hungry and
far from home. His disciples are perplexed by the problem, but Jesus
multiplies the loaves and fishes and feeds four thousand.

Pray as you are led for yourself and others.
"Loving Jesus, feed me with yourself, for you are the Bread of Life . . ."
(Continue in your own words.)

Listen to Jesus.
Beloved disciple, I love your coming to me, our time together. What else is
Jesus saying to you?

Ask God to show you how to live today.

"I wish to do something good for someone else today, Lord. I offer myself to your service. Amen."

Sunday, February 12, 2017
Sixth Sunday in Ordinary Time

Know that God is present with you and ready to converse.

Jesus, the Lamb of God, came to earth to express the love of God by offering himself for all humankind, suffering and dying to save us from sin and death. But he was also a teacher. He taught us how to be happy. He taught us about holiness.

"Eternal Word of God, I will hear you now. Give me grace to understand and obey."

Read the gospel: Matthew 5:17–37.

Jesus said, "Do not think that I have come to abolish the law or the prophets; I have come not to abolish but to fulfill. For truly I tell you, until heaven and earth pass away, not one letter, not one stroke of a letter, will pass from the law until all is accomplished. Therefore, whoever breaks one of the least of these commandments, and teaches others to do the same, will be called least in the kingdom of heaven; but whoever does them and teaches them will be called great in the kingdom of heaven. For I tell you, unless your righteousness exceeds that of the scribes and Pharisees, you will never enter the kingdom of heaven.

"You have heard that it was said to those of ancient times, 'You shall not murder'; and 'whoever murders shall be liable to judgment.' But I say to you that if you are angry with a brother or sister, you will be liable to judgment; and if you insult a brother or sister, you will be liable to the council; and if you say, 'You fool,' you will be liable to the hell of fire. So when you are offering your gift at the altar, if you remember that your brother or sister has something against you, leave your gift there before the altar and go; first be reconciled to your brother or sister, and then come and offer your gift. Come to terms quickly with your accuser while you are on the way to court with him, or your accuser may hand you over to the judge, and the judge to the guard, and you will be thrown into prison. Truly I tell you, you will never get out until you have paid the last penny.

"You have heard that it was said, 'You shall not commit adultery.' But I say to you that everyone who looks at a woman with lust has already committed adultery with her in his heart. If your right eye causes you to sin, tear it out and throw it away; it is better for you to lose one of your members than for your whole body to be thrown into hell. And if your right hand causes you to sin, cut it off and throw it away; it is better for you to lose one of your members than for your whole body to go into hell.

"It was also said, 'Whoever divorces his wife, let him give her a certificate of divorce.' But I say to you that anyone who divorces his wife, except on the ground of unchastity, causes her to commit adultery; and whoever marries a divorced woman commits adultery.

"Again, you have heard that it was said to those of ancient times, 'You shall not swear falsely, but carry out the vows you have made to the Lord.' But I say to you, Do not swear at all, either by heaven, for it is the throne of God, or by the earth, for it is his footstool, or by Jerusalem, for it is the city of the great King. And do not swear by your head, for you cannot make one hair white or black. Let your word be 'Yes, Yes' or 'No, No'; anything more than this comes from the evil one."

Notice what you think and feel as you read the gospel.

Jesus teaches that sin arises in the heart before it expresses itself in actions. He raises the standard for righteousness. He insists on holiness. He wants simple purity of heart.

Pray as you are led for yourself and others.

"Lord, who can achieve this holiness? Pour your Spirit into my heart, dispelling lust, anger, and selfishness before they can manifest themselves . . ." (Continue in your own words.)

Listen to Jesus.

I forgive your sins, and I give you power to overcome sin. Continue to strive for holiness. What else is Jesus saying to you?

Ask God to show you how to live today.

"Lord, I hear your words, but I know I fail often. Please give me your grace when I am tempted. Amen."

Monday, February 13, 2017

Know that God is present with you and ready to converse.

"Lord, you are not a force I can exploit for my own benefit. You are a person, and you are here with me now. I thank you."

Read the gospel: Mark 8:11–13.

The Pharisees came and began to argue with Jesus, asking him for a sign from heaven, to test him. And he sighed deeply in his spirit and said, "Why does this generation ask for a sign? Truly I tell you, no sign will be given to this generation." And he left them, and getting into the boat again, he went across to the other side.

Notice what you think and feel as you read the gospel.

The Pharisees tire Jesus with their insistence that he prove himself with signs. He refuses to be their trick pony.

Pray as you are led for yourself and others.

"Jesus, I know you care for me far beyond my ability to ask or think about my own needs. Let me bring to you the needs of others . . ." (Continue in your own words.)

Listen to Jesus.

I am in your life, beloved servant. Your love for others is my love for others. It is a joy to be of one mind and heart with you. What else is Jesus saying to you?

Ask God to show you how to live today.

"I am just myself, Lord. I feel overwhelmed by the neediness of so many. Guide me to do what I should do today. Amen."

Tuesday, February 14, 2017

Know that God is present with you and ready to converse.

"Lord, you exist, you love, you are here with me now; let me please you by my faith."

Read the gospel: Mark 8:14–21.

Now the disciples had forgotten to bring any bread; and they had only one loaf with them in the boat. And Jesus cautioned them, saying, "Watch out—beware of the yeast of the Pharisees and the yeast of Herod." They said to one another, "It is because we have no bread." And becoming aware of it, Jesus said to them, "Why are you talking about having no bread? Do you still not perceive or understand? Are your hearts hardened? Do you have eyes, and fail to see? Do you have ears, and fail to hear? And do you not remember? When I broke the five loaves for the five thousand, how many baskets full of broken pieces did you collect?" They said to him, "Twelve." "And the seven for the four thousand, how many baskets full of broken pieces did you collect?" And they said to him, "Seven." Then he said to them, "Do you not yet understand?"

Notice what you think and feel as you read the gospel.

When Jesus brings up the yeast of the Pharisees and Herod, the disciples assume he is talking about the fact they forgot to bring bread. He rebukes them for not understanding that he is speaking figuratively. Weak in understanding, weak in faith, they are concerned with worldly things. He reminds them of the miracles multiplying the bread. He wants them to understand that he is Lord.

Pray as you are led for yourself and others.

"Jesus, increase my understanding and my faith. Let me remember the mighty things you have done in my life. Let me be ready to speak of your wonderful ways to all I encounter . . ." (Continue in your own words.)

Listen to Jesus.

Beloved disciple, begin in humble ignorance, but reach out to me in faith. I will teach you the way you should go. What else is Jesus saying to you?

Ask God to show you how to live today.

"Lord, show me how to act upon my small faith so that I can learn how to think, love, pray, and serve as you do. Let this prayer make a positive difference in my day, in my life. Amen."

Wednesday, February 15, 2017

Know that God is present with you and ready to converse.

"Lord, I am blind to your glory. Open my eyes to you and to others."

Read the gospel: Mark 8:22–26.

Jesus and his disciples came to Bethsaida. Some people brought a blind man to him and begged him to touch him. He took the blind man by the hand and led him out of the village; and when he had put saliva on his eyes and laid his hands on him, he asked him, "Can you see anything?" And the man looked up and said, "I can see people, but they look like trees, walking." Then Jesus laid his hands on his eyes again; and he looked intently and his sight was restored, and he saw everything clearly. Then he sent him away to his home, saying, "Do not even go into the village."

Notice what you think and feel as you read the gospel.

The details of Jesus' healing of this blind man are interesting. First he puts his saliva on the man's eyes, lays his hands on the man, and the man's sight is restored partially. He sees people like "trees, walking." Then Jesus lays hands on his eyes again and he is completely healed.

Pray as you are led for yourself and others.

"This healing is so vivid, Lord. Your ways are mysterious, but you do all things well. I pray for my own healing and for the healing of those you have given me . . ." (Continue in your own words.)

Listen to Jesus.

Doing good for others is the secret of joy, my dear servant. Join me in joy. What else is Jesus saying to you?

Ask God to show you how to live today.

"Lord, I aspire to virtue, to walk in your love today. You must fill me with your love and lead me to do good. Let me glorify you in thought, word, and deed. Amen."

Thursday, February 16, 2017

Know that God is present with you and ready to converse.

"Incarnate God, Son of Man, let me know you by your Word."

Read the gospel: Mark 8:27–33.

Jesus went on with his disciples to the villages of Caesarea Philippi; and on the way he asked his disciples, "Who do people say that I am?" And they answered him, "John the Baptist; and others, Elijah; and still others, one of the prophets." He asked them, "But who do you say that I am?" Peter answered him, "You are the Messiah." And he sternly ordered them not to tell anyone about him.

Then he began to teach them that the Son of Man must undergo great suffering, and be rejected by the elders, the chief priests, and the scribes, and be killed, and after three days rise again. He said all this quite openly. And Peter took him aside and began to rebuke him. But turning and looking at his disciples, he rebuked Peter and said, "Get behind me, Satan! For you are setting your mind not on divine things but on human things."

Notice what you think and feel as you read the gospel.

Jesus tests his disciples about his identity. When Peter proclaims him the Messiah, Jesus teaches them that he will have to undergo great suffering. Peter doesn't understand that!

Pray as you are led for yourself and others.

"Lord, you suffered, died, and rose again so that I might follow you. I unite my sufferings to yours, including . . ." (Continue in your own words.)

Listen to Jesus.

I have liberated you from sin and death, beloved disciple. Your life has profound meaning for yourself and those I have given you. What else is Jesus saying to you?

Ask God to show you how to live today.

"Let me live and work today with my mind tuned to yours, my heart tuned to heaven. Thank you, Savior. Amen."

Friday, February 17, 2017

Know that God is present with you and ready to converse.

"Lord, you are here tapping me on the shoulder saying 'follow me.' Help me respond with all my heart and mind."

Read the gospel: Mark 8:34–9:1.

Jesus called the crowd with his disciples, and said to them, "If any want to become my followers, let them deny themselves and take up their cross and follow me. For those who want to save their life will lose it, and those who lose their life for my sake, and for the sake of the gospel, will save it. For what will it profit them to gain the whole world and forfeit their life? Indeed, what can they give in return for their life? Those who are ashamed of me and of my words in this adulterous and sinful generation, of them the Son of Man will also be ashamed when he comes in the glory of his Father with the holy angels." And he said to them, "Truly I tell you, there are some standing here who will not taste death until they see that the kingdom of God has come with power."

Notice what you think and feel as you read the gospel.

What did the phrase "take up their cross" mean to those who heard Jesus? After all, the crucifixion was in the future. But the meaning is clear: followers must suffer and lose their lives and be proud of their association with Jesus.

Pray as you are led for yourself and others.

"Lord, I am ashamed of the times I have been ashamed of you, hiding my love of you, pretending I do not depend on you. Forgive me and give me the boldness and wisdom of your Spirit . . ." (Continue in your own words.)

Listen to Jesus.

Give your suffering to me, and it will contribute to the redemption of your soul and the souls of those I have given you. What else is Jesus saying to you?

Ask God to show you how to live today.

"Help me to remember often today that you and your kingdom will come with power. Come, Lord Jesus. Amen."

Saturday, February 18, 2017

Know that God is present with you and ready to converse.

"You are the One of whom the prophets spoke, the Christ, the Savior of the world. Let me know you in your glory."

Read the gospel: Mark 9:2–13.

Six days later, Jesus took with him Peter and James and John, and led them up a high mountain apart, by themselves. And he was transfigured before them, and his clothes became dazzling white, such as no one on earth could bleach them. And there appeared to them Elijah with Moses, who were talking with Jesus. Then Peter said to Jesus, "Rabbi, it is good for us to be here; let us make three dwellings, one for you, one for Moses, and one for Elijah." He did not know what to say, for they were terrified. Then a cloud overshadowed them, and from the cloud there came a voice, "This is my Son, the Beloved; listen to him!" Suddenly when they looked around, they saw no one with them any more, but only Jesus.

As they were coming down the mountain, he ordered them to tell no one about what they had seen, until after the Son of Man had risen from the dead. So they kept the matter to themselves, questioning what this rising from the dead could mean. Then they asked him, "Why do the scribes say that Elijah must come first?" He said to them, "Elijah is indeed coming first to restore all things. How then is it written about the Son of Man, that he is to go through many sufferings and be treated with contempt? But I tell you that Elijah has come, and they did to him whatever they pleased, as it is written about him."

Notice what you think and feel as you read the gospel.

The transfiguration of Jesus places him in the Jewish historic and prophetic context for he is speaking with Elijah and Moses. The Father speaks to the three disciples out of a cloud. Jesus predicts his rising from the dead, but his disciples don't understand.

Pray as you are led for yourself and others.

"Lord, some of your promises are so great I cannot take them in. You foretold your own resurrection, and you promise me that I also shall be raised. Make this promise real to me . . ." (Continue in your own words.)

Listen to Jesus.

I suffered and died in the flesh so that you could take on my glory and join me in everlasting life. I offer you your heart's desire. What else is Jesus saying to you?

Ask God to show you how to live today.

"Okay, Lord. I am ready to follow you through suffering to obtain your glorious kingdom. Remind me of that when I experience suffering today. Amen."

Sunday, February 19, 2017
Seventh Sunday in Ordinary Time

Know that God is present with you and ready to converse.

In this week of Ordinary Time, Jesus travels among the people, teaching them how to achieve true holiness. His teaching fulfills the law. He teaches his inner circle of disciples as well, helping them understand who he is, what kind of death he is facing, and how they may follow him in humble service to others.

"Jesus, I praise you. Teach me the holiness of God."

Read the gospel: Matthew 5:38–48.

Jesus said, "You have heard that it was said, 'An eye for an eye and a tooth for a tooth.' But I say to you, Do not resist an evildoer. But if anyone strikes you on the right cheek, turn the other also; and if anyone wants to sue you and take your coat, give your cloak as well; and if anyone forces you to go one mile, go also the second mile. Give to everyone who begs from you, and do not refuse anyone who wants to borrow from you.

"You have heard that it was said, 'You shall love your neighbor and hate your enemy.' But I say to you, Love your enemies and pray for those who persecute you, so that you may be children of your Father in heaven; for he makes his sun rise on the evil and on the good, and sends rain on the righteous and on the unrighteous. For if you love those who love you, what reward do you have? Do not even the tax-collectors do the same? And if you greet only your brothers and sisters, what more are you doing than others? Do not even the Gentiles do the same? Be perfect, therefore, as your heavenly Father is perfect."

Notice what you think and feel as you read the gospel.

Rather than negate the laws of Moses, Jesus raises them to a higher level of godliness. He challenges his hearers to love those who hate and abuse them. I recall he did that very thing from the cross. He loved those who were hurting him and asked his Father to forgive them.

Pray as you are led for yourself and others.

"Lord, give me love like yours. Unless you change my heart, I will not be able to love my enemies. By your grace, I beg you, Lord, give me a heart like yours . . ." (Continue in your own words.)

Listen to Jesus.

I pour into you love and mercy, for you have asked for it. I am happy with you. What else is Jesus saying to you?

Ask God to show you how to live today.

"Make me aware today of someone in my life I find it hard to love. Then let me receive love from you for that person. Help me to persevere in that love. Amen."

Monday, February 20, 2017

Know that God is present with you and ready to converse.

"Jesus, you are so good to be present with me now. Let me learn what you want me to learn today in your Word."

Read the gospel: Mark 9:14–29.

When Jesus, Peter, James, and John came to the disciples, they saw a great crowd around them, and some scribes arguing with them. When the whole crowd saw him, they were immediately overcome with awe, and they ran forward to greet him. He asked them, "What are you arguing about with them?" Someone from the crowd answered him, "Teacher, I brought you my son; he has a spirit that makes him unable to speak; and whenever it seizes him, it dashes him down; and he foams and grinds his teeth and becomes rigid; and I asked your disciples to cast it out, but they could not do so." He answered them, "You faithless generation, how much longer must I be among you? How much longer must I put up with you? Bring him to me." And they brought the boy to him. When the spirit saw him, immediately it threw the boy into convulsions, and he fell on the ground and rolled about, foaming at the mouth. Jesus asked the father, "How long has this been happening to him?" And he said, "From childhood. It has often cast him into the fire and into the water, to destroy him; but if you are able to do anything, have pity on us and help us." Jesus said to him, "If you are able!—All things can be done for the one who believes." Immediately the father of the child cried out, "I believe; help my unbelief!" When Jesus saw that a crowd came running together, he rebuked the unclean spirit, saying to it, "You spirit that keep this boy from speaking and hearing, I command you, come out of him, and never enter him again!" After crying out and convulsing him terribly, it came out, and the boy was like a corpse, so that most of them said, "He is dead." But Jesus took him by the hand and lifted him up, and he was able to stand. When he had entered the house, his disciples asked him privately, "Why could we not cast it out?" He said to them, "This kind can come out only through prayer."

Notice what you think and feel as you read the gospel.

Jesus casts out a dumb and violent spirit from a boy. Beforehand, people doubt he can do it. He rebukes their lack of faith. "How much longer must I put up with you?" he asks. The boy's father says, "If you are able . . . ," which Jesus echoes immediately, "If you are able!" The father says, "Help my unbelief."

Pray as you are led for yourself and others.

"Lord, let me know deep within that all things are possible for the one who believes. Help my unbelief. I think of . . ." (Continue in your own words.)

Listen to Jesus.

You are right to ask for faith, dear one. I am pleased to grant your prayer. What would you like me to do for you? What else is Jesus saying to you?

Ask God to show you how to live today.

"Lord, let me focus on the needs of others today and in your power act
to provide for them. Amen."

Tuesday, February 21, 2017

Know that God is present with you and ready to converse.

"Lord, speak to my heart by your mighty Word."

Read the gospel: Mark 9:30–37.

Jesus and his disciples went on from there and passed through Galilee.
He did not want anyone to know it; for he was teaching his disciples,
saying to them, "The Son of Man is to be betrayed into human hands,
and they will kill him, and three days after being killed, he will rise
again." But they did not understand what he was saying and were afraid
to ask him.

  Then they came to Capernaum; and when he was in the house he
asked them, "What were you arguing about on the way?" But they were
silent, for on the way they had argued with one another about who was
the greatest. He sat down, called the twelve, and said to them, "Whoever
wants to be first must be last of all and servant of all." Then he took a
little child and put it among them; and taking it in his arms, he said to
them, "Whoever welcomes one such child in my name welcomes me,
and whoever welcomes me welcomes not me but the one who sent me."

Notice what you think and feel as you read the gospel.

The disciples are unable to understand Jesus' prediction of his passion
and resurrection. They are afraid to ask him for an explanation. Instead
they argue on the way about who is the greatest. They are afraid to admit
it. He teaches them with the little child.

Pray as you are led for yourself and others.

"Lord, I, too, am obtuse, and I often miss your point or forget it before I
can apply it. Let me welcome a little child. Let me be a servant to others
. . ." (Continue in your own words.)

Listen to Jesus.

You will find me in that service, my beloved. You will find me, Jesus. What else
is Jesus saying to you?

Ask God to show you how to live today.
"Let me see situations in which I can put myself last and give me the grace to do so, Lord. Amen."

Wednesday, February 22, 2017
Chair of Saint Peter, Apostle

Know that God is present with you and ready to converse.
"Jesus, by your Word you convey power and authority. Let me understand you well."

Read the gospel: Matthew 16:13–19.

Now when Jesus came into the district of Caesarea Philippi, he asked his disciples, "Who do people say that the Son of Man is?" And they said, "Some say John the Baptist, but others Elijah, and still others Jeremiah or one of the prophets." He said to them, "But who do you say that I am?" Simon Peter answered, "You are the Messiah, the Son of the living God." And Jesus answered him, "Blessed are you, Simon son of Jonah! For flesh and blood has not revealed this to you, but my Father in heaven. And I tell you, you are Peter, and on this rock I will build my church, and the gates of Hades will not prevail against it. I will give you the keys of the kingdom of heaven, and whatever you bind on earth will be bound in heaven, and whatever you loose on earth will be loosed in heaven."

Notice what you think and feel as you read the gospel.
Peter answers Jesus' question well, and Jesus commends him for it. Then he blesses him, promising that he is the rock upon which Jesus will build his Church. Peter is given authority on earth and in heaven.

Pray as you are led for yourself and others.
"Lord, give me a greater appreciation for the authority of the Church. I pray for those who serve you in it, that they may be holy servants of your flocks . . ." (Continue in your own words.)

Listen to Jesus.
I am with my Church until the end of the age. Though some may sin, I will always raise up holy men and women to do my will. Trust me. What else is Jesus saying to you?

Ask God to show you how to live today.

"I wish to support and respect your servants in the Church, Lord. Give
me the opportunity to do so. Amen."

Thursday, February 23, 2017

Know that God is present with you and ready to converse.

"Lord, I read in your presence. Let me be comforted and challenged by
your Word as you deem best for me."

Read the gospel: Mark 9:41–50.

Jesus said, "For truly I tell you, whoever gives you a cup of water to drink
because you bear the name of Christ will by no means lose the reward.

"If any of you put a stumbling-block before one of these little ones
who believe in me, it would be better for you if a great millstone were
hung around your neck and you were thrown into the sea. If your hand
causes you to stumble, cut it off; it is better for you to enter life maimed
than to have two hands and to go to hell, to the unquenchable fire. And
if your foot causes you to stumble, cut it off; it is better for you to enter
life lame than to have two feet and to be thrown into hell., And if your
eye causes you to stumble, tear it out; it is better for you to enter the
kingdom of God with one eye than to have two eyes and to be thrown
into hell, where their worm never dies, and the fire is never quenched.

"For everyone will be salted with fire. Salt is good; but if salt has lost
its saltiness, how can you season it? Have salt in yourselves, and be at
peace with one another."

Notice what you think and feel as you read the gospel.

Jesus urges loving actions, promising rewards, and condemns unloving
actions, threatening punishment. He uses the shocking metaphor of
cutting off a hand or a foot or tearing out an eye if any of those cause us
to sin. He asks us to discipline ourselves, remembering what's at stake.

Pray as you are led for yourself and others.

"Lord, give me that hatred for my own sin. Help me root out my complacency and all habits of sin. Salt me with fire, and I shall enter into your
kingdom . . ." (Continue in your own words.)

Listen to Jesus.

Gaze at me, my beloved disciple, and I will show you your own reflection. If you bring your faults to me, I will cleanse you, heal you, and give you new life. What else is Jesus saying to you?

Ask God to show you how to live today.

"Lord, I accept your discipline in my life. Transform what is displeasing to you into what pleases you. Help me to cooperate with you in this. Amen."

Friday, February 24, 2017

Know that God is present with you and ready to converse.

"Jesus, guide me into your righteousness by your Word. Open my heart to your goodness."

Read the gospel: Mark 10:1–12.

Jesus left that place and went to the region of Judea and beyond the Jordan. And crowds again gathered around him; and, as was his custom, he again taught them.

Some Pharisees came, and to test him they asked, "Is it lawful for a man to divorce his wife?" He answered them, "What did Moses command you?" They said, "Moses allowed a man to write a certificate of dismissal and to divorce her." But Jesus said to them, "Because of your hardness of heart he wrote this commandment for you. But from the beginning of creation, 'God made them male and female. For this reason a man shall leave his father and mother and be joined to his wife, and the two shall become one flesh.' So they are no longer two, but one flesh. Therefore what God has joined together, let no one separate."

Then in the house the disciples asked him again about this matter. He said to them, "Whoever divorces his wife and marries another commits adultery against her; and if she divorces her husband and marries another, she commits adultery."

Notice what you think and feel as you read the gospel.

Jesus responds to the Pharisees' hard question about divorce by affirming a higher morality in marriage than Moses did. He dignifies marriage as the fulfillment of God's purpose in creating man and woman.

Pray as you are led for yourself and others.

"Merciful Lord, you are full of forgiveness when I err or sin. May my heart never harden toward any to whom I have promised my love. Let me keep all my promises . . ." (Continue in your own words.)

Listen to Jesus.

I understand that relationships can be difficult, my child. You may suffer, but you may also find great joy, as God intended. What else is Jesus saying to you?

Ask God to show you how to live today.

"Lord, I do not wish to take any relationship for granted. Give me the wisdom and grace to right any relationship that is faltering. Help me to obey you, Lord. Thank you. Amen."

Saturday, February 25, 2017

Know that God is present with you and ready to converse.

"Jesus, you love the little children. You see yourself in them. Let me learn from your Word."

Read the gospel: Mark 10:13–16.

People were bringing little children to Jesus in order that he might touch them; and the disciples spoke sternly to them. But when Jesus saw this, he was indignant and said to them, "Let the little children come to me; do not stop them; for it is to such as these that the kingdom of God belongs. Truly I tell you, whoever does not receive the kingdom of God as a little child will never enter it." And he took them up in his arms, laid his hands on them, and blessed them.

Notice what you think and feel as you read the gospel.

The disciples seem to think that the children are a distraction from Jesus' serious work. Jesus rebukes them, "indignant," saying that the kingdom of God is populated by the childlike.

Pray as you are led for yourself and others.

"Lord, a child is fun-loving, trusting, and open to love. Show me how to be a child of God . . ." (Continue in your own words.)

Listen to Jesus.

I often call you "child" because you come to me trusting and loving me. I bless you for that, dear child. What else is Jesus saying to you?

Ask God to show you how to live today.

"Reveal to me a moment today when I am not thinking and behaving like a trusting child. Lord, I long for your simplicity in loving. Amen."

Sunday, February 26, 2017
Eighth Sunday in Ordinary Time

Know that God is present with you and ready to converse.

This week of Ordinary Time begins with Jesus commanding us not to worry about our lives for our lives are in the hand of our loving Father. So what shall we do to inherit eternal life? Abandon everything and follow him. Where will he lead us? All the way to the Cross. So begins Lent, a joyous time in which we draw near to God.

"Lord, I wish to draw nearer to you than ever before. Let your sanctifying Word transform my mind and my heart so that I may please you."

Read the gospel: Matthew 6:24–34.

Jesus said, "No one can serve two masters; for a slave will either hate the one and love the other, or be devoted to the one and despise the other. You cannot serve God and wealth.

"Therefore I tell you, do not worry about your life, what you will eat or what you will drink, or about your body, what you will wear. Is not life more than food, and the body more than clothing? Look at the birds of the air; they neither sow nor reap nor gather into barns, and yet your heavenly Father feeds them. Are you not of more value than they? And can any of you by worrying add a single hour to your span of life? And why do you worry about clothing? Consider the lilies of the field, how they grow; they neither toil nor spin, yet I tell you, even Solomon in all his glory was not clothed like one of these. But if God so clothes the grass of the field, which is alive today and tomorrow is thrown into the oven, will he not much more clothe you—you of little faith? Therefore do not worry, saying, 'What will we eat?' or 'What will we drink?' or 'What will we wear?' For it is the Gentiles who strive for all these things; and indeed your heavenly Father knows that you need all these things. But strive first for the kingdom of God and his righteousness, and all these things will be given to you as well.

"So do not worry about tomorrow, for tomorrow will bring worries of its own. Today's trouble is enough for today."

Notice what you think and feel as you read the gospel.

In beautiful images Jesus commends the birds and the flowers. They do not worry for God feeds them and dresses them; in the same way, we should not worry but strive first for the kingdom of God and his righteousness. God will provide for our needs.

Pray as you are led for yourself and others.

"Lord, I have many worries. Help me to put you first, especially in these areas . . ." (Continue in your own words.)

Listen to Jesus.

You desire the peace I give to you. I wish to give you peace and absolute confidence in me, your Shepherd. What else is Jesus saying to you?

Ask God to show you how to live today.

"Don't let me repress my anxieties, Lord. As they rise up in me during my day, let them pop like bubbles for I have put my trust in God. Amen."

Monday, February 27, 2017

Know that God is present with you and ready to converse.

"Lord, I turn to you while you are here with me. I ask you to speak to me in your holy Word."

Read the gospel: Mark 10:17–27.

As Jesus was setting out on a journey, a man ran up and knelt before him, and asked him, "Good Teacher, what must I do to inherit eternal life?" Jesus said to him, "Why do you call me good? No one is good but God alone. You know the commandments: 'You shall not murder; You shall not commit adultery; You shall not steal; You shall not bear false witness; You shall not defraud; Honor your father and mother.'" He said to him, "Teacher, I have kept all these since my youth." Jesus, looking at him, loved him and said, "You lack one thing; go, sell what you own, and give the money to the poor, and you will have treasure in heaven; then come, follow me." When he heard this, he was shocked and went away grieving, for he had many possessions.

Then Jesus looked around and said to his disciples, "How hard it will be for those who have wealth to enter the kingdom of God!" And the disciples were perplexed at these words. But Jesus said to them again, "Children, how hard it is to enter the kingdom of God! It is easier for a camel to go through the eye of a needle than for someone who is rich to enter the kingdom of God." They were greatly astounded and said to one another, "Then who can be saved?" Jesus looked at them and said, "For mortals it is impossible, but not for God; for God all things are possible."

Notice what you think and feel as you read the gospel.

It's all about goodness. The rich young man had obeyed the commandments of Moses, but he is not ready to obey Jesus' higher call to abandon all and follow him. Jesus called him because he loved him, but the man is not yet ready to let go. Jesus comments that wealth can hold a person back from God. Yet with God all things are possible.

Pray as you are led for yourself and others.

"Lord, I do not know that I am able to abandon everything for you. What I do possess, let me hold it lightly, ready to let it go. I think of these things . . ." (Continue in your own words.)

Listen to Jesus.

I provide for you, beloved disciple. I ask you to be generous with those in need. What else is Jesus saying to you?

Ask God to show you how to live today.

"I am ready to be generous, Lord. Help me identify opportunities to give. Amen."

Tuesday, February 28, 2017

Know that God is present with you and ready to converse.

"Jesus, what treasure do you have for me in your Word today? Let me take it to heart."

Read the gospel: Mark 10:28–31.

Peter began to say to Jesus, "Look, we have left everything and followed you." Jesus said, "Truly I tell you, there is no one who has left house or brothers or sisters or mother or father or children or fields, for my sake and for the sake of the good news, who will not receive a hundredfold now in this age—houses, brothers and sisters, mothers and children, and fields, with persecutions—and in the age to come eternal life. But many who are first will be last, and the last will be first."

Notice what you think and feel as you read the gospel.

Peter frankly asks Jesus what they will gain by leaving everything and following him and proclaiming the Good News. Jesus says everyone who abandons his or her former life will receive a "hundredfold" compensation even in this lifetime and eternal life in the next life.

Pray as you are led for yourself and others.

"Lord, you suggest that denying ourselves and serving you is joy, not deprivation. I have tasted some of those joys. Let me give you more and serve you more so that I may enjoy your plenty in this life and the next . . ." (Continue in your own words.)

Listen to Jesus.

Seek out those who love me, and you will have brothers and sisters. Live the Gospel with them, and you will know peace and joy. What else is Jesus saying to you?

Ask God to show you how to live today.

"Lord, I long for close community with those who love and serve you. Lead me among them. Amen."

The Lenten Season

INTRODUCTION

In the gospel, Jesus says his disciples will fast when he, the Bridegroom, is taken from them. We know that Jesus is always with us, but during the season of Lent we honor him in a special way by entering a forty-day period of prayer, fasting, and almsgiving in preparation for the celebration of the resurrection of the Lord, Easter Sunday. The forty days of Lent correspond to the forty days Jesus prayed and fasted in the desert before beginning his earthly ministry. Lent is a time to allow God to help us become holy, to help us look to the needs of others and minister to those needs, and most of all, to grow in faith, hope, and love, for those virtues are of God, motivating and empowering us to live the gospel.

The season of Lent begins on Ash Wednesday, dividing the cycle of Ordinary Time in the Church year. Sundays in Lent are not counted as fast days. Fast days continue through Holy Saturday, the day before Easter. Lent officially ends on Holy Thursday, the beginning of the Easter Triduum.

Wednesday, March 1, 2017
Ash Wednesday

Know that God is present with you and ready to converse.
"Lent has begun, Lord. Draw me nearer to yourself in this season. Open me fully to your Word."

Read the gospel: Matthew 6:1–6, 16–18.
Jesus said, "Beware of practicing your piety before others in order to be seen by them; for then you have no reward from your Father in heaven.

"So whenever you give alms, do not sound a trumpet before you, as the hypocrites do in the synagogues and in the streets, so that they may be praised by others. Truly I tell you, they have received their reward. But when you give alms, do not let your left hand know what your right hand is doing, so that your alms may be done in secret; and your Father who sees in secret will reward you.

"And whenever you pray, do not be like the hypocrites; for they love to stand and pray in the synagogues and at the street corners, so that they may be seen by others. Truly I tell you, they have received their reward. But whenever you pray, go into your room and shut the door and pray to your Father who is in secret; and your Father who sees in secret will reward you. . . .

"And whenever you fast, do not look dismal, like the hypocrites, for they disfigure their faces so as to show others that they are fasting. Truly I tell you, they have received their reward. But when you fast, put oil on your head and wash your face, so that your fasting may be seen not by others but by your Father who is in secret; and your Father who sees in secret will reward you."

Notice what you think and feel as you read the gospel.
Jesus says to pray, fast, and do good works in secret, for to do them before others undercuts their spiritual value. When we desire that others think well of us, we tend to become hypocrites. We should trust God for our reward.

Pray as you are led for yourself and others.
"Lord, help me keep secrets. Let me pray, fast, and give alms in secret today. Let me offer them all for the good of others, especially . . ." (Continue in your own words.)

Listen to Jesus.

I love it when you pray for others. Then our hearts beat together. What else is Jesus saying to you?

Ask God to show you how to live today.

"Lord, I start Lent with great hope. Give me grace to persevere one day at a time. Amen."

Thursday, March 2, 2017

Know that God is present with you and ready to converse.

"Jesus, you have the words of eternal life. What must I do to inherit eternal life?"

Read the gospel: Luke 9:22–25.

Jesus said, "The Son of Man must undergo great suffering, and be rejected by the elders, chief priests, and scribes, and be killed, and on the third day be raised."

Then he said to them all, "If any want to become my followers, let them deny themselves and take up their cross daily and follow me. For those who want to save their life will lose it, and those who lose their life for my sake will save it. What does it profit them if they gain the whole world, but lose or forfeit themselves?"

Notice what you think and feel as you read the gospel.

Jesus predicts his passion, death, and resurrection, then urges his followers to take up their own crosses daily. He says if we try to save our lives, we will lose them, but those who lose their lives for his sake will save them.

Pray as you are led for yourself and others.

"Lord, teach me your way of denying myself and losing my life for your sake, for I long for eternal life with you. I give you everything, including . . ." (Continue in your own words.)

Listen to Jesus.

You have nothing to fear, beloved. As long as I am with you, you have everything you need. What else is Jesus saying to you?

Ask God to show you how to live today.

"Put me in situations today, Lord, where I can see my choice of saving or losing my life, and let me choose the way of self-denial, not for my sake but for yours. Amen."

Friday, March 3, 2017

Know that God is present with you and ready to converse.

"Father, Son, and Holy Spirit, one Lord, you are present before me in the Spirit and in the Word. I glorify you."

Read the gospel: Matthew 9:14–15.

Then the disciples of John came to Jesus, saying, "Why do we and the Pharisees fast often, but your disciples do not fast?" And Jesus said to them, "The wedding-guests cannot mourn as long as the bridegroom is with them, can they? The days will come when the bridegroom is taken away from them, and then they will fast."

Notice what you think and feel as you read the gospel.

Jesus answers the question posed to him by the disciples of John: Why don't your disciples fast? Jesus' answer points to who he is: the Messiah, the Bridegroom. As wedding guests, his disciples cannot fast.

Pray as you are led for yourself and others.

"Jesus, you are always with me, yet I long to look upon your face. With that hope, let me rejoice as I fast, developing hunger for your loveliness . . ." (Continue in your own words.)

Listen to Jesus.

I am the Bridegroom who embraces you and loves you, dear one. Ask of me what you will. What else is Jesus saying to you?

Ask God to show you how to live today.

"Lord, I cannot do much in my own strength and discipline. I depend upon your grace. I thank you for it, Lord. Amen."

Saturday, March 4, 2017

Know that God is present with you and ready to converse.

"Lord, Creator of all, you made humans in the image of God. You know me inside and out. Let me respond to your call."

Read the gospel: Luke 5:27–32.

After this Jesus went out and saw a tax-collector named Levi, sitting at the tax booth; and he said to him, "Follow me." And he got up, left everything, and followed him.

Then Levi gave a great banquet for him in his house; and there was a large crowd of tax-collectors and others sitting at the table with them. The Pharisees and their scribes were complaining to his disciples, saying, "Why do you eat and drink with tax-collectors and sinners?" Jesus answered, "Those who are well have no need of a physician, but those who are sick; I have come to call not the righteous but sinners to repentance."

Notice what you think and feel as you read the gospel.

Jesus must have known Levi's willingness of heart when he called him, for Levi simply left everything and followed him immediately. Or did Jesus speak with such authority that his invitation was irresistible? The way the Pharisees and the scribes grumble about Jesus' eating with him suggest that they, at least, assume that Levi was a great sinner. Jesus doesn't deny it. He says he came to call sinners, not the righteous, to repentance.

Pray as you are led for yourself and others.

"Lord, I am a sinner. Call me. Levi became Matthew and served you well. What will you make of me?" (Continue in your own words.)

Listen to Jesus.

Beloved, I will make you my lover, more than spouse, friend, sister, or brother. Our work together starts with our love for one another. What else is Jesus saying to you?

Ask God to show you how to live today.

"If I see someone I judge to be a sinner today, let me pray for him or her, knowing that you love that person and call him or her to yourself. Inspire me to speak or act in a loving way toward that person. Amen."

Sunday, March 5, 2017
First Sunday of Lent

Know that God is present with you and ready to converse.

Lent is a season set aside to root out habits of sin in our lives. First we must acknowledge our sins, then we must confess them, and then we must develop strategies to avoid them in the future. We need Jesus to help us in this noble quest. Having been tempted himself, he knows how to help us.

"Lord, here with me now, let me receive your Word, your Spirit, deep into my soul that I may stand in the hour of my temptation."

Read the gospel: Matthew 4:1–11.

Then Jesus was led up by the Spirit into the wilderness to be tempted by the devil. He fasted for forty days and forty nights, and afterwards he was famished. The tempter came and said to him, "If you are the Son of God, command these stones to become loaves of bread." But he answered, "It is written,

> 'One does not live by bread alone,
>> but by every word that comes
> from the mouth of God.'"

Then the devil took him to the holy city and placed him on the pinnacle of the temple, saying to him, "If you are the Son of God, throw yourself down; for it is written,

> 'He will command his angels concerning you,'
>> and 'On their hands they will bear you up,
> so that you will not dash your foot against a stone.'"

Jesus said to him, "Again it is written, 'Do not put the Lord your God to the test.'"

Again, the devil took him to a very high mountain and showed him all the kingdoms of the world and their splendor; and he said to him, "All these I will give you, if you will fall down and worship me." Jesus said to him, "Away with you, Satan! for it is written,

> 'Worship the Lord your God,
>> and serve only him.'"

Then the devil left him, and suddenly angels came and waited on him.

Notice what you think and feel as you read the gospel.

Jesus resists all the temptations of the devil, out-dueling him with scripture. The devil betrays what he himself desires, but Jesus desires only to do the will of his Father. We, too, are to live by every word that proceeds from the mouth of God.

Pray as you are led for yourself and others.

"Lord, I wish to live by your Word. That is why I am praying with today's gospel. In your name, Jesus, give me power over these temptations in my life . . ." (Continue in your own words.)

Listen to Jesus.

I give you power, dear disciple, to do what you cannot do on your own. Receive the Holy Spirit and overcome temptation. What else is Jesus saying to you?

Ask God to show you how to live today.

"Lord, help me to replace sins and temptations with good and lovely things. Let them be my gifts to others. Amen."

Monday, March 6, 2017

Know that God is present with you and ready to converse.

"Lord, I entrust my personal salvation to you. By your Word, help me to serve you and others in my community."

Read the gospel: Matthew 25:31–40 (Mt 25:31–46).

Jesus said, "When the Son of Man comes in his glory, and all the angels with him, then he will sit on the throne of his glory. All the nations will be gathered before him, and he will separate people one from another as a shepherd separates the sheep from the goats, and he will put the sheep at his right hand and the goats at the left. Then the king will say to those at his right hand, 'Come, you that are blessed by my Father, inherit the kingdom prepared for you from the foundation of the world; for I was hungry and you gave me food, I was thirsty and you gave me something to drink, I was a stranger and you welcomed me, I was naked and you gave me clothing, I was sick and you took care of me, I was in prison and you visited me.' Then the righteous will answer him, 'Lord, when was it that we saw you hungry and gave you food, or thirsty and gave you something to drink? And when was it that we saw you a stranger and welcomed you, or naked and gave you clothing? And when was it that we saw you sick or in prison and visited you?' And the king will answer them, 'Truly I tell you, just as you did it to one of the least of these who are members of my family, you did it to me.'"

Notice what you think and feel as you read the gospel.

In Jesus' prophetic judgment of the nations, the Son of Man will commend those peoples who served the poor and needy, for he identifies with them. The Lord of Judgment will condemn those nations who ignored the poor and needy. Ours is the age of redemption and grace. Afterward comes judgment.

Pray as you are led for yourself and others.

"Lord, what can I do to serve you in the hungry, poor, homeless, lost, or lonely? Give me eyes to see you . . ." (Continue in your own words.)

Listen to Jesus.

Your love for me will express itself in service to those who suffer. I will show you opportunities, dear disciple. What else is Jesus saying to you?

Ask God to show you how to live today.

"Lord, open my eyes and my heart to opportunities. Let me see you. Thank you. Amen."

Tuesday, March 7, 2017

Know that God is present with you and ready to converse.

"Lord, teach me to pray."

Read the gospel: Matthew 6:7–15.

Jesus said, "When you are praying, do not heap up empty phrases as the Gentiles do; for they think that they will be heard because of their many words. Do not be like them, for your Father knows what you need before you ask him.

"Pray then in this way:

Our Father in heaven,
        hallowed be your name.
        Your kingdom come.
        Your will be done,
            on earth as it is in heaven.
        Give us this day our daily bread.
        And forgive us our debts,
            as we also have forgiven our debtors.
        And do not bring us to the time of trial,
            but rescue us from the evil one.

For if you forgive others their trespasses, your heavenly Father will also forgive you; but if you do not forgive others, neither will your Father forgive your trespasses."

Notice what you think and feel as you read the gospel.

Jesus' great prayer seems to express priorities in our relationship with God and others. First we glorify the Father, seeking the kingdom, embracing God's will on earth. Then we ask for bread, the necessities of our lives. We ask God's forgiveness and offer our own forgiveness of others' sins against us. Finally, we ask for endurance in the time of trial and rescue from evil.

Pray as you are led for yourself and others.

"Jesus, after you teach the prayer, you point out especially our need to forgive others. As I examine my heart, I forgive these people who have hurt me . . ." (Continue in your own words.)

Listen to Jesus.

The love in your life must often take the form of mercy, my child. Do not judge others. I give you eyes of mercy. What else is Jesus saying to you?

Ask God to show you how to live today.

"Chances are that someone will offend me today, Jesus. Give me grace to forgive that person immediately. Make mercy a habit of my heart. Amen."

Wednesday, March 8, 2017

Know that God is present with you and ready to converse.

"Jesus, no one ever spoke as you did. Speak to me by your Word."

Read the gospel: Luke 11:29–32.

When the crowds were increasing, Jesus began to say, "This generation is an evil generation; it asks for a sign, but no sign will be given to it except the sign of Jonah. For just as Jonah became a sign to the people of Nineveh, so the Son of Man will be to this generation. The queen of the South will rise at the judgment with the people of this generation and condemn them, because she came from the ends of the earth to listen to the wisdom of Solomon, and see, something greater than Solomon is here! The people of Nineveh will rise up at the judgment with this generation and condemn it, because they repented at the proclamation of Jonah, and see, something greater than Jonah is here!"

Notice what you think and feel as you read the gospel.

Jesus deplores those who seek a sign from him. He likens himself to Jonah who preached repentance and spent three days in the belly of a whale before he emerged. He tells them he is greater than Jonah, greater even than Solomon, for he is the Son of God.

Pray as you are led for yourself and others.

"Lord, you are here. Let me repent at your command and listen to your wisdom. I open myself to understand what you are saying to me now . . ." (Continue in your own words.)

Listen to Jesus.

I am, beloved disciple, the Son of the Father. My words have the power to save you. I have some things I want you to do. What else is Jesus saying to you?

Ask God to show you how to live today.

"Although I am a sinner, I give myself to you for forgiveness, cleansing, and service today. Let me please you, Blessed Lord. Amen."

Thursday, March 9, 2017

Know that God is present with you and ready to converse.

"Gracious Father, always near me, let me pray well and learn by your Word to do your will."

Read the gospel: Matthew 7:7–12.

Jesus said, "Ask, and it will be given to you; search, and you will find; knock, and the door will be opened for you. For everyone who asks receives, and everyone who searches finds, and for everyone who knocks, the door will be opened. Is there anyone among you who, if your child asks for bread, will give a stone? Or if the child asks for a fish, will give a snake? If you then, who are evil, know how to give good gifts to your children, how much more will your Father in heaven give good things to those who ask him!

"In everything do to others as you would have them do to you; for this is the law and the prophets."

Notice what you think and feel as you read the gospel.

Jesus urges us to ask, search, and knock, requesting from God what we desire. God will give us only good things. Our job? To do unto others as we would have them do to us.

Pray as you are led for yourself and others.

"Lord, focus me on what I may do for others first. Let me do those things and then return to ask you for the good things I need . . ." (Continue in your own words.)

Listen to Jesus.

It is sweet to be in conversation with you, dear one. Through our intimacy, our friendship will grow into everlasting life in the kingdom of my Father. Desire that. Ask for it. What else is Jesus saying to you?

Ask God to show you how to live today.

"Help me to discern between good things and those things that only appear good. Then let me ask for the good things, Lord. Praise your holy name! Amen."

Friday, March 10, 2017

Know that God is present with you and ready to converse.

"Holy Lord, you are just. Teach me by your Word lest I sin against you or my brother or my sister."

Read the gospel: Matthew 5:20–26.

Jesus said, "For I tell you, unless your righteousness exceeds that of the scribes and Pharisees, you will never enter the kingdom of heaven.

"You have heard that it was said to those of ancient times, 'You shall not murder'; and 'whoever murders shall be liable to judgment.' But I say to you that if you are angry with a brother or sister, you will be liable to judgment; and if you insult a brother or sister, you will be liable to the council; and if you say, 'You fool,' you will be liable to the hell of fire. So when you are offering your gift at the altar, if you remember that your brother or sister has something against you, leave your gift there before the altar and go; first be reconciled to your brother or sister, and then come and offer your gift. Come to terms quickly with your accuser while you are on the way to court with him, or your accuser may hand you over to the judge, and the judge to the guard, and you will be thrown into prison. Truly I tell you, you will never get out until you have paid the last penny."

Notice what you think and feel as you read the gospel.

Jesus raises the standard set by Moses' commandments. Anger in the heart is akin to murder and to indulge it is to risk judgment. The solution is to go to a brother or sister who has something against us and reconcile. Jesus asks us to take the initiative even when the other person is angry toward us.

Pray as you are led for yourself and others.

"Lord, who in my life is angry with me, harboring grudges against me, offended by me? Lord, I think of these . . ." (Continue in your own words.)

Listen to Jesus.

I will give you opportunities to reconcile with those with whom you need to reconcile. Be open to these opportunities as there can be healing. What else is Jesus saying to you?

Ask God to show you how to live today.

"My life is complicated, Lord. Sometimes I feel I drag my sins along with me. Help me to have hope and break free by your power. I cannot do it alone, Jesus. Amen."

Saturday, March 11, 2017

Know that God is present with you and ready to converse.

"Jesus, risen Lord, I listen to your Word today. Let me also be a doer of your Word."

Read the gospel: Matthew 5:43–48.

Jesus said, "You have heard that it was said, 'You shall love your neighbor and hate your enemy.' But I say to you, Love your enemies and pray for those who persecute you, so that you may be children of your Father in heaven; for he makes his sun rise on the evil and on the good, and sends rain on the righteous and on the unrighteous. For if you love those who love you, what reward do you have? Do not even the tax-collectors do the same? And if you greet only your brothers and sisters, what more are you doing than others? Do not even the Gentiles do the same? Be perfect, therefore, as your heavenly Father is perfect."

Notice what you think and feel as you read the gospel.
Again Jesus raises the bar of holiness. He calls us to holiness, the very
perfection of the heavenly Father. The holiness of God requires us to
love our enemies and our persecutors. God does. Jesus wouldn't ask us
to do something impossible.

Pray as you are led for yourself and others.
"Lord, I am far from your holiness, but I open my heart for your enabling
grace. Who is my enemy, who persecutes me? These people will I
love . . ." (Continue in your own words.)

Listen to Jesus.
*In humility you learn to love those who oppose you. See others with the mercy
I give you.* What else is Jesus saying to you?

Ask God to show you how to live today.
"Every day is a new chance to obey your Spirit and act in love. Prepare
me for those moments today. Let me succeed in loving someone who
hates me, hurts me. Amen."

Sunday, March 12, 2017
Second Sunday of Lent

Know that God is present with you and ready to converse.
Lent is the season in which we focus on moral correction, aligning our-
selves with the commandments of Jesus. They are summed up in loving
God with all one's might and loving one's neighbor as one's self, but
Jesus details what this means in various contexts in the Lenten gospels.
He wills to heal our blindness to our sins, especially those habitual sins
we rationalize or despair of amending.
"Jesus, you were God among us, and your glory was to die for us.
Thank you for being with me now as I read your Word."

Read the gospel: Matthew 17:1–9.
Six days later, Jesus took with him Peter and James and his brother John
and led them up a high mountain, by themselves. And he was transfigured before them, and his face shone like the sun, and his clothes became
dazzling white. Suddenly there appeared to them Moses and Elijah,
talking with him. Then Peter said to Jesus, "Lord, it is good for us to be
here; if you wish, I will make three dwellings here, one for you, one for
Moses, and one for Elijah." While he was still speaking, suddenly a bright

cloud overshadowed them, and from the cloud a voice said, "This is my Son, the Beloved; with him I am well pleased; listen to him!" When the disciples heard this, they fell to the ground and were overcome by fear. But Jesus came and touched them, saying, "Get up and do not be afraid." And when they looked up, they saw no one except Jesus himself alone.

As they were coming down the mountain, Jesus ordered them, "Tell no one about the vision until after the Son of Man has been raised from the dead."

Notice what you think and feel as you read the gospel.

Peter, James, and John are amazed by Jesus' transfiguration before them and his meeting with Moses and Elijah. Then the voice from the cloud proclaims the Father's love for the Son and commands that they "listen to him." Later, Jesus asks them to tell no one until he has been raised from the dead.

Pray as you are led for yourself and others.

"Jesus, your divinity keeps breaking through in the gospels. I believe you are the Son of God, and I put my trust in you. Will you help me do your will? . . ." (Continue in your own words.)

Listen to Jesus.

Lean on my grace, my child, for you are beloved of my Father, too. What else is Jesus saying to you?

Ask God to show you how to live today.

"If I feel your presence with me today, let me praise you and do your will. If I do not feel your presence today, let me praise you and do your will. You are Lord! Amen."

Monday, March 13, 2017

Know that God is present with you and ready to converse.

"Merciful God, I depend on your mercy for repentance, forgiveness, reinstatement as your child, and sanctification. How shall I proceed?"

Read the gospel: Luke 6:36–38.

Jesus said, "Be merciful, just as your Father is merciful.

"Do not judge, and you will not be judged; do not condemn, and you will not be condemned. Forgive, and you will be forgiven; give, and it will be given to you. A good measure, pressed down, shaken together, running over, will be put into your lap; for the measure you give will be the measure you get back."

Notice what you think and feel as you read the gospel.

Jesus commands us to be merciful toward others as God is. He commands us not to judge or condemn so we will not be condemned. He commands us to forgive and to give, promising that we will receive more than we can give.

Pray as you are led for yourself and others.

"Lord, I see faults in others often. I cannot help but judge. Cleanse me of this judgmental mindset. Give me your true mercy for . . ." (Continue in your own words.)

Listen to Jesus.

I love your sincere efforts to be made new and pleasing to God. You must rely on my grace at every step. As you allow me to work holiness in you, I shall work. What else is Jesus saying to you?

Ask God to show you how to live today.

"Lord, help me strive to avoid sin and to do good today. Pick me up when I fall and put me back on your path by your grace. Amen."

Tuesday, March 14, 2017

Know that God is present with you and ready to converse.

"Lord, you are high and lifted up in glory even as you are here with me now. I seek your lesson for me today in your Word."

Read the gospel: Matthew 23:1–12.

Then Jesus said to the crowds and to his disciples, "The scribes and the Pharisees sit on Moses' seat; therefore, do whatever they teach you and follow it; but do not do as they do, for they do not practice what they teach. They tie up heavy burdens, hard to bear, and lay them on the shoulders of others; but they themselves are unwilling to lift a finger to move them. They do all their deeds to be seen by others; for they make their phylacteries broad and their fringes long. They love to have the place of honor at banquets and the best seats in the synagogues, and to be greeted with respect in the market-places, and to have people call them rabbi. But you are not to be called rabbi, for you have one teacher, and you are all students. And call no one your father on earth, for you have one Father—the one in heaven. Nor are you to be called instructors, for you have one instructor, the Messiah. The greatest among you will be your servant. All who exalt themselves will be humbled, and all who humble themselves will be exalted."

Notice what you think and feel as you read the gospel.

Jesus notices that religious people love to exalt themselves and be honored and respected by those they command. Jesus turns the crowd's attention to the one Teacher, the Messiah, and to the one Father, God in heaven. Only those who humble themselves will be exalted.

Pray as you are led for yourself and others.

"Only you, Lord, are exalted above all forever—you who came to serve us and die for us. Humility is not a pose before you, Lord; it is our only rational response to who you are. Lord, give me clarity so that I may always know my place as your servant . . ." (Continue in your own words.)

Listen to Jesus.

If you want joy, my child, embrace the role of the servant with all your heart. What else is Jesus saying to you?

Ask God to show you how to live today.

"How may I serve today, Lord? Open my eyes and heart to serving you in others. Thank you for your light, Lord. Amen."

Wednesday, March 15, 2017

Know that God is present with you and ready to converse.

"Lord, let your Word today take my mind off of me and place it on you. Let me hold you in my heart with gratitude and love."

Read the gospel: Matthew 20:17–28.

While Jesus was going up to Jerusalem, he took the twelve disciples aside by themselves, and said to them on the way, "See, we are going up to Jerusalem, and the Son of Man will be handed over to the chief priests and scribes, and they will condemn him to death; then they will hand him over to the Gentiles to be mocked and flogged and crucified; and on the third day he will be raised."

Then the mother of the sons of Zebedee came to him with her sons, and kneeling before him, she asked a favor of him. And he said to her,

"What do you want?" She said to him, "Declare that these two sons of mine will sit, one at your right hand and one at your left, in your kingdom." But Jesus answered, "You do not know what you are asking. Are you able to drink the cup that I am about to drink?" They said to him, "We are able." He said to them, "You will indeed drink my cup, but to sit at my right hand and at my left, this is not mine to grant, but it is for those for whom it has been prepared by my Father."

When the ten heard it, they were angry with the two brothers. But Jesus called them to him and said, "You know that the rulers of the Gentiles lord it over them, and their great ones are tyrants over them. It will not be so among you; but whoever wishes to be great among you must be your servant, and whoever wishes to be first among you must be your slave; just as the Son of Man came not to be served but to serve, and to give his life a ransom for many."

Notice what you think and feel as you read the gospel.
The disciples don't really hear Jesus' announcement of his coming passion, death, and resurrection in Jerusalem. They are caught up in their own jockeying for honor and authority. Jesus tells them that the one who would be great must be a servant, a slave, just like the Son of Man.

Pray as you are led for yourself and others.
"I give myself to you and to others today, Lord. I want to serve as you served. Guide me . . ." (Continue in your own words.)

Listen to Jesus.
Dearly beloved, I am here to serve you still. You wish to be like me in serving others. I will show you how and give you grace to do it. What else is Jesus saying to you?

Ask God to show you how to live today.
"Lord, first I need a servant's attitude. Then I need opportunities to serve. You will help me! I have a new start every day in your grace. Glory to you, Lord. Amen."

Thursday, March 16, 2017

Know that God is present with you and ready to converse.
"Lord, you intervened in human history to save us from ourselves. Let me respond to your Word in the manner you would have me. Let me learn from you."

Read the gospel: Luke 16:19–31.

Jesus said, "There was a rich man who was dressed in purple and fine linen and who feasted sumptuously every day. And at his gate lay a poor man named Lazarus, covered with sores, who longed to satisfy his hunger with what fell from the rich man's table; even the dogs would come and lick his sores. The poor man died and was carried away by the angels to be with Abraham. The rich man also died and was buried. In Hades, where he was being tormented, he looked up and saw Abraham far away with Lazarus by his side. He called out, 'Father Abraham, have mercy on me, and send Lazarus to dip the tip of his finger in water and cool my tongue; for I am in agony in these flames.' But Abraham said, 'Child, remember that during your lifetime you received your good things, and Lazarus in like manner evil things; but now he is comforted here, and you are in agony. Besides all this, between you and us a great chasm has been fixed, so that those who might want to pass from here to you cannot do so, and no one can cross from there to us.' He said, 'Then, father, I beg you to send him to my father's house—for I have five brothers—that he may warn them, so that they will not also come into this place of torment.' Abraham replied, 'They have Moses and the prophets; they should listen to them.' He said, 'No, father Abraham; but if someone goes to them from the dead, they will repent.' He said to him, 'If they do not listen to Moses and the prophets, neither will they be convinced even if someone rises from the dead.'"

Notice what you think and feel as you read the gospel.

By this parable Jesus shows how blind the rich can be to those suffering nearby. Their blindness is a moral failing for which they will be judged and sentenced at death. The rich man discovers it's too late for him now. Abraham tells him that many who are alive will not repent even if they hear from one who has risen from the dead.

Pray as you are led for yourself and others.

"Lord, many do not believe that you have risen from the dead, and they do not see any need to repent. I pray for mercy, repentance, and conversion for them today, including . . ." (Continue in your own words.)

Listen to Jesus.

Your growth in grace is a progression of belief, faith, conviction, assurance. Ask for deepening in faith, hope, and love. This is the way to joy. What else is Jesus saying to you?

Ask God to show you how to live today.

"As I pray for others, Lord, let me deepen in my understanding of you, that I may be truly useful to you and your works of grace. Amen."

Friday, March 17, 2017

Know that God is present with you and ready to converse.

"Jesus, sometimes people do not understand you; sometimes they do and yet fail to respond. Let me understand your Word and respond as you would have me respond."

Read the gospel: Matthew 21:33–41 (Mt 21:33–43, 45–46).

Jesus said, "Listen to another parable. There was a landowner who planted a vineyard, put a fence around it, dug a wine press in it, and built a watch-tower. Then he leased it to tenants and went to another country. When the harvest time had come, he sent his slaves to the tenants to collect his produce. But the tenants seized his slaves and beat one, killed another, and stoned another. Again he sent other slaves, more than the first; and they treated them in the same way. Finally he sent his son to them, saying, 'They will respect my son.' But when the tenants saw the son, they said to themselves, 'This is the heir; come, let us kill him and get his inheritance.' So they seized him, threw him out of the vineyard, and killed him. Now when the owner of the vineyard comes, what will he do to those tenants?" They said to him, "He will put those wretches to a miserable death, and lease the vineyard to other tenants who will give him the produce at the harvest time."

Notice what you think and feel as you read the gospel.

In this parable, the tenants wish to exploit the property of the land-owner. They reject all emissaries who assert the landowner's claim on the vineyard. When the landowner sends his son, they kill him. Even Jesus' hearers recognize the injustice in that.

Pray as you are led for yourself and others.

"Jesus, you know people so well. You speak so clearly to us about our nature. I come to you asking for a new nature, the one you suffered and died to give me. I ask for . . ." (Continue in your own words.)

Listen to Jesus.

I am pleased to give you what you ask for, beloved disciple. Come to me often with simple sincerity. What else is Jesus saying to you?

Ask God to show you how to live today.

"Jesus, let me work for you today, pleasing you and leaving the results to you. Let me trust in the power of acting in love even if I do not see results. Amen."

Saturday, March 18, 2017

Know that God is present with you and ready to converse.

"Father, your Son proclaimed your mercy and your greatness to the world. Give me a fresh love for you by his Word."

Read the gospel: Luke 15:11-24 (Lk 15:1-3, 11-32).

Then Jesus said, "There was a man who had two sons. The younger of them said to his father, 'Father, give me the share of the property that will belong to me.' So he divided his property between them. A few days later the younger son gathered all he had and travelled to a distant country, and there he squandered his property in dissolute living. When he had spent everything, a severe famine took place throughout that country, and he began to be in need. So he went and hired himself out to one of the citizens of that country, who sent him to his fields to feed the pigs. He would gladly have filled himself with the pods that the pigs were eating; and no one gave him anything. But when he came to himself he said, 'How many of my father's hired hands have bread enough and to spare, but here I am dying of hunger! I will get up and go to my father, and I will say to him, "Father, I have sinned against heaven and before you; I am no longer worthy to be called your son; treat me like one of your hired hands."' So he set off and went to his father. But while he was still far off, his father saw him and was filled with compassion; he ran and put his arms around him and kissed him. Then the son said to him, 'Father, I have sinned against heaven and before you; I am no longer worthy to be called your son.' But the father said to his slaves, 'Quickly, bring out a robe—the best one—and put it on him; put a ring on his finger and sandals on his feet. And get the fatted calf and kill it, and let us eat and celebrate; for this son of mine was dead and is alive again; he was lost and is found!' And they began to celebrate."

Notice what you think and feel as you read the gospel.

In this great parable, the younger son does something young people have always done: leave home to waste their time and money in self-indulgence. When he finds misery instead of freedom and pleasure, he returns repentant to his father, who welcomes him with joy.

Pray as you are led for yourself and others.

"Lord, I am a sinner, craving your mercy and love. I am aware that I deserve neither. How many ways can I praise you? . . ." (Continue in your own words.)

Listen to Jesus.

God is always good—do not forget it. Let God's mercy draw you back home. What else is Jesus saying to you?

Ask God to show you how to live today.

"Thank you for your mercy to me, Lord. Let me never forget how you have lifted me out of selfishness to depend on you and serve you all the days of my life. Amen."

Sunday, March 19, 2017
Third Sunday of Lent

Know that God is present with you and ready to converse.

Jesus, the One sent to reconcile us to the God, had natural parents and grew up in a natural family. This Holy Family now includes all who believe in the Christ. Our Father has a hand on us, shepherding us through our lives, always providing for us what is good, even if we don't always understand it as such. What a privilege to be a child of the Most High God, a brother or sister to our Lord Jesus Christ!

"Jesus, you bought me with your blood. Quench my thirst for you by your Word."

Read the gospel: John 4:5–26, 39–42 (Jn 4:5–42).

So Jesus came to a Samaritan city called Sychar, near the plot of ground that Jacob had given to his son Joseph. Jacob's well was there, and Jesus, tired out by his journey, was sitting by the well. It was about noon.

A Samaritan woman came to draw water, and Jesus said to her, "Give me a drink." (His disciples had gone to the city to buy food.) The Samaritan woman said to him, "How is it that you, a Jew, ask a drink of me, a woman of Samaria?" (Jews do not share things in common with Samaritans.) Jesus answered her, "If you knew the gift of God, and who it is that is saying to you, 'Give me a drink,' you would have asked him, and he would have given you living water." The woman said to him, "Sir, you have no bucket, and the well is deep. Where do you get that living water? Are you greater than our ancestor Jacob, who gave us the well, and with his sons and his flocks drank from it?" Jesus said to her,

"Everyone who drinks of this water will be thirsty again, but those who drink of the water that I will give them will never be thirsty. The water that I will give will become in them a spring of water gushing up to eternal life." The woman said to him, "Sir, give me this water, so that I may never be thirsty or have to keep coming here to draw water."

Jesus said to her, "Go, call your husband, and come back." The woman answered him, "I have no husband." Jesus said to her, "You are right in saying, 'I have no husband'; for you have had five husbands, and the one you have now is not your husband. What you have said is true!" The woman said to him, "Sir, I see that you are a prophet. Our ancestors worshipped on this mountain, but you say that the place where people must worship is in Jerusalem." Jesus said to her, "Woman, believe me, the hour is coming when you will worship the Father neither on this mountain nor in Jerusalem. You worship what you do not know; we worship what we know, for salvation is from the Jews. But the hour is coming, and is now here, when the true worshippers will worship the Father in spirit and truth, for the Father seeks such as these to worship him. God is spirit, and those who worship him must worship in spirit and truth." The woman said to him, "I know that Messiah is coming (who is called Christ). When he comes, he will proclaim all things to us." Jesus said to her, "I am he, the one who is speaking to you." . . .

Many Samaritans from that city believed in him because of the woman's testimony, "He told me everything I have ever done." So when the Samaritans came to him, they asked him to stay with them; and he stayed there for two days. And many more believed because of his word. They said to the woman, "It is no longer because of what you said that we believe, for we have heard for ourselves, and we know that this is truly the Savior of the world."

Notice what you think and feel as you read the gospel.
Jesus lays aside all religious and cultural rules to speak to the Samaritan woman. It's all about water, developed as a symbol of eternal life. The woman is suspicious, but she is convinced because Jesus knows her past. She departs to tell the village that she may have found the Messiah.

Pray as you are led for yourself and others.
"Lord, I do not deserve a spring in me gushing up to eternal life, but you offer it to those who believe. Jesus, I believe. Let your waters flow through me to others . . ." (Continue in your own words.)

Listen to Jesus.
See, my child, it is not in yourself you find life but in me. Worship God from the depths of your heart and soul, and you will live forever. What else is Jesus saying to you?

Ask God to show you how to live today.
"Lord, I do not always recognize when I am worshipping you in Spirit and in truth. Help me to do so. Help me to worship you often today and all my life. Amen."

Monday, March 20, 2017
Saint Joseph, Spouse of the Blessed Virgin Mary

Know that God is present with you and ready to converse.
"Lord, your ways are so high above my ways. Let me be guided, not by my own understanding, but by your Word and your Spirit."

Read the gospel: Matthew 1:16, 18–21, 24.
Joseph the husband of Mary, of whom Jesus was born, who is called the Messiah. . . .

   Now the birth of Jesus the Messiah took place in this way. When his mother Mary had been engaged to Joseph, but before they lived together, she was found to be with child from the Holy Spirit. Her husband Joseph, being a righteous man and unwilling to expose her to public disgrace, planned to dismiss her quietly. But just when he had resolved to do this, an angel of the Lord appeared to him in a dream and said, "Joseph, son of David, do not be afraid to take Mary as your wife, for the child conceived in her is from the Holy Spirit. She will bear a son, and you are to name him Jesus, for he will save his people from their sins." . . . When Joseph awoke from sleep, he did as the angel of the Lord commanded him; he took her as his wife.

Notice what you think and feel as you read the gospel.
Joseph needs divine guidance to change his reasonable and compassionate plans about Mary, now pregnant by the Holy Spirit. It takes an angel to convince him of that and to take Mary as his wife despite her pregnancy with a child not his own. The child, he is told, will save the people from their sins.

Pray as you are led for yourself and others.

"St. Joseph, guardian of the Child Jesus and his Mother, the Blessed Virgin Mary, pray for me and help me be a loving child in the Holy Family and a faithful member of the Church, the Body of Christ, which you protect by your intercession. I pray also for those in my family . . ." (Continue in your own words.)

Listen to Jesus.

Stronger than the family of blood is the family of the Spirit, beloved disciple. I have won you a place at the table of the family of God. What else is Jesus saying to you?

Ask God to show you how to live today.

"As a child of God, let me live today as a child—believing, trusting, giving myself for the good of others. Amen."

Tuesday, March 21, 2017

Know that God is present with you and ready to converse.

"Father, let me eat the food your Son, Jesus Christ, gives to me. He is the Word, and he feeds me with himself."

Read the gospel: John 4:5–10, 27–42 (Jn 4:5–42).

So Jesus came to a Samaritan city called Sychar, near the plot of ground that Jacob had given to his son Joseph. Jacob's well was there, and Jesus, tired out by his journey, was sitting by the well. It was about noon.

A Samaritan woman came to draw water, and Jesus said to her, "Give me a drink." (His disciples had gone to the city to buy food.) The Samaritan woman said to him, "How is it that you, a Jew, ask a drink of me, a woman of Samaria?" (Jews do not share things in common with Samaritans.) Jesus answered her, "If you knew the gift of God, and who it is that is saying to you, 'Give me a drink,' you would have asked him, and he would have given you living water." . . .

Just then his disciples came. They were astonished that he was speaking with a woman, but no one said, "What do you want?" or, "Why are you speaking with her?" Then the woman left her water-jar and went back to the city. She said to the people, "Come and see a man who told me everything I have ever done! He cannot be the Messiah, can he?" They left the city and were on their way to him.

Meanwhile the disciples were urging him, "Rabbi, eat something." But he said to them, "I have food to eat that you do not know about."

So the disciples said to one another, "Surely no one has brought him something to eat?" Jesus said to them, "My food is to do the will of him who sent me and to complete his work. Do you not say, 'Four months more, then comes the harvest'? But I tell you, look around you, and see how the fields are ripe for harvesting. The reaper is already receiving wages and is gathering fruit for eternal life, so that sower and reaper may rejoice together. For here the saying holds true, 'One sows and another reaps.' I sent you to reap that for which you did not labor. Others have labored, and you have entered into their labor."

Many Samaritans from that city believed in him because of the woman's testimony, "He told me everything I have ever done." So when the Samaritans came to him, they asked him to stay with them; and he stayed there for two days. And many more believed because of his word. They said to the woman, "It is no longer because of what you said that we believe, for we have heard for ourselves, and we know that this is truly the Savior of the world."

Notice what you think and feel as you read the gospel.

While the disciples go to find food in the Samaritan village, Jesus speaks to the woman at the well outside of town. He turns her life upside down. The disciples return astonished he is speaking with her but don't dare ask about it. When they offer him food, Jesus tells them that his food is to do the will of God, which is to announce the kingdom. The woman and many Samaritans come to believe in him.

Pray as you are led for yourself and others.

"Lord, I pray for both the living water and the food of God. Let me believe and do God's will. Help me see and do God's will in these matters . . ." (Continue in your own words.)

Listen to Jesus.

This is the journey of faith, dear disciple. Entrust yourself entirely to God, giving up your own will and seeking God's. God will work in your life and bless you. What else is Jesus saying to you?

Ask God to show you how to live today.

"Lord, I abandon all to you today. Take all of me and do with me what you will. I seek your power to do what pleases you. Amen."

Wednesday, March 22, 2017

Know that God is present with you and ready to converse.

"Lord, give me deep understanding of your commandments by your Word. You are present now to teach me by the Word of your Son."

Read the gospel: Matthew 5:17–19.

Jesus said, "Do not think that I have come to abolish the law or the prophets; I have come not to abolish but to fulfill. For truly I tell you, until heaven and earth pass away, not one letter, not one stroke of a letter, will pass from the law until all is accomplished. Therefore, whoever breaks one of the least of these commandments, and teaches others to do the same, will be called least in the kingdom of heaven; but whoever does them and teaches them will be called great in the kingdom of heaven."

Notice what you think and feel as you read the gospel.

Jesus says he fulfills the law and the prophets, and all they have said will come to pass. Those who break their commandments will be called least in the kingdom, especially those who teach others to break them.

Pray as you are led for yourself and others.

"Lord, let me not abuse the liberty of your law of love, which comprises all of the law and the prophets. Let me understand deeply that God's morality is exacting, and I am called to obedience, not for the sake of legality but for the sake of love. Keep me from leading any of these into error . . ." (Continue in your own words.)

Listen to Jesus.

The proper fear of God is to guard yourself and your heart that you may not offend God. If you sin, you may come to the infinite forgiveness I offer. I will wash you white as snow. What else is Jesus saying to you?

Ask God to show you how to live today.

"Lord, I place my sinful self in your hands. Only you can forgive and cleanse me. Give me your Spirit that I may walk in your grace and reflect your grace upon others. Amen."

Thursday, March 23, 2017

Know that God is present with you and ready to converse.
"Lord, I live in a world full of spiritual forces. I seek only you by the Holy Spirit. Let the Spirit illuminate your Word to me."

Read the gospel: Luke 11:14–23.

Now Jesus was casting out a demon that was mute; when the demon had gone out, the one who had been mute spoke, and the crowds were amazed. But some of them said, "He casts out demons by Beelzebul, the ruler of the demons." Others, to test him, kept demanding from him a sign from heaven. But he knew what they were thinking and said to them, "Every kingdom divided against itself becomes a desert, and house falls on house. If Satan also is divided against himself, how will his kingdom stand?—for you say that I cast out the demons by Beelzebul. Now if I cast out the demons by Beelzebul, by whom do your exorcists cast them out? Therefore they will be your judges. But if it is by the finger of God that I cast out the demons, then the kingdom of God has come to you. When a strong man, fully armed, guards his castle, his property is safe. But when one stronger than he attacks him and overpowers him, he takes away his armor in which he trusted and divides his plunder. Whoever is not with me is against me, and whoever does not gather with me scatters."

Notice what you think and feel as you read the gospel.
Seeing his power over evil spirits, some in the crowd accuse Jesus of being in league with Satan, Beelzebul. Jesus repudiates that idea, pointing out that a divided kingdom cannot stand. He describes himself as a man stronger than the strong man for he exercises the power of God.

Pray as you are led for yourself and others.
"Lord, protect me and those I love from evil. Vanquish evil by your power, and let us all gather with you . . ." (Continue in your own words.)

Listen to Jesus.
Dearest soul, I am your protector. Sometimes you will be opposed by powers greater than yourself. Always turn to me, trusting me and praying for my protection, for there is no power greater than I. What else is Jesus saying to you?

Ask God to show you how to live today.

"Lord, if there is any evil jeopardizing me or those you have given me, direct me to pray. Give me discernment that I may turn to you for all rescue and protection. Thank you, mighty Savior. Amen."

Friday, March 24, 2017

Know that God is present with you and ready to converse.

"Lord, I am here before you, hungry for your Word."

Read the gospel: Mark 12:28–34.

One of the scribes came near and heard them disputing with one another, and seeing that Jesus answered them well, he asked Jesus, "Which commandment is the first of all?" Jesus answered, "The first is, 'Hear, O Israel: the Lord our God, the Lord is one; you shall love the Lord your God with all your heart, and with all your soul, and with all your mind, and with all your strength.' The second is this, 'You shall love your neighbor as yourself.' There is no other commandment greater than these." Then the scribe said to him, "You are right, Teacher; you have truly said that 'he is one, and besides him there is no other'; and 'to love him with all the heart, and with all the understanding, and with all the strength,' and 'to love one's neighbor as oneself,'—this is much more important than all whole burnt-offerings and sacrifices." When Jesus saw that he answered wisely, he said to him, "You are not far from the kingdom of God." After that no one dared to ask him any question.

Notice what you think and feel as you read the gospel.

Jesus must have loved the scribe who understood the greatest commandments of the law. Loving God and one's neighbor includes all the commandments of the law and the prophets. Jesus assures the scribe he is "not far" from the kingdom.

Pray as you are led for yourself and others.

"Lord, I embrace your law of love. Fill me with the love in your own heart. Let me love others as you loved the scribe . . ." (Continue in your own words.)

Listen to Jesus.

In love is all your power, dear disciple. Take up your cross and follow me in your journey of love. What else is Jesus saying to you?

Ask God to show you how to live today.

"Lord, if you walk with me, I can bear my cross today. Fill me with love for others so that I may love with your love. I glorify your name, blessed Savior. Amen."

Saturday, March 25, 2017
Annunciation of the Lord

Know that God is present with you and ready to converse.

"Here am I before you, Lord God of Hosts. Teach me by your Word to do your will."

Read the gospel: Luke 1:26–38.

In the sixth month the angel Gabriel was sent by God to a town in Galilee called Nazareth, to a virgin engaged to a man whose name was Joseph, of the house of David. The virgin's name was Mary. And he came to her and said, "Greetings, favored one! The Lord is with you." But she was much perplexed by his words and pondered what sort of greeting this might be. The angel said to her, "Do not be afraid, Mary, for you have found favor with God. And now, you will conceive in your womb and bear a son, and you will name him Jesus. He will be great, and will be called the Son of the Most High, and the Lord God will give to him the throne of his ancestor David. He will reign over the house of Jacob forever, and of his kingdom there will be no end." Mary said to the angel, "How can this be, since I am a virgin?" The angel said to her, "The Holy Spirit will come upon you, and the power of the Most High will overshadow you; therefore the child to be born will be holy; he will be called Son of God. And now, your relative Elizabeth in her old age has also conceived a son; and this is the sixth month for her who was said to be barren. For nothing will be impossible with God." Then Mary said, "Here am I, the servant of the Lord; let it be with me according to your word." Then the angel departed from her.

Notice what you think and feel as you read the gospel.

Usually in scripture people who see angels are stricken with fear. Not so Mary, a young teenager dedicated to God. Mary is not afraid of the angel, but she is perplexed by the greeting and by the prophetic message that she would be the Mother of the Son of the Most High God. But her spirit was open and she said yes to the Holy Spirit.

Pray as you are led for yourself and others.

"Mary, I honor you for your willingness to be the Mother of God. I bless you. I ask your prayers, Mother, for these . . ." (Continue in your own words.)

Listen to Jesus.

I love my Mother, too, and honor her as you do. She prays for you and all her children. God hears her. What else is Jesus saying to you?

Ask God to show you how to live today.

"Lord, by your grace help me to say yes to your will today. Show me that nothing is impossible with God. Amen."

Sunday, March 26, 2017
Fourth Sunday of Lent

Know that God is present with you and ready to converse.

In this week of Lent, the gospels show Jesus at work, healing and preaching. The disputes against him are getting more intense as the scribes and Pharisees get a clearer understanding that he is claiming that God is his Father and that they are one. Jesus encounters blindness in many forms on his way to the cross.

"Lord, open my eyes that I may see you in your holy Word."

Read the gospel: John 9:1–7, 13–17, 39–41 (Jn 9:1–41).

As Jesus walked along, he saw a man blind from birth. His disciples asked him, "Rabbi, who sinned, this man or his parents, that he was born blind?" Jesus answered, "Neither this man nor his parents sinned; he was born blind so that God's works might be revealed in him. We must work the works of him who sent me while it is day; night is coming when no one can work. As long as I am in the world, I am the light of the world." When he had said this, he spat on the ground and made mud with the saliva and spread the mud on the man's eyes, saying to him, "Go, wash in the pool of Siloam" (which means Sent). Then he went and washed and came back able to see. . . .

They brought to the Pharisees the man who had formerly been blind. Now it was a sabbath day when Jesus made the mud and opened his eyes. Then the Pharisees also began to ask him how he had received his sight. He said to them, "He put mud on my eyes. Then I washed, and now I see." Some of the Pharisees said, "This man is not from God, for he does not observe the sabbath." But others said, "How can a man who is a sinner perform such signs?" And they were divided. So they said again to the blind man, "What do you say about him? It was your eyes he opened." He said, "He is a prophet." . . .

Jesus said, "I came into this world for judgement so that those who do not see may see, and those who do see may become blind." Some of the Pharisees near him heard this and said to him, "Surely we are not blind, are we?" Jesus said to them, "If you were blind, you would not have sin. But now that you say, 'We see,' your sin remains."

Notice what you think and feel as you read the gospel.

The disciples ask Jesus who has sinned that a man is born blind. Jesus says it is not about sin but about revealing the glory of God. Then he heals the blind man. The Pharisees interrogate the man who had been blind, and when they hear his story they deny that Jesus could be from God. Jesus says that those who think they see but deny him are blind.

Pray as you are led for yourself and others.

"Lord, I cannot pretend to see. I long to see your face. Heal me deep within, and heal those you have given me . . ." (Continue in your own words.)

Listen to Jesus.

It is my joy to open your heart, mind, and soul to me, my child. Give yourself to me every day, and I will change your life. What else is Jesus saying to you?

Ask God to show you how to live today.

"Lead me by the hand, Lord. Lead me into your light. And let me do something that pleases you today. Amen."

Monday, March 27, 2017

Know that God is present with you and ready to converse.

"Lord, let me find you in the darkness of the world and even within my own darkness. You are the Light of the world."

Read the gospel: John 9:13–16, 18–21, 24–38 (Jn 9:1–41).

They brought to the Pharisees the man who had formerly been blind. Now it was a sabbath day when Jesus made the mud and opened his eyes. Then the Pharisees also began to ask him how he had received his sight. He said to them, "He put mud on my eyes. Then I washed, and now I see." Some of the Pharisees said, "This man is not from God, for he does not observe the sabbath." But others said, "How can a man who is a sinner perform such signs?" And they were divided. . . .

The Jews did not believe that he had been blind and had received his sight until they called the parents of the man who had received his sight and asked them, "Is this your son, who you say was born blind? How then does he now see?" His parents answered, "We know that this is our son, and that he was born blind; but we do not know how it is that now he sees, nor do we know who opened his eyes. Ask him; he is of age. He will speak for himself." . . .

So for the second time they called the man who had been blind, and they said to him, "Give glory to God! We know that this man is a sinner." He answered, "I do not know whether he is a sinner. One thing I do know, that though I was blind, now I see." They said to him, "What did he do to you? How did he open your eyes?" He answered them, "I have told you already, and you would not listen. Why do you want to hear it again? Do you also want to become his disciples?" Then they reviled him, saying, "You are his disciple, but we are disciples of Moses. We know that God has spoken to Moses, but as for this man, we do not know where he comes from." The man answered, "Here is an astonishing thing! You do not know where he comes from, and yet he opened my eyes. We know that God does not listen to sinners, but he does listen to one who worships him and obeys his will. Never since the world began has it been heard that anyone opened the eyes of a person born blind. If this man were not from God, he could do nothing." They answered him, "You were born entirely in sins, and are you trying to teach us?" And they drove him out.

Jesus heard that they had driven him out, and when he found him, he said, "Do you believe in the Son of Man?" He answered, "And who is he, sir? Tell me, so that I may believe in him." Jesus said to him, "You have seen him, and the one speaking with you is he." He said, "Lord, I believe." And he worshipped him.

Notice what you think and feel as you read the gospel.

This passage is a study of human nature. All are in the dark whether they realize it or not. The disciples don't understand. The blind man doesn't see anything. His parents can't explain his healing. The Pharisees cannot see past the fact that Jesus breaks the Sabbath according to their laws. They are blinded by their theology. Meanwhile, the man restored to sight believes in Jesus, the Messiah.

Pray as you are led for yourself and others.

"Lord, though all the world be wrong, you are right. I believe in you and worship you. As we have a personal relationship, I pray the same for others, especially those in deepest darkness . . ." (Continue in your own words.)

Listen to Jesus.

I cannot do my work in those who deny their sins, beloved disciple. Give all your sins to me and let me wash you. You will know my joy. What else is Jesus saying to you?

Ask God to show you how to live today.

"What sacrifice can I make today to show my love for you, my gratitude that you are with me, Savior? Amen."

Tuesday, March 28, 2017

Know that God is present with you and ready to converse.

Lord of heaven and earth, stir up my heart to receive your Word today.

Read the gospel: John 5:1–9a, 14–16 (Jn 5:1–16).

After this there was a festival of the Jews, and Jesus went up to Jerusalem.

Now in Jerusalem by the Sheep Gate there is a pool, called in Hebrew Beth-zatha, which has five porticoes. In these lay many invalids—blind, lame, and paralyzed. One man was there who had been ill for thirty-eight years. When Jesus saw him lying there and knew that he had been there a long time, he said to him, "Do you want to be made well?" The sick man answered him, "Sir, I have no one to put me into the pool when the water is stirred up; and while I am making my way, someone else steps down ahead of me." Jesus said to him, "Stand up, take your mat and walk." At once the man was made well, and he took up his mat and began to walk. . . .

Later Jesus found him in the temple and said to him, "See, you have been made well! Do not sin anymore, so that nothing worse happens to you." The man went away and told the Jews that it was Jesus who had made him well. Therefore the Jews started persecuting Jesus, because he was doing such things on the sabbath.

Notice what you think and feel as you read the gospel.

On this Sabbath, Jesus tells the paralyzed man to take up his mat and walk, and he does so. Some Jews tell the man that it is unlawful for him to carry his mat on the Sabbath. These Jews started persecuting Jesus for healing on the Sabbath.

Pray as you are led for yourself and others.

"How narrow is the human heart, Lord! How easily we reject your free ways of love and allow ourselves to be imprisoned by human rules and expectations. Free us from this sin . . ." (Continue in your own words.)

Listen to Jesus.

If you offer yourself to act upon my love, you, too, will meet opposition. But I will be with you, and I will work through you, dear disciple. What else is Jesus saying to you?

Ask God to show you how to live today.

"Lord, all I ask is to walk in your grace, following you, doing small acts of love. Amen."

Wednesday, March 29, 2017

Know that God is present with you and ready to converse.

"Father, in the unity of the Holy Spirit you are one with your Son, Jesus, who is the everlasting Word. Let me join you in your love."

Read the gospel: John 5:17–24 (Jn 5:17–30).

But Jesus answered them, "My Father is still working, and I also am working." For this reason the Jews were seeking all the more to kill him, because he was not only breaking the sabbath, but was also calling God his own Father, thereby making himself equal to God.

Jesus said to them, "Very truly, I tell you, the Son can do nothing on his own, but only what he sees the Father doing; for whatever the Father does, the Son does likewise. The Father loves the Son and shows him all that he himself is doing; and he will show him greater works than these, so that you will be astonished. Indeed, just as the Father raises the dead and gives them life, so also the Son gives life to whomsoever he wishes. The Father judges no one but has given all judgment to the Son, so that all may honor the Son just as they honor the Father. Anyone who does not honor the Son does not honor the Father who sent him. Very truly, I tell you, anyone who hears my word and believes him who sent me has eternal life, and does not come under judgment, but has passed from death to life."

Notice what you think and feel as you read the gospel.

Some of the Jews want to kill Jesus now not just because he breaks the Sabbath but even more because he makes himself equal to God by healing, forgiving, raising the dead, and proclaiming that in the end he will judge all humanity. He and the Father are one; he does only the Father's will.

Pray as you are led for yourself and others.

"I can imagine how stunned people were to hear your words, Lord. You spoke the truth, but it was too much for many to take in. Open my spirit to humility to receive and believe the truth, your perfect unity with the Father, your life-giving authority . . ." (Continue in your own words.)

Listen to Jesus.

My work of redemption is a complete work, still in process. I did not come to give temporary relief to a fallen race; I came to raise all who trust in me to eternal life with God. Let me work in you, beloved. What else is Jesus saying to you?

Ask God to show you how to live today.

"Jesus, make your saving power real in me. Let me extend it by your grace and guidance to someone else today. I am grateful to you, blessed Lord. Amen."

Thursday, March 30, 2017

Know that God is present with you and ready to converse.

"Word of God, Savior, Jesus, let me hear you and know your voice today."

Read the gospel: John 5:31–38 (Jn 5:31–47).

Jesus said, "If I testify about myself, my testimony is not true. There is another who testifies on my behalf, and I know that his testimony to me is true. You sent messengers to John, and he testified to the truth. Not that I accept such human testimony, but I say these things so that you may be saved. He was a burning and shining lamp, and you were willing to rejoice for a while in his light. But I have a testimony greater than John's. The works that the Father has given me to complete, the very works that I am doing, testify on my behalf that the Father has sent me. And the Father who sent me has himself testified on my behalf. You have never heard his voice or seen his form, and you do not have his word abiding in you, because you do not believe him whom he has sent."

Notice what you think and feel as you read the gospel.

Jesus points out the things that testify to him as the Messiah. These are not his own testimony but God's he says. John the Baptist, the mighty works Jesus did, and the scriptures all testify to Jesus as the Messiah. But many who hear him do not believe because they do not have the love of God in them.

Pray as you are led for yourself and others.

"Lord, how can I keep the love of God within myself and share it with others? I need your grace, and I pray you give grace to these you have given me . . ." (Continue in your own words.)

Listen to Jesus.

Beloved, I have made life easy for you: merely love me. As long as you love me, we journey together, you are safe, you can do God's will, and your prayers are powerful. What else is Jesus saying to you?

Ask God to show you how to live today.

"Lord, increase my love of God and neighbor, that I may bring glory to you. Thank you! Amen."

Friday, March 31, 2017

Know that God is present with you and ready to converse.

"One God, I am before you, in awe at your wonderful works in the universe, in history, in the salvation of your people. Teach me by your Word."

Read the gospel: John 7:1–2, 10, 25–30.

After this Jesus went about in Galilee. He did not wish to go about in Judea because the Jews were looking for an opportunity to kill him. Now the Jewish festival of Booths was near. . . .

But after his brothers had gone to the festival, then he also went, not publicly but as it were in secret. . . .

Now some of the people of Jerusalem were saying, "Is not this the man whom they are trying to kill? And here he is, speaking openly, but they say nothing to him! Can it be that the authorities really know that this is the Messiah? Yet we know where this man is from; but when the Messiah comes, no one will know where he is from." Then Jesus cried out as he was teaching in the temple, "You know me, and you know where I am from. I have not come on my own. But the one who sent me is true, and you do not know him. I know him, because I am from him, and he sent me." Then they tried to arrest him, but no one laid hands on him, because his hour had not yet come.

Notice what you think and feel as you read the gospel.
In Jerusalem now, Jesus is in great danger. He moves about in secret. Meanwhile, people of Jerusalem speculate about his being the Messiah. Others argue against that idea. Jesus now cries out in the temple that he has been sent by God, whom they do not know. They try but fail to arrest him for his hour had not yet come.

Pray as you are led for yourself and others.
"Lord, I, too, give myself to your timing and the events you have destined in my life. Let me be true to you and embrace your will. Let it be for the good of others . . ." (Continue in your own words.)

Listen to Jesus.
It was my glory to be crucified in shame before men and women. I did it for love. My cross is also your glory, dear disciple. Take up your own cross in love and follow me to glory. What else is Jesus saying to you?

Ask God to show you how to live today.
"Let me make a small or great sacrifice in love today, Lord. Let it be to glorify you. I praise the way of the cross, Jesus. Thank you for teaching me. Amen."

Saturday, April 1, 2017

Know that God is present with you and ready to converse.
"Lord, as I come into your presence, let all doubt and disputation die in me, and let me receive the truth of your Word."

Read the gospel: John 7:40–53.
When they heard Jesus' words, some in the crowd said, "This is really the prophet." Others said, "This is the Messiah." But some asked, "Surely the Messiah does not come from Galilee, does he? Has not the scripture said that the Messiah is descended from David and comes from Bethlehem, the village where David lived?" So there was a division in the crowd because of him. Some of them wanted to arrest him, but no one laid hands on him.

Then the temple police went back to the chief priests and Pharisees, who asked them, "Why did you not arrest him?" The police answered, "Never has anyone spoken like this!" Then the Pharisees replied, "Surely you have not been deceived too, have you? Has any one of the authorities or of the Pharisees believed in him? But this crowd, which does not know the law—they are accursed." Nicodemus, who had gone to Jesus before, and who was one of them, asked, "Our law does not judge people without first giving them a hearing to find out what they are doing, does it?" They replied, "Surely you are not also from Galilee, are you? Search and you will see that no prophet is to arise from Galilee."

Notice what you think and feel as you read the gospel.

The people of Jerusalem are arguing about Jesus. They speak from partial knowledge, and they form their opinions based on self-interest, not regard for the truth. The Pharisees condemn the crowd's ignorance of the law, but Nicodemus points out that they themselves unfairly judge Jesus contrary to the law.

Pray as you are led for yourself and others.

"Lord, I can get swept into confusion by all the arguments of my own day. My knowledge is partial, my prejudices hold sway, and I am distracted from having a pure encounter with you. Let me know you and worship you with all my heart . . ." (Continue in your own words.)

Listen to Jesus.

My beloved servant, I give you my heart as you have given me yours. By faith you see me, by love you know me. What else do you ask of me today? What else is Jesus saying to you?

Ask God to show you how to live today.

"Thank you for your wonderful love for me, Lord. Let nothing ever come between us. I humbly ask that I may radiate your love to others today. Amen."

Sunday, April 2, 2017
Fifth Sunday of Lent

Know that God is present with you and ready to converse.

Lent continues with gospels showing intensifying opposition to Jesus who, for his part, continues to work great miracles and speak more and more plainly even to those who wish to kill him. He shows no fear for he walks in the light of his Father and he wholly trusts the providence of God. Though he journeys toward his death, he has come to bring life.

"Jesus, you who began my salvation, I ask you to finish it according to your will. Let me follow you in your Word."

Read the gospel: John 11:1–6, 38–45 (Jn 11:1–45).

Now a certain man was ill, Lazarus of Bethany, the village of Mary and her sister Martha. Mary was the one who anointed the Lord with perfume and wiped his feet with her hair; her brother Lazarus was ill. So the sisters sent a message to Jesus, "Lord, he whom you love is ill." But when Jesus heard it, he said, "This illness does not lead to death; rather it is for God's glory, so that the Son of God may be glorified through it." Accordingly, though Jesus loved Martha and her sister and Lazarus, after having heard that Lazarus was ill, he stayed two days longer in the place where he was. . . .

Then Jesus, again greatly disturbed, came to the tomb. It was a cave, and a stone was lying against it. Jesus said, "Take away the stone." Martha, the sister of the dead man, said to him, "Lord, already there is a stench because he has been dead for four days." Jesus said to her, "Did I not tell you that if you believed, you would see the glory of God?" So they took away the stone. And Jesus looked upwards and said, "Father, I thank you for having heard me. I knew that you always hear me, but I have said this for the sake of the crowd standing here, so that they may believe that you sent me." When he had said this, he cried with a loud voice, "Lazarus, come out!" The dead man came out, his hands and feet bound with strips of cloth, and his face wrapped in a cloth. Jesus said to them, "Unbind him, and let him go."

Many of the Jews therefore, who had come with Mary and had seen what Jesus did, believed in him.

Notice what you think and feel as you read the gospel.

Fearlessly, Jesus moves among the people and here does one of his greatest miracles, raising Lazarus from the grave. Seeing it, many of the mourners at the tomb believe in Jesus. In his grief, Jesus shows his love for his friend. In his prayer, he shows his union with his Father.

Pray as you are led for yourself and others.

"Lord, you will also raise me from death to everlasting life. I feel you asking me to pray for those who do not yet believe in you. I think of these . . ." (Continue in your own words.)

Listen to Jesus.

Your life is a walk of faith, my child. But do not cling to your faith; cling to me, for I am your Resurrection and your Life. I also hold in my hand those for whom you pray. What else is Jesus saying to you?

Ask God to show you how to live today.

"I offer myself to you today, Lord, to use me as you will. I want to serve and please you, but I cannot unless you work through me. Work through me, Jesus. Amen."

Monday, April 3, 2017

Know that God is present with you and ready to converse.

"Lord, write on my heart your laws of love. I thank you for your presence here now."

Read the gospel: John 8:1–11.

Jesus went to the Mount of Olives. Early in the morning he came again to the temple. All the people came to him and he sat down and began to teach them. The scribes and the Pharisees brought a woman who had been caught in adultery; and making her stand before all of them, they said to him, "Teacher, this woman was caught in the very act of committing adultery. Now in the law Moses commanded us to stone such women. Now what do you say?" They said this to test him, so that they might have some charge to bring against him. Jesus bent down and wrote with his finger on the ground. When they kept on questioning him, he straightened up and said to them, "Let anyone among you who is without sin be the first to throw a stone at her." And once again he bent down and wrote on the ground. When they heard it, they went away, one by one, beginning with the elders; and Jesus was left alone with the woman standing before him. Jesus straightened up and said to her, "Woman, where are they? Has no one condemned you?" She said, "No one, sir." And Jesus said, "Neither do I condemn you. Go your way, and from now on do not sin again."

Notice what you think and feel as you read the gospel.

The story of the woman taken in adultery seems to illuminate several principles. First, the law of Moses needs to be open to interpretation in its application to specific cases. Second, we should focus our moral scrutiny on ourselves before we judge and condemn others. Third, the Lord is full of mercy and forgiveness of sin. Fourth, the Lord asks the sinner to turn from sin and to obey the law of Moses.

Pray as you are led for yourself and others.

"Lord, my heart is quick to judge others and to excuse myself. By your Spirit, let me seek your forgiveness and let me show only mercy to others. Instead of condemnation, I have mercy upon . . ." (Continue in your own words.)

Listen to Jesus.

Beloved, you strive for much that is contrary to the human heart. You are right to seek holiness by my Spirit, for only in God is it possible to achieve true mercy. What else is Jesus saying to you?

Ask God to show you how to live today.

"Open my eyes and mind to how I can be judgmental. Lord, show me how to put my judgments far from me, case by case. All praise to you, Lord Jesus Christ. Amen."

Tuesday, April 4, 2017

Know that God is present with you and ready to converse.

"Master of the Universe, Holy Trinity, One God, I cannot take you in. Take me into yourself. Capture me by your Word."

Read the gospel: John 8:21–30.

Again Jesus said to them, "I am going away, and you will search for me, but you will die in your sin. Where I am going, you cannot come." Then the Jews said, "Is he going to kill himself? Is that what he means by saying, 'Where I am going, you cannot come'?" He said to them, "You are from below, I am from above; you are of this world, I am not of this world. I told you that you would die in your sins, for you will die in your sins unless you believe that I am he." They said to him, "Who are you?" Jesus said to them, "Why do I speak to you at all? I have much to say about you and much to condemn; but the one who sent me is true, and I declare to the world what I have heard from him." They did not understand that he was speaking to them about the Father. So Jesus said, "When you have lifted up the Son of Man, then you will realize that I am he, and that I do nothing on my own, but I speak these things as the Father instructed me. And the one who sent me is with me; he has not left me alone, for I always do what is pleasing to him." As he was saying these things, many believed in him.

Notice what you think and feel as you read the gospel.

Jesus is thinking of his passion, death, resurrection, and ascension. He shows urgency on behalf of his hearers. He warns them they will die in their sins because they are worldly while he is from heaven, the obedient Son of the Father. He exhorts them to believe in him lest they die in their sins. He tells them they will realize who he is when they lift him up on the cross.

Pray as you are led for yourself and others.

"Lord, I know I am of this world, full of human weakness. Let me believe and come to you. I pray for all those who resist you . . ." (Continue in your own words.)

Listen to Jesus.

Your faithfulness to me touches me, dear friend. You want others to know your peace in knowing me. Our prayers for them have power with our Father. Thank you for praying with me. What else is Jesus saying to you?

Ask God to show you how to live today.

"I offer you all my thoughts, words, deeds, joys, and sorrows this day that you may count them as a prayer for those you have given me. Keep my mind on you. Amen."

Wednesday, April 5, 2017

Know that God is present with you and ready to converse.

Jesus, give me your Spirit to know your truth and freedom.

Read the gospel: John 8:31–38 (Jn 8:31–42).

Then Jesus said to the Jews who had believed in him, "If you continue in my word, you are truly my disciples; and you will know the truth, and the truth will make you free." They answered him, "We are descendants of Abraham and have never been slaves to anyone. What do you mean by saying, 'You will be made free'?"

Jesus answered them, "Very truly, I tell you, everyone who commits sin is a slave to sin. The slave does not have a permanent place in the household; the son has a place there forever. So if the Son makes you free, you will be free indeed. I know that you are descendants of Abraham;

yet you look for an opportunity to kill me, because there is no place in you for my word. I declare what I have seen in the Father's presence; as for you, you should do what you have heard from the Father."

Notice what you think and feel as you read the gospel.

Jesus declares the truth of his Word: it will make us free. How will we be free? Free from sin. Loving God the Father is also loving Jesus.

Pray as you are led for yourself and others.

"Jesus, let me use the freedom you give me to avoid sin. Let me love God and desire to please God in all things. I wish to help others to see the truth of your Word and person, Jesus . . ." (Continue in your own words.)

Listen to Jesus.

Examine your life, beloved disciple, in the light of my Word and the freedom it gives you. As you give yourself to me, turning from sin, you will rejoice in the love of God. What else is Jesus saying to you?

Ask God to show you how to live today.

"How am I free, Lord? Make me aware of moments of freedom in this day so that I may choose goodness, truth, love, and God. Amen."

Thursday, April 6, 2017

Know that God is present with you and ready to converse.

"You are here with me now, Jesus. You are always with me. Let me know you in your Word and carry you forth into my day by your Spirit."

Read the gospel: John 8:51–59.

Jesus said, "Very truly, I tell you, whoever keeps my word will never see death." The Jews said to him, "Now we know that you have a demon. Abraham died, and so did the prophets; yet you say, 'Whoever keeps my word will never taste death.' Are you greater than our father Abraham, who died? The prophets also died. Who do you claim to be?" Jesus answered, "If I glorify myself, my glory is nothing. It is my Father who glorifies me, he of whom you say, 'He is our God,' though you do not know him. But I know him; if I were to say that I do not know him, I would be a liar like you. But I do know him and I keep his word. Your ancestor Abraham rejoiced that he would see my day; he saw it and was glad." Then the Jews said to him, "You are not yet fifty years old, and have you seen Abraham?" Jesus said to them, "Very truly, I tell you, before Abraham was, I am." So they picked up stones to throw at him, but Jesus hid himself and went out of the temple.

Notice what you think and feel as you read the gospel.

The Jews scorn Jesus' claims of having a special relationship with God, his Father, and his claims of conferring eternal life to those who keep his Word. Jesus puts himself above Abraham, for before Abraham was, Jesus existed. He knows they will turn on him for what seems blasphemy to them, but he is compelled to tell the truth about himself.

Pray as you are led for yourself and others.

"Word of the Father, Light of the World, grant me your Life, your Truth, your Way. I glorify you for your goodness and your generous grace to me and mine . . ." (Continue in your own words.)

Listen to Jesus.

My Father glorified my suffering. I obeyed God for love because God's purposes are all love. Let love operate in your life, child, and God will glorify your suffering as well. What else is Jesus saying to you?

Ask God to show you how to live today.

"I do suffer, Lord, in small and great ways as the days pass. I offer this suffering to our Father for love of those you have given me. Let me love as you do, Jesus. Amen."

Friday, April 7, 2017

Know that God is present with you and ready to converse.

"Jesus, Son of the Father and one with the Father in the unity of the Holy Spirit, lift me to God by your Word."

Read the gospel: John 10:31–39 (Jn 10:31–42).

The Jews took up stones again to stone him. Jesus replied, "I have shown you many good works from the Father. For which of these are you going to stone me?" The Jews answered, "It is not for a good work that we are going to stone you, but for blasphemy, because you, though only a human being, are making yourself God." Jesus answered, "Is it not written in your law, 'I said, you are gods'? If those to whom the word of God came were called 'gods'—and the scripture cannot be annulled— can you say that the one whom the Father has sanctified and sent into the world is blaspheming because I said, 'I am God's Son'? If I am not doing the works of my Father, then do not believe me. But if I do them, even though you do not believe me, believe the works, so that you may know and understand that the Father is in me and I am in the Father." Then they tried to arrest him again, but he escaped from their hands.

Notice what you think and feel as you read the gospel.

Jesus faces stoning by the many who cannot abide the notion that he is God's Son. Jesus appeals to scripture and then to his mighty works as reasons to believe in him. He affirms again that the Father is in him and he is in the Father. He escapes arrest.

Pray as you are led for yourself and others.

"Lord, what is the difference between those who believe your Word and those who don't? I believe. Help my unbelief. I pray for those who do not believe or who suffer from doubts . . ." (Continue in your own words.)

Listen to Jesus.

Your faith is my gift to you, beloved disciple. Treasure it. Put it to use in your prayers and in your actions. Let it grow and bear fruit. What else is Jesus saying to you?

Ask God to show you how to live today.

"Lord, today when I find myself in a situation in which I may act on faith in God, let me do so. Let me remember your words to me and walk in the faith you have given me. Amen."

Saturday, April 8, 2017

Know that God is present with you and ready to converse.

"I am looking for you, Jesus, and ask you to let me find you, know you, and love you in your Word. Speak to me, Lord."

Read the gospel: John 11:45–53 (Jn 11:45–56).

Many of the Jews therefore, who had come with Mary and had seen what Jesus did, believed in him. But some of them went to the Pharisees and told them what he had done. So the chief priests and the Pharisees called a meeting of the council, and said, "What are we to do? This man is performing many signs. If we let him go on like this, everyone will believe in him, and the Romans will come and destroy both our holy place and our nation." But one of them, Caiaphas, who was high priest that year, said to them, "You know nothing at all! You do not understand that it is better for you to have one man die for the people than to have the whole nation destroyed." He did not say this on his own, but being high priest that year he prophesied that Jesus was about to die for the nation, and not for the nation only, but to gather into one the dispersed children of God. So from that day on they planned to put him to death.

Notice what you think and feel as you read the gospel.

Feeling threatened by the many who believe in Jesus, the Pharisees call a meeting. They are worried that the many conversions to Jesus will provoke the Romans to destroy their religious traditions. The chief priest, Caiaphas, suggests that Jesus may make a good scapegoat for the nation; his comment is truer than he realized at the time.

Pray as you are led for yourself and others.

"Jesus, you hide yourself and you show yourself in obedience to God, not for fear of others. Let me be as you were, led only by the will of God. Give me grace to do God's will . . ." (Continue in your own words.)

Listen to Jesus.

Servant of God, I come to you with love this moment, and I will be close to you all day. As you give yourself to God, God's will is done. Follow me. What else is Jesus saying to you?

Ask God to show you how to live today.

"Jesus, you came to earth and changed history. Work with me in my life to change things, that I may hasten the coming of the kingdom of God. Thank you. Amen."

Sunday, April 9, 2017
Palm Sunday of the Lord's Passion

Know that God is present with you and ready to converse.

The story of God made flesh, coming into the world to proclaim his Father's love for all humanity and to save us from sin and death now turns grim. Jesus faces his destiny: to be captured, tortured, and crucified by his enemies while also abandoned by his friends. What do these awful events mean? The Word is open to us that we may understand.

"Jesus, let me enter into your passion with open eyes and heart that I may love you more and serve you better than I ever have."

Read the gospel: Matthew 27:24–37, 45–54 (Mt 26:14–27:66).

So when Pilate saw that he could do nothing, but rather that a riot was beginning, he took some water and washed his hands before the crowd, saying, "I am innocent of this man's blood; see to it yourselves." Then the people as a whole answered, "His blood be on us and on our children." So he released Barabbas for them; and after flogging Jesus, he handed him over to be crucified.

Then the soldiers of the governor took Jesus into the governor's headquarters, and they gathered the whole cohort around him. They stripped him and put a scarlet robe on him, and after twisting some thorns into a crown, they put it on his head. They put a reed in his right hand and knelt before him and mocked him, saying, "Hail, King of the Jews!" They spat on him, and took the reed and struck him on the head. After mocking him, they stripped him of the robe and put his own clothes on him. Then they led him away to crucify him.

As they went out, they came upon a man from Cyrene named Simon; they compelled this man to carry his cross. And when they came to a place called Golgotha (which means Place of a Skull), they offered him wine to drink, mixed with gall; but when he tasted it, he would not drink it. And when they had crucified him, they divided his clothes among themselves by casting lots; then they sat down there and kept watch over him. Over his head they put the charge against him, which read, "This is Jesus, the King of the Jews." . . .

From noon on, darkness came over the whole land until three in the afternoon. And about three o'clock Jesus cried with a loud voice, "Eli, Eli, lema sabachthani?" that is, "My God, my God, why have you forsaken me?" When some of the bystanders heard it, they said, "This man is calling for Elijah." At once one of them ran and got a sponge, filled it with sour wine, put it on a stick, and gave it to him to drink. But the others said, "Wait, let us see whether Elijah will come to save him." Then Jesus cried again with a loud voice and breathed his last. At that moment the curtain of the temple was torn in two, from top to bottom. The earth shook, and the rocks were split. The tombs also were opened, and many bodies of the saints who had fallen asleep were raised. After his resurrection they came out of the tombs and entered the holy city and appeared to many. Now when the centurion and those with him, who were keeping watch over Jesus, saw the earthquake and what took place, they were terrified and said, "Truly this man was God's Son!"

Notice what you think and feel as you read the gospel.

This is an account of Jesus' passion. He is arrested, flogged, crowned with thorns, stripped, forced to carry his cross, and crucified. This is what Jesus had come to do.

Pray as you are led for yourself and others.

"Lord, I have desired to follow you. Help me to take up my own cross and follow you all the way to God. What a privilege you give me that I can join you in acts of love . . ." (Continue in your own words.)

Listen to Jesus.

You will be tried and tested, dearest beloved, as I was. Turn to me, for I have power to redeem your sufferings. By them, you will glorify God and help others. Continue in my love. What else is Jesus saying to you?

Ask God to show you how to live today.

"God, I cannot face suffering unless you are with me. Be with me. Be with all who suffer. Let us not suffer needlessly but for the good of ourselves and others. Amen."

Monday, April 10, 2017

Know that God is present with you and ready to converse.

"Jesus, Word of the Father, enter my heart, mind, soul, and spirit as I read and pray today."

Read the gospel: Luke 4:16–21.

When Jesus came to Nazareth, where he had been brought up, he went to the synagogue on the sabbath day, as was his custom. He stood up to read, and the scroll of the prophet Isaiah was given to him. He unrolled the scroll and found the place where it was written:

> "The Spirit of the Lord is upon me,
>   because he has anointed me
>   to bring good news to the poor.
> He has sent me to proclaim release to the captives
>   and recovery of sight to the blind,
>   to let the oppressed go free,
> to proclaim the year of the Lord's favor."

And he rolled up the scroll, gave it back to the attendant, and sat down. The eyes of all in the synagogue were fixed on him. Then he began to say to them, "Today this scripture has been fulfilled in your hearing."

Notice what you think and feel as you read the gospel.

What a stunning event for those who attended the synagogue of Nazareth that day! Here the young man Jesus, whom they all knew well, stands up to read the prophetic words of Isaiah. The Messiah would bring good news to the poor, release captives, give sight to the blind, and free the oppressed. Who is this Messiah? Jesus says it is he.

Pray as you are led for yourself and others.

"Lord, fill me with wonder that you are real, true God made man, the Savior of the world. Be my Savior, too, Lord, today and tomorrow. Extend your mercy upon . . ." (Continue in your own words.)

Listen to Jesus.

If you want to know who you are, beloved, follow me. No one else is like you. That is why I love you and need you to be who you are. What else is Jesus saying to you?

Ask God to show you how to live today.

"Lord, you declared your identity clearly at the start of your ministry. Help me be genuine, authentic, and honest with myself and all I encounter, for that is what you call me to do. Thank you. Amen."

Tuesday, April 11, 2017

Know that God is present with you and ready to converse.

"Jesus, let me know you better so that I may follow you more closely. Teach me by your Word."

Read the gospel: John 13:21–33, 36–38.

After saying this Jesus was troubled in spirit, and declared, "Very truly, I tell you, one of you will betray me." The disciples looked at one another, uncertain of whom he was speaking. One of his disciples—the one whom Jesus loved—was reclining next to him; Simon Peter therefore motioned to him to ask Jesus of whom he was speaking. So while reclining next to Jesus, he asked him, "Lord, who is it?" Jesus answered, "It is the one to whom I give this piece of bread when I have dipped it in the dish." So when he had dipped the piece of bread, he gave it to Judas son of Simon

Iscariot. After he received the piece of bread, Satan entered into him. Jesus said to him, "Do quickly what you are going to do." Now no one at the table knew why he said this to him. Some thought that, because Judas had the common purse, Jesus was telling him, "Buy what we need for the festival"; or, that he should give something to the poor. So, after receiving the piece of bread, he immediately went out. And it was night.

When he had gone out, Jesus said, "Now the Son of Man has been glorified, and God has been glorified in him. If God has been glorified in him, God will also glorify him in himself and will glorify him at once. Little children, I am with you only a little longer. You will look for me; and as I said to the Jews so now I say to you, 'Where I am going, you cannot come.'" . . .

Simon Peter said to him, "Lord, where are you going?" Jesus answered, "Where I am going, you cannot follow me now; but you will follow afterwards." Peter said to him, "Lord, why can I not follow you now? I will lay down my life for you." Jesus answered, "Will you lay down your life for me? Very truly, I tell you, before the cock crows, you will have denied me three times."

Notice what you think and feel as you read the gospel.

Jesus begins the evening of the Passover troubled by his impending betrayal, but when Judas finally goes out, Jesus speaks of his glory and his coming departure to a place they cannot follow. Peter protests, but Jesus predicts his denial. Yet Peter would follow Jesus, laying down his life.

Pray as you are led for yourself and others.

"Lord, I have denied you, and I'm sorry. But I ask you to let me follow you, dying to myself and forsaking all for you. Show me how to do that . . ." (Continue in your own words.)

Listen to Jesus.

If I am the love of your life, if you give your whole heart to me, I will guide you in my path of service. Will you suffer? Yes, but you will also share my glory. What else is Jesus saying to you?

Ask God to show you how to live today.

"Help me to get my eyes off of myself, Lord, and look upon you, the crucified and risen King of Glory. I praise your holy name. Amen."

Wednesday, April 12, 2017

Know that God is present with you and ready to converse.

"Lord, I have been close to you, and you are with me now. Keep me from all betrayal; let me never turn away from you."

Read the gospel: Matthew 26:14–25.

Then one of the twelve, who was called Judas Iscariot, went to the chief priests and said, "What will you give me if I betray him to you?" They paid him thirty pieces of silver. And from that moment he began to look for an opportunity to betray him.

On the first day of Unleavened Bread the disciples came to Jesus, saying, "Where do you want us to make the preparations for you to eat the Passover?" He said, "Go into the city to a certain man, and say to him, 'The Teacher says, My time is near; I will keep the Passover at your house with my disciples.'" So the disciples did as Jesus had directed them, and they prepared the Passover meal.

When it was evening, he took his place with the twelve; and while they were eating, he said, "Truly I tell you, one of you will betray me." And they became greatly distressed and began to say to him one after another, "Surely not I, Lord?" He answered, "The one who has dipped his hand into the bowl with me will betray me. The Son of Man goes as it is written of him, but woe to that one by whom the Son of Man is betrayed! It would have been better for that one not to have been born." Judas, who betrayed him, said, "Surely not I, Rabbi?" He replied, "You have said so."

Notice what you think and feel as you read the gospel.

Judas, though he had traveled with Jesus, heard his preaching, seen his miracles, and was given a position of trust, agrees to betray Jesus to the chief priests for money. All people are subject to temptation. He must have deluded himself about what he was doing. He lied to the Lord.

Pray as you are led for yourself and others.

"Lord, let me never forget that I am weak, easily tempted to value things other than you. In my weakness, love me and let me do what pleases you . . ." (Continue in your own words.)

Listen to Jesus.

I do love you, my dear child. Open yourself in all your failure and weakness to me. I understand. I will wash and heal you and make you strong. What else is Jesus saying to you?

Ask God to show you how to live today.

"I need you, Lord. Today I need you to see well, to love well, to speak well, and to do well. Thank you. Amen."

Thursday, April 13, 2017
Holy Thursday

Know that God is present with you and ready to converse.

"Jesus, Son of the Father, you show me how you live by your Word. Let your lessons be bound to my heart."

Read the gospel: John 13:2b–15 (Jn 13:1–15).

And during supper Jesus, knowing that the Father had given all things into his hands, and that he had come from God and was going to God, got up from the table, took off his outer robe, and tied a towel around himself. Then he poured water into a basin and began to wash the disciples' feet and to wipe them with the towel that was tied around him. He came to Simon Peter, who said to him, "Lord, are you going to wash my feet?" Jesus answered, "You do not know now what I am doing, but later you will understand." Peter said to him, "You will never wash my feet." Jesus answered, "Unless I wash you, you have no share with me." Simon Peter said to him, "Lord, not my feet only but also my hands and my head!" Jesus said to him, "One who has bathed does not need to wash, except for the feet, but is entirely clean. And you are clean, though not all of you." For he knew who was to betray him; for this reason he said, "Not all of you are clean."

After he had washed their feet, had put on his robe, and had returned to the table, he said to them, "Do you know what I have done to you? You call me Teacher and Lord—and you are right, for that is what I am. So if I, your Lord and Teacher, have washed your feet, you also ought to wash one another's feet. For I have set you an example, that you also should do as I have done to you."

Notice what you think and feel as you read the gospel.

Jesus teaches by example that the greatest ones will wash the feet of those they serve. Not just in the washing of the feet but throughout his ministry Jesus served others.

Pray as you are led for yourself and others.

"How shall I put your lesson into action, Lord? These are people I intend to serve, so help me God . . ." (Continue in your own words.)

Listen to Jesus.
You will find great joy in humble service. Don't talk about it. Don't pat yourself on the back. You are only doing what I have commanded. What else is Jesus saying to you?

Ask God to show you how to live today.
"Give me the skill, Jesus, to know how to serve others without embarrassing them or striking a false pose of humility. Amen."

Friday, April 14, 2017
Good Friday

Know that God is present with you and ready to converse.
"Lord, I come to you on this day with awe and trembling. You willingly went to your death for love of me."

Read the gospel: John 19:25b–37 (Jn 18:1–19:42).
Meanwhile, standing near the cross of Jesus were his mother, and his mother's sister, Mary the wife of Clopas, and Mary Magdalene. When Jesus saw his mother and the disciple whom he loved standing beside her, he said to his mother, "Woman, here is your son." Then he said to the disciple, "Here is your mother." And from that hour the disciple took her into his own home.

After this, when Jesus knew that all was now finished, he said (in order to fulfill the scripture), "I am thirsty." A jar full of sour wine was standing there. So they put a sponge full of the wine on a branch of hyssop and held it to his mouth. When Jesus had received the wine, he said, "It is finished." Then he bowed his head and gave up his spirit.

Since it was the day of Preparation, the Jews did not want the bodies left on the cross during the sabbath, especially because that sabbath was a day of great solemnity. So they asked Pilate to have the legs of the crucified men broken and the bodies removed. Then the soldiers came and broke the legs of the first and of the other who had been crucified with him. But when they came to Jesus and saw that he was already dead, they did not break his legs. Instead, one of the soldiers pierced his side with a spear, and at once blood and water came out. (He who saw this has testified so that you also may believe. His testimony is true, and he knows that he tells the truth.) These things occurred so that the scripture might be fulfilled, "None of his bones shall be broken." And again another passage of scripture says, "They will look on the one whom they have pierced."

Notice what you think and feel as you read the gospel.

How brave and good Jesus was throughout that horrible ordeal, his torture and death. In the end, blood and water flowed out of his pierced side.

Pray as you are led for yourself and others.

"Jesus, I am not worthy, but you died for love of me. Let me be washed clean of all sin by your blood. Let me thank you and glorify you this moment . . ." (Continue in your own words.)

Listen to Jesus.

My child, I love you now as I loved you then. Do you love me? What else is Jesus saying to you?

Ask God to show you how to live today.

"Lord, I am burdened and broken by my own crosses, even today. Give me your courage and your heart to journey today until the end. Amen."

Saturday, April 15, 2017
Holy Saturday

Know that God is present with you and ready to converse.

"Jesus, you live. Live in me and guide me by your Word."

Read the gospel: Matthew 28:1–10.

After the sabbath, as the first day of the week was dawning, Mary Magdalene and the other Mary went to see the tomb. And suddenly there was a great earthquake; for an angel of the Lord, descending from heaven, came and rolled back the stone and sat on it. His appearance was like lightning, and his clothing white as snow. For fear of him the guards shook and became like dead men. But the angel said to the women, "Do not be afraid; I know that you are looking for Jesus who was crucified. He is not here; for he has been raised, as he said. Come, see the place where he lay. Then go quickly and tell his disciples, 'He has been raised from the dead, and indeed he is going ahead of you to Galilee; there you will see him.' This is my message for you." So they left the tomb quickly with fear and great joy, and ran to tell his disciples. Suddenly Jesus met them and said, "Greetings!" And they came to him, took hold of his feet, and worshipped him. Then Jesus said to them, "Do not be afraid; go and tell my brothers to go to Galilee; there they will see me."

Notice what you think and feel as you read the gospel.
The women are the first to know and believe Jesus is alive. They understood. They worshiped. They obeyed.

Pray as you are led for yourself and others.
"Lord, strengthen my faith in the miracle of your resurrection. Let it be so real to me that the living Jesus becomes the center of my life. Let others see you through me . . ." (Continue in your own words.)

Listen to Jesus.
I take care of you, beloved. Trust in me. Let others know you do. Ask me for whatever you need. What else is Jesus saying to you?

Ask God to show you how to live today.
"Show me in many little ways how to recognize you, worship you, and obey you. I need you, Lord. Amen."

Sunday, April 16, 2017
Easter Sunday

Know that God is present with you and ready to converse.
After his passion, death, and burial, Jesus rises bodily from the dead. This is the fulfillment of his ministry on earth. What he had told his disciples would happen has happened. They cannot easily take it in. But they come to believe this great mystery.

Risen Lord, you have revealed yourself to many. Reveal yourself to me.

Read the gospel: John 20:1–9.
Early on the first day of the week, while it was still dark, Mary Magdalene came to the tomb and saw that the stone had been removed from the tomb. So she ran and went to Simon Peter and the other disciple, the one whom Jesus loved, and said to them, "They have taken the Lord out of the tomb, and we do not know where they have laid him." Then Peter and the other disciple set out and went towards the tomb. The two were running together, but the other disciple outran Peter and reached the tomb first. He bent down to look in and saw the linen wrappings lying there, but he did not go in. Then Simon Peter came, following him, and went into the tomb. He saw the linen wrappings lying there, and the cloth that had been on Jesus' head, not lying with the linen wrappings but rolled up in a place by itself. Then the other disciple, who reached

the tomb first, also went in, and he saw and believed; for as yet they did not understand the scripture, that he must rise from the dead.

Notice what you think and feel as you read the gospel.

The scene in the tomb with the wrappings and the head cloth is very specific. When the other disciple, John, sees it, he believes.

Pray as you are led for yourself and others.

"The world has never seen such a miracle as your resurrection, Lord. Alleluia! You are my Shepherd and you will lead me into your life . . ." (Continue in your own words.)

Listen to Jesus.

You may follow me with confidence, dear one. With me you will do well, and those around you will notice. What else is Jesus saying to you?

Ask God to show you how to live today.

"I would like to help others believe in you, Lord. Let me see the opportunities to say and do things that reveal you. You are one with Almighty God, Father, Son, and Holy Spirit. Amen."

The Easter Season

INTRODUCTION

Easter is the greatest feast of the Church year because it celebrates the victory of Jesus Christ over sin and death, a victory not just for himself but for all who believe in him. Jesus is the pioneer who leads us into eternal life. "Just as in Adam all die," wrote St. Paul, "so in Christ all will come to life again . . . Christ the first fruits and then, at his coming, all those who belong to him" (1 Cor 15:22–23). In the risen Christ, we are reconciled with God now and forever.

Our hearts and minds may wonder at the great mystery of resurrection. In the gospels, we read how the disciples received the amazing news that Jesus was not dead but lives. At first, many of them are skeptical, but they come to believe as Jesus shows himself to them again and again. For modern readers, their skepticism that turns to faith helps us to believe in this greatest of all miracles.

The season ends with Pentecost, the descent of the Holy Spirit to empower the disciples of Jesus to carry on his great work. The Spirit is given to us, too, as is the work. Let us pray the gospels of this season with joy and thanksgiving.

Monday, April 17, 2017

Know that God is present with you and ready to converse.
"Jesus, where are you? Why do I worry? You are here. I will not be afraid."

Read the gospel: Matthew 28:8–15.
So the women left the tomb quickly with fear and great joy, and ran to tell his disciples. Suddenly Jesus met them and said, "Greetings!" And they came to him, took hold of his feet, and worshipped him. Then Jesus said to them, "Do not be afraid; go and tell my brothers to go to Galilee; there they will see me."

While they were going, some of the guard went into the city and told the chief priests everything that had happened. After the priests had assembled with the elders, they devised a plan to give a large sum of money to the soldiers, telling them, "You must say, 'His disciples came by night and stole him away while we were asleep.' If this comes to the governor's ears, we will satisfy him and keep you out of trouble." So they took the money and did as they were directed. And this story is still told among the Jews to this day.

Notice what you think and feel as you read the gospel.
The empty tomb fills Mary Magdalene and the other Mary with fear and great joy. What were they afraid of? What were they joyful about? Jesus meets them and they worship him.

Pray as you are led for yourself and others.
"Lord, the world is full of lies and lost without God. I pray that your truth and resurrection be revealed to all that they may come to believe in you, know you, and be saved. I think of certain people who need you . . ." (Continue in your own words.)

Listen to Jesus.
Dear disciple, you love as I love. People of every time shall know this truth: I am Lord. Pray for the coming of my kingdom. What else is Jesus saying to you?

Ask God to show you how to live today.
"I desire to live according to my faith today, Jesus, seeing situations as you do and doing what you would do. Help me to do that, Jesus. Amen."

Tuesday, April 18, 2017

Know that God is present with you and ready to converse.
"Risen Lord, you have been waiting for me here. Tell me what I need to know today."

Read the gospel: John 20:11–18.
But Mary stood weeping outside the tomb. As she wept, she bent over to look into the tomb; and she saw two angels in white, sitting where the body of Jesus had been lying, one at the head and the other at the feet. They said to her, "Woman, why are you weeping?" She said to them, "They have taken away my Lord, and I do not know where they have laid him." When she had said this, she turned round and saw Jesus standing there, but she did not know that it was Jesus. Jesus said to her, "Woman, why are you weeping? For whom are you looking?" Supposing him to be the gardener, she said to him, "Sir, if you have carried him away, tell me where you have laid him, and I will take him away." Jesus said to her, "Mary!" She turned and said to him in Hebrew, "Rabbouni!" (which means Teacher). Jesus said to her, "Do not hold on to me, because I have not yet ascended to the Father. But go to my brothers and say to them, 'I am ascending to my Father and your Father, to my God and your God.'" Mary Magdalene went and announced to the disciples, "I have seen the Lord"; and she told them that he had said these things to her.

Notice what you think and feel as you read the gospel.
Mary is privileged to see and speak with the risen Jesus, whom she loves so much. He sends his message to the disciples through her: "I am ascending to my Father and your Father, to my God and your God." Because of Jesus, God is my Father, too.

Pray as you are led for yourself and others.
"Father in heaven, give me understanding to walk with you as a trusting child, for you have my life in your loving hand and will lead me all the way. Let me strengthen others on the way . . ." (Continue in your own words.)

Listen to Jesus.
This Word is Truth, my child. Lean on my Word every day, and I will accompany you hour by hour. What else is Jesus saying to you?

Ask God to show you how to live today.

"I love being present with you like this, Lord. Help me to find you during the distractions of my day. Teach me to abide in you. Amen."

Wednesday, April 19, 2017

Know that God is present with you and ready to converse.

"Lord, open my eyes to you, to your truth, to your Word."

Read the gospel: Luke 24:13–35.

Now on that same day two of them were going to a village called Emmaus, about seven miles from Jerusalem, and talking with each other about all these things that had happened. While they were talking and discussing, Jesus himself came near and went with them, but their eyes were kept from recognizing him. And he said to them, "What are you discussing with each other while you walk along?" They stood still, looking sad. Then one of them, whose name was Cleopas, answered him, "Are you the only stranger in Jerusalem who does not know the things that have taken place there in these days?" He asked them, "What things?" They replied, "The things about Jesus of Nazareth, who was a prophet mighty in deed and word before God and all the people, and how our chief priests and leaders handed him over to be condemned to death and crucified him. But we had hoped that he was the one to redeem Israel. Yes, and besides all this, it is now the third day since these things took place. Moreover, some women of our group astounded us. They were at the tomb early this morning, and when they did not find his body there, they came back and told us that they had indeed seen a vision of angels who said that he was alive. Some of those who were with us went to the tomb and found it just as the women had said; but they did not see him." Then he said to them, "Oh, how foolish you are, and how slow of heart to believe all that the prophets have declared! Was it not necessary that the Messiah should suffer these things and then enter into his glory?" Then beginning with Moses and all the prophets, he interpreted to them the things about himself in all the scriptures.

As they came near the village to which they were going, he walked ahead as if he were going on. But they urged him strongly, saying, "Stay with us, because it is almost evening and the day is now nearly over." So he went in to stay with them. When he was at the table with them, he took bread, blessed and broke it, and gave it to them. Then their eyes were opened, and they recognized him; and he vanished from their sight. They said to each other, "Were not our hearts burning within us while he was talking to us on the road, while he was opening the scriptures to us?" That same hour they got up and returned to Jerusalem; and they found the eleven and their companions gathered together. They were saying, "The Lord has risen indeed, and he has appeared to Simon!" Then they told what had happened on the road, and how he had been made known to them in the breaking of the bread.

Notice what you think and feel as you read the gospel.

I have felt my heart burning within me reading the scriptures. I know this is the power of the Holy Spirit, to recognize Truth even when shrouded in high mystery. The Lord is risen indeed!

Pray as you are led for yourself and others.

"Let your Truth be food and drink to me, Jesus Christ. Reign over me and those I love and pray for . . ." (Continue in your own words.)

Listen to Jesus.

I love you, beloved. I will increase your faith and strengthen you in wisdom and grace as you seek me and pray. Come to me often. What else is Jesus saying to you?

Ask God to show you how to live today.

"Jesus, when I forget you during the day, come to me, open my eyes to your presence, feed me with the Bread of Life. Amen."

Thursday, April 20, 2017

Know that God is present with you and ready to converse.

"If I saw you here with me, Jesus, I would be afraid. Give me eyes to see you, a mind to understand, and a heart full of your peace."

Read the gospel: Luke 24:35–48.

Then they told what had happened on the road, and how Jesus had been made known to them in the breaking of the bread.

While they were talking about this, Jesus himself stood among them and said to them, "Peace be with you." They were startled and terrified, and thought that they were seeing a ghost. He said to them, "Why are you frightened, and why do doubts arise in your hearts? Look at my hands and my feet; see that it is I myself. Touch me and see; for a ghost does not have flesh and bones as you see that I have." And when he had said this, he showed them his hands and his feet. While in their joy they were disbelieving and still wondering, he said to them, "Have you anything here to eat?" They gave him a piece of broiled fish, and he took it and ate in their presence.

Then he said to them, "These are my words that I spoke to you while I was still with you—that everything written about me in the law of Moses, the prophets, and the psalms must be fulfilled." Then he opened their minds to understand the scriptures, and he said to them, "Thus it is written, that the Messiah is to suffer and to rise from the dead on the third day, and that repentance and forgiveness of sins is to be proclaimed in his name to all nations, beginning from Jerusalem. You are witnesses of these things."

Notice what you think and feel as you read the gospel.

Look at his hands and his feet, still bearing the imprint of the nails of the cross. Touch him and see. He is alive. All that is written about him is true, and all shall be fulfilled.

Pray as you are led for yourself and others.

"I cling to your promise of forgiveness, Lord. For by your cross and resurrection you have set me free. I pray for those who need forgiveness today, that they may repent and turn to you for everlasting life . . ." (Continue in your own words.)

Listen to Jesus.

Loving God is a daily act. Love me all the time. Give me your fears, your doubts. Give me those who need me every day. We are walking and working side by side. What else is Jesus saying to you?

Ask God to show you how to live today.

"I cannot know what will happen in my life today, but I want to face it in your company, Lord. You will help me do that. Thank you. Amen."

Friday, April 21, 2017

Know that God is present with you and ready to converse.

"I know you are with me always, Lord, but I do not always recognize you. Let me do so now."

Read the gospel: John 21:1–14.

After these things Jesus showed himself again to the disciples by the Sea of Tiberias; and he showed himself in this way. Gathered there together were Simon Peter, Thomas called the Twin, Nathanael of Cana in Galilee, the sons of Zebedee, and two others of his disciples. Simon Peter said to them, "I am going fishing." They said to him, "We will go with you." They went out and got into the boat, but that night they caught nothing.

Just after daybreak, Jesus stood on the beach; but the disciples did not know that it was Jesus. Jesus said to them, "Children, you have no fish, have you?" They answered him, "No." He said to them, "Cast the net to the right side of the boat, and you will find some." So they cast it, and now they were not able to haul it in because there were so many fish. That disciple whom Jesus loved said to Peter, "It is the Lord!" When Simon Peter heard that it was the Lord, he put on some clothes, for he was naked, and jumped into the lake. But the other disciples came in the boat, dragging the net full of fish, for they were not far from the land, only about a hundred yards off.

When they had gone ashore, they saw a charcoal fire there, with fish on it, and bread. Jesus said to them, "Bring some of the fish that you have just caught." So Simon Peter went aboard and hauled the net ashore, full of large fish, a hundred and fifty-three of them; and though there were so many, the net was not torn. Jesus said to them, "Come and have breakfast." Now none of the disciples dared to ask him, "Who are you?" because they knew it was the Lord. Jesus came and took the bread and gave it to them, and did the same with the fish. This was now the third time that Jesus appeared to the disciples after he was raised from the dead.

Notice what you think and feel as you read the gospel.

How did Jesus look after his resurrection? His disciples have difficulty recognizing him as he appears to them in different ways in different places. Here he cooks them breakfast on the shore.

Pray as you are led for yourself and others.

"Jesus, feed me, too. Feed me with the truth of your resurrection, mighty Lord and King. Let me give to you all my circumstances. Let me entrust to you all those you have given me . . ." (Continue in your own words.)

Listen to Jesus.

I will provide for all your needs, dear friend, for you have placed your trust in me. What else is Jesus saying to you?

Ask God to show you how to live today.

"How shall I behave, Lord? Now that I have seen you with eyes of faith, show me how to be in this world. How may I glorify you, Jesus, my Rock and my Redeemer? Amen."

Saturday, April 22, 2017

Know that God is present with you and ready to converse.

The reality of your resurrection takes time to sink into one's being. Banish my doubts with your presence, Lord Jesus.

Read the gospel: Mark 16:9–15.

Now after Jesus rose early on the first day of the week, he appeared first to Mary Magdalene, from whom he had cast out seven demons. She went out and told those who had been with him, while they were mourning and weeping. But when they heard that he was alive and had been seen by her, they would not believe it.

After this he appeared in another form to two of them, as they were walking into the country. And they went back and told the rest, but they did not believe them.

Later he appeared to the eleven themselves as they were sitting at the table; and he upbraided them for their lack of faith and stubbornness, because they had not believed those who saw him after he had risen. And he said to them, "Go into all the world and proclaim the good news to the whole creation."

Notice what you think and feel as you read the gospel.

Jesus tells those who have been slow to believe to go into all the world and proclaim the Good News to all. Even when we doubt, he sends us with a message of faith to others.

Pray as you are led for yourself and others.

"Lord, send me. Even today, let me be a messenger of your love and your truth. Let me walk and speak in your power, Lord, and by your Spirit. Though I doubt myself, let me trust in you. I give you . . ." (Continue in your own words.)

Listen to Jesus.

You are blessed to believe in me. Your heart aches for those who still have not come to me. I join you in praying for them. With God all things are possible. What else is Jesus saying to you?

Ask God to show you how to live today.

"Give me the right words to say at the right time, Lord. Give me work to do and let me do it with you. Amen."

Sunday, April 23, 2017
Second Sunday of Easter

Know that God is present with you and ready to converse.

Jesus continues to appear to his disciples after his resurrection. They need many signs. He says to Thomas, "Do not doubt but believe." Thomas answers him, "My Lord and my God!"

"Breathe your holy truth upon me, Lord, as I read your word. I seek your blessing. I seek you, Son of God."

Read the gospel: John 20:19–31.

When it was evening on that day, the first day of the week, and the doors of the house where the disciples had met were locked for fear of the Jews, Jesus came and stood among them and said, "Peace be with you." After he said this, he showed them his hands and his side. Then the disciples rejoiced when they saw the Lord. Jesus said to them again, "Peace be with you. As the Father has sent me, so I send you." When he had said this, he breathed on them and said to them, "Receive the Holy Spirit. If you forgive the sins of any, they are forgiven them; if you retain the sins of any, they are retained."

But Thomas (who was called the Twin), one of the twelve, was not with them when Jesus came. So the other disciples told him, "We have seen the Lord." But he said to them, "Unless I see the mark of the nails in his hands, and put my finger in the mark of the nails and my hand in his side, I will not believe."

A week later his disciples were again in the house, and Thomas was with them. Although the doors were shut, Jesus came and stood among them and said, "Peace be with you." Then he said to Thomas, "Put your finger here and see my hands. Reach out your hand and put it in my side. Do not doubt but believe." Thomas answered him, "My Lord and my God!" Jesus said to him, "Have you believed because you have seen me? Blessed are those who have not seen and yet have come to believe."

Now Jesus did many other signs in the presence of his disciples, which are not written in this book. But these are written so that you may come to believe that Jesus is the Messiah, the Son of God, and that through believing you may have life in his name.

Notice what you think and feel as you read the gospel.

Jesus breathes on his disciples and tells them to receive the Holy Spirit; he then sends them out to continue his work on earth. We, too, are sent to do the work of the Father.

Pray as you are led for yourself and others.

"Lord, you know I am a weak and flawed person, yet I offer myself to you. Give me your Holy Spirit that I may serve you well. I am a sinner restored to grace by your power, Lord. Let me be a vessel of grace for others . . ." (Continue in your own words.)

Listen to Jesus.

You are right to rely on me. Do not be afraid. I have work for you that only you can do. I love you. What else is Jesus saying to you?

Ask God to show you how to live today.

"I resolve to lean on the Lord today with my heart open to him. Let my eyes be open to seeing the Lord in others. Amen."

Monday, April 24, 2017

Know that God is present with you and ready to converse.

"Who has seen the wind? Who can control the Spirit of God? I am here with you now, Spirit of Christ. Do with me what you will."

Read the gospel: John 3:1–8.

Now there was a Pharisee named Nicodemus, a leader of the Jews. He came to Jesus by night and said to him, "Rabbi, we know that you are a teacher who has come from God; for no one can do these signs that you do apart from the presence of God." Jesus answered him, "Very truly, I tell you, no one can see the kingdom of God without being born from above." Nicodemus said to him, "How can anyone be born after having grown old? Can one enter a second time into the mother's womb and be born?" Jesus answered, "Very truly, I tell you, no one can enter the kingdom of God without being born of water and Spirit. What is born of the flesh is flesh, and what is born of the Spirit is spirit. Do not be astonished that I said to you, 'You must be born from above.' The wind blows where it chooses, and you hear the sound of it, but you do not know where it comes from or where it goes. So it is with everyone who is born of the Spirit."

Notice what you think and feel as you read the gospel.
Becoming a child of God requires a spiritual birth. We must be born from above. It is not our doing but God's.

Pray as you are led for yourself and others.
"Lord, I often strive by my own efforts to be the person I want to be. Let me allow you to transform me and guide me by your Spirit. I wish to do your will, Lord . . ." (Continue in your own words.)

Listen to Jesus.
I will that you worship God in Spirit and in Truth, dear follower. Ask me for the grace you need. Look around you and see what we can do together. What else is Jesus saying to you?

Ask God to show you how to live today.
"Whatever happens today, Lord, I surrender to you in trust. I know that you work in all my circumstances and that nothing is more than you and I can manage together. I am yours, Jesus. Amen."

Tuesday, April 25, 2017
Saint Mark, Evangelist

Know that God is present with you and ready to converse.
"You who sit at the right hand of the Father are here with me now. Open me to your holy Word, Jesus."

Read the gospel: Mark 16:15–20.
And Jesus said to them, "Go into all the world and proclaim the good news to the whole creation. The one who believes and is baptized will be saved; but the one who does not believe will be condemned. And these signs will accompany those who believe: by using my name they will cast out demons; they will speak in new tongues; they will pick up snakes in their hands, and if they drink any deadly thing, it will not hurt them; they will lay their hands on the sick, and they will recover."

So then the Lord Jesus, after he had spoken to them, was taken up into heaven and sat down at the right hand of God. And they went out and proclaimed the good news everywhere, while the Lord worked with them and confirmed the message by the signs that accompanied it.

Notice what you think and feel as you read the gospel.

Jesus gives his disciples power. He says these signs will accompany those who believe. They will have his protection in the world and will do mighty things in his name.

Pray as you are led for yourself and others.

"Give me that simple faith, Lord, for I long to live as you command. Give me the awareness that this is a serious age and souls are at stake. I pray for these people . . ." (Continue in your own words.)

Listen to Jesus.

Life is short, my dear child. You believe and wish to serve me and those I have put in your life. I am with you in this. What else is Jesus saying to you?

Ask God to show you how to live today.

"Do not let me create barriers to you by my own ways of thinking, Lord. Help me to entrust myself to your mysterious power. Let me do your will and give glory to God! Amen."

Wednesday, April 26, 2017

Know that God is present with you and ready to converse.

"Lord, I know what it is to be in darkness. I turn toward your light at this moment."

Read the gospel: John 3:16–21.

Jesus said, "For God so loved the world that he gave his only Son, so that everyone who believes in him may not perish but may have eternal life.

"Indeed, God did not send the Son into the world to condemn the world, but in order that the world might be saved through him. Those who believe in him are not condemned; but those who do not believe are condemned already, because they have not believed in the name of the only Son of God. And this is the judgement, that the light has come into the world, and people loved darkness rather than light because their deeds were evil. For all who do evil hate the light and do not come to the light, so that their deeds may not be exposed. But those who do what is true come to the light, so that it may be clearly seen that their deeds have been done in God."

Notice what you think and feel as you read the gospel.

People love darkness rather than light because we do not want our evil deeds to be exposed. It is our deeds that keep us from the light of God. But we can choose to believe. We can come to the light and receive forgiveness and eternal life.

Pray as you are led for yourself and others.

"Lord, I pray for all those who are afraid of the light, as I myself have been afraid of the light. Let us all turn toward you and behold your glory . . ." (Continue in your own words.)

Listen to Jesus.

I am the light for your feet, and we will walk together on a path of love and goodness. What else is Jesus saying to you?

Ask God to show you how to live today.

"Let my eyes be fixed upon your light, Lord, and let me walk in it all day. Amen."

Thursday, April 27, 2017

Know that God is present with you and ready to converse.

"You have come down from heaven for me, Lord. Thank you."

Read the gospel: John 3:31–36.

The one who comes from above is above all; the one who is of the earth belongs to the earth and speaks about earthly things. The one who comes from heaven is above all. He testifies to what he has seen and heard, yet no one accepts his testimony. Whoever has accepted his testimony has certified this, that God is true. He whom God has sent speaks the words of God, for he gives the Spirit without measure. The Father loves the Son and has placed all things in his hands. Whoever believes in the Son has eternal life; whoever disobeys the Son will not see life, but must endure God's wrath.

Notice what you think and feel as you read the gospel.

God is true, and Jesus speaks the words of God. God is all truth, all love, and all life. In him we have eternal life.

Pray as you are led for yourself and others.

"What blessedness you give to me, dear Lord. Pour out your Spirit and renew the earth. Kindle hearts with love for God, for you alone are worthy of worship . . ." (Continue in your own words.)

Listen to Jesus.

I quicken hearts like yours to hunger for God, in whom is all infinite perfection. When you feel the need to pray, it is I calling you, my beloved disciple. What else is Jesus saying to you?

Ask God to show you how to live today.

"Teach me obedience to you, Jesus. Reveal to me whatever is not pleasing to you and give me your Spirit to obey you well. Glory be to the Father, the Son, and the Holy Spirit. Amen."

Friday, April 28, 2017

Know that God is present with you and ready to converse.

"Jesus, you yourself are the great sign from God. You are the Lord of glory. Come in."

Read the gospel: John 6:1–15.

After this Jesus went to the other side of the Sea of Galilee, also called the Sea of Tiberias. A large crowd kept following him, because they saw the signs that he was doing for the sick. Jesus went up the mountain and sat down there with his disciples. Now the Passover, the festival of the Jews, was near. When he looked up and saw a large crowd coming towards him, Jesus said to Philip, "Where are we to buy bread for these people to eat?" He said this to test him, for he himself knew what he was going to do. Philip answered him, "Six months' wages would not buy enough bread for each of them to get a little." One of his disciples, Andrew, Simon Peter's brother, said to him, "There is a boy here who has five barley loaves and two fish. But what are they among so many people?" Jesus said, "Make the people sit down." Now there was a great deal of grass in the place; so they sat down, about five thousand in all. Then Jesus took the loaves, and when he had given thanks, he distributed them to those who were seated; so also the fish, as much as they wanted. When they were satisfied, he told his disciples, "Gather up the fragments left over, so that nothing may be lost." So they gathered them up, and from the fragments of the five barley loaves, left by those who had eaten, they filled twelve baskets. When the people saw the sign that he had done, they began to say, "This is indeed the prophet who is to come into the world."

When Jesus realized that they were about to come and take him by force to make him king, he withdrew again to the mountain by himself.

Notice what you think and feel as you read the gospel.

God is not bound by our mathematics. Jesus can feed five thousand people with five loaves and two fish, and there were twelve baskets left over. How the people must have marveled at the ongoing miraculous multiplication of food!

Pray as you are led for yourself and others.

"Lord, I know my own limits sometimes. Let me trust your abundant generosity. Let me show your generosity to others, especially those in need . . ." (Continue in your own words.)

Listen to Jesus.

The earth is the Lord's, and I give to you whatever you need. What you receive, give freely, my child. What else is Jesus saying to you?

Ask God to show you how to live today.

"How may I translate your request of me into action today? I would be a cheerful giver. Thank you, Master. Amen."

Saturday, April 29, 2017

Know that God is present with you and ready to converse.

"You are with me, Lord. What have I to fear?"

Read the gospel: John 6:16–21.

When evening came, Jesus' disciples went down to the lake, got into a boat, and started across the lake to Capernaum. It was now dark, and Jesus had not yet come to them. The lake became rough because a strong wind was blowing. When they had rowed about three or four miles, they saw Jesus walking on the lake and coming near the boat, and they were terrified. But he said to them, "It is I; do not be afraid." Then they wanted to take him into the boat, and immediately the boat reached the land towards which they were going.

Notice what you think and feel as you read the gospel.

Jesus is off by himself praying while the disciples are rowing toward Capernaum in the dark. The waters are rough, but what seems to scare the disciples is the sight of Jesus walking toward them on the lake. He calms their fears.

Pray as you are led for yourself and others.

"Jesus, sometimes I labor in rough seas. Come to me and calm my fears . . ." (Continue in your own words.)

Listen to Jesus.

Tell me all that frightens you, my child. Tell me all your concerns for others as well. Then receive my peace and my reassurance that all shall be well. What else is Jesus saying to you?

Ask God to show you how to live today.

"Hold me in your peace today especially as I deal with rough matters. Prince of Peace, keep me in your presence all day long. Amen."

Sunday, April 30, 2017
Third Sunday of Easter

Know that God is present with you and ready to converse.

The Lord is risen, risen indeed. He can now give himself to greater crowds than ever all over the world, for he works through his Holy Spirit which reigns in the hearts of those who love him.

"Lord, I rejoice in your presence this moment. Let me know you better by your Word."

Read the gospel: Luke 24:13–35.

Now on that same day two of Jesus' disciples were going to a village called Emmaus, about seven miles from Jerusalem, and talking with each other about all these things that had happened. While they were talking and discussing, Jesus himself came near and went with them, but their eyes were kept from recognizing him. And he said to them, "What are you discussing with each other while you walk along?" They stood still, looking sad. Then one of them, whose name was Cleopas, answered him, "Are you the only stranger in Jerusalem who does not know the things that have taken place there in these days?" He asked them, "What things?" They replied, "The things about Jesus of Nazareth, who was a prophet mighty in deed and word before God and all the people, and how our chief priests and leaders handed him over to be condemned to death and crucified him. But we had hoped that he was the one to redeem Israel. Yes, and besides all this, it is now the third day since these things took place. Moreover, some women of our group astounded us. They were at the tomb early this morning, and when they did not find his body there, they came back and told us that they had indeed seen a vision of angels who said that he was alive. Some of those who were with us went to the tomb and found it just as the women had said; but they did not see him." Then he said to them, "Oh, how foolish you are, and how slow of heart to believe all that the prophets have declared! Was it not necessary that the Messiah should suffer these things and then enter into his glory?" Then beginning with Moses and all the prophets, he interpreted to them the things about himself in all the scriptures.

As they came near the village to which they were going, he walked ahead as if he were going on. But they urged him strongly, saying, "Stay with us, because it is almost evening and the day is now nearly over." So he went in to stay with them. When he was at the table with them, he took bread, blessed and broke it, and gave it to them. Then their eyes were opened, and they recognized him; and he vanished from their sight. They said to each other, "Were not our hearts burning within us while he was talking to us on the road, while he was opening the scriptures to us?" That same hour they got up and returned to Jerusalem; and they found the eleven and their companions gathered together. They were saying, "The Lord has risen indeed, and he has appeared to Simon!" Then they told what had happened on the road, and how he had been made known to them in the breaking of the bread.

Notice what you think and feel as you read the gospel.

Jesus vanishes when the disciples recognize him in the breaking of the bread. But he leaves them in joy for they have seen the Lord, now risen from the dead. They return to Jerusalem to tell the apostles and the other disciples what they have seen. But those in Jerusalem are already saying that the Lord has risen.

Pray as you are led for yourself and others.

"Let witnesses of your resurrection multiply, Lord, that those near and far may believe in you, know you, and love you . . ." (Continue in your own words.)

Listen to Jesus.

I want to share my life with all humanity. I give it to those who follow me. You may share it with others. What else is Jesus saying to you?

Ask God to show you how to live today.

"Make a difference in my day, Lord. Let me touch someone with your love. Amen."

Monday, May 1, 2017
Saint Joseph the Worker

Know that God is present with you and ready to converse.

"It is human to take blessings for granted. Lord, wake me up to your wonderful working in my life."

Read the gospel: Matthew 13:54–58.

Jesus came to his home town and began to teach the people in their synagogue, so that they were astounded and said, "Where did this man get this wisdom and these deeds of power? Is not this the carpenter's son? Is not his mother called Mary? And are not his brothers James and Joseph and Simon and Judas? And are not all his sisters with us? Where then did this man get all this?" And they took offence at him. But Jesus said to them, "Prophets are not without honor except in their own country and in their own house." And he did not do many deeds of power there, because of their unbelief.

Notice what you think and feel as you read the gospel.

It is not surprising that the townspeople who knew Jesus and his family take offense at his words and deeds. They wonder where he got the authority, the wisdom, and the power to work miracles. Jesus seems hindered by their disbelief.

Pray as you are led for yourself and others.

"Do not let me fail to recognize you, Lord. Give me a strong faith so that you can work in me and through me. Let me recognize you in your mighty deeds. I think of these needs . . ." (Continue in your own words.)

Listen to Jesus.

You are in my service, beloved. Do your work humbly and faithfully, as did Joseph. God is with you. What else is Jesus saying to you?

Ask God to show you how to live today.

"Let me work like Joseph, Lord. Help me not to seek recognition for good deeds or accomplishments. Help me to stick faithfully to the tasks you have given me. Amen."

Tuesday, May 2, 2017

Know that God is present with you and ready to converse.
"Jesus, I hunger for God. Give me the bread of heaven today."

Read the gospel: John 6:30–35.

So the crowd said to Jesus, "What sign are you going to give us then, so that we may see it and believe you? What work are you performing? Our ancestors ate the manna in the wilderness; as it is written, 'He gave them bread from heaven to eat.'" Then Jesus said to them, "Very truly, I tell you, it was not Moses who gave you the bread from heaven, but it is my Father who gives you the true bread from heaven. For the bread of God is that which comes down from heaven and gives life to the world." They said to him, "Sir, give us this bread always."

Jesus said to them, "I am the bread of life. Whoever comes to me will never be hungry, and whoever believes in me will never be thirsty."

Notice what you think and feel as you read the gospel.

People in the crowd want Jesus to prove himself a prophet by a sign as Moses did with the manna in the wilderness. Jesus says that he himself is the true bread from heaven.

Pray as you are led for yourself and others.

"Jesus, you nourish me with the bread of your Word and with your Body and Blood of the Eucharist. Thank you for giving yourself to me. I offer you myself in response. How may I serve you?" (Continue in your own words.)

Listen to Jesus.

There is joy and freedom in giving yourself to me. I will take care of you. You and I may become very close. What else is Jesus saying to you?

Ask God to show you how to live today.

"Thank you for being my food and drink, Lord. Send me out to do your will. Amen."

Wednesday, May 3, 2017
Saints Philip and James, Apostles

Know that God is present with you and ready to converse.

"Lord, let me know you by the reading of your Word. Let me give you my love and worship."

Read the gospel: John 14:6–14.

Jesus said to Thomas, "I am the way, and the truth, and the life. No one comes to the Father except through me. If you know me, you will know my Father also. From now on you do know him and have seen him."

Philip said to him, "Lord, show us the Father, and we will be satisfied." Jesus said to him, "Have I been with you all this time, Philip, and you still do not know me? Whoever has seen me has seen the Father. How can you say, 'Show us the Father'? Do you not believe that I am in the Father and the Father is in me? The words that I say to you I do not speak on my own; but the Father who dwells in me does his works. Believe me that I am in the Father and the Father is in me; but if you do not, then believe me because of the works themselves. Very truly, I tell you, the one who believes in me will also do the works that I do and, in fact, will do greater works than these, because I am going to the Father. I will do whatever you ask in my name, so that the Father may be glorified in the Son. If in my name you ask me for anything, I will do it."

Notice what you think and feel as you read the gospel.

Jesus and the Father are one, yet they are two persons. Jesus promises to do great works among us if we ask him.

Pray as you are led for yourself and others.

"Jesus, I ask in your name for the salvation of the world and the coming of your kingdom. Let the whole earth glorify your name . . ." (Continue in your own words.)

Listen to Jesus.

I hear your prayers, and I will do what you ask. Believe in me with all your heart, and you will see great good come upon you and those for whom you pray. What else is Jesus saying to you?

Ask God to show you how to live today.

"Give me the faith I need to pray and act in your name, Lord. I want to do all for the glory of God. Amen."

Thursday, May 4, 2017

Know that God is present with you and ready to converse.
"Father, you have drawn me to Jesus, the very Word of God before me."

Read the gospel: John 6:44–51.
Jesus said, "No one can come to me unless drawn by the Father who sent me; and I will raise that person up on the last day. It is written in the prophets, 'And they shall all be taught by God.' Everyone who has heard and learned from the Father comes to me. Not that anyone has seen the Father except the one who is from God; he has seen the Father. Very truly, I tell you, whoever believes has eternal life. I am the bread of life. Your ancestors ate the manna in the wilderness, and they died. This is the bread that comes down from heaven, so that one may eat of it and not die. I am the living bread that came down from heaven. Whoever eats of this bread will live for ever; and the bread that I will give for the life of the world is my flesh."

Notice what you think and feel as you read the gospel.
Jesus says those who come to him are drawn by the Father, and he will raise us up on the last day. He himself is the life-giving bread of heaven, his flesh.

Pray as you are led for yourself and others.
"Jesus, your promise is great; your words are strong. Let me understand and act upon them. Your Father draws me to you . . ." (Continue in your own words.)

Listen to Jesus.
You shall be taught by God, dear one, for you are coming to me. In me is life for you and all you pray for. What else is Jesus saying to you?

Ask God to show you how to live today.
"Let me remember today that in you is life. Let me remain in you, Jesus, and live forever. Amen."

Friday, May 5, 2017

Know that God is present with you and ready to converse.
"Lord, let me read your Word with eyes of faith. I long to know you and to understand all the truth you have for me."

Read the gospel: John 6:52–59.

The Jews then disputed among themselves, saying, "How can this man give us his flesh to eat?" So Jesus said to them, "Very truly, I tell you, unless you eat the flesh of the Son of Man and drink his blood, you have no life in you. Those who eat my flesh and drink my blood have eternal life, and I will raise them up on the last day; for my flesh is true food and my blood is true drink. Those who eat my flesh and drink my blood abide in me, and I in them. Just as the living Father sent me, and I live because of the Father, so whoever eats me will live because of me. This is the bread that came down from heaven, not like that which your ancestors ate, and they died. But the one who eats this bread will live for ever." He said these things while he was teaching in the synagogue at Capernaum.

Notice what you think and feel as you read the gospel.

Those who listen to Jesus cannot understand how he can give them his flesh to eat. Jesus repeats in very literal terms that one must eat his flesh and drink his blood to abide in him and have everlasting life.

Pray as you are led for yourself and others.

"Jesus, let me receive your flesh and blood in the Eucharist with growing faith and appreciation. I pray for all who cannot receive the truth of this gospel . . ." (Continue in your own words.)

Listen to Jesus.

Child, do you see that my devotion to you is total, involving all that I am? I can give you no more than myself. What do you say to that? What else is Jesus saying to you?

Ask God to show you how to live today.

"Lord, I am following you. I want to give as you give. I ask that your life flow through me to others today. Amen."

Saturday, May 6, 2017

Know that God is present with you and ready to converse.

"Lord, you challenge me by your Word, but I have nowhere else to go for truth and life. Let me receive it now."

Read the gospel: John 6:60–69.

When many of Jesus' disciples heard it, they said, "This teaching is difficult; who can accept it?" But Jesus, being aware that his disciples were complaining about it, said to them, "Does this offend you? Then what if you were to see the Son of Man ascending to where he was before? It is the spirit that gives life; the flesh is useless. The words that I have spoken to you are spirit and life. But among you there are some who do not believe." For Jesus knew from the first who were the ones that did not believe, and who was the one that would betray him. And he said, "For this reason I have told you that no one can come to me unless it is granted by the Father."

Because of this many of his disciples turned back and no longer went about with him. So Jesus asked the twelve, "Do you also wish to go away?" Simon Peter answered him, "Lord, to whom can we go? You have the words of eternal life. We have come to believe and know that you are the Holy One of God."

Notice what you think and feel as you read the gospel.

Jesus asks his disciples to believe in mysteries—that he himself is the bread of heaven, that he is one with the Father, that he will ascend to his Father, and that the Spirit alone gives life, eternal life. Overwhelmed by his teaching, some turn back.

Pray as you are led for yourself and others

"Jesus, with your help I will not turn back. You ask for great faith and great commitment. Increase both in me. Father, draw me into Jesus. I pray also for . . ." (Continue in your own words.)

Listen to Jesus.

Great work is being done in your spirit as you seek me and contemplate my words. They are the words of eternal life for you, my beloved disciple. Keep following me. What else is Jesus saying to you?

Ask God to show you how to live today.

"I have chosen life, Lord. I am all in with you. Purify me that I may be truly single-minded in my devotion to you and to your work on earth. I offer myself again, Lord. Use me. Amen."

Sunday, May 7, 2017
Fourth Sunday of Easter

Know that God is present with you and ready to converse.

Jesus often speaks in metaphors and parables as he tries to make the spiritual truths of himself, his Father, and the Holy Spirit understandable to his followers. In so doing, he makes the mysteries of God and eternal life approachable, reassuring, and wonderful.

"Dear Lord, let me read and understand all that you have for me here today."

Read the gospel: John 10:1–10.

Jesus said, "Very truly, I tell you, anyone who does not enter the sheepfold by the gate but climbs in by another way is a thief and a bandit. The one who enters by the gate is the shepherd of the sheep. The gatekeeper opens the gate for him, and the sheep hear his voice. He calls his own sheep by name and leads them out. When he has brought out all his own, he goes ahead of them, and the sheep follow him because they know his voice. They will not follow a stranger, but they will run from him because they do not know the voice of strangers." Jesus used this figure of speech with them, but they did not understand what he was saying to them.

So again Jesus said to them, "Very truly, I tell you, I am the gate for the sheep. All who came before me are thieves and bandits; but the sheep did not listen to them. I am the gate. Whoever enters by me will be saved, and will come in and go out and find pasture. The thief comes only to steal and kill and destroy. I came that they may have life, and have it abundantly."

Notice what you think and feel as you read the gospel.

Jesus uses two figures of speech to describe himself in relation to us. He is the shepherd who knows his sheep and is known by them, and they follow him. He is also the gate through which the sheep may enter into abundant life.

Pray as you are led for yourself and others.

"Let me follow you alone, Lord, and not strangers or thieves. Thank you for the life you give me. Thank you for your holy Word that transforms me from within. I pray that others may know you and go into your pasture . . ." (Continue in your own words.)

Listen to Jesus.

I speak to hearts in many ways. I gather my sheep and I do it well. You may trust me with your life and with the lives of those I have given you. What else is Jesus saying to you?

Ask God to show you how to live today.

"Let me take what you show me in the spirit and bring it to practical uses in this day-to-day world of matter and practicality. I thank you for your faithful care for me and all those you have given me. Amen."

Monday, May 8, 2017

Know that God is present with you and ready to converse.

"Who is here with me? It is you, Lord. Always you. Alleluia."

Read the gospel: John 10:11–18.

Jesus said, "I am the good shepherd. The good shepherd lays down his life for the sheep. The hired hand, who is not the shepherd and does not own the sheep, sees the wolf coming and leaves the sheep and runs away—and the wolf snatches them and scatters them. The hired hand runs away because a hired hand does not care for the sheep. I am the good shepherd. I know my own and my own know me, just as the Father knows me and I know the Father. And I lay down my life for the sheep. I have other sheep that do not belong to this fold. I must bring them also, and they will listen to my voice. So there will be one flock, one shepherd. For this reason the Father loves me, because I lay down my life in order to take it up again. No one takes it from me, but I lay it down of my own accord. I have power to lay it down, and I have power to take it up again. I have received this command from my Father."

Notice what you think and feel as you read the gospel.

Jesus, the Good Shepherd, freely and willingly lays down his life for his sheep. He has many sheep, and they will all be one flock, one shepherd.

Pray as you are led for yourself and others.

"Jesus, I come into your fold and listen to your voice. I pray for those who have wandered away from you or who are afraid to come in . . ." (Continue in your own words.)

Listen to Jesus.
Rely on me, my beloved, and I will keep you safe at all times. As you abide in me, you will know me more and more. You may pray for those you love with confidence. I love them, too. What else is Jesus saying to you?

Ask God to show you how to live today.
"Jesus, you do so much for me and mine that I long to do something for you. Give me work that pleases you. Amen."

Tuesday, May 9, 2017

Know that God is present with you and ready to converse.
"Jesus, as I read your Word, give me your Spirit of understanding and faith."

Read the gospel: John 10:22–30.
At that time the festival of the Dedication took place in Jerusalem. It was winter, and Jesus was walking in the temple, in the portico of Solomon. So the Jews gathered around him and said to him, "How long will you keep us in suspense? If you are the Messiah, tell us plainly." Jesus answered, "I have told you, and you do not believe. The works that I do in my Father's name testify to me; but you do not believe, because you do not belong to my sheep. My sheep hear my voice. I know them, and they follow me. I give them eternal life, and they will never perish. No one will snatch them out of my hand. What my Father has given me is greater than all else, and no one can snatch it out of the Father's hand. The Father and I are one."

Notice what you think and feel as you read the gospel.
Not all who hear Jesus' words believe him. He is unfazed. He is gathering his sheep, for they hear his voice and follow him. No one can snatch his sheep out of his hand or his Father's hand for they are one.

Pray as you are led for yourself and others.
"You promise me eternal life; you have already given it to me. Let me treasure that life and rest in my security. You are my security, Lord. I love you . . ." (Continue in your own words.)

Listen to Jesus.
I love you, child. My Father has drawn you to me. You hear my voice. What else is Jesus saying to you?

Ask God to show you how to live today.
"Jesus, let me hear your voice often as I go about my day. And let me obey you completely. Give me grace to obey you always. Amen."

Wednesday, May 10, 2017

Know that God is present with you and ready to converse.
"Jesus, you speak the Word of your Father. Save me."

Read the gospel: John 12:44–50.

Then Jesus cried aloud: "Whoever believes in me believes not in me but in him who sent me. And whoever sees me sees him who sent me. I have come as light into the world, so that everyone who believes in me should not remain in the darkness. I do not judge anyone who hears my words and does not keep them, for I came not to judge the world, but to save the world. The one who rejects me and does not receive my word has a judge; on the last day the word that I have spoken will serve as judge, for I have not spoken on my own, but the Father who sent me has himself given me a commandment about what to say and what to speak. And I know that his commandment is eternal life. What I speak, therefore, I speak just as the Father has told me."

Notice what you think and feel as you read the gospel.

Jesus proclaims that he is one with the Father, that he comes as light into the world, and that he brings salvation, not judgment. On the last day the Word he has spoken will judge all people.

Pray as you are led for yourself and others.

"Jesus, let your light continue to shine in our darkness. I pray for those in darkness. Let them come into your marvelous light . . ." (Continue in your own words.)

Listen to Jesus.

Your life and all history are very brief. All the time that ever was or will be cannot fill up eternity. You walk in time toward eternal life, my child. Follow me. What else is Jesus saying to you?

Ask God to show you how to live today.

"Keep my eyes and mind on heavenly things, Lord. Let me do what is good today. Amen."

Thursday, May 11, 2017

Know that God is present with you and ready to converse.
"Jesus, let me hear, learn, and know you in your Word."

Read the gospel: John 13:16–20.

Jesus said, "Very truly, I tell you, servants are not greater than their master, nor are messengers greater than the one who sent them. If you know these things, you are blessed if you do them. I am not speaking of all of you; I know whom I have chosen. But it is to fulfill the scripture, 'The one who ate my bread has lifted his heel against me.' I tell you this now, before it occurs, so that when it does occur, you may believe that I am he. Very truly, I tell you, whoever receives one whom I send receives me; and whoever receives me receives him who sent me."

Notice what you think and feel as you read the gospel.

Jesus says we are blessed if we do the things we know from him. As his servants, we are to do what Jesus did and serve others. This is the will of the Father.

Pray as you are led for yourself and others.

"Lord, I resolve to do what you would have me do. I place myself and my day in your hands to do with whatever you will. Let me do your work . . ." (Continue in your own words.)

Listen to Jesus.

Whatever you do for love of me and for love of others is a great thing. Do not be discouraged that your deeds are small or ordinary. Do them with love and you shall be as I am. What else is Jesus saying to you?

Ask God to show you how to live today.

"Master, help me receive those you send to me, and let me be sent to those you wish to receive you. Give me wisdom to do this. I glorify you, Lord. Amen."

Friday, May 12, 2017

Know that God is present with you and ready to converse.
"Jesus, I seek God: Father, Son, and Holy Spirit. I seek God now in your Word."

Read the gospel: John 14:1–6.

Jesus said, "Do not let your hearts be troubled. Believe in God, believe also in me. In my Father's house there are many dwelling-places. If it were not so, would I have told you that I go to prepare a place for you? And if I go and prepare a place for you, I will come again and will take you to myself, so that where I am, there you may be also. And you know the way to the place where I am going." Thomas said to him, "Lord, we do not know where you are going. How can we know the way?" Jesus said to him, "I am the way, and the truth, and the life. No one comes to the Father except through me."

Notice what you think and feel as you read the gospel.

Jesus speaks peace to his troubled disciples. He is going away so he can return and bring them to himself in his Father's house. Thomas questions him further about how this will work. Jesus assures Thomas that he is the Way, the Truth, and the Life.

Pray as you are led for yourself and others.

"Jesus, thank you for your reassurances. I long for your Father's house. May I dwell with God forever with all those you have given me . . ." (Continue in your own words.)

Listen to Jesus.

All those in your life I have given you. Look upon each one with love as I look upon you. Do unto them what I would do. What else is Jesus saying to you?

Ask God to show you how to live today.

"Jesus, you challenge me to love and to act upon it. My love is imperfect. Strengthen me to love others as you love and to do for others what you would do. Amen."

Saturday, May 13, 2017

Know that God is present with you and ready to converse.

"Jesus, you are my way to God. Let me know you through your Word and your Spirit."

Read the gospel: John 14:7–14.

Jesus said, "If you know me, you will know my Father also. From now on you do know him and have seen him."

Philip said to him, "Lord, show us the Father, and we will be satisfied." Jesus said to him, "Have I been with you all this time, Philip, and
you still do not know me? Whoever has seen me has seen the Father.
How can you say, 'Show us the Father'? Do you not believe that I am
in the Father and the Father is in me? The words that I say to you I do
not speak on my own; but the Father who dwells in me does his works.
Believe me that I am in the Father and the Father is in me; but if you do
not, then believe me because of the works themselves. Very truly, I tell
you, the one who believes in me will also do the works that I do and, in
fact, will do greater works than these, because I am going to the Father. I
will do whatever you ask in my name, so that the Father may be glorified
in the Son. If in my name you ask me for anything, I will do it."

Notice what you think and feel as you read the gospel.

Jesus wants his disciples to know his Father for he and his Father are
one, and he speaks for his Father. The ones who believe in him will do
the works he does and pray as he does, in the power and the glory of
the Father.

Pray as you are led for yourself and others.

"Lord, thank you for the power of prayer in your name. I pray for these
needs and these people . . ." (Continue in your own words.)

Listen to Jesus.

*I hear your prayers and thank you for them. By prayer you are doing my works
and glorifying my Father. You will know the power of your prayers.* What else
is Jesus saying to you?

Ask God to show you how to live today.

"Let me see you and know you today in others, Lord, and do what you
want me to do for them. Let me do it as unto you. Amen."

Sunday, May 14, 2017
Fifth Sunday of Easter

Know that God is present with you and ready to converse.

"Jesus, Word of the Father, united by and with God the Holy Spirit, you
came as the Way, the Truth, and the Life, leading us to heaven. We long
for that perfect, everlasting communion with God. By prayer, Jesus says
we can participate in the communion already and do the works that he
does.

"Lord, speak to my heart and soul with power, that I may love you and do your holy will."

Read the gospel: John 14:1–12.

Jesus said, "Do not let your hearts be troubled. Believe in God, believe also in me. In my Father's house there are many dwelling-places. If it were not so, would I have told you that I go to prepare a place for you? And if I go and prepare a place for you, I will come again and will take you to myself, so that where I am, there you may be also. And you know the way to the place where I am going." Thomas said to him, "Lord, we do not know where you are going. How can we know the way?" Jesus said to him, "I am the way, and the truth, and the life. No one comes to the Father except through me. If you know me, you will know my Father also. From now on you do know him and have seen him."

Philip said to him, "Lord, show us the Father, and we will be satisfied." Jesus said to him, "Have I been with you all this time, Philip, and you still do not know me? Whoever has seen me has seen the Father. How can you say, 'Show us the Father'? Do you not believe that I am in the Father and the Father is in me? The words that I say to you I do not speak on my own; but the Father who dwells in me does his works. Believe me that I am in the Father and the Father is in me; but if you do not, then believe me because of the works themselves. Very truly, I tell you, the one who believes in me will also do the works that I do and, in fact, will do greater works than these, because I am going to the Father."

Notice what you think and feel as you read the gospel.

Though he is God, Jesus obeys and glorifies his Father. He speaks and does what his Father wills. He says that we can, too.

Pray as you are led for yourself and others.

"Lord, you grant me access to God through you. I am in your presence to worship you. Guide my prayers for those you have given me . . ." (Continue in your own words.)

Listen to Jesus.

I rejoice in your faith, my dear one. Water it with your desire for God, and it will grow. What else is Jesus saying to you?

Ask God to show you how to live today.

"I believe in you, Lord, and I offer myself to do the works that you do. Be my companion today, Jesus. Amen."

Monday, May 15, 2017

Know that God is present with you and ready to converse.

"Holy Spirit, author of the Word of God, teach me what I need to know. Quicken me."

Read the gospel: John 14:21–26.

Jesus said, "They who have my commandments and keep them are those who love me; and those who love me will be loved by my Father, and I will love them and reveal myself to them." Judas (not Iscariot) said to him, "Lord, how is it that you will reveal yourself to us, and not to the world?" Jesus answered him, "Those who love me will keep my word, and my Father will love them, and we will come to them and make our home with them. Whoever does not love me does not keep my words; and the word that you hear is not mine, but is from the Father who sent me.

"I have said these things to you while I am still with you. But the Advocate, the Holy Spirit, whom the Father will send in my name, will teach you everything, and remind you of all that I have said to you."

Notice what you think and feel as you read the gospel.

Jesus says he will reveal himself to those who love him. If we love him, we obey him, and he and the Father will love us and make their home with us.

Pray as you are led for yourself and others.

"Lord, be the reality of my life. Help me love and obey you for I long to know you and be the dwelling place of God. Holy Spirit, work in me ..." (Continue in your own words.)

Listen to Jesus.

The love I put in your heart is for you and for others, my child. I will remind you today that the love of God is the way and the destination. Follow me. What else is Jesus saying to you?

Ask God to show you how to live today.

"I give myself to your love, Lord Jesus Christ. I give myself to your truth, Holy Spirit. Father in heaven, I glorify you and come to do your will. Amen."

Tuesday, May 16, 2017

Know that God is present with you and ready to converse.
"Lord, I open my heart to your Word of peace. Fill me with your love."

Read the gospel: John 14:27–31.
Jesus said, "Peace I leave with you; my peace I give to you. I do not give to you as the world gives. Do not let your hearts be troubled, and do not let them be afraid. You heard me say to you, 'I am going away, and I am coming to you.' If you loved me, you would rejoice that I am going to the Father, because the Father is greater than I. And now I have told you this before it occurs, so that when it does occur, you may believe. I will no longer talk much with you, for the ruler of this world is coming. He has no power over me; but I do as the Father has commanded me, so that the world may know that I love the Father. Rise, let us be on our way."

Notice what you think and feel as you read the gospel.
Jesus tells his disciples he is going away to the Father and he is also coming back to them. He says he does what his Father commands so the world may know that he loves his Father.

Pray as you are led for yourself and others.
"Lord, I love the Father, too, and wish to do what he commands of me. Touch me and those you have given me with faith, hope, and love . . ." (Continue in your own words.)

Listen to Jesus.
I enjoy you, beloved disciple. There is no one else like you. Come to me often and we shall become very close. Rise, let us be on our way. What else is Jesus saying to you?

Ask God to show you how to live today.
"Lord, I am following. By your grace, I shall walk in your peace today. Amen."

Wednesday, May 17, 2017

Know that God is present with you and ready to converse.
"You seek me constantly, Lord. I turn my attention from myself to you now. What do you ask of me, Lord?"

Read the gospel: John 15:1–8.

Jesus said, "I am the true vine, and my Father is the vine-grower. He removes every branch in me that bears no fruit. Every branch that bears fruit he prunes to make it bear more fruit. You have already been cleansed by the word that I have spoken to you. Abide in me as I abide in you. Just as the branch cannot bear fruit by itself unless it abides in the vine, neither can you unless you abide in me. I am the vine, you are the branches. Those who abide in me and I in them bear much fruit, because apart from me you can do nothing. Whoever does not abide in me is thrown away like a branch and withers; such branches are gathered, thrown into the fire, and burned. If you abide in me, and my words abide in you, ask for whatever you wish, and it will be done for you. My Father is glorified by this, that you bear much fruit and become my disciples."

Notice what you think and feel as you read the gospel.

Jesus is the vine and we are the branches bearing fruit. The Father removes the unfruitful branches and prunes the fruitful ones to bear more fruit. It's a process. The way and the goal are to abide in him, the True Vine, where we will bear much fruit and so glorify the Father.

Pray as you are led for yourself and others.

"Lord, I would be more fruitful. I offer myself for pruning. I place all my trust in you. May I glorify the Lord by my life . . ." (Continue in your own words.)

Listen to Jesus.

We abide in each other, you and I. So ask for whatever you wish, and I will do it. What else is Jesus saying to you?

Ask God to show you how to live today.

"Lord, give me the gift of prayer. Let me pray as you would have me pray, and let others be blessed by my prayers. I want to bear fruit for the glory of God. Thank you for letting me serve, Lord. Amen."

Thursday, May 18, 2017

Know that God is present with you and ready to converse.

"My desire is to abide in your love, Jesus. Teach me how to do that."

Read the gospel: John 15:9–11.

Jesus said, "As the Father has loved me, so I have loved you; abide in my love. If you keep my commandments, you will abide in my love, just as I have kept my Father's commandments and abide in his love. I have said these things to you so that my joy may be in you, and that your joy may be complete."

Notice what you think and feel as you read the gospel.

Loving—abiding in God's love—is not primarily an emotion; it is obedience to the commandments of love. It is in doing acts of love that we know the joy of God.

Pray as you are led for yourself and others.

"Open my eyes to your commandments, Lord, that I may walk in them. Let my obedience prove my love for you. Let me abide in your love. I pray that others may also know the joy of abiding in your love . . ." (Continue in your own words.)

Listen to Jesus.

Just as my peace is not the peace of the world, so my joy is far above what the world can give you. I give you my peace and my joy for you serve me. What else is Jesus saying to you?

Ask God to show you how to live today.

"Lord, I thank you for your blessings. You have given me so many. Give me the blessing of serving others as you do, giving them peace and joy. Amen."

Friday, May 19, 2017

Know that God is present with you and ready to converse.

"Teach me your commandments, Lord, that I may obey and abide in you."

Read the gospel: John 15:12–17.

Jesus said, "This is my commandment, that you love one another as I have loved you. No one has greater love than this, to lay down one's life for one's friends. You are my friends if you do what I command you. I do not call you servants any longer, because the servant does not know what the master is doing; but I have called you friends, because I have made known to you everything that I have heard from my Father. You did not choose me but I chose you. And I appointed you to go and bear fruit, fruit that will last, so that the Father will give you whatever you ask him in my name. I am giving you these commands so that you may love one another."

Notice what you think and feel as you read the gospel.

Jesus commands us to love one another as he loves us. What is love? What is the greatest love? To lay down one's life for one's friends as he did. We are his friends, so let us also love one another in thought, word, and deed.

Pray as you are led for yourself and others.

"Lord, I rejoice to be your friend and that you have appointed me to go and bear fruit that will last. I pray in your name to the Father for these people . . ." (Continue in your own words.)

Listen to Jesus.

I am teaching you the mystery of true love. Love like mine is full of power to do good in the world, though the world will not understand it. Do what I command you: love one another. What else is Jesus saying to you?

Ask God to show you how to live today.

"You would not give me a commandment I could not keep. But, Jesus, only by your Holy Spirit can I love others as you love them. Give me grace to love and to pray. Amen."

Saturday, May 20, 2017

Know that God is present with you and ready to converse.

"Jesus, you came into the world to take us out of this world. Teach me what that means."

Read the gospel: John 15:18–21.

Jesus said, "If the world hates you, be aware that it hated me before it hated you. If you belonged to the world, the world would love you as its own. Because you do not belong to the world, but I have chosen you out of the world—therefore the world hates you. Remember the word that I said to you, 'Servants are not greater than their master.' If they persecuted me, they will persecute you; if they kept my word, they will keep yours also. But they will do all these things to you on account of my name, because they do not know him who sent me."

Notice what you think and feel as you read the gospel.

The world is hostile to Jesus Christ and his followers. What they did to him they will do to us. They will hate us. We belong to Christ, not to the world. That is a hard truth.

Pray as you are led for yourself and others.

"Lord, strengthen me against persecution. Let me be bold in your Spirit and walk in love, even loving those who hate me. I pray for . . ." (Continue in your own words.)

Listen to Jesus.

It is impossible to love your enemies, your persecutors, in your own power. I give you my love, which perseveres through hatred and persecution. As you follow me and do my work, you will experience rejection, but I will never leave you. What else is Jesus saying to you?

Ask God to show you how to live today.

"Lord, remove all fear from me. Please let me walk in full confidence of your love and protection, even when I face hostility. Let me be blameless as you were and suffer nobly as you did, praying for them. Amen."

Sunday, May 21, 2017
Sixth Sunday of Easter

Know that God is present with you and ready to converse.

Jesus did many miracles during his ministry, but near the end, before he gave his life to save us, he did much teaching. He wanted to prepare his disciples—and us—for life after his departure. What did it mean that he would rise again and leave them? How could they carry on without him? He told them and us what we need to know.

"Eternal Word of God, impress upon me the profound truths of your way. Give me ears to hear."

Read the gospel: John 14:15–21.

Jesus said, "If you love me, you will keep my commandments. And I will ask the Father, and he will give you another Advocate, to be with you for ever. This is the Spirit of truth, whom the world cannot receive, because it neither sees him nor knows him. You know him, because he abides with you, and he will be in you.

"I will not leave you orphaned; I am coming to you. In a little while the world will no longer see me, but you will see me; because I live, you also will live. On that day you will know that I am in my Father, and you in me, and I in you. They who have my commandments and keep them are those who love me; and those who love me will be loved by my Father, and I will love them and reveal myself to them."

Notice what you think and feel as you read the gospel.

Jesus says he will go and send to us the Spirit of truth to abide with us; he will abide in us as well, and we in him. As we keep his commandments of love, we are enfolded in the infinite love of God even as we live.

Pray as you are led for yourself and others.

"What greater gift could you have given us, Lord? Let me appreciate it more and more. Let others come to you and know your love . . ." (Continue in your own words.)

Listen to Jesus.

Your power to act and to pray comes from God, beloved disciple. Abandon yourself to God, loving, obeying, and praying. What else is Jesus saying to you?

Ask God to show you how to live today.

"I give myself to you, Lord. How may I love, obey, and pray? I want to serve you all day long. Amen."

Monday, May 22, 2017

Know that God is present with you and ready to converse.

"What have you to say to me today, Lord? Open me up to receive your Word in the depths of my being."

Read the gospel: John 15:26–16:4a.

Jesus said, "When the Advocate comes, whom I will send to you from the Father, the Spirit of truth who comes from the Father, he will testify on my behalf. You also are to testify because you have been with me from the beginning.

"I have said these things to you to keep you from stumbling. They will put you out of the synagogues. Indeed, an hour is coming when those who kill you will think that by doing so they are offering worship to God. And they will do this because they have not known the Father or me. But I have said these things to you so that when their hour comes you may remember that I told you about them.

"I did not say these things to you from the beginning, because I was with you."

Notice what you think and feel as you read the gospel.

Jesus wants to keep his disciples from stumbling after he is gone for the time is coming when those who kill them will think they are offering worship to God in so doing.

Pray as you are led for yourself and others.

"Lord, send me your Spirit that I may testify on your behalf. I will not be surprised if they reject you and me. Let me remember what you say to me today . . ." (Continue in your own words.)

Listen to Jesus.

Trust the Holy Spirit to be your Advocate and Teacher. You can walk in that Truth without fear. What else is Jesus saying to you?

Ask God to show you how to live today.

"How do I testify to those who have not known the Father or you, Jesus? Give me wisdom and courage today as I seek to share your love. Amen."

Tuesday, May 23, 2017

Know that God is present with you and ready to converse.

"Jesus, speak to me today. I need your Spirit and your Truth."

Read the gospel: John 16:5–11.

Jesus said, "But now I am going to him who sent me; yet none of you asks me, 'Where are you going?' But because I have said these things to you, sorrow has filled your hearts. Nevertheless, I tell you the truth: it is to your advantage that I go away, for if I do not go away, the Advocate will not come to you; but if I go, I will send him to you. And when he comes, he will prove the world wrong about sin and righteousness and judgement: about sin, because they do not believe in me; about righteousness, because I am going to the Father and you will see me no longer; about judgement, because the ruler of this world has been condemned."

Notice what you think and feel as you read the gospel.

Jesus promises his disciples that the Advocate will come to them, and he prophesies what the Advocate will accomplish: the Holy Spirit will prove the world wrong about sin, righteousness, and judgment.

Pray as you are led for yourself and others.

"Lord, the fulfillment of the mission of the Holy Spirit is yet to come. May your Spirit renew the face of the earth; may your Spirit gather your people into God. I think of . . ." (Continue in your own words.)

Listen to Jesus.

I abide in joy with my Father, but I am not far off from you, beloved. Ask for my Holy Spirit to replace all your sorrow with enduring joy. I will not refuse you. What else is Jesus saying to you?

Ask God to show you how to live today.

"Lord, I need your Holy Spirit to live well for you. I abandon myself to the Spirit to do in me and through me what is pleasing to God. Amen."

Wednesday, May 24, 2017

Know that God is present with you and ready to converse.

"Holy Spirit, declare to me by your Word all the truth I need, for I long to know, love, and serve God."

Read the gospel: John 16:12–15.

Jesus said, "I still have many things to say to you, but you cannot bear them now. When the Spirit of truth comes, he will guide you into all the truth; for he will not speak on his own, but will speak whatever he hears, and he will declare to you the things that are to come. He will glorify me, because he will take what is mine and declare it to you. All that the Father has is mine. For this reason I said that he will take what is mine and declare it to you."

Notice what you think and feel as you read the gospel.

Knowledge of God, Jesus makes clear, can come to us only by the Holy Spirit for the Spirit is one with the Father and the Son.

Pray as you are led for yourself and others.

"Lord, raise me above earthly knowledge and give me godly knowledge by your Spirit, for it is my desire to know you as I am known by you. In your power, Lord, I pray for . . ." (Continue in your own words.)

Listen to Jesus.

By the Spirit, you recognize truth. The Spirit can declare to you the deep wisdom of God, and you will know God more and more. What else is Jesus saying to you?

Ask God to show you how to live today.

"Thank you, Jesus, for the gift of your Spirit. Let me receive all you have for me and let me glorify the Father, the Son, and the Holy Spirit in all I think, say, and do today. Amen."

Thursday, May 25, 2017

Know that God is present with you and ready to converse.

"I cannot see you, Lord, but you have promised to be here with me. I take you at your Word."

Read the gospel: John 16:16–20.

Jesus said, "A little while, and you will no longer see me, and again a little while, and you will see me." Then some of his disciples said to one another, "What does he mean by saying to us, 'A little while, and you will no longer see me, and again a little while, and you will see me'; and 'Because I am going to the Father'?" They said, "What does he mean by this 'a little while'? We do not know what he is talking about." Jesus knew that they wanted to ask him, so he said to them, "Are you discussing among yourselves what I meant when I said, 'A little while, and you will no longer see me, and again a little while, and you will see me'? Very truly, I tell you, you will weep and mourn, but the world will rejoice; you will have pain, but your pain will turn into joy."

Notice what you think and feel as you read the gospel.

Jesus is preparing his disciples for his death and resurrection. He tells them the truth, but they cannot imagine what he means. They will no longer see him in a little while, and then they will? He seems to be speaking in riddles again when he says they will mourn but the world will rejoice and then their pain will turn to joy. Something unheard of is about to happen, and they will be first-hand witnesses.

Pray as you are led for yourself and others.

"Jesus, the events of my own life are often hard to make sense of. Sometimes you allow things to happen that seem contrary to the way things should go. Help me to trust in your loving providence, knowing that all things work together for good for those who love God . . ." (Continue in your own words.)

Listen to Jesus.

Yes, you may trust me with everything: your life, your loved ones, your work, your health. When things seem to go bad for you, look to me, for your redemption is near. What else is Jesus saying to you?

Ask God to show you how to live today.

"Jesus, let me be patient and grateful to you in both hardship and blessing. You are Lord. Let me praise you all day long. Amen."

Friday, May 26, 2017

Know that God is present with you and ready to converse.

"You are there for me when I am mourning; you are there for me when I am rejoicing. Thank you, Lord. You are here with me now."

Read the gospel: John 16:20–23.

Jesus said, "Very truly, I tell you, you will weep and mourn, but the world will rejoice; you will have pain, but your pain will turn into joy. When a woman is in labor, she has pain, because her hour has come. But when her child is born, she no longer remembers the anguish because of the joy of having brought a human being into the world. So you have pain now; but I will see you again, and your hearts will rejoice, and no one will take your joy from you. On that day you will ask nothing of me. Very truly, I tell you, if you ask anything of the Father in my name, he will give it to you."

Notice what you think and feel as you read the gospel.

After their time of mourning his passion and death, Jesus tells them their pain will turn to joy, comparing their experience to a woman who gives birth after a painful delivery. Her anguish turns to joy and so will theirs.

Pray as you are led for yourself and others.

"Father, in Jesus' name I ask you to be with me today and with all those you have given me, whether they are experiencing pain or joy. I especially think of . . ." (Continue in your own words.)

Listen to Jesus.

You are easy for me to love, beloved friend. Your prayers for others are heard, and my Father will give them what is best for them. What else is Jesus saying to you?

Ask God to show you how to live today.

"If there is anyone I can touch with kindness today, Lord, let me do it. Amen."

Saturday, May 27, 2017

Know that God is present with you and ready to converse.

"I come with joy into your presence, Lord. You are calling me to yourself, healing me by your Word."

Read the gospel: John 16:23–28.

Jesus said, "On that day you will ask nothing of me. Very truly, I tell you, if you ask anything of the Father in my name, he will give it to you. Until now you have not asked for anything in my name. Ask and you will receive, so that your joy may be complete.

"I have said these things to you in figures of speech. The hour is coming when I will no longer speak to you in figures, but will tell you plainly of the Father. On that day you will ask in my name. I do not say to you that I will ask the Father on your behalf; for the Father himself loves you, because you have loved me and have believed that I came from God. I came from the Father and have come into the world; again, I am leaving the world and am going to the Father."

Notice what you think and feel as you read the gospel.

How many times in these readings from John has Jesus reminded his disciples that if they ask anything of the Father in his name, he will give it to them? Here he says it again. Why should they pray to the Father? So their joy may be complete.

Pray as you are led for yourself and others.

"Father, thank you for your Son. I ask that I and all those you have given me respond with love to his great love for us. That will complete my joy . . ." (Continue in your own words.)

Listen to Jesus.

My Father is Love. God is the power behind the mysteries of creation and salvation. My Father loves you as he loves me. I love you, too. What else is Jesus saying to you?

Ask God to show you how to live today.

"Knowing of your love for me, I wish to love others, especially those who need a kindness or a favor. Place me in those situations, Lord, and give me grace to share your love. Amen."

Sunday, May 28, 2017
Ascension of the Lord

Know that God is present with you and ready to converse.

He is risen, and there are many witnesses to that fact, but he has not yet ascended to his Father. His speech is full of the future now, for he has established his Church among a band of rough and unlearned men. What shall they do? How shall they do it without Jesus to teach and to do wonders among the people?

"Risen Lord, you are with us always, even to the end of the age. Raise me up to do your will."

Read the gospel: Matthew 28:16–20.

Now the eleven disciples went to Galilee, to the mountain to which Jesus had directed them. When they saw him, they worshipped him; but some doubted. And Jesus came and said to them, "All authority in heaven and on earth has been given to me. Go therefore and make disciples of all nations, baptizing them in the name of the Father and of the Son and of the Holy Spirit, and teaching them to obey everything that I have commanded you. And remember, I am with you always, to the end of the age."

Notice what you think and feel as you read the gospel.

The eleven have done what Jesus directed through Mary Magdalene when she encountered him in the garden after his resurrection. They meet him on a mountain in Galilee. He commands them to make disciples of all nations, baptizing believers in the name of the Trinity. Yet he is not leaving them alone. He says he will be with them always.

Pray as you are led for yourself and others.

"Jesus, you ask us to evangelize, yet you yourself must draw souls to seek and find you. Your Church, now spread throughout the world, is much more than the work of human hands. It is you, your Body. Let it continue to gather souls into your kingdom . . ." (Continue in your own words.)

Listen to Jesus.

I am with you, beloved disciple, as I was with my first disciples. I ask you to continue my work in the ways I show you. Draw near to me and I will guide you in the way. What else is Jesus saying to you?

Ask God to show you how to live today.

"I am just one weak person, Lord. I depend on you to lead me and help me do what pleases you. Thank you for being with me today. Amen."

Monday, May 29, 2017

Know that God is present with you and ready to converse.

"Who is with me now, here to strengthen and guide me? It is you, Jesus Christ, conqueror of the world."

Read the gospel: John 16:29–33.

Jesus' disciples said, "Yes, now you are speaking plainly, not in any figure of speech! Now we know that you know all things, and do not need to have anyone question you; by this we believe that you came from God." Jesus answered them, "Do you now believe? The hour is coming, indeed it has come, when you will be scattered, each one to his home, and you will leave me alone. Yet I am not alone because the Father is with me. I have said this to you, so that in me you may have peace. In the world you face persecution. But take courage; I have conquered the world!"

Notice what you think and feel as you read the gospel.

Just when the disciples get comfortable with his messages, Jesus disrupts their complacency by telling them that they will be scattered. But the Father will always remain with him. They will face persecution in the world, but he has conquered the world. How were they to understand that? He would soon be crucified by the world.

Pray as you are led for yourself and others.

"Lord, disrupt my complacency today and prepare me for what is to come. Let me be vigilant, too, for all those you have given me. I pray for . . ." (Continue in your own words.)

Listen to Jesus.

Ask me for peace, dear one; ask me for courage. I gladly give you whatever you need on your journey to my eternal kingdom. What else is Jesus saying to you?

Ask God to show you how to live today.

"Every day is another challenge, my Jesus. Let me turn and face every difficulty with peaceful courage, knowing you have overcome the world. You are at my side. Amen."

Tuesday, May 30, 2017

Know that God is present with you and ready to converse.

"Jesus, Savior, mighty God, let me know you and love you better through the power of the Word."

Read the gospel: John 17:1–11a.

After Jesus had spoken these words, he looked up to heaven and said, "Father, the hour has come; glorify your Son so that the Son may glorify you, since you have given him authority over all people, to give eternal life to all whom you have given him. And this is eternal life, that they may know you, the only true God, and Jesus Christ whom you have sent. I glorified you on earth by finishing the work that you gave me to do. So now, Father, glorify me in your own presence with the glory that I had in your presence before the world existed.

"I have made your name known to those whom you gave me from the world. They were yours, and you gave them to me, and they have kept your word. Now they know that everything you have given me is from you; for the words that you gave to me I have given to them, and they have received them and know in truth that I came from you; and they have believed that you sent me. I am asking on their behalf; I am not asking on behalf of the world, but on behalf of those whom you gave me, because they are yours. All mine are yours, and yours are mine; and I have been glorified in them. And now I am no longer in the world, but they are in the world, and I am coming to you. Holy Father, protect them in your name that you have given me, so that they may be one, as we are one."

Notice what you think and feel as you read the gospel.

Jesus' prayer declares that what is most important is that his followers know the Father, the only true God, and God's Son. Now all who believe in him belong to the Father. Jesus prays for their protection, that they may be one as God is one.

Pray as you are led for yourself and others.

"Lord, I embrace the mysteries of oneness: God is one and God's worshippers are one with God. I pray that many, many souls may join this blessed oneness. For it is the nature of love to give the good it has to others. I pray for . . ." (Continue in your own words.)

Listen to Jesus.

Do you wish to please me, beloved? See others through my eyes. Do not place limits on what you can do for those in need. What else is Jesus saying to you?

Ask God to show you how to live today.

"Jesus, let my hands serve you today. Thank you for giving me life to do what pleases you, Lord. I worship you and glorify you for your great goodness. Amen."

Wednesday, May 31, 2017
Visitation of the Blessed Virgin Mary

Know that God is present with you and ready to converse.

"Holy Spirit, you testify of Jesus in the inspired Word of God. Fill me with joy in the knowledge of my Lord."

Read the gospel: Luke 1:39–56.

In those days Mary set out and went with haste to a Judean town in the hill country, where she entered the house of Zechariah and greeted Elizabeth. When Elizabeth heard Mary's greeting, the child leapt in her womb. And Elizabeth was filled with the Holy Spirit and exclaimed with a loud cry, "Blessed are you among women, and blessed is the fruit of your womb. And why has this happened to me, that the mother of my Lord comes to me? For as soon as I heard the sound of your greeting, the child in my womb leapt for joy. And blessed is she who believed that there would be a fulfillment of what was spoken to her by the Lord."

And Mary said,

> "My soul magnifies the Lord,
>> and my spirit rejoices in God my Savior,
> for he has looked with favor on the lowliness of his servant.
>> Surely, from now on all generations will call me blessed;
> for the Mighty One has done great things for me,
>> and holy is his name.
> His mercy is for those who fear him
>> from generation to generation.
> He has shown strength with his arm;
>> he has scattered the proud in the thoughts of their
>> hearts.
> He has brought down the powerful from their thrones,
>> and lifted up the lowly;
> he has filled the hungry with good things,
>> and sent the rich away empty.
> He has helped his servant Israel,
>> in remembrance of his mercy,
> according to the promise he made to our ancestors,
>> to Abraham and to his descendants for ever."

And Mary remained with her for about three months and then returned to her home.

Notice what you think and feel as you read the gospel.

Mary, now pregnant with Jesus by the Holy Spirit, greets her cousin Elizabeth. The child in Elizabeth's womb leaps, and Elizabeth becomes filled with the Spirit and blesses Mary and the fruit of her womb, Jesus. Then Mary, Spouse of the Holy Spirit, prays her inspired prayer.

Pray as you are led for yourself and others.

"Pray through me, Holy Spirit, in praise and thanksgiving for God and God's mighty works. Pray for those you have given me . . ." (Continue in your own words.)

Listen to Jesus.

The joy in heaven is the joy of love, child. There your treasure is. Let your heart be there, too. You are beloved of God. What else is Jesus saying to you?

Ask God to show you how to live today.

"Lord, I am lifted high by your blessings and goodness. Help me to pass on this all-consuming love. Amen."

Thursday, June 1, 2017

Know that God is present with you and ready to converse.

"Father, let me join Jesus as he prays for those you have given him. Let his prayer also be for those you have given me."

Read the gospel: John 17:20–26.

Jesus said, "I ask not only on behalf of these, but also on behalf of those who will believe in me through their word, that they may all be one. As you, Father, are in me and I am in you, may they also be in us, so that the world may believe that you have sent me. The glory that you have given me I have given them, so that they may be one, as we are one, I in them and you in me, that they may become completely one, so that the world may know that you have sent me and have loved them even as you have loved me. Father, I desire that those also, whom you have given me, may be with me where I am, to see my glory, which you have given me because you loved me before the foundation of the world.

"Righteous Father, the world does not know you, but I know you; and these know that you have sent me. I made your name known to them, and I will make it known, so that the love with which you have loved me may be in them, and I in them."

Notice what you think and feel as you read the gospel.

As we are one in God, like Jesus, we know that we have been loved before the foundation of the world. That love is in us.

Pray as you are led for yourself and others.

"Lord, let me desire to be one with all who love you. Let me pray and work for unity, for that is your sign to those who do not yet believe. I pray for . . ." (Continue in your own words.)

Listen to Jesus.

The world is full of strife and selfishness, dear disciple. You have no part in those. Cling to me and my promises with faith, hope, and love. What else is Jesus saying to you?

Ask God to show you how to live today.

"You light my path, Lord. You set me on high ground. Let me walk with you today, doing what pleases you. Amen."

Friday, June 2, 2017

Know that God is present with you and ready to converse.
"Master, I invite you into my day and my prayers. Let me draw near to you and listen to your words with my heart."

Read the gospel: John 21:15–19.
When they had finished breakfast, Jesus said to Simon Peter, "Simon son of John, do you love me more than these?" He said to him, "Yes, Lord; you know that I love you." Jesus said to him, "Feed my lambs." A second time he said to him, "Simon son of John, do you love me?" He said to him, "Yes, Lord; you know that I love you." Jesus said to him, "Tend my sheep." He said to him the third time, "Simon son of John, do you love me?" Peter felt hurt because he said to him the third time, "Do you love me?" And he said to him, "Lord, you know everything; you know that I love you." Jesus said to him, "Feed my sheep. Very truly, I tell you, when you were younger, you used to fasten your own belt and to go wherever you wished. But when you grow old, you will stretch out your hands, and someone else will fasten a belt around you and take you where you do not wish to go." (He said this to indicate the kind of death by which he would glorify God.) After this he said to him, "Follow me."

Notice what you think and feel as you read the gospel.
Jesus commissions Peter to feed his sheep as the natural result of Peter's love for the Lord. Then he predicts Peter's death at the hands of men. Peter would follow his beloved Lord to martyrdom.

Pray as you are led for yourself and others.
"You ask us to die to self and to worldly desires, Lord. That is the necessary condition to receive and give your love. Remove from me all fear of death and dying. Give me confidence that I am coming to you. I pray for those I know who are sick or dying . . ." (Continue in your own words.)

Listen to Jesus.
Death for those who love me is a translation to a better place and even a better self, my child, and we will share our love and joy forever. That love and joy begins here. Receive them and lose your fears. What else is Jesus saying to you?

Ask God to show you how to live today.
"Lord, you know that I love you. How may I feed your lambs and tend your sheep today? Amen."

Saturday, June 3, 2017

Know that God is present with you and ready to converse.
"Master of the Universe, your will is shrouded, your ways far above our ways. Reveal to me what I need to know to love and serve you."

Read the gospel: John 21:20–25.

Peter turned and saw the disciple whom Jesus loved following them; he was the one who had reclined next to Jesus at the supper and had said, "Lord, who is it that is going to betray you?" When Peter saw him, he said to Jesus, "Lord, what about him?" Jesus said to him, "If it is my will that he remain until I come, what is that to you? Follow me!" So the rumor spread in the community that this disciple would not die. Yet Jesus did not say to him that he would not die, but, "If it is my will that he remain until I come, what is that to you?"

   This is the disciple who is testifying to these things and has written them, and we know that his testimony is true. But there are also many other things that Jesus did; if every one of them were written down, I suppose that the world itself could not contain the books that would be written.

Notice what you think and feel as you read the gospel.
Jesus does not reveal how or when that other disciple (John, the writer of today's gospel) will die. John ends his testimony affirming the truth of what he has written even though it is only a partial account of the many things Jesus did, which was enough to fill many books.

Pray as you are led for yourself and others.
"Lord, much of your life remains unknown, especially your early life. My future life remains unknown. Let me be faithful to you until the end. I pray now for . . ." (Continue in your own words.)

Listen to Jesus.
No one alive knows the wisdom of God, but when you see God you will know as you are known. What else is Jesus saying to you?

Ask God to show you how to live today.
"Let me take to heart about what I do not know, Lord, that I may all the more trust and rely upon you, day by day, hour by hour. I glorify the ways of God Almighty. Amen."

Sunday, June 4, 2017
Pentecost Sunday

Know that God is present with you and ready to converse.

Jesus asked his disciples to wait for the Holy Spirit, who would lead them into all truth and give them power to do his work on earth. What is the Holy Spirit? It is like the wind: unseen and going where it will. The Holy Spirit is the Creator, the power of Jesus, one with the Father and the Son, yet distinct in person.

"Holy Spirit, God with me now, open to me the Word and impress it upon me."

Read the gospel: John 20:19–23.

When it was evening on that day, the first day of the week, and the doors of the house where the disciples had met were locked for fear of the Jews, Jesus came and stood among them and said, "Peace be with you." After he said this, he showed them his hands and his side. Then the disciples rejoiced when they saw the Lord. Jesus said to them again, "Peace be with you. As the Father has sent me, so I send you." When he had said this, he breathed on them and said to them, "Receive the Holy Spirit. If you forgive the sins of any, they are forgiven them; if you retain the sins of any, they are retained."

Notice what you think and feel as you read the gospel.

The risen Jesus mysteriously appears in the locked room where the disciples had met for fear of the Jews. He gives them his peace and shows them his wounds. As they rejoice, he commissions them to continue to do his works—breathing on them and saying, "Receive the Holy Spirit"— with his power to forgive sins.

Pray as you are led for yourself and others.

"Jesus, you were crucified because you made yourself equal to God, able to forgive sins. Then you gave that power to us. I pray for forgiveness for myself and all those you have given me. Wash us all of our sins . . ." (Continue in your own words.)

Listen to Jesus.

Do you hold unforgiven any sins against you, beloved disciple? First forgive with all your heart, and you, too, will be forgiven and blessed by God. What else is Jesus saying to you?

Ask God to show you how to live today.

"As I go through my day, Lord, and all my days, let me understand and practice the power of forgiveness. Whom may I forgive? Amen."

Ordinary Time

INTRODUCTION

The second period of Ordinary Time immediately follows Pentecost. The Holy Spirit has fallen upon the disciples while they prayed in the upper room. For the disciples, Pentecost was even more transforming than Easter, for the Holy Spirit gave them, as Jesus had promised, power to carry the Good News to every nation on earth. So began the age of grace.

Our own journeys are similarly wrapped up with Christ's command to follow him every day. This is our own time of grace as we seek to do his work in today's world. By praying with the Word of God in this season, we may discover how we, too, can serve the Master. The last Sunday of Ordinary Time is the Feast of Christ the King, whose coming and kingdom we await.

Monday, June 5, 2017

Know that God is present with you and ready to converse.

"Jesus, sometimes even in your parables you speak plainly. Speak plainly to me today."

Read the gospel: Mark 12:1–12.

Then Jesus began to speak to them in parables. "A man planted a vineyard, put a fence around it, dug a pit for the wine press, and built a watch-tower; then he leased it to tenants and went to another country. When the season came, he sent a slave to the tenants to collect from them his share of the produce of the vineyard. But they seized him, and beat him, and sent him away empty-handed. And again he sent another slave to them; this one they beat over the head and insulted. Then he sent another, and that one they killed. And so it was with many others; some they beat, and others they killed. He had still one other, a beloved son. Finally he sent him to them, saying, 'They will respect my son.' But those tenants said to one another, 'This is the heir; come, let us kill him, and the inheritance will be ours.' So they seized him, killed him, and threw him out of the vineyard. What then will the owner of the vineyard do? He will come and destroy the tenants and give the vineyard to others. Have you not read this scripture:

> 'The stone that the builders rejected
>   has become the cornerstone;
> this was the Lord's doing,
>   and it is amazing in our eyes'?"

When they realized that he had told this parable against them, they wanted to arrest him, but they feared the crowd. So they left him and went away.

Notice what you think and feel as you read the gospel.

This is a powerful portrayal of what may seem the upside-down logic of God because the owner of the vineyard seems so slow to understand that his tenants are evil. After sending many servants to ask for his share of the vineyard, he sends his son, whom they kill. What will the owner do now? He will destroy the tenants and give the vineyard to others, and that rejected stone, the son of the owner, will somehow become the cornerstone predicted by scripture, amazing in our eyes.

Pray as you are led for yourself and others.

"Only love can explain your slowness to anger, Lord, for the people of this world are ignorant, selfish, and violent. Yet you sent your Son to save us by his death. I pray in his name for all those who are ignorant, selfish, and violent. Redeem us all, Lord . . ." (Continue in your own words.)

Listen to Jesus.

God can use the stone the builders reject, dear disciple. I can use even your weaknesses to serve others. Do not fear your weakness. Give it to me. What else is Jesus saying to you?

Ask God to show you how to live today.

"Jesus, you allowed yourself to be weak before the cruel power of people, yet in your suffering and dying you were victorious, reconciling sinful humanity with God. Help me understand how my own weakness can serve others today. Thank you, Lord. Amen."

Tuesday, June 6, 2017

Know that God is present with you and ready to converse.

"Lord, you confound the understanding of people who seek to dismiss you. Enlighten this one who seeks to know and love you."

Read the gospel: Mark 12:13–17.

Then they sent to Jesus some Pharisees and some Herodians to trap him in what he said. And they came and said to him, "Teacher, we know that you are sincere, and show deference to no one; for you do not regard people with partiality, but teach the way of God in accordance with truth. Is it lawful to pay taxes to the emperor, or not? Should we pay them, or should we not?" But knowing their hypocrisy, he said to them, "Why are you putting me to the test? Bring me a denarius and let me see it." And they brought one. Then he said to them, "Whose head is this, and whose title?" They answered, "The emperor's." Jesus said to them, "Give to the emperor the things that are the emperor's, and to God the things that are God's." And they were utterly amazed at him.

Notice what you think and feel as you read the gospel.

Why were the Herodians amazed? That he answered the question well, or that he saw through their flattering, two-faced trap and evaded it? He poses to them the implicit challenge: What belongs to God? Obviously, all things.

Pray as you are led for yourself and others.

"Jesus, you amaze me, too. You are not a man to be trifled with. I pray for all those who seek to avoid God and God's commandments . . ." (Continue in your own words.)

Listen to Jesus.

I AM. I am the Alpha and the Omega, and I shall come again in power and glory to gather my own into my kingdom. Prepare your heart, my beloved. What else is Jesus saying to you?

Ask God to show you how to live today.

"Teach me simplicity and truthfulness, Lord, in all I do. Let me find your lessons in the circumstances of my day so that I may please you. Amen."

Wednesday, June 7, 2017

Know that God is present with you and ready to converse.

"Jesus, you read hearts and offer them what they need: love and truth. Read my heart today and feed me by your Word."

Read the gospel: Mark 12:18–27.

Some Sadducees, who say there is no resurrection, came to Jesus and asked him a question, saying, "Teacher, Moses wrote for us that if a man's brother dies, leaving a wife but no child, the man shall marry the widow and raise up children for his brother. There were seven brothers; the first married and, when he died, left no children; and the second married her and died, leaving no children; and the third likewise; none of the seven left children. Last of all the woman herself died. In the resurrection whose wife will she be? For the seven had married her."

Jesus said to them, "Is not this the reason you are wrong, that you know neither the scriptures nor the power of God? For when they rise from the dead, they neither marry nor are given in marriage, but are like angels in heaven. And as for the dead being raised, have you not read in the book of Moses, in the story about the bush, how God said to him, 'I am the God of Abraham, the God of Isaac, and the God of Jacob'? He is God not of the dead, but of the living; you are quite wrong."

Notice what you think and feel as you read the gospel.

Jesus thwarts the sophism of the Sadducees and their absurd, legalistic question—hypocritical as well, for they do not believe in the resurrection.

In the end, he exposes their error in limiting God's power to raise the dead, for God is a God of the living.

Pray as you are led for yourself and others.

"Lord, how sad that people rebel against your order, your goodness, and yourself. Remove from me my blindness and vanity because I want to love you in truth and walk in your way. I pray for those who resist you ..." (Continue in your own words.)

Listen to Jesus.

Those who hunger for truth will find it. Those who seek God find God. All shall be well. What else is Jesus saying to you?

Ask God to show you how to live today.

"In the meantime, Lord, let me focus my efforts on my own journey. Let me hunger after your goodness and truth, whatever it may cost me. Amen."

Thursday, June 8, 2017

Know that God is present with you and ready to converse.

"Lord, you train me in the way that I should go. Command me by your holy Word."

Read the gospel: Mark 12:28–34.

One of the scribes came near and heard them disputing with one another, and seeing that Jesus answered them well, he asked him, "Which commandment is the first of all?" Jesus answered, "The first is, 'Hear, O Israel: the Lord our God, the Lord is one; you shall love the Lord your God with all your heart, and with all your soul, and with all your mind, and with all your strength.' The second is this, 'You shall love your neighbor as yourself.' There is no other commandment greater than these." Then the scribe said to him, "You are right, Teacher; you have truly said that 'he is one, and besides him there is no other'; and 'to love him with all the heart, and with all the understanding, and with all the strength,' and 'to love one's neighbor as oneself,'—this is much more important than all whole burnt-offerings and sacrifices." When Jesus saw that he answered wisely, he said to him, "You are not far from the kingdom of God." After that no one dared to ask him any question.

Notice what you think and feel as you read the gospel.

This scribe, unlike those who tried to trap Jesus, has a heart hungry for truth. That wise scribe understands the scripture rightly, and Jesus compliments him by inviting him to come into the kingdom of God.

Pray as you are led for yourself and others.

"Lord, I pray for wisdom for myself, my loved ones, and all leaders throughout the world. Let us take to heart your commandments of love for God and for one another . . ." (Continue in your own words.)

Listen to Jesus.

This is why I say that the kingdom of God is already among you. Dear disciple, my kingdom is a world of perfect love. Enter it here and now. What else is Jesus saying to you?

Ask God to show you how to live today.

"Jesus, I do love God and others, but my love is not perfect. Help me to love with your heart and to remain in your love. Amen."

Friday, June 9, 2017

Know that God is present with you and ready to converse.

"Lord, your Word is a mystery. Let me read it in the light of the Holy Spirit, who inspired it."

Read the gospel: Mark 12:35–37.

While Jesus was teaching in the temple, he said, "How can the scribes say that the Messiah is the son of David? David himself, by the Holy Spirit, declared,

> 'The Lord said to my Lord,
> "Sit at my right hand,
>   until I put your enemies under your feet."'

David himself calls him Lord; so how can he be his son?" And the large crowd was listening to him with delight.

Notice what you think and feel as you read the gospel.

Jesus teaches religious education in the temple, quizzing his students about scripture while a large crowd watches. He quotes a psalm of David to show that, by the Spirit, David prophesies that his son would be his Lord, as indeed Jesus is.

Pray as you are led for yourself and others.

"God, your salvation is a work in progress until whoever will comes into your kingdom and all evil is banished for eternity. I, too, am a work in progress. Let me be your work and not my own. I pray in the same way for these . . ." (Continue in your own words.)

Listen to Jesus.

This is the season of God's mercy and grace, my child. But the time is coming when God will judge each one with perfect justice. What else is Jesus saying to you?

Ask God to show you how to live today.

"Let me extend mercy to others today, for I wish to place myself under your mercy, Lord. I praise you for your mercy, loving Father. Amen."

Saturday, June 10, 2017

Know that God is present with you and ready to converse.

"Holy Spirit, I invite you into my heart today so that I may receive the truth of the Word and apply it where I need it. I seek an authentic encounter with God."

Read the gospel: Mark 12:38–44.

As he taught, Jesus said, "Beware of the scribes, who like to walk around in long robes, and to be greeted with respect in the market-places, and to have the best seats in the synagogues and places of honor at banquets! They devour widows' houses and for the sake of appearance say long prayers. They will receive the greater condemnation."

He sat down opposite the treasury, and watched the crowd putting money into the treasury. Many rich people put in large sums. A poor widow came and put in two small copper coins, which are worth a penny. Then he called his disciples and said to them, "Truly I tell you, this poor widow has put in more than all those who are contributing to the treasury. For all of them have contributed out of their abundance; but she out of her poverty has put in everything she had, all she had to live on."

Notice what you think and feel as you read the gospel.

Jesus warns the people to beware of religious hypocrites, full of arrogance and greed and fake piety. Meanwhile he commends a poor widow and her contribution of a penny. Blessed are the poor in spirit.

Pray as you are led for yourself and others.

"Lord, do not let me be ruled by selfishness. Let me share the riches you have given me with the needy. Let me give not only above and beyond my excess but of my very substance . . ." (Continue in your own words.)

Listen to Jesus.

Trust God, my beloved, trust God alone, and you will possess all you need, here and for eternity. What else is Jesus saying to you?

Ask God to show you how to live today.

"Give me wisdom today, Lord, to plan and perform some substantial generosity. Let me give without fear for myself. Amen."

Sunday, June 11, 2017
The Most Holy Trinity

Know that God is present with you and ready to converse.

The gospels frequently talk about the loving relationship among the Father, Son, and Holy Spirit. Jesus loves his Father and does his Father's will, moving in the power of the Holy Spirit throughout his earthly ministry. Yet God is one. Praise Father, Son, and Holy Spirit.

"Jesus, you have the Word of salvation. What must I do to be saved?"

Read the gospel: John 3:16–18.

Jesus said, "For God so loved the world that he gave his only Son, so that everyone who believes in him may not perish but may have eternal life.

"Indeed, God did not send the Son into the world to condemn the world, but in order that the world might be saved through him. Those who believe in him are not condemned; but those who do not believe are condemned already, because they have not believed in the name of the only Son of God."

Notice what you think and feel as you read the gospel.

Love is the motive behind God's offer of salvation. Love is a relationship. God loves humanity, so God gives his Son. Those who believe and receive the Son have eternal life. Those who do not sadly remain in condemnation.

Pray as you are led for yourself and others.

"Lord, I pray earnestly today for all those who do not believe in the Son of God. Faith is a gift of God. Give these people that gift . . ." (Continue in your own words.)

Listen to Jesus.

I continue to invite all to come to me for life. What can be done to ensure that my invitation does not fall upon deaf ears? What else is Jesus saying to you?

Ask God to show you how to live today.

"Let me be part of your invitation to love and eternal life, Lord. Let me pray for those who need you today. Let me speak of your goodness to me without fear. Amen."

Monday, June 12, 2017

Know that God is present with you and ready to converse.

"Lord, I know you want what is best for me. I seek your happiness, now and forever. Teach me by your Word."

Read the gospel: Matthew 5:1–12.

When Jesus saw the crowds, he went up the mountain; and after he sat down, his disciples came to him. Then he began to speak, and taught them, saying:

"Blessed are the poor in spirit, for theirs is the kingdom of heaven.

"Blessed are those who mourn, for they will be comforted.

"Blessed are the meek, for they will inherit the earth.

"Blessed are those who hunger and thirst for righteousness, for they will be filled.

"Blessed are the merciful, for they will receive mercy.

"Blessed are the pure in heart, for they will see God.

"Blessed are the peacemakers, for they will be called children of God.

"Blessed are those who are persecuted for righteousness' sake, for theirs is the kingdom of heaven.

"Blessed are you when people revile you and persecute you and utter all kinds of evil against you falsely on my account. Rejoice and be glad, for your reward is great in heaven, for in the same way they persecuted the prophets who were before you."

Notice what you think and feel as you read the gospel.

Is blessedness happiness? Blessedness is finding favor with God, even in poverty, grief, and humility. Blessedness is striving against evil, vengeance, and war; blessedness is suffering persecution. In those situations, we are to rejoice because we have found favor with God!

Pray as you are led for yourself and others.

"Lord, let me experience my troubles with a pure heart, rejoicing in the confidence that you are working your will through me, whatever befalls me. Let me pray for those who suffer in any way, knowing that nothing is impossible for God . . ." (Continue in your own words.)

Listen to Jesus.

I love to give you my view of things, dear disciple. Your love for another is never wasted. Your acts of love will always bear fruit for good. Live in that blessedness. What else is Jesus saying to you?

Ask God to show you how to live today.

"Open my eyes to your view of things, Lord. Sometimes I glimpse your heart of love for all. Let me be in the world today as you were in the world, Jesus. Thank you. Amen."

Tuesday, June 13, 2017

Know that God is present with you and ready to converse.

"Ever-present Lord of the universe, let me bask in the love and light of your Word, Jesus."

Read the gospel: Matthew 5:13–16.

Jesus said, "You are the salt of the earth; but if salt has lost its taste, how can its saltiness be restored? It is no longer good for anything, but is thrown out and trampled under foot.

"You are the light of the world. A city built on a hill cannot be hidden. No one after lighting a lamp puts it under the bushel basket, but on the lampstand, and it gives light to all in the house. In the same way, let your light shine before others, so that they may see your good works and give glory to your Father in heaven."

Notice what you think and feel as you read the gospel.

Jesus affirms the people who have come out to hear him. He exhorts them to be what they are: salt and light in a dark world. Let others see the goodness you are and do, he says, that they may glorify your Father in heaven.

Pray as you are led for yourself and others.

"Jesus, let me not neglect the working of your grace within me. Let me not be afraid to shine in thought, word, and deed to the glory of God, the Father . . ." (Continue in your own words.)

Listen to Jesus.

Many come to God because of the example of others, dear disciple. Virtue is a light that draws others to God. Humility is a virtue. What else is Jesus saying to you?

Ask God to show you how to live today.

"You challenge me every day, Lord, to do something good. With your help, I shall do something good today. Stay with me, Jesus. I thank you, praise you, and worship you, my King. Amen."

Wednesday, June 14, 2017

Know that God is present with you and ready to converse.

"Lord, often in your Word you are forceful and commanding. Let me receive your Word in holy fear."

Read the gospel: Matthew 5:17–19.

Jesus said, "Do not think that I have come to abolish the law or the prophets; I have come not to abolish but to fulfill. For truly I tell you, until heaven and earth pass away, not one letter, not one stroke of a letter, will pass from the law until all is accomplished. Therefore, whoever breaks one of the least of these commandments, and teaches others to do the same, will be called least in the kingdom of heaven; but whoever does them and teaches them will be called great in the kingdom of heaven."

Notice what you think and feel as you read the gospel.

Jesus recognizes the enduring force of the law and the prophets in the scriptures. All they speak of will be accomplished. We are to obey the commandments and teach others to do the same.

Pray as you are led for yourself and others.

"Lord, give me grace to examine my conscience in light of your commandments. Root out all my sin and renew me in grace. I pray also for those you have given me . . ." (Continue in your own words.)

Listen to Jesus.

I ask you to do your best, child, just for today. Remember that I am always near and you may touch my hand whenever you need me. What else is Jesus saying to you?

Ask God to show you how to live today.

"I need you, Lord, more than I know, as I get distracted by the business of the day. Let me find those moments to reach out to you. Amen."

Thursday, June 15, 2017

Know that God is present with you and ready to converse.

"Lord, teach me to obey you by your Word. You are here now to lead me on my way."

Read the gospel: Matthew 5:20–26.

Jesus said, "For I tell you, unless your righteousness exceeds that of the scribes and Pharisees, you will never enter the kingdom of heaven.

"You have heard that it was said to those of ancient times, 'You shall not murder'; and 'whoever murders shall be liable to judgement.' But I say to you that if you are angry with a brother or sister, you will be liable to judgement; and if you insult a brother or sister, you will be liable to the council; and if you say, 'You fool,' you will be liable to the hell of fire. So when you are offering your gift at the altar, if you remember that your brother or sister has something against you, leave your gift there before the altar and go; first be reconciled to your brother or sister, and then come and offer your gift. Come to terms quickly with your accuser while you are on the way to court with him, or your accuser may hand you over to the judge, and the judge to the guard, and you will be thrown into prison. Truly I tell you, you will never get out until you have paid the last penny."

Notice what you think and feel as you read the gospel.

Jesus brings the great commandments of Moses down to ordinary life and every day relationships. He makes sin a matter of the heart. He recommends swift and practical action to undo our offenses against others.

Pray as you are led for yourself and others.

"Give me insight to apply your words today, Savior. What lesson shall I take away for myself? I pray for myself and for these . . ." (Continue in your own words.)

Listen to Jesus.

I want to speak to your heart, beloved. First, know that I love you. How may I help you love your neighbor? What else is Jesus saying to you?

Ask God to show you how to live today.

"Jesus, continue to speak to my heart. I am very weak and shaky without you. Strengthen me to follow you today and do what pleases you. Thank you! Amen."

Friday, June 16, 2017

Know that God is present with you and ready to converse.

"Lord, I come into your presence looking for love, longing to learn about love. Teach me."

Read the gospel: Matthew 5:27–32.

Jesus said, "You have heard that it was said, 'You shall not commit adultery.' But I say to you that everyone who looks at a woman with lust has already committed adultery with her in his heart. If your right eye causes you to sin, tear it out and throw it away; it is better for you to lose one of your members than for your whole body to be thrown into hell. And if your right hand causes you to sin, cut it off and throw it away; it is better for you to lose one of your members than for your whole body to go into hell.

"It was also said, 'Whoever divorces his wife, let him give her a certificate of divorce.' But I say to you that anyone who divorces his wife, except on the ground of unchastity, causes her to commit adultery; and whoever marries a divorced woman commits adultery."

Notice what you think and feel as you read the gospel.

Jesus speaks of sexual lust, its power and its danger. Lust begins in the human heart, hurting people and destroying marriages and families. We must fight against it with all our might.

Pray as you are led for yourself and others.

"Lord, so many are slaves of lust. I ask you to remove all lust from my heart, and I pray for those whose lust is causing damage to themselves and others . . ." (Continue in your own words.)

Listen to Jesus.

There is no happiness in sin. My faithful followers learn that. In me you have power over all sin. Ask me for that power. What else is Jesus saying to you?

Ask God to show you how to live today.

"Lord, give me hatred for all my sins because they hurt me, hurt others, and hurt my relationship with you. Let me be converted, washed, and set free. Amen."

Saturday, June 17, 2017

Know that God is present with you and ready to converse.

"Lord, bind your Word upon my heart. Let it be clear and bright by your grace. You are here to teach me now."

Read the gospel: Matthew 5:33–37.

Jesus said, "Again, you have heard that it was said to those of ancient times, 'You shall not swear falsely, but carry out the vows you have made to the Lord.' But I say to you, Do not swear at all, either by heaven, for it is the throne of God, or by the earth, for it is his footstool, or by Jerusalem, for it is the city of the great King. And do not swear by your head, for you cannot make one hair white or black. Let your word be 'Yes, Yes' or 'No, No'; anything more than this comes from the evil one."

Notice what you think and feel as you read the gospel.

Jesus asks us to live simply and responsibly, with just judgment about our own limitations. We are not to make grand promises but to speak with a simple yes and no.

Pray as you are led for yourself and others.

"Lord, what promises have I made to you and to others? Let me review those promises in simplicity and humility and make amends for what is false . . ." (Continue in your own words.)

Listen to Jesus.

The Holy Spirit searches hearts, my beloved. We seek your holiness, for that is how you can best love and know God. What else is Jesus saying to you?

Ask God to show you how to live today.

"Search my heart as often as you wish, Lord. Let me cast away from me all that is false and walk in simple truth with you, my Good Shepherd. Amen."

Sunday, June 18, 2017
The Most Holy Body and Blood of Christ

Know that God is present with you and ready to converse.

Jesus Christ, the Word of God, fulfills the scriptures handed down to his own generation. He is the prophet like Moses; he is the Son of David, the Suffering Servant by whose stripes we are healed. Much of his teaching reinterpreted the scriptures without negating it. At the same time, he continuously challenged those who heard him to understand who he was—the Son of the Father—and to believe.

"When you are ready, open yourself to the Word of God."

Read the gospel: John 6:51–58.

Jesus said, "I am the living bread that came down from heaven. Whoever eats of this bread will live for ever; and the bread that I will give for the life of the world is my flesh."

The Jews then disputed among themselves, saying, "How can this man give us his flesh to eat?" So Jesus said to them, "Very truly, I tell you, unless you eat the flesh of the Son of Man and drink his blood, you have no life in you. Those who eat my flesh and drink my blood have eternal life, and I will raise them up on the last day; for my flesh is true food and my blood is true drink. Those who eat my flesh and drink my blood abide in me, and I in them. Just as the living Father sent me, and I live because of the Father, so whoever eats me will live because of me. This is the bread that came down from heaven, not like that which your ancestors ate, and they died. But the one who eats this bread will live for ever."

Notice what you think and feel as you read the gospel.

Jesus, who would soon offer his life to save humanity, here offers his flesh and blood as food and drink. He is the bread of life, much more than the manna in the desert the Israelites ate. Those who eat his body and drink his blood abide in him and live forever.

Pray as you are led for yourself and others.

"Lord, let me receive your body and blood with faith in your promises, for I long to abide with you forever. I pray for those who do not yet believe your words . . ." (Continue in your own words.)

Listen to Jesus.

As I am bread for others, dear follower, so are you. Draw near to me often, and I shall use you. What else is Jesus saying to you?

Ask God to show you how to live today.

"Lord, I offer you my day and my whole life. Use me as you will, but be with me in the work. I do not want to be striving vainly by my own efforts without you. Amen."

Monday, June 19, 2017

Know that God is present with you and ready to converse.

"You guide your saints, Lord, and show them what to do. What shall I do?"

Read the gospel: Matthew 5:38–42.

Jesus said, "You have heard that it was said, 'An eye for an eye and a tooth for a tooth.' But I say to you, Do not resist an evildoer. But if anyone strikes you on the right cheek, turn the other also; and if anyone wants to sue you and take your coat, give your cloak as well; and if anyone forces you to go one mile, go also the second mile. Give to everyone who begs from you, and do not refuse anyone who wants to borrow from you."

Notice what you think and feel as you read the gospel.

Jesus imposes what seem like impossibly high standards of ethical behavior. He speaks without qualification with words such as "anyone" and "everyone." He speaks with authority.

Pray as you are led for yourself and others.

"Lord, let me receive your strong words with humility and apply them to my own actions. Evildoers cannot harm me because you have my life in your hands . . ." (Continue in your own words.)

Listen to Jesus.

You have the freedom to follow me even to your death, for in me you will not see death. Do not fear anyone. I am your sword and shield. What else is Jesus saying to you?

Ask God to show you how to live today.

"Let me live humbly and fearlessly today in you, Lord. Give me courage to turn the other cheek. Amen."

Tuesday, June 20, 2017

Know that God is present with you and ready to converse.

"Heavenly Father, you loved me so much you sent your Son to save me even when I was opposed to you. Teach me to love as you do."

Read the gospel: Matthew 5:43–48.

Jesus said, "You have heard that it was said, 'You shall love your neighbor and hate your enemy.' But I say to you, Love your enemies and pray for those who persecute you, so that you may be children of your Father in heaven; for he makes his sun rise on the evil and on the good, and sends rain on the righteous and on the unrighteous. For if you love those who love you, what reward do you have? Do not even the tax-collectors do the same? And if you greet only your brothers and sisters, what more are you doing than others? Do not even the Gentiles do the same? Be perfect, therefore, as your heavenly Father is perfect."

Notice what you think and feel as you read the gospel.

Jesus' model for holiness is his Father. We are to be perfect as the Father is perfect. That means loving everyone, even the evil, for they stumble in darkness now but soon may see the light.

Pray as you are led for yourself and others.

"Lord, I will fail, but give me grace to strive continuously to be perfect as you are perfect. I entrust you with my life and the lives of those you have given me . . ." (Continue in your own words.)

Listen to Jesus.

Your Father and my Father sends the sun and the rain for all. Do not judge others; love them. You are a child of the Father. What else is Jesus saying to you?

Ask God to show you how to live today.

"Jesus, when my petty heart inclines to judge or look down upon someone today, remind me of what you are teaching me now. Help me to love, not judge. Amen."

Wednesday, June 21, 2017

Know that God is present with you and ready to converse.

"Lord, you understand the human heart. You know me better than I know myself. Let me learn from you."

Read the gospel: Matthew 6:1–6, 16–18.

Jesus said, "Beware of practicing your piety before others in order to be seen by them; for then you have no reward from your Father in heaven.

"So whenever you give alms, do not sound a trumpet before you, as the hypocrites do in the synagogues and in the streets, so that they may be praised by others. Truly I tell you, they have received their reward. But when you give alms, do not let your left hand know what your right hand is doing, so that your alms may be done in secret; and your Father who sees in secret will reward you. . . .

"And whenever you pray, do not be like the hypocrites; for they love to stand and pray in the synagogues and at the street corners, so that they may be seen by others. Truly I tell you, they have received their reward. But whenever you pray, go into your room and shut the door and pray to your Father who is in secret; and your Father who sees in secret will reward you.

"And whenever you fast, do not look dismal, like the hypocrites, for they disfigure their faces so as to show others that they are fasting. Truly I tell you, they have received their reward. But when you fast, put oil on your head and wash your face, so that your fasting may be seen not by others but by your Father who is in secret; and your Father who sees in secret will reward you."

Notice what you think and feel as you read the gospel.

Jesus knows that many practice religion to be seen as religious by others. Giving alms, praying, and fasting are good, but they can become worthless acts if done for show. Jesus urges us to do these things in secret, not for earthly esteem but for God's rewards.

Pray as you are led for yourself and others.

"Strip away my vanity, Lord, and let me worship you in truth. What secret good may I do today for love of you?" (Continue in your own words.)

Listen to Jesus.

In truth is simplicity, my child. There is great joy in dropping all pretense before others and just being who you are. What else is Jesus saying to you?

Ask God to show you how to live today.

"Help me monitor my words and my actions today, Jesus, so that I can speak and live in your truth. Holy Spirit, I need your light and your strength in this. Thank you. Amen."

Thursday, June 22, 2017

Know that God is present with you and ready to converse.

"Praise to you, Lord God of Hosts, heaven and earth are full of your glory. Teach me to pray."

Read the gospel: Matthew 6:7–15.

Jesus said, "When you are praying, do not heap up empty phrases as the Gentiles do; for they think that they will be heard because of their many words. Do not be like them, for your Father knows what you need before you ask him.

"Pray then in this way:

> Our Father in heaven,
>> hallowed be your name.
>> Your kingdom come.
>> Your will be done,
>>> on earth as it is in heaven.
>> Give us this day our daily bread.
>> And forgive us our debts,
>>> as we also have forgiven our debtors.
>> And do not bring us to the time of trial,
>>> but rescue us from the evil one.

For if you forgive others their trespasses, your heavenly Father will also forgive you; but if you do not forgive others, neither will your Father forgive your trespasses."

Notice what you think and feel as you read the gospel.

Jesus' prayer is rich in meaning, yet he chooses to emphasize the need for us to forgive others. We must do that to be forgiven ourselves. Jesus knows that forgiving others who have hurt us can be very difficult, yet it is our way to God.

Pray as you are led for yourself and others.

"Lord, it is easy for me to harbor grudges toward those who have hurt me in my distant and recent past. At times I don't even realize that I am refusing to forgive. Shine your light upon my hard heart and give me your Spirit of true forgiveness . . ." (Continue in your own words.)

Listen to Jesus.

When you forgive, remember what you have done. Renew forgiveness as often as you need to. You can forgive because you are mine. What else is Jesus saying to you?

Ask God to show you how to live today.

"Lord, walking with you is sometimes difficult. Help me hear and do what pleases you today. I can do all things with you. Amen."

Friday, June 23, 2017
The Most Sacred Heart of Jesus

Know that God is present with you and ready to converse.

"Father, you reveal your truths not to the wise but to infants. I am a child before you today."

Read the gospel: Matthew 11:25–30.

At that time Jesus said, "I thank you, Father, Lord of heaven and earth, because you have hidden these things from the wise and the intelligent and have revealed them to infants; yes, Father, for such was your gracious will. All things have been handed over to me by my Father; and no one knows the Son except the Father, and no one knows the Father except the Son and anyone to whom the Son chooses to reveal him.

"Come to me, all you that are weary and are carrying heavy burdens, and I will give you rest. Take my yoke upon you, and learn from me; for I am gentle and humble in heart, and you will find rest for your souls. For my yoke is easy, and my burden is light."

Notice what you think and feel as you read the gospel.

Jesus invites the weary to come to him for rest. That rest is found in his heart, gentle and humble. This is the Sacred Heart of Jesus who has loved us so much!

Pray as you are led for yourself and others.

"I seek rest in your heart, Lord. How may I bear your burden today? I begin by praying for others who are weary . . ." (Continue in your own words.)

Listen to Jesus.

The secret of this life is to see others and yourself with my eyes and with my heart. When you do, you will love them as God loves them and you will bear much fruit to the glory of God. What else is Jesus saying to you?

Ask God to show you how to live today.

"I believe your promises to me. Make my heart like your heart, Lord, so that I may find rest for my soul and do as you do. Amen."

Saturday, June 24, 2017
Nativity of Saint John the Baptist

Know that God is present with you and ready to converse.

"Lord, you do great things through your lowly servants. I offer myself to you today. Feed me by your Word."

Read the gospel: Luke 1:57–66, 80.

Now the time came for Elizabeth to give birth, and she bore a son. Her neighbors and relatives heard that the Lord had shown his great mercy to her, and they rejoiced with her.

On the eighth day they came to circumcise the child, and they were going to name him Zechariah after his father. But his mother said, "No; he is to be called John." They said to her, "None of your relatives has this name." Then they began motioning to his father to find out what name he wanted to give him. He asked for a writing-tablet and wrote, "His name is John." And all of them were amazed. Immediately his mouth was opened and his tongue freed, and he began to speak, praising God. Fear came over all their neighbors, and all these things were talked about throughout the entire hill country of Judea. All who heard them pondered them and said, "What then will this child become?" For, indeed, the hand of the Lord was with him. . . .

The child grew and became strong in spirit, and he was in the wilderness until the day he appeared publicly to Israel.

Notice what you think and feel as you read the gospel.

The story of the public naming of John is full of human details. When his father writes "His name is John" he regains the power of speech and praises God. Throughout the hill country, people wondered what the child would become, for the Lord was with him.

Pray as you are led for yourself and others.

"Lord, be with me and those you have given me. Let us be patient in waiting until you are ready to use us for your good and glorious purposes, great and small . . ." (Continue in your own words.)

Listen to Jesus.

God favored John, but you are a child of the Father, a member of the holy family and the kingdom of heaven. Even small things you do in God are great things. What else is Jesus saying to you?

Ask God to show you how to live today.

"Give me something small to do for someone today, Lord, for I would like to do something great for you. Amen."

Sunday, June 25, 2017
Twelfth Sunday in Ordinary Time

Know that God is present with you and ready to converse.

Jesus teaches the wisdom of the Father. He performs the works of the Father. He gives his wisdom and does his work for simple men and women. Through Jesus, we are dignified by the Father, each of us made like him to be a child of God.

"Lord, though I am poor and weak, I would be rich in the things of God. Let me learn from you."

Read the gospel: Matthew 10:26–33.

Jesus said, "So have no fear of them; for nothing is covered up that will not be uncovered, and nothing secret that will not become known. What I say to you in the dark, tell in the light; and what you hear whispered, proclaim from the housetops. Do not fear those who kill the body but cannot kill the soul; rather fear him who can destroy both soul and body in hell. Are not two sparrows sold for a penny? Yet not one of them will fall to the ground unperceived by your Father. And even the hairs of your head are all counted. So do not be afraid; you are of more value than many sparrows.

"Everyone therefore who acknowledges me before others, I also will acknowledge before my Father in heaven; but whoever denies me before others, I also will deny before my Father in heaven."

Notice what you think and feel as you read the gospel.

Speaking to his followers, Jesus dispels all fears of violence and persecution, reminding them that no one can really hurt them. They will live forever in God who values us more than "many sparrows."

Pray as you are led for yourself and others.

"You urge me to talk of you, Lord, and to have no fears about doing so. Free my heart and free my tongue to tell others of your love for me . . ." (Continue in your own words.)

Listen to Jesus.

I set you free by my truth, dear disciple. As you walk in my way, you will see my truth ever more clearly. Trust me. What else is Jesus saying to you?

Ask God to show you how to live today.

"I am ready to walk with you today, Lord. How may I show you that I trust you? Amen."

Monday, June 26, 2017

Know that God is present with you and ready to converse.

"Lord, you will come again to judge the living and the dead. Teach me about judgment."

Read the gospel: Matthew 7:1–5.

Jesus said, "Do not judge, so that you may not be judged. For with the judgement you make you will be judged, and the measure you give will be the measure you get. Why do you see the speck in your neighbor's eye, but do not notice the log in your own eye? Or how can you say to your neighbor, 'Let me take the speck out of your eye,' while the log is in your own eye? You hypocrite, first take the log out of your own eye, and then you will see clearly to take the speck out of your neighbor's eye."

Notice what you think and feel as you read the gospel.

Jesus commands us not to judge others. We are blind to our own faults. We have no right to judge.

Pray as you are led for yourself and others.

"Let me be generous in my opinions of others, Lord. Let me measure each one with love. I pour my love now upon those you have given me . . ." (Continue in your own words.)

Listen to Jesus.

Day after day passes and then you come to the end of life, my beloved. You have today to love. What else is Jesus saying to you?

Ask God to show you how to live today.

"You are the only judge, Lord, yet you are all mercy toward me. How may I show mercy to someone today? Amen."

Tuesday, June 27, 2017

Know that God is present with you and ready to converse.

"God, thank you for being here with me now and teaching me what I need to know by your Word. Let it penetrate to the depths of my soul."

Read the gospel: Matthew 7:6, 12–14.

Jesus said, "Do not give what is holy to dogs; and do not throw your pearls before swine, or they will trample them under foot and turn and maul you. . . .

"In everything do to others as you would have them do to you; for this is the law and the prophets.

"Enter through the narrow gate; for the gate is wide and the road is easy that leads to destruction, and there are many who take it. For the gate is narrow and the road is hard that leads to life, and there are few who find it."

Notice what you think and feel as you read the gospel.

The narrow gate is doing to others as we would have them do to us. Who lives this way? Jesus says only a few, yet this is the way to life.

Pray as you are led for yourself and others.

"Almighty Lord of Love, in your mercy lead many through your narrow gate. I pray for . . ." (Continue in your own words.)

Listen to Jesus.

Though you cannot see it, child, I am drawing all people to myself. You are my witness, living your days in the power of my love. Take heart. What else is Jesus saying to you?

Ask God to show you how to live today.

"Thank you for being with me, Lord, and letting me serve you by serving others. I pray today for faithfulness in your service. Amen."

Wednesday, June 28, 2017

Know that God is present with you and ready to converse.

"God, you are present with me in times of tranquility and in times of danger. You are here with me now. Hallowed be your name."

Read the gospel: Matthew 7:15–20.

Jesus said, "Beware of false prophets, who come to you in sheep's clothing but inwardly are ravenous wolves. You will know them by their fruits. Are grapes gathered from thorns, or figs from thistles? In the same way, every good tree bears good fruit, but the bad tree bears bad fruit. A good tree cannot bear bad fruit, nor can a bad tree bear good fruit. Every tree that does not bear good fruit is cut down and thrown into the fire. Thus you will know them by their fruits."

Notice what you think and feel as you read the gospel.

Jesus warns his followers to beware of false prophets. They can look like sheep, but they might be wolves. We can know them by their fruits.

Pray as you are led for yourself and others.

"Lord, give me grace to discern those I may truly trust. I pray for those who are victims of false prophets . . ." (Continue in your own words.)

Listen to Jesus.

If you remain in me I remain in you, and you have nothing to fear from false prophets and violent people. In fact, you yourself will bear good fruit. What else is Jesus saying to you?

Ask God to show you how to live today.

"If today I am drawn to admire anyone, remind me that you alone are good, Lord. Let me set my heart on you and none other. Amen."

Thursday, June 29, 2017
Saints Peter and Paul, Apostles

Know that God is present with you and ready to converse.

"Word of the Father, Jesus, you are the Son of the living God. Pour out your grace upon me."

Read the gospel: Matthew 16:13–19.

Now when Jesus came into the district of Caesarea Philippi, he asked his disciples, "Who do people say that the Son of Man is?" And they said, "Some say John the Baptist, but others Elijah, and still others Jeremiah or one of the prophets." He said to them, "But who do you say that I am?" Simon Peter answered, "You are the Messiah, the Son of the living God." And Jesus answered him, "Blessed are you, Simon son of Jonah! For flesh and blood has not revealed this to you, but my Father in heaven. And I tell you, you are Peter, and on this rock I will build my church, and the gates of Hades will not prevail against it. I will give you the keys of the kingdom of heaven, and whatever you bind on earth will be bound in heaven, and whatever you loose on earth will be loosed in heaven."

Notice what you think and feel as you read the gospel.

Jesus rejoices that Peter recognizes him as the Messiah, the Lord. It is the Father who has revealed this to Peter. Jesus proclaims that Peter is the rock upon which he will build his Church and he will have power on earth and in heaven to bind and to loose.

Pray as you are led for yourself and others.

"Lord, let your Church wield the great power you gave to Peter. I pray for all those who feed your sheep that they may serve in your power . . ." (Continue in your own words.)

Listen to Jesus.

I am with you always, beloved disciple. Pray, but do not fear, for I have overcome the world. What else is Jesus saying to you?

Ask God to show you how to live today.

"I offer myself to you today, Lord, to pray for those who serve you and your flock. Amen."

Friday, June 30, 2017

Know that God is present with you and ready to converse.
"Lord of Love, let me trust you as I come to your Word, for you have the words of eternal life."

Read the gospel: Matthew 8:1–4.
When Jesus had come down from the mountain, great crowds followed him; and there was a leper who came to him and knelt before him, saying, "Lord, if you choose, you can make me clean." He stretched out his hand and touched him, saying, "I do choose. Be made clean!" Immediately his leprosy was cleansed. Then Jesus said to him, "See that you say nothing to anyone; but go, show yourself to the priest, and offer the gift that Moses commanded, as a testimony to them."

Notice what you think and feel as you read the gospel.
The leper's faith is qualified by the words "if you choose." Jesus shores up his doubts by proclaiming, "I do choose. Be made clean!" God always wills good for us, and God will always do for us what is good if we put ourselves in God's care.

Pray as you are led for yourself and others.
"I place myself in your care, good and loving God, knowing you will always choose to heal me, and I entrust to you these whom you have given me . . ." (Continue in your own words.)

Listen to Jesus.
I hear your prayers, my child, and I shall care for you and those for whom you pray. You cannot know now, but someday you will see the power of your prayers. What else is Jesus saying to you?

Ask God to show you how to live today.
"If something goes wrong or is not right today, give me faith that you choose to do good by it and even to use it for good for me and for others. We are your children, Lord. I praise you! Amen."

Saturday, July 1, 2017

Know that God is present with you and ready to converse.

"Lord, there is power in your Word to save, to heal, and to bless. What a privilege for me that you are here now to open it to me! I am listening, Jesus."

Read the gospel: Matthew 8:5–17.

When he entered Capernaum, a centurion came to Jesus, appealing to him and saying, "Lord, my servant is lying at home paralyzed, in terrible distress." And he said to him, "I will come and cure him." The centurion answered, "Lord, I am not worthy to have you come under my roof; but only speak the word, and my servant will be healed. For I also am a man under authority, with soldiers under me; and I say to one, 'Go,' and he goes, and to another, 'Come,' and he comes, and to my slave, 'Do this,' and the slave does it." When Jesus heard him, he was amazed and said to those who followed him, "Truly I tell you, in no one in Israel have I found such faith. I tell you, many will come from east and west and will eat with Abraham and Isaac and Jacob in the kingdom of heaven, while the heirs of the kingdom will be thrown into the outer darkness, where there will be weeping and gnashing of teeth." And to the centurion Jesus said, "Go; let it be done for you according to your faith." And the servant was healed in that hour.

When Jesus entered Peter's house, he saw his mother-in-law lying in bed with a fever; he touched her hand, and the fever left her, and she got up and began to serve him. That evening they brought to him many who were possessed by demons; and he cast out the spirits with a word, and cured all who were sick. This was to fulfill what had been spoken through the prophet Isaiah, "He took our infirmities and bore our diseases."

Notice what you think and feel as you read the gospel.

Jesus heals the centurion's servant by dismissing the centurion with a simple "Go." He heals Peter's mother "with a word." Who is worthy of such divine attention? How can it be that God takes our infirmities and bears our diseases?

Pray as you are led for yourself and others.

"Lord, I am not worthy, but you are merciful. There is no shadow in you. I ask for the humility and faith of the centurion for my own healing and for the healing of these others . . ." (Continue in your own words.)

Listen to Jesus.

I am gathering my people, beloved. I rejoice you have come to me with your needs. I hear your prayer. What else is Jesus saying to you?

Ask God to show you how to live today.

"Give me the strength to serve you, Master, and give praise and thanks to you all day long. Amen."

Sunday, July 2, 2017
Thirteenth Sunday in Ordinary Time

Know that God is present with you and ready to converse.

The gospels tell us what Jesus taught and what he did. He said surprising truths with authority; he performed mighty deeds with power. This was the moment when God had finally come to walk among people.

"Lord, you are here with me too. Give me grace to respond to your holy Word."

Read the gospel: Matthew 10:37–42.

Jesus said, "Whoever loves father or mother more than me is not worthy of me; and whoever loves son or daughter more than me is not worthy of me; and whoever does not take up the cross and follow me is not worthy of me. Those who find their life will lose it, and those who lose their life for my sake will find it.

"Whoever welcomes you welcomes me, and whoever welcomes me welcomes the one who sent me. Whoever welcomes a prophet in the name of a prophet will receive a prophet's reward; and whoever welcomes a righteous person in the name of a righteous person will receive the reward of the righteous; and whoever gives even a cup of cold water to one of these little ones in the name of a disciple—truly I tell you, none of these will lose their reward."

Notice what you think and feel as you read the gospel.

Jesus asks his followers for love that is greater than family love and commitment to him that is greater than love of life. He demands everything. He also promises great rewards even for the ordinary acts of love we can perform any day.

Pray as you are led for yourself and others.

"Lord, I don't know how to lose my life for your sake. I long to find my life in you. Take my life. Let it be lost in you. Then let me serve others . . ." (Continue in your own words.)

Listen to Jesus.

Your time of service is short, beloved disciple. Use it to do what good you can do. Your time of reward is long. What else is Jesus saying to you?

Ask God to show you how to live today.

"Whom may I welcome today, Lord? To whom may I give a cup of cold water? I offer myself to your service because I love you. Amen."

Monday, July 3, 2017
Saint Thomas, Apostle

Know that God is present with you and ready to converse.

"Almighty God, you are invisible Spirit. Jesus Christ, you are God and a man who walked on the earth, but I have never seen you. Let me see you in the Word you have spread before me today."

Read the gospel: John 20:24–29.

But Thomas (who was called the Twin), one of the twelve, was not with them when Jesus came. So the other disciples told him, "We have seen the Lord." But he said to them, "Unless I see the mark of the nails in his hands, and put my finger in the mark of the nails and my hand in his side, I will not believe."

A week later his disciples were again in the house, and Thomas was with them. Although the doors were shut, Jesus came and stood among them and said, "Peace be with you." Then he said to Thomas, "Put your finger here and see my hands. Reach out your hand and put it in my side. Do not doubt but believe." Thomas answered him, "My Lord and my God!" Jesus said to him, "Have you believed because you have seen me? Blessed are those who have not seen and yet have come to believe."

Notice what you think and feel as you read the gospel.

Jesus personally reveals himself to the doubtful Thomas by his wounds, causing Thomas to believe and worship. When Thomas pronounces his faith, Jesus mentions you and me, the ones who have not seen him and yet believe. We are blessed!

Pray as you are led for yourself and others.

"My Lord and my God! Jesus, perfect my faith in you. I pray for . . ."
(Continue in your own words.)

Listen to Jesus.

Your life, child of the Father, is in God's hands for you are mine. I give you
strength to live and serve others by my Spirit. What else may I do for you today?
What else is Jesus saying to you?

Ask God to show you how to live today.

"Help me to communicate the blessedness of faith—the faith you give
me through your Spirit and your Word, Lord. You love me so much! I
wish to show that love to others. Amen."

Tuesday, July 4, 2017

Know that God is present with you and ready to converse.

"Lord, you have found me today needing you and afraid of many things.
I need assurance of your strong hand in my life. Calm me, Lord, and set
me straight."

Read the gospel: Matthew 8:23–27.

And when Jesus got into the boat, his disciples followed him. A gale arose
on the lake, so great that the boat was being swamped by the waves; but
he was asleep. And they went and woke him up, saying, "Lord, save
us! We are perishing!" And he said to them, "Why are you afraid, you
of little faith?" Then he got up and rebuked the winds and the sea; and
there was a dead calm. They were amazed, saying, "What sort of man is
this, that even the winds and the sea obey him?"

Notice what you think and feel as you read the gospel.

Jesus has not fallen asleep on the boat by accident. The storm is no accident either. He may have been testing their faith, but the final result is
to increase their faith. For they see that even the winds and the sea obey
him.

Pray as you are led for yourself and others.

"Are you testing my faith, Lord? With what little faith I have I ask you
to save me and to save those you have given me. I believe in you. Let
me see your power . . ." (Continue in your own words.)

Listen to Jesus.

When you are distressed, dear disciple, come to me and spend time with me, sharing all that troubles you, every detail. I will hear it all, and then I will take it all from you. You will be amazed. What else is Jesus saying to you?

Ask God to show you how to live today.

"Lord, I am ready to walk with you today. I worship and adore you, Jesus, and wish to glorify God as pleases you. Amen."

Wednesday, July 5, 2017

Know that God is present with you and ready to converse.

"Lord, before you created the universe world you existed as eternal Spirit in the mystery of the Trinity. I live in a fallen world of sin. Rescue me."

Read the gospel: Matthew 8:28–34.

When Jesus came to the other side, to the country of the Gadarenes, two demoniacs coming out of the tombs met him. They were so fierce that no one could pass that way. Suddenly they shouted, "What have you to do with us, Son of God? Have you come here to torment us before the time?" Now a large herd of swine was feeding at some distance from them. The demons begged him, "If you cast us out, send us into the herd of swine." And he said to them, "Go!" So they came out and entered the swine; and suddenly, the whole herd rushed down the steep bank into the lake and perished in the water. The swineherds ran off, and on going into the town, they told the whole story about what had happened to the demoniacs. Then the whole town came out to meet Jesus; and when they saw him, they begged him to leave their neighborhood.

Notice what you think and feel as you read the gospel.

What a ghastly scene among the tombs with two possessed of demons who recognize the Son of God and speak to him! He casts the demons into the swine, which then stampede into the lake and drown. Everyone is frightened, and they ask Jesus to leave.

Pray as you are led for yourself and others.

"Lord, there are dangers in the spiritual world I cannot see or control. But you can. Do not leave my neighborhood, but protect me from all evil. Protect these I now pray for, as well . . ." (Continue in your own words.)

Listen to Jesus.

Child, it is good for you to turn to me with things you do not understand and cannot control. I understand, and I am protecting you. What else is Jesus saying to you?

Ask God to show you how to live today.

"I give myself to you, Lord, to teach me to walk in your way despite spiritual forces that assail me and those I love. You will defend us. Keep us safe, Great Shepherd. Amen."

Thursday, July 6, 2017

Know that God is present with you and ready to converse.

"Lord, when I come to you I don't always know what I need or what I want. I leave it to you to give me what is best."

Read the gospel: Matthew 9:1–8.

And after getting into a boat Jesus crossed the water and came to his own town.

And just then some people were carrying a paralyzed man lying on a bed. When Jesus saw their faith, he said to the paralytic, "Take heart, son; your sins are forgiven." Then some of the scribes said to themselves, "This man is blaspheming." But Jesus, perceiving their thoughts, said, "Why do you think evil in your hearts? For which is easier, to say, 'Your sins are forgiven,' or to say, 'Stand up and walk'? But so that you may know that the Son of Man has authority on earth to forgive sins"—he then said to the paralytic—"Stand up, take your bed and go to your home." And he stood up and went to his home. When the crowds saw it, they were filled with awe, and they glorified God, who had given such authority to human beings.

Notice what you think and feel as you read the gospel.

Some people brought a paralyzed man to Jesus for healing. A crowd gathers to see what will happen. Jesus does not heal the man but instead forgives his sins to the horror of some scribes, though they dare not say anything. Jesus knows they think he has sinned by putting himself forward as God, for only God can forgive sins. He says simply that he wants them to know he has that authority. And then he heals the paralytic. The crowd is filled with awe.

Pray as you are led for yourself and others.

"Lord, I have many favors to ask of you for myself and for others. First forgive my many sins and wash me clean. Now lead me as I pray . . ." (Continue in your own words.)

Listen to Jesus.

I know your heart, my child. I know every part of you, and I love you. I work in you to make you holy that you may be worthy of eternal life with God. This is most important. What else is Jesus saying to you?

Ask God to show you how to live today.

"Jesus, go ahead and work in me as you see fit. Then be with me as I seek to serve others and let them know your power to forgive sins and to heal. Amen."

Friday, July 7, 2017

Know that God is present with you and ready to converse.

"Lord, questions about life and the ways of God often come to me. Clarify my mind and heart and guide me in your truth. Your Word is truth."

Read the gospel: Matthew 9:9–13.

As Jesus was walking along, he saw a man called Matthew sitting at the tax booth; and he said to him, "Follow me." And he got up and followed him.

And as he sat at dinner in the house, many tax-collectors and sinners came and were sitting with him and his disciples. When the Pharisees saw this, they said to his disciples, "Why does your teacher eat with tax-collectors and sinners?" But when he heard this, he said, "Those who are well have no need of a physician, but those who are sick. Go and learn what this means, 'I desire mercy, not sacrifice.' For I have come to call not the righteous but sinners."

Notice what you think and feel as you read the gospel.

Jesus calls Matthew, a tax collector and sinner, to follow him; Matthew does so without hesitation. When Jesus goes to dinner at Matthew's house, the Pharisees have critical questions. Jesus points out to them that only sick people need doctors, that God desires mercy not sacrifice, and that Jesus calls not the righteous but sinners.

Pray as you are led for yourself and others.

"Lord, I am a sinner among sinners. Teach me mercy. Free me from all phony religiosity. I pray for those you have given me . . ." (Continue in your own words.)

Listen to Jesus.

I call people of all kinds, at all times, and everywhere. I have called you, dear disciple. Thank you for following me. There is work only you can do. What else is Jesus saying to you?

Ask God to show you how to live today.

"Give me the work you have for me, Lord. Give me grace to do it well and faithfully because I desire to please you and glorify you by my life. Amen."

Saturday, July 8, 2017

Know that God is present with you and ready to converse.

"Lord, your mercies are new every morning. Thank you for calling me here to be with you now. Renew me by your Word."

Read the gospel: Matthew 9:14–17.

Then the disciples of John came to Jesus, saying, "Why do we and the Pharisees fast often, but your disciples do not fast?" And Jesus said to them, "The wedding-guests cannot mourn as long as the bridegroom is with them, can they? The days will come when the bridegroom is taken away from them, and then they will fast. No one sews a piece of unshrunk cloth on an old cloak, for the patch pulls away from the cloak, and a worse tear is made. Neither is new wine put into old wineskins; otherwise, the skins burst, and the wine is spilled, and the skins are destroyed; but new wine is put into fresh wineskins, and so both are preserved."

Notice what you think and feel as you read the gospel.

Jesus answers the question John's disciples ask him about fasting. How can his disciples fast when he, the Bridegroom, is among them? They will fast later when he's gone. Then he uses the images of the new patch on an old cloak and the new wine in old wineskins. What is new, he seems to be saying, requires a new container.

Pray as you are led for yourself and others.

"Lord, renew in me whatever needs renewing; you know what I need. I am yours. I also give to you those you have given me . . ." (Continue in your own words.)

Listen to Jesus.

When I come into a person's life, I bring new ways of thinking, feeling, and behaving. New life stirs within, and it is my life in you. Walk in newness of life, rejoicing, depending on me for everything. What else is Jesus saying to you?

Ask God to show you how to live today.

"Refresh my heart with joy and thanksgiving, Lord, for you are my constant companion. I praise you and thank you for your wonderful blessings. Amen."

Sunday, July 9, 2017
Fourteenth Sunday in Ordinary Time

Know that God is present with you and ready to converse.

Jesus' followers see him do great works of compassion. He speaks and acts in the power of love at all times, for he is the Son of Love. Do his followers realize that he is preparing them to do what he has been doing? Do I realize that God is preparing me also by his mighty Word?

"Great Trinity, Father, Son, and Holy Spirit, I am clay in your hands. Make me what you will."

Read the gospel: Matthew 11:25-30.

At that time Jesus said, "I thank you, Father, Lord of heaven and earth, because you have hidden these things from the wise and the intelligent and have revealed them to infants; yes, Father, for such was your gracious will. All things have been handed over to me by my Father; and no one knows the Son except the Father, and no one knows the Father except the Son and anyone to whom the Son chooses to reveal him.

"Come to me, all you that are weary and are carrying heavy burdens, and I will give you rest. Take my yoke upon you, and learn from me; for I am gentle and humble in heart, and you will find rest for your souls. For my yoke is easy, and my burden is light."

Notice what you think and feel as you read the gospel.

The Son has special knowledge of the Father, and the Father has given to the Son all things. As the Father reveals the Son to those he chooses (not to the wise and the intelligent), so the Son reveals the Father to those he chooses. The Son also reveals himself by inviting all who are weary to come and learn from him, the gentle and humble Jesus. In him we will find rest.

Pray as you are led for yourself and others.

"I was created to know and love you, Lord. Draw me by your love and reveal yourself to me, for I am not wise or intelligent. I wait for you, Lord ..." (Continue in your own words.)

Listen to Jesus.

I choose you. I chose you from all eternity. Before the universe was created, you were in my heart. What else is Jesus saying to you?

Ask God to show you how to live today.

"Teach me to walk in your gentleness, Jesus, and with your humble heart let me serve others. Amen."

Monday, July 10, 2017

Know that God is present with you and ready to converse.

"Lord, I know that to call on you for help takes faith. You have called me here to call on you. Increase my faith."

Read the gospel: Matthew 9:18–26.

While he was saying these things to them, suddenly a leader of the synagogue came in and knelt before Jesus, saying, "My daughter has just died; but come and lay your hand on her, and she will live." And Jesus got up and followed him, with his disciples. Then suddenly a woman who had been suffering from hemorrhages for twelve years came up behind him and touched the fringe of his cloak, for she said to herself, "If I only touch his cloak, I will be made well." Jesus turned, and seeing her he said, "Take heart, daughter; your faith has made you well." And instantly the woman was made well. When Jesus came to the leader's house and saw the flute-players and the crowd making a commotion, he said, "Go away; for the girl is not dead but sleeping." And they laughed at him. But when the crowd had been put outside, he went in and took her by the hand, and the girl got up. And the report of this spread throughout that district.

Notice what you think and feel as you read the gospel.

This passage presents a story within a story, both concerning faith. Jesus responds to the faith of the leader of the synagogue and goes with him to heal his daughter. Meanwhile, a long-suffering woman comes up behind him believing that if she can touch his cloak she will be healed. Jesus stops in the crowd and turns to her, saying, "Take heart, daughter; your faith has made you well." She is healed on the spot. But by now the daughter of the leader of the synagogue has died. When Jesus tells the crowd she is only sleeping, they laugh. Jesus takes the girl by the hand, and she gets up. His fame spreads.

Pray as you are led for yourself and others.

"Lord, it often amazes me how important faith is to knowing, loving, and serving you. Faith is not of the head but the heart. Touch my heart with faith, Lord, and touch others . . ." (Continue in your own words.)

Listen to Jesus.

When you ask me for faith, I give it to you. Keep asking, for the world will drain your faith. With faith in God, you can accomplish anything. What else is Jesus saying to you?

Ask God to show you how to live today.

"I want to accomplish what pleases you, precious Lord. Give me whatever faith I need to serve you. Keep me from setting limits upon the power of God in my life and the lives of others. Amen."

Tuesday, July 11, 2017

Know that God is present with you and ready to converse.

"I am here with you, Lord. I come to do your will. Open my heart to your Word."

Read the gospel: Matthew 9:32–38.

After they had gone away, a demoniac who was mute was brought to Jesus. And when the demon had been cast out, the one who had been mute spoke; and the crowds were amazed and said, "Never has anything like this been seen in Israel." But the Pharisees said, "By the ruler of the demons he casts out the demons."

Then Jesus went about all the cities and villages, teaching in their synagogues, and proclaiming the good news of the kingdom, and curing every disease and every sickness. When he saw the crowds, he had compassion for them, because they were harassed and helpless, like sheep without a shepherd. Then he said to his disciples, "The harvest is plentiful, but the laborers are few; therefore ask the Lord of the harvest to send out laborers into his harvest."

Notice what you think and feel as you read the gospel.

While the Pharisees criticize him, Jesus does his healing miracles and proclaims the kingdom of God. He loves these people because they need him as sheep need a shepherd. He turns to his disciples and asks them to pray that the Lord send workers to bring in his harvest. It starts with prayer!

Pray as you are led for yourself and others.

"Father, send laborers to bring in your harvest for people are wandering aimlessly in the dark without you. Deputize me to serve others in your compassion. I pray also for . . ." (Continue in your own words.)

Listen to Jesus.

This is the work of my Father: loving. There are many ways to love. When your heart is full of love, do whatever God gives you to do. What else is Jesus saying to you?

Ask God to show you how to live today.

"I need love like yours to serve others as you did, Jesus. Thank you for giving me this high and worthy work of loving. I resolve to be faithful in this service. Amen."

Wednesday, July 12, 2017

Know that God is present with you and ready to converse.

"Almighty God, you yourself are the kingdom of heaven and you have drawn near to me. Speak to me by your Word."

Read the gospel: Matthew 10:1–7.

Then Jesus summoned his twelve disciples and gave them authority over unclean spirits, to cast them out, and to cure every disease and every sickness. These are the names of the twelve apostles: first, Simon, also known as Peter, and his brother Andrew; James son of Zebedee, and his brother John; Philip and Bartholomew; Thomas and Matthew the tax-collector; James son of Alphaeus, and Thaddaeus; Simon the Cananaean, and Judas Iscariot, the one who betrayed him.

These twelve Jesus sent out with the following instructions: "Go nowhere among the Gentiles, and enter no town of the Samaritans, but go rather to the lost sheep of the house of Israel. As you go, proclaim the good news, 'The kingdom of heaven has come near.'"

Notice what you think and feel as you read the gospel.

Jesus gives his disciples power to cast out unclean spirits and to heal diseases among the Jews. Later, the Church would understand his command to preach the Gospel to all people. What is this Gospel? That the kingdom of heaven has come near.

Pray as you are led for yourself and others.

"Lord Jesus Christ, you are present with your Church, with your followers, and with me. Let me bear your good news to others in authentic ways. I pray for all those who preach the Gospel . . ." (Continue in your own words.)

Listen to Jesus.

I raise up servants to proclaim the Gospel in every generation, beloved. Some are persecuted and martyred. They need your prayers. What else is Jesus saying to you?

Ask God to show you how to live today.

"Lord, remind me of the sacrifices of those who preach and live the Gospel in difficult places and let me return often to pray for them. Amen."

Thursday, July 13, 2017

Know that God is present with you and ready to converse.

"Unchanging God, you make all things new through your Son, our Lord Jesus Christ. Renew me by your Word."

Read the gospel: Matthew 10:7–15.

Jesus said, "As you go, proclaim the good news, 'The kingdom of heaven has come near.' Cure the sick, raise the dead, cleanse the lepers, cast out demons. You received without payment; give without payment. Take no gold, or silver, or copper in your belts, no bag for your journey, or two tunics, or sandals, or a staff; for laborers deserve their food. Whatever town or village you enter, find out who in it is worthy, and stay there until you leave. As you enter the house, greet it. If the house is worthy, let your peace come upon it; but if it is not worthy, let your peace return to you. If anyone will not welcome you or listen to your words, shake off the dust from your feet as you leave that house or town. Truly I tell you, it will be more tolerable for the land of Sodom and Gomorrah on the day of judgement than for that town."

Notice what you think and feel as you read the gospel.

Sending them out, Jesus commands his disciples to use the authority he has given them to work wonders as they proclaim the Good News of the kingdom. They are to give as they received: without pay. If people receive you, stay; if people do not receive you, go. The consequences are dire for those who reject the Gospel, but the preachers must move on.

Pray as you are led for yourself and others.

"Lord, I am not worthy to serve you in carrying your Gospel to others, but I seek to obey you. Give me the power I need to do that bravely, selflessly, and honestly. I pray for these people . . ." (Continue in your own words.)

Listen to Jesus.

Beloved disciple, I work through you. You are working, but it is I who am bringing in the harvest and gathering the fruit of your efforts. Do not be discouraged by what seems like small results. I do all things well. What else is Jesus saying to you?

Ask God to show you how to live today.

"Lord, I give you all that I am and all that I have to use as you see fit today. Thank you for this wonderful privilege to work for you and with you for the good of others. Amen."

Friday, July 14, 2017

Know that God is present with you and ready to converse.

"God in heaven, still center of peace and love, you expand your presence to engulf me here and now. I praise your holy name."

Read the gospel: Matthew 10:16–23.

Jesus said, "See, I am sending you out like sheep into the midst of wolves; so be wise as serpents and innocent as doves. Beware of them, for they will hand you over to councils and flog you in their synagogues; and you will be dragged before governors and kings because of me, as a testimony to them and the Gentiles. When they hand you over, do not worry about how you are to speak or what you are to say; for what you are to say will be given to you at that time; for it is not you who speak, but the Spirit of your Father speaking through you. Brother will betray brother to death, and a father his child, and children will rise against parents and have them put to death; and you will be hated by all because of my name. But the one who endures to the end will be saved. When they persecute you in one town, flee to the next; for truly I tell you, you will not have gone through all the towns of Israel before the Son of Man comes."

Notice what you think and feel as you read the gospel.

Jesus describes the great turmoil of the missionary life of his Church on earth. His followers are sheep in the midst of wolves. He wants them to be wise to reality but innocent. They don't need to prepare their speeches but only trust that the Spirit of God the Father will speak through them in every situation.

Pray as you are led for yourself and others.

"Jesus, Son of Man, you are coming again. No one knows when. I pray for all those who witness to you throughout the world. Spirit of God, protect, inspire, and strengthen them . . ." (Continue in your own words.)

Listen to Jesus.

The world longs for peace, dear disciple, but peace is found only in God. As the world abandons God, it reverts to sin and violence, for evil cannot abide the good. What else is Jesus saying to you?

Ask God to show you how to live today.

"Lord, make me an instrument of your peace. How may I make peace in my own world? Amen."

Saturday, July 15, 2017

Know that God is present with you and ready to converse.

"God, you are so high and great that no mind can grasp you or know your ways. Yet you invite me into your presence. Give me ears to hear your Word."

Read the gospel: Matthew 10:24–33.

Jesus said, "A disciple is not above the teacher, nor a slave above the master; it is enough for the disciple to be like the teacher, and the slave like the master. If they have called the master of the house Beelzebul, how much more will they malign those of his household!

"So have no fear of them; for nothing is covered up that will not be uncovered, and nothing secret that will not become known. What I say to you in the dark, tell in the light; and what you hear whispered, proclaim from the housetops. Do not fear those who kill the body but cannot kill the soul; rather fear him who can destroy both soul and body in hell. Are not two sparrows sold for a penny? Yet not one of them will fall to the ground unperceived by your Father. And even the hairs of your head are all counted. So do not be afraid; you are of more value than many sparrows.

"Everyone therefore who acknowledges me before others, I also will acknowledge before my Father in heaven; but whoever denies me before others, I also will deny before my Father in heaven."

Notice what you think and feel as you read the gospel.

Jesus instructs his followers to have no fear. Yes, the world will treat them as it treated him, maligning, persecuting, and even killing them. But God values those who do God's work, and death cannot separate the servant from the Master's reward. Meanwhile, those who hear the Gospel must decide either to receive it or reject it.

Pray as you are led for yourself and others.

"Lord, there are so many distractions from the message of your Gospel. I pray that you clear the air so your simple message can go out. I pray that many will choose you . . ." (Continue in your own words.)

Listen to Jesus.

My sheep hear my voice, as you do, gentle disciple. I call my own, and they come to me. Be at peace. What else is Jesus saying to you?

Ask God to show you how to live today.

"Help me to be fearless today, Master, for who can hurt me if you are with me? I offer myself to do your works of love and mercy. Amen."

Sunday, July 16, 2017
Fifteenth Sunday in Ordinary Time

Know that God is present with you and ready to converse.

The gospels tell of the words and actions of God-with-us. God loved us so much that God came to us as one of us to save us from the death we brought upon ourselves through sin. In Jesus, God does what a true Father would do. Jesus, God's own Son, speaks and does whatever his Father asks of him.

"Mysterious Lord, what wonders you have done and are doing! I marvel that I am included among your friends. Let me love you and your Word."

Read the gospel: Matthew 13:1–23.

That same day Jesus went out of the house and sat beside the lake. Such great crowds gathered around him that he got into a boat and sat there, while the whole crowd stood on the beach. And he told them many things in parables, saying: "Listen! A sower went out to sow. And as he sowed, some seeds fell on the path, and the birds came and ate them up. Other seeds fell on rocky ground, where they did not have much soil, and they sprang up quickly, since they had no depth of soil. But when the sun rose, they were scorched; and since they had no root, they withered away. Other seeds fell among thorns, and the thorns grew up and choked them. Other seeds fell on good soil and brought forth grain, some a hundredfold, some sixty, some thirty. Let anyone with ears listen!"

Then the disciples came and asked him, "Why do you speak to them in parables?" He answered, "To you it has been given to know the secrets of the kingdom of heaven, but to them it has not been given. For to those who have, more will be given, and they will have an abundance; but from those who have nothing, even what they have will be taken away. The reason I speak to them in parables is that 'seeing they do not perceive, and hearing they do not listen, nor do they understand.' With them indeed is fulfilled the prophecy of Isaiah that says:

'You will indeed listen, but never understand,
and you will indeed look, but never perceive.
For this people's heart has grown dull,
and their ears are hard of hearing,
and they have shut their eyes;
so that they might not look with their eyes,
and listen with their ears,
and understand with their heart and turn—
and I would heal them.'

But blessed are your eyes, for they see, and your ears, for they hear. Truly I tell you, many prophets and righteous people longed to see what you see, but did not see it, and to hear what you hear, but did not hear it.

"Hear then the parable of the sower. When anyone hears the word of the kingdom and does not understand it, the evil one comes and snatches away what is sown in the heart; this is what was sown on the path. As for what was sown on rocky ground, this is the one who hears the word and immediately receives it with joy; yet such a person has no root, but endures only for a while, and when trouble or persecution arises on account of the word, that person immediately falls away. As for what was sown among thorns, this is the one who hears the word, but the cares of the world and the lure of wealth choke the word, and it yields nothing. But as for what was sown on good soil, this is the one who hears the word and understands it, who indeed bears fruit and yields, in one case a hundredfold, in another sixty, and in another thirty."

Notice what you think and feel as you read the gospel.

The parable of the sower is a challenge to all who hear God's Word—one must take it in deeply for it to grow and bear fruit. The words of Isaiah describe people whose hearts are dull, eyes are blind, and ears are deaf to the Word of God. Too bad, because God has the power to teach and heal them.

Pray as you are led for yourself and others.

"Lord, do not allow me to be smug in thinking I am not one of those who resists your words. I, too, am vulnerable to the world, the flesh, and the devil. Let your Word be deeply rooted in me . . ." (Continue in your own words.)

Listen to Jesus.

You are blessed, my child. I plant my Word in you, and it cannot return to me void. Let it grow within you and your blessing shall flow to others. What else is Jesus saying to you?

Ask God to show you how to live today.

"I thank you, Lord, for calling me your child, for that is what I long to be. Simplify me that I may see and hear and understand only you. Amen."

Monday, July 17, 2017

Know that God is present with you and ready to converse.

"Lord, what would you have me learn from you today? Be present for me in your Word."

Read the gospel: Matthew 10:34–11:1.

Jesus said, "Do not think that I have come to bring peace to the earth; I have not come to bring peace, but a sword.

"For I have come to set a man against his father, and a daughter against her mother, and a daughter-in-law against her mother-in-law; and one's foes will be members of one's own household.

"Whoever loves father or mother more than me is not worthy of me; and whoever loves son or daughter more than me is not worthy of me; and whoever does not take up the cross and follow me is not worthy of me. Those who find their life will lose it, and those who lose their life for my sake will find it.

"Whoever welcomes you welcomes me, and whoever welcomes me welcomes the one who sent me. Whoever welcomes a prophet in the name of a prophet will receive a prophet's reward; and whoever welcomes a righteous person in the name of a righteous person will receive the reward of the righteous; and whoever gives even a cup of cold water to one of these little ones in the name of a disciple—truly I tell you, none of these will lose their reward."

Now when Jesus had finished instructing his twelve disciples, he went on from there to teach and proclaim his message in their cities.

Notice what you think and feel as you read the gospel.

Jesus teaches his disciples that his Gospel will divide people. Jesus asks for complete devotion from his followers—that they choose him before all family, that they take up their cross and follow him, and that they understand that only in losing their life for his sake will they find it. Such devoted followers will be rewarded by God.

Pray as you are led for yourself and others.

"Lord, I fall short of such single-minded devotion, but I offer myself to you all the same. Strengthen me in my inner self to embrace my cross and follow you . . ." (Continue in your own words.)

Listen to Jesus.

Following me, dear disciple, is not easy but I will help you. I ask you for everything, but I give you everything, too. I give you myself. Walk with me. What else is Jesus saying to you?

Ask God to show you how to live today.

"Let me walk today in the awareness that you are in me and I am in you. Let me be a blessing to those you have given me. Amen."

Tuesday, July 18, 2017

Know that God is present with you and ready to converse.
"Almighty God, you will judge all people, the living and the dead. Lord, what must I do to be saved?"

Read the gospel: Matthew 11:20–24.
Then Jesus began to reproach the cities in which most of his deeds of power had been done, because they did not repent. "Woe to you, Chorazin! Woe to you, Bethsaida! For if the deeds of power done in you had been done in Tyre and Sidon, they would have repented long ago in sackcloth and ashes. But I tell you, on the day of judgement it will be more tolerable for Tyre and Sidon than for you. And you, Capernaum, will you be exalted to heaven? No, you will be brought down to Hades. For if the deeds of power done in you had been done in Sodom, it would have remained until this day. But I tell you that on the day of judgement it will be more tolerable for the land of Sodom than for you."

Notice what you think and feel as you read the gospel.
Jesus pronounces woe upon the cities that witnessed his works of power but did not repent. He reproaches those who do not see their need to repent and the danger of not repenting. He speaks here of cities and their collective guilt.

Pray as you are led for yourself and others.
"Lord, I am part of a community—several communities, in fact. Let me be one of those who hears you and obeys you for the good of the whole community. At the judgment, let my community stand and live. I pray for these . . ." (Continue in your own words.)

Listen to Jesus.
You see how people, nations, and cities ignore my warnings. People, nations, and cities also heed my warnings, repent, and escape judgment. What else is Jesus saying to you?

Ask God to show you how to live today.
"Lord, make me mindful of the guilt of my community, and let me join with those who take the lead in repenting and making amends. I ask you to help me live this way always. May your goodness spread over all the earth. Amen."

Wednesday, July 19, 2017

Know that God is present with you and ready to converse.

"God, you are here to draw me into love and knowledge of yourself. I seek to respond to your initiative."

Read the gospel: Matthew 11:25–27.

At that time Jesus said, "I thank you, Father, Lord of heaven and earth, because you have hidden these things from the wise and the intelligent and have revealed them to infants; yes, Father, for such was your gracious will. All things have been handed over to me by my Father; and no one knows the Son except the Father, and no one knows the Father except the Son and anyone to whom the Son chooses to reveal him."

Notice what you think and feel as you read the gospel.

Jesus is grateful that God reveals divine truth to infants, not to those who are wise in their own eyes. The Father's gracious will is to be revealed to whomever the Son chooses to reveal him.

Pray as you are led for yourself and others.

"I rejoice with you, Jesus, in the wise and loving ways of your and my Father. Continue to reveal the Father to me and to those you have given me . . ." (Continue in your own words.)

Listen to Jesus.

Beloved, you can know God and love God more and more. I give you that gift, a gift unto eternity. What else is Jesus saying to you?

Ask God to show you how to live today.

"Lord, I receive what you give me though I cannot take it in. Increase my capacity for God moment by moment, hour by hour. Amen."

Thursday, July 20, 2017

Know that God is present with you and ready to converse.

"Gentle Jesus, I am carrying some heavy burdens. Come and give me rest. I listen, Lord."

Read the gospel: Matthew 11:28–30.

Jesus said, "Come to me, all you that are weary and are carrying heavy burdens, and I will give you rest. Take my yoke upon you, and learn from me; for I am gentle and humble in heart, and you will find rest for your souls. For my yoke is easy, and my burden is light."

Notice what you think and feel as you read the gospel.

Jesus invites to himself all who are weary and overwhelmed by their burdens. Promising us rest, he asks us to take up his yoke, for his yoke is easy and his burden light. At the heart of his message is his description of himself as gentle and humble of heart. We can learn that from him.

Pray as you are led for yourself and others.

"Lord, give me your gentle, humble heart. That will make my burden light. I pray that I may love others with the love that you gave me . . ." (Continue in your own words.)

Listen to Jesus.

The yoke I offer you, beloved, is love: love for God and love for others. This is where you will find rest. What else is Jesus saying to you?

Ask God to show you how to live today.

"Today you make it sound so easy, Lord. Let me come to you morning, noon, and night, loving you and loving others. Amen."

Friday, July 21, 2017

Know that God is present with you and ready to converse.

"Without you, Lord, people misunderstand and thwart your purposes. Thank you for being present with me now as I receive your Word."

Read the gospel: Matthew 12:1–8.

At that time Jesus went through the cornfields on the sabbath; his disciples were hungry, and they began to pluck heads of grain and to eat. When the Pharisees saw it, they said to him, "Look, your disciples are doing what is not lawful to do on the sabbath." He said to them, "Have you not read what David did when he and his companions were hungry? He entered the house of God and ate the bread of the Presence, which it was not lawful for him or his companions to eat, but only for the priests. Or have you not read in the law that on the sabbath the priests in the temple break the sabbath and yet are guiltless? I tell you, something greater than the temple is here. But if you had known what this means, 'I desire mercy and not sacrifice,' you would not have condemned the guiltless. For the Son of Man is lord of the sabbath."

Notice what you think and feel as you read the gospel.

Earnest people can misunderstand the freedoms of God. Jesus allows his disciples freedoms because he is with them. It's not about laws and temples and prescribed observances, he says. Knowing God is the purpose of all religious practices. We are to practice mercy first.

Pray as you are led for yourself and others.

"Lord, let me not judge others in their religious practices. Let me regard them with mercy, praying that they find you in all they do . . ." (Continue in your own words.)

Listen to Jesus.

I will that all people come to know God, for God exists and rewards all who seek God. In God's Son you may find the truth that sets you free. What else is Jesus saying to you?

Ask God to show you how to live today.

"Breathe yourself into all I do today, Lord. Let me know the freedom of walking with you in obedience. Amen."

Saturday, July 22, 2017
Saint Mary Magdalene

Know that God is present with you and ready to converse.

"Jesus, you are present. Teacher, speak my name."

Read the gospel: John 20:1–2, 11–18.

Early on the first day of the week, while it was still dark, Mary Magdalene came to the tomb and saw that the stone had been removed from the tomb. So she ran and went to Simon Peter and the other disciple, the one whom Jesus loved, and said to them, "They have taken the Lord out of the tomb, and we do not know where they have laid him." . . .

But Mary stood weeping outside the tomb. As she wept, she bent over to look into the tomb; and she saw two angels in white, sitting where the body of Jesus had been lying, one at the head and the other at the feet. They said to her, "Woman, why are you weeping?" She said to them, "They have taken away my Lord, and I do not know where they have laid him." When she had said this, she turned round and saw Jesus standing there, but she did not know that it was Jesus. Jesus said to her, "Woman, why are you weeping? For whom are you looking?" Supposing him to be the gardener, she said to him, "Sir, if you have carried him away, tell me where you have laid him, and I will take him away." Jesus said to her, "Mary!" She turned and said to him in Hebrew, "Rabbouni!" (which means Teacher). Jesus said to her, "Do not hold on to me, because I have not yet ascended to the Father. But go to my brothers and say to them, 'I am ascending to my Father and your Father, to my God and your God.'" Mary Magdalene went and announced to the disciples, "I have seen the Lord"; and she told them that he had said these things to her.

Notice what you think and feel as you read the gospel.

On the day of his resurrection, Jesus reveals himself to his friend Mary. It's odd that she doesn't recognize him at first, but then when he speaks her name she does. He gives her the privilege of announcing to the disciples that she has seen the Lord, risen from the dead. This indeed was a reality that would take a while to sink in. It would soon change the world.

Pray as you are led for yourself and others.

"Lord, I have not seen you risen from the dead as Mary did, yet I believe in you. By your Spirit you now walk with me and talk with me. Thank you, dear Jesus . . ." (Continue in your own words.)

Listen to Jesus.

I am with you, beloved. I am. How may I bless you? What else is Jesus saying to you?

Ask God to show you how to live today.

"Let me more fully grasp the wonderful truth of your resurrection, Jesus. I feel that if I can really take it in, I will be changed forever for the better. Amen."

Sunday, July 23, 2017
Sixteenth Sunday in Ordinary Time

Know that God is present with you and ready to converse.

Spiritual truth: How is it learned and how is it taught? Jesus Christ came to tell us the truth. Yet he spoke to critics, skeptics, unbelievers, and the simple-minded, as well as to those who received him readily. His method was to speak in many parables. His parables present everyday stories or realities to teach the great spiritual truths about God and the kingdom of heaven.

"Word of God, I have confidence that you will lead me into the truth I need; the Holy Spirit is here to teach me."

Read the gospel: Matthew 13:24–43.

Jesus put before them another parable: "The kingdom of heaven may be compared to someone who sowed good seed in his field; but while everybody was asleep, an enemy came and sowed weeds among the wheat, and then went away. So when the plants came up and bore grain, then the weeds appeared as well. And the slaves of the householder came and said to him, 'Master, did you not sow good seed in your field? Where, then, did these weeds come from?' He answered, 'An enemy has done this.' The slaves said to him, 'Then do you want us to go and gather them?' But he replied, 'No; for in gathering the weeds you would uproot the wheat along with them. Let both of them grow together until the harvest; and at harvest time I will tell the reapers, Collect the weeds first and bind them in bundles to be burned, but gather the wheat into my barn.'"

He put before them another parable: "The kingdom of heaven is like a mustard seed that someone took and sowed in his field; it is the smallest of all the seeds, but when it has grown it is the greatest of shrubs and becomes a tree, so that the birds of the air come and make nests in its branches."

He told them another parable: "The kingdom of heaven is like yeast that a woman took and mixed in with three measures of flour until all of it was leavened."

Jesus told the crowds all these things in parables; without a parable he told them nothing. This was to fulfill what had been spoken through the prophet:

> "I will open my mouth to speak in parables;
> I will proclaim what has been hidden from the founda-
> tion of the world."

Then he left the crowds and went into the house. And his disciples approached him, saying, "Explain to us the parable of the weeds of the field." He answered, "The one who sows the good seed is the Son of Man; the field is the world, and the good seed are the children of the kingdom; the weeds are the children of the evil one, and the enemy who sowed them is the devil; the harvest is the end of the age, and the reapers are angels. Just as the weeds are collected and burned up with fire, so will it be at the end of the age. The Son of Man will send his angels, and they will collect out of his kingdom all causes of sin and all evildoers, and they will throw them into the furnace of fire, where there will be weeping and gnashing of teeth. Then the righteous will shine like the sun in the kingdom of their Father. Let anyone with ears listen!"

Notice what you think and feel as you read the gospel.

These parables speak of good and evil existing together in this life, especially the parable of the wheat and the weeds, which Jesus explains to his inner circle of disciples. The truth that has been hidden from the foundation of the world is that God is good. The righteous will shine like the sun in the kingdom of their Father, but the evil will perish. In the meantime, wheat and weeds grow up together.

Pray as you are led for yourself and others.

"Lord, make me worthy to shine like the sun in your kingdom, though I am a sinner. I entrust myself to your care. I also entrust to you those you have given me . . ." (Continue in your own words.)

Listen to Jesus.

Be patient, beloved disciple. These things will come to pass. Your task is to persevere in this time of mercy, for my Father would gather all people into the kingdom. Pray and work as I show you. What else is Jesus saying to you?

Ask God to show you how to live today.

"You came to save sinners, Jesus. A saved sinner myself, how may I join you in this work? Amen."

Monday, July 24, 2017

Know that God is present with you and ready to converse.

"Jesus, let your words, familiar or new, enflame my heart and transform me. Make of me what you will."

Read the gospel: Matthew 12:38–42.

Then some of the scribes and Pharisees said to Jesus, "Teacher, we wish to see a sign from you." But he answered them, "An evil and adulterous generation asks for a sign, but no sign will be given to it except the sign of the prophet Jonah. For just as Jonah was for three days and three nights in the belly of the sea monster, so for three days and three nights the Son of Man will be in the heart of the earth. The people of Nineveh will rise up at the judgement with this generation and condemn it, because they repented at the proclamation of Jonah, and see, something greater than Jonah is here! The queen of the South will rise up at the judgement with this generation and condemn it, because she came from the ends of the earth to listen to the wisdom of Solomon, and see, something greater than Solomon is here!"

Notice what you think and feel as you read the gospel.

It seems so natural to ask for a sign from Jesus—after all, he has been performing many miracles. But Jesus refuses, pointing cryptically to a sign that is yet to come: his rising from the dead. This is the sign of Jonah. He, standing before them, is greater than Jonah, greater than wise Solomon, yet they do not repent.

Pray as you are led for yourself and others.

"Reveal to me all my faults, Savior, so I may repent of all my sins. I am truly sorry for the evil I have done and do. Make me clean and pleasing to you, fit to serve in your name . . ." (Continue in your own words.)

Listen to Jesus.

I forgive you, beloved disciple, and wash you. I am preparing you for eternal life with God, who is holy. What else is Jesus saying to you?

Ask God to show you how to live today.

"Lord, let me walk in your life today, confident of your work in me, always attentive to your correction and your leading. Amen."

Tuesday, July 25, 2017
Saint James, Apostle

Know that God is present with you and ready to converse.

"Lord of heaven and earth, give me a heart to understand what you have for me today. Nourish me with the bread of your Word."

Read the gospel: Matthew 20:20–28.

Then the mother of the sons of Zebedee came to Jesus with her sons, and kneeling before him, she asked a favor of him. And he said to her, "What do you want?" She said to him, "Declare that these two sons of mine will sit, one at your right hand and one at your left, in your kingdom." But Jesus answered, "You do not know what you are asking. Are you able to drink the cup that I am about to drink?" They said to him, "We are able." He said to them, "You will indeed drink my cup, but to sit at my right hand and at my left, this is not mine to grant, but it is for those for whom it has been prepared by my Father."

When the ten heard it, they were angry with the two brothers. But Jesus called them to him and said, "You know that the rulers of the Gentiles lord it over them, and their great ones are tyrants over them. It will not be so among you; but whoever wishes to be great among you must be your servant, and whoever wishes to be first among you must be your slave; just as the Son of Man came not to be served but to serve, and to give his life a ransom for many."

Notice what you think and feel as you read the gospel.

The sons of Zebedee and their mother are ambitious. They want to be seated next to Jesus in the kingdom. Jesus tells them that that is something only his Father can grant. When the other disciples become angry with the two, Jesus gives them all a lesson in greatness. Among his followers, the great are servants, even as he came to serve and give his life for others.

Pray as you are led for yourself and others.

"Lord, I, too, wish to be great in your kingdom. Let me drink your cup of service, even if it involves suffering. I offer it all to you for the good of others, especially . . ." (Continue in your own words.)

Listen to Jesus.

I rejoice in your prayers, beloved. I love you and also those I have given you. Continue to pray and to serve in the joy I give you. What else is Jesus saying to you?

Ask God to show you how to live today.

"Jesus, you give my life meaning and purpose. Keep me tuned to that as I fulfill my duties today. All for you, Lord. Amen."

Wednesday, July 26, 2017

Know that God is present with you and ready to converse.

"Lord, let me listen to your Word. Let it take root in me."

Read the gospel: Matthew 13:1–9.

That same day Jesus went out of the house and sat beside the lake. Such great crowds gathered around him that he got into a boat and sat there, while the whole crowd stood on the beach. And he told them many things in parables, saying: "Listen! A sower went out to sow. And as he sowed, some seeds fell on the path, and the birds came and ate them up.

Other seeds fell on rocky ground, where they did not have much soil, and they sprang up quickly, since they had no depth of soil. But when the sun rose, they were scorched; and since they had no root, they withered away. Other seeds fell among thorns, and the thorns grew up and choked them. Other seeds fell on good soil and brought forth grain, some a hundredfold, some sixty, some thirty. Let anyone with ears listen!"

Notice what you think and feel as you read the gospel.

This familiar parable understands the great power of the Word of God to bear fruit. But much of the seed the sower casts is wasted: the seeds and the plants are eaten up, scorched, and choked before they can bring forth grain. The seeds that fall on good soil yield abundant grain. This is the way it is and always has been.

Pray as you are led for yourself and others.

"You know what you are doing, Lord, sowing your seeds among all people and all nations, and I pray for the harvest. Let many have ears to hear your saving words, and let those many bear much fruit throughout the world . . ." (Continue in your own words.)

Listen to Jesus.

My Father often accomplishes his purposes through the agency of people. If some refuse to do God's work my Father raises up others who will. Pray for the coming of God's kingdom. What else is Jesus saying to you?

Ask God to show you how to live today.

"Lord, I offer myself to you today for the work of the kingdom. By your grace I shall do my work well today, even the most menial tasks. Thank you for allowing me to serve you in others. Amen."

Thursday, July 27, 2017

Know that God is present with you and ready to converse.

"Lord, how mysterious is the working of your Word! I wish to know the secrets of the kingdom, how to enter it. Instruct me now."

Read the gospel: Matthew 13:10–17.

Then the disciples came and asked Jesus, "Why do you speak to them in parables?" He answered, "To you it has been given to know the secrets of the kingdom of heaven, but to them it has not been given. For to those who have, more will be given, and they will have an abundance;

but from those who have nothing, even what they have will be taken away. The reason I speak to them in parables is that 'seeing they do not perceive, and hearing they do not listen, nor do they understand.' With them indeed is fulfilled the prophecy of Isaiah that says:

> 'You will indeed listen, but never understand,
>   and you will indeed look, but never perceive.
> For this people's heart has grown dull,
>   and their ears are hard of hearing,
>   and they have shut their eyes;
>   so that they might not look with their eyes,
>   and listen with their ears,
> and understand with their heart and turn—
>   and I would heal them.'

But blessed are your eyes, for they see, and your ears, for they hear. Truly I tell you, many prophets and righteous people longed to see what you see, but did not see it, and to hear what you hear, but did not hear it."

Notice what you think and feel as you read the gospel.

Jesus explains to his disciples that through parables he can reach those who will listen and confound those who will not. Those who will hear them will have more; those who do not will have less and finally nothing. It seems to be all about one's willingness to hear the Word of the Lord. We are privileged to have the words of Jesus.

Pray as you are led for yourself and others.

"Lord, you bless me with your words of truth. Let me never become dull of heart and deaf to you. I pray also for those you have given me . . ." (Continue in your own words.)

Listen to Jesus.

Do not give up on people, even those who scorn me or are indifferent to what I have to say. Your role is to be salt and light in the world. Love them as I love them and pray for them. What else is Jesus saying to you?

Ask God to show you how to live today.

"Let me see the world and the people in it with eyes of hope, Lord, as you have instructed me. Thank you for showing me your kingdom. Amen."

Friday, July 28, 2017

Know that God is present with you and ready to converse.

"Open your Word to me, Lord. You are with me now to give me what I need. Thank you."

Read the gospel: Matthew 13:18–23.

Jesus said, "Hear then the parable of the sower. When anyone hears the word of the kingdom and does not understand it, the evil one comes and snatches away what is sown in the heart; this is what was sown on the path. As for what was sown on rocky ground, this is the one who hears the word and immediately receives it with joy; yet such a person has no root, but endures only for a while, and when trouble or persecution arises on account of the word, that person immediately falls away. As for what was sown among thorns, this is the one who hears the word, but the cares of the world and the lure of wealth choke the word, and it yields nothing. But as for what was sown on good soil, this is the one who hears the word and understands it, who indeed bears fruit and yields, in one case a hundredfold, in another sixty, and in another thirty."

Notice what you think and feel as you read the gospel.

Jesus explains the parable of the sower. The birds who snatch away the seed represent the evil one. Rocky ground represents the person who is a superficial hearer, who withers under trouble or persecution. As for thorns, they represent the cares of the world and lure of wealth choking the Word. Good soil represents the one who hears and understands it. That one will bear fruit.

Pray as you are led for yourself and others.

"I myself can be superficial or beset by the cares of the world. Prepare my heart to hear and understand your Word, Lord. Let it bring forth fruit . . ." (Continue in your own words.)

Listen to Jesus.

Your concern about your own heart is a good thing. The heart can lead one astray. Rely on me, beloved, and I will carry you through all your troubles so that you will bear fruit to the glory of God. What else is Jesus saying to you?

Ask God to show you how to live today.

"Teach me how to walk in the proper fear of the Lord, not trusting myself but in all things consulting you. Let me lose myself to find you. I glorify you, King of heaven. Amen."

Saturday, July 29, 2017
Saint Martha

Know that God is present with you and ready to converse.

"I turn to your Word, my God, that my faith, hope, and love may grow by it. All those things come from you."

Read the gospel: Luke 10:38–42.

Now as they went on their way, Jesus entered a certain village, where a woman named Martha welcomed him into her home. She had a sister named Mary, who sat at the Lord's feet and listened to what he was saying. But Martha was distracted by her many tasks; so she came to him and asked, "Lord, do you not care that my sister has left me to do all the work by myself? Tell her then to help me." But the Lord answered her, "Martha, Martha, you are worried and distracted by many things; there is need of only one thing. Mary has chosen the better part, which will not be taken away from her."

Notice what you think and feel as you read the gospel.

Jesus' friend Martha runs the house and does all the work. After all, they have guests. Her sister Mary just wants to sit at Jesus' feet and listen. Martha wants Jesus to ask Mary to help her. Jesus is sympathetic but gently corrects her. Only one thing is important, and Mary has chosen it rightly.

Pray as you are led for yourself and others.

"When I am prone to judge my brother or sister, Lord, correct me. Is it possible for me to serve others and listen to you at the same time?" (Continue in your own words.)

Listen to Jesus.

I call people in different ways and give my disciples different tasks. You are one of a kind, my child, and I have placed you where you are for many good reasons. Commit your ways to me, and I will lead you and help you in your work. What else is Jesus saying to you?

Ask God to show you how to live today.

"I follow you, Lord. I rejoice in your care for me and your guidance. How may I please you today? Amen."

Sunday, July 30, 2017
Seventeenth Sunday in Ordinary Time

Know that God is present with you and ready to converse.

Eternal God, Creator and Sustainer of all that is, you sent your Son to save us. He gave his life to save mine and the lives of all who come to him. He spoke your words to teach us how to live and walk in your presence. What love you have shown to us, Lord!

"Your Word is a treasure. I am ready to hear your Word and draw nearer to you."

Read the gospel: Matthew 13:44–52.

Jesus said, "The kingdom of heaven is like treasure hidden in a field, which someone found and hid; then in his joy he goes and sells all that he has and buys that field.

"Again, the kingdom of heaven is like a merchant in search of fine pearls; on finding one pearl of great value, he went and sold all that he had and bought it.

"Again, the kingdom of heaven is like a net that was thrown into the sea and caught fish of every kind; when it was full, they drew it ashore, sat down, and put the good into baskets but threw out the bad. So it will be at the end of the age. The angels will come out and separate the evil from the righteous and throw them into the furnace of fire, where there will be weeping and gnashing of teeth.

"Have you understood all this?" They answered, "Yes." And he said to them, "Therefore every scribe who has been trained for the kingdom of heaven is like the master of a household who brings out of his treasure what is new and what is old."

Notice what you think and feel as you read the gospel.

Finding God, knowing God, is the treasure that outshines all other things, for through God we enter the kingdom of heaven. Even now we participate in the kingdom even though life is full of good and bad. We can trust that in the end good will prevail and evil will perish. The treasure we find is eternal life with God.

Pray as you are led for yourself and others.

"Sometimes I am discouraged by difficulties, Lord, but I rejoice to possess your treasure, the pearl of greatest value, yourself. Keep my eyes on you, Jesus. I pray now for those I know who labor under difficulties . . ." (Continue in your own words.)

Listen to Jesus.

Your job is to pray. I give you precious souls to pray for. Give them to me as often as I put it into your heart. This is great service for the kingdom of God. What else is Jesus saying to you?

Ask God to show you how to live today.

"Prayer is my gate to you, Lord. Prayer is our ongoing friendship. Keep me in prayer all day, dear Jesus. Amen."

Monday, July 31, 2017

Know that God is present with you and ready to converse.

"Lord, your Word has power when received in your Spirit. I call upon the Holy Spirit to quicken your Word in me."

Read the gospel: Matthew 13:31–35.

Jesus put before them another parable: "The kingdom of heaven is like a mustard seed that someone took and sowed in his field; it is the smallest of all the seeds, but when it has grown it is the greatest of shrubs and becomes a tree, so that the birds of the air come and make nests in its branches."

He told them another parable: "The kingdom of heaven is like yeast that a woman took and mixed in with three measures of flour until all of it was leavened."

Jesus told the crowds all these things in parables; without a parable he told them nothing. This was to fulfill what had been spoken through the prophet:

> "I will open my mouth to speak in parables;
> I will proclaim what has been hidden from the foundation of the world."

Notice what you think and feel as you read the gospel.

The kingdom Jesus preaches is like a mustard seed or yeast. It starts small but soon magnifies itself in the world. This is a great secret we now know, and a reason for our hope.

Pray as you are led for yourself and others.

"Lord, you work in the world in mysterious ways, making the small great and the great small. You can even take me in my brokenness and restore me to love and serve others to the glory of God. In gratitude I pray for these . . ." (Continue in your own words.)

Listen to Jesus.

I am pleased to give you the kingdom, beloved servant. Let us continue on the way together. What else is Jesus saying to you?

Ask God to show you how to live today.

"Even in suffering and sorrow, your closeness is a joy to me, Lord. Let me be mindful today of that, especially when I am hurting. I love you, Jesus, Savior and Shepherd. Amen."

Tuesday, August 1, 2017

Know that God is present with you and ready to converse.

"Jesus, you said those who love and obey you hear your voice. Let me hear it now as I pray with this gospel."

Read the gospel: Matthew 13:36–43.

Then Jesus left the crowds and went into the house. And his disciples approached him, saying, "Explain to us the parable of the weeds of the field." He answered, "The one who sows the good seed is the Son of Man; the field is the world, and the good seed are the children of the kingdom; the weeds are the children of the evil one, and the enemy who sowed them is the devil; the harvest is the end of the age, and the reapers are angels. Just as the weeds are collected and burned up with fire, so will it be at the end of the age. The Son of Man will send his angels, and they will collect out of his kingdom all causes of sin and all evildoers, and they will throw them into the furnace of fire, where there will be weeping and gnashing of teeth. Then the righteous will shine like the sun in the kingdom of their Father. Let anyone with ears listen!"

Notice what you think and feel as you read the gospel.

Having left the crowds and gone into the house, the disciples ask Jesus to explain the parable of the weeds. Jesus tells them directly that there will be a judgment at the end of the age. The righteous will be united with the Father in the kingdom; the evildoers thrown into the furnace of fire.

Pray as you are led for yourself and others.

"Lord, perhaps you delay coming back because you want evildoers to repent and come into your kingdom. I adore you for your mercy, not just to me but to these I pray for . . ." (Continue in your own words.)

Listen to Jesus.

God is the judge of the whole earth, my child, and God is just. Justice is the remedy of sin. But now my grace is strong to save those who come to me. What else is Jesus saying to you?

Ask God to show you how to live today.

"Let your justice quicken my obedience to you, Lord, as I seek to walk in your way today. I praise you for your righteous judgments, my God. Amen."

Wednesday, August 2, 2017

Know that God is present with you and ready to converse.

"Renew in me the joy of my salvation as I attend to your Word, Lord God."

Read the gospel: Matthew 13:44–46.

Jesus said, "The kingdom of heaven is like treasure hidden in a field, which someone found and hid; then in his joy he goes and sells all that he has and buys that field.

"Again, the kingdom of heaven is like a merchant in search of fine pearls; on finding one pearl of great value, he went and sold all that he had and bought it."

Notice what you think and feel as you read the gospel.

These parables suggest not only that finding the kingdom of heaven is of great value but also that finding it entails selling (or perhaps letting go of) all that one has formerly considered valuable.

Pray as you are led for yourself and others.

"As you have loved me and called me to your kingdom, I love you and seek to please you. Thank you for your goodness, Savior, to me and to those you have given me . . ." (Continue in your own words.)

Listen to Jesus.

I am so happy that you have received my gifts, beloved disciple. Rejoice with me. What else is Jesus saying to you?

Ask God to show you how to live today.

"How can I keep from singing, since Love is Lord of heaven and earth? Stay close to me all day long, Jesus. Amen."

Thursday, August 3, 2017

Know that God is present with you and ready to converse.

"Lord, your Word is old, but you make all things new. Renew me by your Word."

Read the gospel: Matthew 13:47–53.

Jesus said, "Again, the kingdom of heaven is like a net that was thrown into the sea and caught fish of every kind; when it was full, they drew it ashore, sat down, and put the good into baskets but threw out the bad. So it will be at the end of the age. The angels will come out and separate the evil from the righteous and throw them into the furnace of fire, where there will be weeping and gnashing of teeth.

"Have you understood all this?" They answered, "Yes." And he said to them, "Therefore every scribe who has been trained for the kingdom of heaven is like the master of a household who brings out of his treasure what is new and what is old." When Jesus had finished these parables, he left that place.

Notice what you think and feel as you read the gospel.

The parable of the net concludes like the parable of the weeds, with judgment coming at the end of the age. The parable of the master of the house suggests that the kingdom of heaven is comprised of treasures both old and new.

Pray as you are led for yourself and others.

"Lord, let me not be closed to any of the treasures of your kingdom, neither the old nor the new. Whatever gifts you give, all are good. I thank you for these . . ." (Continue in your own words.)

Listen to Jesus.

I have given you myself, beloved. I am all you need. Give me yourself entirely, and we will journey together. What else is Jesus saying to you?

Ask God to show you how to live today.

"I am yours, Jesus. I will walk with you today if you will lead me. Amen."

Friday, August 4, 2017

Know that God is present with you and ready to converse.

"Stir up my spirit, Lord, and refresh me as I ponder your Word."

Read the gospel: Matthew 13:54–58.

Jesus came to his home town and began to teach the people in their synagogue, so that they were astounded and said, "Where did this man get this wisdom and these deeds of power? Is not this the carpenter's son? Is not his mother called Mary? And are not his brothers James and Joseph and Simon and Judas? And are not all his sisters with us? Where then did this man get all this?" And they took offence at him. But Jesus said to them, "Prophets are not without honor except in their own country and in their own house." And he did not do many deeds of power there, because of their unbelief.

Notice what you think and feel as you read the gospel.

The people who had known Jesus longest are astounded and offended by his words and deeds. Jesus notes their rejection, and because of their unbelief, he does not do many miracles among them.

Pray as you are led for yourself and others.

"Banish from me any familiarity that may breed contempt. You make all things new, Jesus. Open my eyes to your wisdom and power . . ." (Continue in your own words.)

Listen to Jesus.

I will do as you ask, child. Come to me and stay with me a long while, and I will show you wonderful things. What else is Jesus saying to you?

Ask God to show you how to live today.

"Give me the gift of prayer, Lord, for it is the key to our love for one another, and your love will lead me in my work and prayer. Amen."

Saturday, August 5, 2017

Know that God is present with you and ready to converse.

"You know the hearts of all, my God. You are here with me now to search me by your Word."

Read the gospel: Matthew 14:1–12.

At that time Herod the ruler heard reports about Jesus; and he said to his servants, "This is John the Baptist; he has been raised from the dead, and for this reason these powers are at work in him." For Herod had arrested John, bound him, and put him in prison on account of Herodias, his brother Philip's wife, because John had been telling him, "It is not lawful for you to have her." Though Herod wanted to put him to death, he feared the crowd, because they regarded him as a prophet. But when Herod's birthday came, the daughter of Herodias danced before the company, and she pleased Herod so much that he promised on oath to grant her whatever she might ask. Prompted by her mother, she said, "Give me the head of John the Baptist here on a platter." The king was grieved, yet out of regard for his oaths and for the guests, he commanded it to be given; he sent and had John beheaded in the prison. The head was brought on a platter and given to the girl, who brought it to her mother. His disciples came and took the body and buried it; then they went and told Jesus.

Notice what you think and feel as you read the gospel.

This passage shows a deep understanding of Herod's twisted mind. When he hears of Jesus, he guiltily thinks it is John the Baptist, risen from the dead. Herod makes Jesus and his work about himself. Herod had wanted to kill John because he called him an adulterer, but he didn't dare because the crowd considered John a prophet. But Herodias, his unlawful wife, finds a way to manipulate her husband before some guests at his birthday party. Herod orders John's beheading.

Pray as you are led for yourself and others.

"Lord, I pray for those who are corrupt in their power, lust, and violence. Let them repent and make amends. Comfort their victims . . ." (Continue in your own words.)

Listen to Jesus.

So it has ever been that the wicked inflict suffering upon the innocent and the good. I hate their evil deeds, and I come with sure justice. What else is Jesus saying to you?

Ask God to show you how to live today.

"Lord, what can I do today to help those who suffer unjustly at the hands of evildoers? I offer my service. Amen."

Sunday, August 6, 2017
Transfiguration of the Lord

Know that God is present with you and ready to converse.

Jesus Christ revealed to his disciples that he was the Lord, God-with-us, Son of the Father, King of all creation. By their testimony of his words and deeds, they transmit that revelation to us. Jesus Christ is revealed by the Word of God. The revelation of his Truth comes to us through the Holy Spirit.

"Great Trinity of Love and Power, speak to me in the inner recesses of my heart and mind, and let me proclaim you my Lord and my God."

Read the gospel: Matthew 17:1-9.

Six days later, Jesus took with him Peter and James and his brother John and led them up a high mountain, by themselves. And he was transfigured before them, and his face shone like the sun, and his clothes became dazzling white. Suddenly there appeared to them Moses and Elijah, talking with him. Then Peter said to Jesus, "Lord, it is good for us to be here; if you wish, I will make three dwellings here, one for you, one for Moses, and one for Elijah." While he was still speaking, suddenly a bright cloud overshadowed them, and from the cloud a voice said, "This is my Son, the Beloved; with him I am well pleased; listen to him!" When the disciples heard this, they fell to the ground and were overcome by fear. But Jesus came and touched them, saying, "Get up and do not be afraid." And when they looked up, they saw no one except Jesus himself alone.

As they were coming down the mountain, Jesus ordered them, "Tell no one about the vision until after the Son of Man has been raised from the dead."

Notice what you think and feel as you read the gospel.

Jesus calls their experience of his transfiguration a vision, and it is mysterious. Jesus assumes a glorified appearance while he speaks with Moses and Elijah, great prophets of the Jewish scriptures. Then the voice out of the cloud confirms that Jesus is the Son, Beloved of the Father. That experience surely changed the lives of Peter, James, and John forever. They were there. They lived it.

Pray as you are led for yourself and others.

"I seek you, too, Jesus, in all your power and glory. I seek to be beloved of your Father as you are. Lord, satisfy my hunger for God . . ." (Continue in your own words.)

Listen to Jesus.

Your desire for me is my desire for you, dear child. You are beloved of God, and God seeks your love in return. Do you love me? What else is Jesus saying to you?

Ask God to show you how to live today.

"Lord, let me walk today as a beloved child of the Father. Let me know it in my inner being and live it in my life. Amen."

Monday, August 7, 2017

Know that God is present with you and ready to converse.

"Lord, I have all I need when I have you. You give yourself to me by your Spirit and your Word. I praise you!"

Read the gospel: Matthew 14:13–21.

Now when Jesus heard this, he withdrew from there in a boat to a deserted place by himself. But when the crowds heard it, they followed him on foot from the towns. When he went ashore, he saw a great crowd; and he had compassion for them and cured their sick. When it was evening, the disciples came to him and said, "This is a deserted place, and the hour is now late; send the crowds away so that they may go into the villages and buy food for themselves." Jesus said to them, "They need not go away; you give them something to eat." They replied, "We have nothing here but five loaves and two fish." And he said, "Bring them here to me." Then he ordered the crowds to sit down on the grass. Taking the five loaves and the two fish, he looked up to heaven, and blessed and broke the loaves, and gave them to the disciples, and the disciples gave them to the crowds. And all ate and were filled; and they took up what was left over of the broken pieces, twelve baskets full. And those who ate were about five thousand men, besides women and children.

Notice what you think and feel as you read the gospel.

Jesus' disciples are very practical about crowd management. Jesus sees the situation as a further opportunity to show his compassion. First he heals the sick, and then he feeds them all, far more than five thousand people. He blesses the food, but he asks the disciples to distribute it among the crowd. They had to have been amazed!

Pray as you are led for yourself and others.

"Lord Jesus, Bread of Life, let me share the Bread you give to me with others. Pour out your compassion through me as so many are sick and hungry . . ." (Continue in your own words.)

Listen to Jesus.
You offer yourself in service of others, in service of me. You are my servant, beloved disciple. I promise to work through you. Stay close to me. What else is Jesus saying to you?

Ask God to show you how to live today.
"I am not worthy of serving you, Lord, and I fail often. Yet I will obey you and serve others with you by my side. Amen."

Tuesday, August 8, 2017

Know that God is present with you and ready to converse.
"Almighty Father, you are the source of faith, which comes to me by hearing the Word of God. Refresh my faith today. Be real to me now."

Read the gospel: Matthew 14:22–36.
Immediately Jesus made the disciples get into the boat and go on ahead to the other side, while he dismissed the crowds. And after he had dismissed the crowds, he went up the mountain by himself to pray. When evening came, he was there alone, but by this time the boat, battered by the waves, was far from the land, for the wind was against them. And early in the morning he came walking towards them on the lake. But when the disciples saw him walking on the lake, they were terrified, saying, "It is a ghost!" And they cried out in fear. But immediately Jesus spoke to them and said, "Take heart, it is I; do not be afraid."
Peter answered him, "Lord, if it is you, command me to come to you on the water." He said, "Come." So Peter got out of the boat, started walking on the water, and came towards Jesus. But when he noticed the strong wind, he became frightened, and beginning to sink, he cried out, "Lord, save me!" Jesus immediately reached out his hand and caught him, saying to him, "You of little faith, why did you doubt?" When they got into the boat, the wind ceased. And those in the boat worshipped him, saying, "Truly you are the Son of God."
When they had crossed over, they came to land at Gennesaret. After the people of that place recognized him, they sent word throughout the region and brought all who were sick to him, and begged him that they might touch even the fringe of his cloak; and all who touched it were healed.

Notice what you think and feel as you read the gospel.
Jesus walks on the stormy waters toward the disciples in the boat. He tells them not to be afraid. Peter asks Jesus to let him come to him on the water, and Jesus permits it. When he starts to sink, Jesus asks him why he doubts. Back in the boat, they all confess that truly he is the Son of God.

Pray as you are led for yourself and others.
"Let me come to you, too, Lord, and let every storm strengthen my confidence in you. You are the Lord of the wind and the waves . . ." (Continue in your own words.)

Listen to Jesus.
Your faith, even the little you have, has power to do good for others. Act in faith, beloved servant, and I will bring forth good things. What else is Jesus saying to you?

Ask God to show you how to live today.
"I give myself to you today, Lord, and ask you to show me ways, large or small, in which I can act in faith in service of others. Amen."

Wednesday, August 9, 2017

Know that God is present with you and ready to converse.
"God, you are present in all things. Let me see and know you in your holy Word."

Read the gospel: Matthew 15:21–28.
Jesus left that place and went away to the district of Tyre and Sidon. Just then a Canaanite woman from that region came out and started shouting, "Have mercy on me, Lord, Son of David; my daughter is tormented by a demon." But he did not answer her at all. And his disciples came and urged him, saying, "Send her away, for she keeps shouting after us." He answered, "I was sent only to the lost sheep of the house of Israel." But she came and knelt before him, saying, "Lord, help me." He answered, "It is not fair to take the children's food and throw it to the dogs." She said, "Yes, Lord, yet even the dogs eat the crumbs that fall from their masters' table." Then Jesus answered her, "Woman, great is your faith! Let it be done for you as you wish." And her daughter was healed instantly.

Notice what you think and feel as you read the gospel.

As he often does, Jesus challenges someone's faith and then rewards it by healing her daughter. It doesn't matter that the woman is not a Jew. Her love for her daughter gives her a desperate faith in this Jewish Messiah, and he approves her.

Pray as you are led for yourself and others.

"Lord, instill in me such love for others that I come to you desperate for their healing, full of faith in you. I pray for those you have given me ..." (Continue in your own words.)

Listen to Jesus.

I hear your prayers, beloved disciple. I grant you what you have asked. What else may I do for you? What else is Jesus saying to you?

Ask God to show you how to live today.

"Let today be another small step in my life toward you and with you. I love you, praise you, and worship you for allowing me to walk with you today. Amen."

Thursday, August 10, 2017
Saint Lawrence, Deacon and Martyr

Know that God is present with you and ready to converse.

"Lord, your servant is here with you. I come to do your will."

Read the gospel: John 12:24–26.

Jesus said, "Very truly, I tell you, unless a grain of wheat falls into the earth and dies, it remains just a single grain; but if it dies, it bears much fruit. Those who love their life lose it, and those who hate their life in this world will keep it for eternal life. Whoever serves me must follow me, and where I am, there will my servant be also. Whoever serves me, the Father will honor."

Notice what you think and feel as you read the gospel.

Jesus teaches the paradox that life comes from death both in this world and the next. He invites us to follow him even into death so that we may live with God forever. Nothing else matters.

Pray as you are led for yourself and others.

"Give me that singleness of vision that you demand, Lord. I will follow you and serve you, for you have given me people I care for. I pray for them . . ." (Continue in your own words.)

Listen to Jesus.

Love is stronger than death, dear one. Let all my love flow out from you and death will have no power over you. What else is Jesus saying to you?

Ask God to show you how to live today.

"Jesus, be the love in me today. Show me how to die to myself as you ask, even today, that I may please you and our Father. Glory be to God. Amen."

Friday, August 11, 2017

Know that God is present with you and ready to converse.

"Lord of Life, you loved me before the foundation of the world and give me life in this moment. Give me wisdom to live it as you will."

Read the gospel: Matthew 16:24–28.

Then Jesus told his disciples, "If any want to become my followers, let them deny themselves and take up their cross and follow me. For those who want to save their life will lose it, and those who lose their life for my sake will find it. For what will it profit them if they gain the whole world but forfeit their life? Or what will they give in return for their life?

"For the Son of Man is to come with his angels in the glory of his Father, and then he will repay everyone for what has been done. Truly I tell you, there are some standing here who will not taste death before they see the Son of Man coming in his kingdom."

Notice what you think and feel as you read the gospel.

Jesus makes sense. Even the whole world is nothing to us if we lose our lives. He asks us to abandon all our natural inclinations not to preserve our lives but to freely embrace losing our lives for his sake. What does that mean? We must take up our cross and follow him.

Pray as you are led for yourself and others.

"Lord, my very life is a cross. As I carry it, let me deny myself and follow you into the eternal life of your kingdom. Make me one of your followers . . ." (Continue in your own words.)

Listen to Jesus.

You cannot imagine the reward of eternal life in my kingdom, beloved. Set your heart upon it. Set your heart upon me, your Savior. What else is Jesus saying to you?

Ask God to show you how to live today.

"Let me see you today in others, Lord, and show them sincere love in words and in action, for I value only the things of God, who is Love. Amen."

Saturday, August 12, 2017

Know that God is present with you and ready to converse.

"Mysterious God, you are the great I AM, eternal, present everywhere at all times, even with me now. Let me respond to you in faith."

Read the gospel: Matthew 17:14–20.

When they came to the crowd, a man came to Jesus, knelt before him, and said, "Lord, have mercy on my son, for he is an epileptic and he suffers terribly; he often falls into the fire and often into the water. And I brought him to your disciples, but they could not cure him." Jesus answered, "You faithless and perverse generation, how much longer must I be with you? How much longer must I put up with you? Bring him here to me." And Jesus rebuked the demon, and it came out of him, and the boy was cured instantly. Then the disciples came to Jesus privately and said, "Why could we not cast it out?" He said to them, "Because of your little faith. For truly I tell you, if you have faith the size of a mustard seed, you will say to this mountain, 'Move from here to there,' and it will move; and nothing will be impossible for you."

Notice what you think and feel as you read the gospel.

Faith activates the power of God to do good, Jesus says, but even a tiny amount of faith can move a mountain. Nothing is impossible to us with faith in God.

Pray as you are led for yourself and others.

"Lord, I pray for many good things for those you have given me. Give me the faith to pray with power . . ." (Continue in your own words.)

Listen to Jesus.

I grant you the faith you need, my child. I know your struggles. I love those I have given you. I have them in my care. What else is Jesus saying to you?

Ask God to show you how to live today.

"If I am presented with a situation in which I can react with faith in your goodness and power, let me react in faith. Make me conscious of you all day, Lord. Thank you. Amen."

Sunday, August 13, 2017
Nineteenth Sunday in Ordinary Time

Know that God is present with you and ready to converse.

The scriptures say that without faith it is impossible to please God. In his earthly ministry, Jesus always looked for faith in those who sought favors of him, and he frequently rebuked those who lacked faith. Faith means believing in God, in God's love and care, and that Jesus is the Christ, God's Son, come to save us from sin and death.

"O eternal God of love and power, I believe in you. Help my unbelief as I encounter your holy Word today."

Read the gospel: Matthew 14:22–33.

Immediately Jesus made the disciples get into the boat and go on ahead to the other side, while he dismissed the crowds. And after he had dismissed the crowds, he went up the mountain by himself to pray. When evening came, he was there alone, but by this time the boat, battered by the waves, was far from the land, for the wind was against them. And early in the morning he came walking towards them on the lake. But when the disciples saw him walking on the lake, they were terrified, saying, "It is a ghost!" And they cried out in fear. But immediately Jesus spoke to them and said, "Take heart, it is I; do not be afraid."

Peter answered him, "Lord, if it is you, command me to come to you on the water." He said, "Come." So Peter got out of the boat, started walking on the water, and came towards Jesus. But when he noticed the strong wind, he became frightened, and beginning to sink, he cried out, "Lord, save me!" Jesus immediately reached out his hand and caught him, saying to him, "You of little faith, why did you doubt?" When they got into the boat, the wind ceased. And those in the boat worshipped him, saying, "Truly you are the Son of God."

Notice what you think and feel as you read the gospel.

Why is Jesus walking on the lake in the storm? Is it necessary or convenient? No, it appears he is doing this to teach his disciples, particularly Peter, something about faith, and something about who he is. This lesson is also for us.

Pray as you are led for yourself and others.

"Lord, command me to come to you on the water of faith. Hold me up as I pray for those you have given me . . ." (Continue in your own words.)

Listen to Jesus.

Seize the faith you have and keep your eyes on me, beloved. I will not let you perish. What else is Jesus saying to you?

Ask God to show you how to live today.

"Let me see you in all my work and challenges today, Lord. Let me trust you to see me through it all. I thank you, dear Lord. I love you. Amen."

Monday, August 14, 2017

Know that God is present with you and ready to converse.

"Lord of all, you came to us to be tortured and killed for us, so that you could also be raised for us. You have reconciled me with God, now and for all eternity. I will listen to your Word with my heart."

Read the gospel: Matthew 17:22–27.

As they were gathering in Galilee, Jesus said to them, "The Son of Man is going to be betrayed into human hands, and they will kill him, and on the third day he will be raised." And they were greatly distressed.

When they reached Capernaum, the collectors of the temple tax came to Peter and said, "Does your teacher not pay the temple tax?" He said, "Yes, he does." And when he came home, Jesus spoke of it first, asking, "What do you think, Simon? From whom do kings of the earth take toll or tribute? From their children or from others?" When Peter said, "From others," Jesus said to him, "Then the children are free. However, so that we do not give offence to them, go to the lake and cast a hook; take the first fish that comes up; and when you open its mouth, you will find a coin; take that and give it to them for you and me."

Notice what you think and feel as you read the gospel.

The disciples are distressed when Jesus speaks of his passion and death. Apparently they don't understand that he will be raised from death, victorious and glorious. I, too, am distressed that the Son of God had to suffer and die for my sins. What great love!

Pray as you are led for yourself and others.

"Jesus, you found an amusing solution for Peter's tax problem. Nothing is impossible for you. I pray for these needs . . ." (Continue in your own words.)

Listen to Jesus.

The things that trouble you are often petty compared to the great things of God. Be a spiritual person, dear disciple, that you can grow in the love and knowledge of God, which is your sole duty and the only lasting good. What else is Jesus saying to you?

Ask God to show you how to live today.

"Let me be responsible in my earthly affairs, Lord, but keep my focus on you and heavenly things all day long. You are my everything, Jesus. Amen."

Tuesday, August 15, 2017
Assumption of the Blessed Virgin Mary

Know that God is present with you and ready to converse.

"Hail Mary, full of grace, the Lord is with you and with me! I bless you, Mother. Pray with me."

Read the gospel: Luke 1:39–56.

In those days Mary set out and went with haste to a Judean town in the hill country, where she entered the house of Zechariah and greeted Elizabeth. When Elizabeth heard Mary's greeting, the child leapt in her womb. And Elizabeth was filled with the Holy Spirit and exclaimed with a loud cry, "Blessed are you among women, and blessed is the fruit of your womb. And why has this happened to me, that the mother of my Lord comes to me? For as soon as I heard the sound of your greeting, the child in my womb leapt for joy. And blessed is she who believed that there would be a fulfillment of what was spoken to her by the Lord."

And Mary said,

> "My soul magnifies the Lord,
>> and my spirit rejoices in God my Savior,
> for he has looked with favor on the lowliness of his servant.
>> Surely, from now on all generations will call me blessed;
> for the Mighty One has done great things for me,
>> and holy is his name.
> His mercy is for those who fear him
>> from generation to generation.
> He has shown strength with his arm;
>> he has scattered the proud in the thoughts of their
>> hearts.
> He has brought down the powerful from their thrones,
>> and lifted up the lowly;
> he has filled the hungry with good things,
>> and sent the rich away empty.
> He has helped his servant Israel,
>> in remembrance of his mercy,
> according to the promise he made to our ancestors,
>> to Abraham and to his descendants for ever."

And Mary remained with her for about three months and then returned to her home.

Notice what you think and feel as you read the gospel.

Mary goes "with haste" to visit Elizabeth. She must be excited by the news of her elderly cousin's pregnancy. She must also be excited about the momentous message of the angel to herself. When the two women meet, even the babies in their wombs share their joy in the Holy Spirit. Elizabeth calls Mary "the mother of my Lord"; Mary responds with her beautiful prayer.

Pray as you are led for yourself and others.

"God, your ways are perfect. Like Mary, I give myself to you to manage my life, today and always. I also give you the lives of those you wish me to pray for . . ." (Continue in your own words.)

Listen to Jesus.

You are mine, beloved. Because you have given yourself to God, you are included in God's family. We love those you love. What else is Jesus saying to you?

Ask God to show you how to live today.

"I thank you for accepting me, loving me, and forming me according to your good pleasure. Help me to cooperate with you today and please you. Amen."

Wednesday, August 16, 2017

Know that God is present with you and ready to converse.

"Lord Jesus, Wisdom of the Father, you lived among us to tell us the truth. You are here with me now to teach me by your Word."

Read the gospel: Matthew 18:15–20.

Jesus said, "If another member of the church sins against you, go and point out the fault when the two of you are alone. If the member listens to you, you have regained that one. But if you are not listened to, take one or two others along with you, so that every word may be confirmed by the evidence of two or three witnesses. If the member refuses to listen to them, tell it to the church; and if the offender refuses to listen even to the church, let such a one be to you as a Gentile and a tax-collector. Truly I tell you, whatever you bind on earth will be bound in heaven, and whatever you loose on earth will be loosed in heaven. Again, truly I tell you, if two of you agree on earth about anything you ask, it will be done for you by my Father in heaven. For where two or three are gathered in my name, I am there among them."

Notice what you think and feel as you read the gospel.

Jesus gives some practical advice about resolving disputes among members of the Church. He has given his Church authority to settle matters both on earth and in heaven; if two or more agree in prayer, his Father in heaven will do it, for Jesus is present with them.

Pray as you are led for yourself and others.

"Lord, let the Church exercise the wisdom that comes from you. May we unite in prayer and be one with you. I pray now for these . . ." (Continue in your own words.)

Listen to Jesus.

You are easy to love, dear one. I created you to love you; I also created the people you struggle to love so I could love them. Ask me to teach you how to love those you struggle to like. What else is Jesus saying to you?

Ask God to show you how to live today.

"Guide my steps today, God, and let my mind return often to you. Amen."

Thursday, August 17, 2017

Know that God is present with you and ready to converse.

"Merciful Father, I wish to understand your mercy. Teach me and form me in your likeness."

Read the gospel: Matthew 18:21–19:1.

Then Peter came and said to Jesus, "Lord, if another member of the church sins against me, how often should I forgive? As many as seven times?" Jesus said to him, "Not seven times, but, I tell you, seventy-seven times.

"For this reason the kingdom of heaven may be compared to a king who wished to settle accounts with his slaves. When he began the reckoning, one who owed him ten thousand talents was brought to him; and, as he could not pay, his lord ordered him to be sold, together with his wife and children and all his possessions, and payment to be made. So the slave fell on his knees before him, saying, 'Have patience with me, and I will pay you everything.' And out of pity for him, the lord of that slave released him and forgave him the debt. But that same slave, as he went out, came upon one of his fellow-slaves who owed him a hundred denarii; and seizing him by the throat, he said, 'Pay what you owe.' Then his fellow-slave fell down and pleaded with him, 'Have patience with me, and I will pay you.' But he refused; then he went and threw him into prison until he should pay the debt. When his fellow-slaves saw what had happened, they were greatly distressed, and they went and reported to their lord all that had taken place. Then his lord summoned him and said to him, 'You wicked slave! I forgave you all that debt because you pleaded with me. Should you not have had mercy on your fellow-slave, as I had mercy on you?' And in anger his lord handed him over to be tortured until he should pay his entire debt. So my heavenly Father will also do to every one of you, if you do not forgive your brother or sister from your heart."

When Jesus had finished saying these things, he left Galilee and went to the region of Judea beyond the Jordan.

Notice what you think and feel as you read the gospel.

Peter wonders at what point does one stop forgiving someone: After the seventh offense? Jesus' answer commands us to extend endless forgiveness to others. The parable of the king and his indebted slaves explains why we must forgive: because God has forgiven us our great debt. His mercy is boundless.

Pray as you are led for yourself and others.

"Lord, let me seek forgiveness as often as I offend you or others. Help me to forgive others even before they ask or even if they never ask. I think of . . ." (Continue in your own words.)

Listen to Jesus.

Mercy is mine, and I give it gladly to you. Regard all people with mercy, and our hearts will be one. What else is Jesus saying to you?

Ask God to show you how to live today.

"Open to me opportunities to forgive others today, to regard others in the light of your infinite mercy. Who am I to judge? Thank you, loving God. I adore you. Amen."

Friday, August 18, 2017

Know that God is present with you and ready to converse.

"Lord, I come to you in the midst of the complications of life. Bind your precepts upon my heart that I may walk justly in your ways."

Read the gospel: Matthew 19:3–12.

Some Pharisees came to him, and to test Jesus they asked, "Is it lawful for a man to divorce his wife for any cause?" He answered, "Have you not read that the one who made them at the beginning 'made them male and female,' and said, 'For this reason a man shall leave his father and mother and be joined to his wife, and the two shall become one flesh'? So they are no longer two, but one flesh. Therefore what God has joined together, let no one separate." They said to him, "Why then did Moses command us to give a certificate of dismissal and to divorce her?" He said to them, "It was because you were so hard-hearted that Moses allowed you to divorce your wives, but at the beginning it was not so. And I say to you, whoever divorces his wife, except for unchastity, and marries another commits adultery."

His disciples said to him, "If such is the case of a man with his wife, it is better not to marry." But he said to them, "Not everyone can accept this teaching, but only those to whom it is given. For there are eunuchs who have been so from birth, and there are eunuchs who have been made eunuchs by others, and there are eunuchs who have made themselves eunuchs for the sake of the kingdom of heaven. Let anyone accept this who can."

Notice what you think and feel as you read the gospel.

Jesus ends this teaching about marriage, divorce, and the single life by inviting his disciples to accept what they can, for difficult personal discernments are involved. Yet he has affirmed the ideal of marriage as it was "at the beginning."

Pray as you are led for yourself and others.

"Lord, help me not to judge others for choices they make in relationships. Guide me and those you have given me to make choices that please you . . ." (Continue in your own words.)

Listen to Jesus.

You need others in your life, beloved. Open yourself to love and virtuous intimacy. Begin with me. What else is Jesus saying to you?

Ask God to show you how to live today.

"Help me to be authentic today in all my dealings with others, beginning with you. Shepherd me in speaking the truth in love. Amen."

Saturday, August 19, 2017

Know that God is present with you and ready to converse.

"Lord, you are Father and Mother to me. I am happy to be your child."

Read the gospel: Matthew 19:13–15.

Then little children were being brought to Jesus in order that he might lay his hands on them and pray. The disciples spoke sternly to those who brought them; but Jesus said, "Let the little children come to me, and do not stop them; for it is to such as these that the kingdom of heaven belongs." And he laid his hands on them and went on his way.

Notice what you think and feel as you read the gospel.

Little children need Jesus to lay his hands on them and pray. Welcoming them, Jesus adds that the kingdom of heaven belongs to "such as these."

Pray as you are led for yourself and others.

"Jesus, like a child I abandon myself to your care. May I show my love for you by obedience. Today I bring to you these children . . ." (Continue in your own words.)

Listen to Jesus.

Adults tend to think they are sufficient in themselves; children know they are dependent. I care for all, the faithful and the unbelieving. I call all to the kingdom of heaven. Who will come? What else is Jesus saying to you?

Ask God to show you how to live today.

"Lord, let me be aware of the needs of children today. Let me find ways to care for them. Thank you for being with me today and leading me in your joyful way. Amen."

Sunday, August 20, 2017
Twentieth Sunday in Ordinary Time

Know that God is present with you and ready to converse.

Jesus came to reconcile all humanity to God through his atoning passion, death, and resurrection. He is the Lamb of God who takes away the sins of the world. He is also the Good Shepherd who tends the sheep and the lambs. His own know his voice. He speaks often of following him.

"Lord, I am ready to listen to your voice. Teach me your way."

Read the gospel: Matthew 15:21–28.

Jesus left that place and went away to the district of Tyre and Sidon. Just then a Canaanite woman from that region came out and started shouting, "Have mercy on me, Lord, Son of David; my daughter is tormented by a demon." But he did not answer her at all. And his disciples came and urged him, saying, "Send her away, for she keeps shouting after us." He answered, "I was sent only to the lost sheep of the house of Israel." But she came and knelt before him, saying, "Lord, help me." He answered, "It is not fair to take the children's food and throw it to the dogs." She said, "Yes, Lord, yet even the dogs eat the crumbs that fall from their masters' table." Then Jesus answered her, "Woman, great is your faith! Let it be done for you as you wish." And her daughter was healed instantly.

Notice what you think and feel as you read the gospel.

The disciples must have been shocked at Jesus' treatment of the boisterous Canaanite woman who demanded healing for her daughter. She has a lot of nerve. She is not a Jew and has no right to confront Jesus. Jesus plays into their prejudices and challenges the woman, even implying she is a dog. Undaunted, the woman cleverly presses her plea. Jesus commends her great faith and heals her daughter on the spot.

Pray as you are led for yourself and others.

"Jesus, you love the faith of those who come to you. I pray that you increase my faith and the faith of those you have given me . . ." (Continue in your own words.)

Listen to Jesus.

Faith is not just something I give you, beloved; it is something you do. When you act in faith, that act is planted and will bear fruit for you and for others. One act of faith leads to another. What else is Jesus saying to you?

Ask God to show you how to live today.

"Lord, you know I have needs, and those you have given me also have needs. Present clear-cut opportunities for us to act on our faith in you, and give us grace to respond as pleases you. May we bear fruit to the great glory of God. Amen."

Monday, August 21, 2017

Know that God is present with you and ready to converse.

"Lord, your servant is here with you now. I am ready to learn what you would have me do to inherit eternal life."

Read the gospel: Matthew 19:16–22.

Then someone came to Jesus and said, "Teacher, what good deed must I do to have eternal life?" And he said to him, "Why do you ask me about what is good? There is only one who is good. If you wish to enter into life, keep the commandments." He said to him, "Which ones?" And Jesus said, "You shall not murder; You shall not commit adultery; You shall not steal; You shall not bear false witness; Honor your father and mother; also, You shall love your neighbor as yourself." The young man said to him, "I have kept all these; what do I still lack?" Jesus said to him, "If you wish to be perfect, go, sell your possessions, and give the money to the poor, and you will have treasure in heaven; then come, follow me." When the young man heard this word, he went away grieving, for he had many possessions.

Notice what you think and feel as you read the gospel.

Jesus meets the young man where he is. He raises the question of what is good and then points to the commandments, listing many. When the man asks if he needs to do more, Jesus tells him the way of full commitment: abandon all and follow him. Grieving, the young man leaves Jesus. He is not ready for that.

Pray as you are led for yourself and others.

"Jesus, let me never turn away from you. Let me not be deterred from following you by things of this world. I wish to lay up treasure in heaven for myself and those I pray for . . ." (Continue in your own words.)

Listen to Jesus.

The way of the world is hard, despite appearances. Beloved disciple, my way is good. Do not be afraid of what you are missing by following me. You possess the kingdom. What else is Jesus saying to you?

Ask God to show you how to live today.

"Reveal to me the things I have put before you, Lord, and let me turn from them to follow you more closely. I depend on you, Good Master, to give me the power to do this. I give myself to you today. Amen."

Tuesday, August 22, 2017

Know that God is present with you and ready to converse.

"Savior, I need saving every day. Save me from myself and from the traps around me. I welcome you into my day through the power of your holy Word."

Read the gospel: Matthew 19:23–30.

Then Jesus said to his disciples, "Truly I tell you, it will be hard for a rich person to enter the kingdom of heaven. Again I tell you, it is easier for a camel to go through the eye of a needle than for someone who is rich to enter the kingdom of God." When the disciples heard this, they were greatly astounded and said, "Then who can be saved?" But Jesus looked at them and said, "For mortals it is impossible, but for God all things are possible."

Then Peter said in reply, "Look, we have left everything and followed you. What then will we have?" Jesus said to them, "Truly I tell you, at the renewal of all things, when the Son of Man is seated on the throne of his glory, you who have followed me will also sit on twelve thrones, judging the twelve tribes of Israel. And everyone who has left houses or brothers or sisters or father or mother or children or fields, for my name's sake, will receive a hundredfold, and will inherit eternal life. But many who are first will be last, and the last will be first."

Notice what you think and feel as you read the gospel.

Jesus talks about the danger of riches for those who would enter the kingdom of heaven. Yet with God all things are possible. Peter wants to know what rewards his disciples will have for abandoning everything and following him. Jesus promises them great rewards, including eternal life. But many who are first will be last, and the last will be first. It seems he doesn't want anyone to take the kingdom for granted.

Pray as you are led for yourself and others.

"Lord, give me healthy fear and seriousness as I journey after you to the kingdom of heaven. Let me know you more and more as I follow you. I pray for these things and these people . . ." (Continue in your own words.)

Listen to Jesus.

Beloved, I have you in my hand. Come to me often, love me, and I will care for you until the end. What else is Jesus saying to you?

Ask God to show you how to live today.

"I love you, Jesus Christ, my Redeemer and King. Let me walk in your loving way. Show me where to step and stand today, Lord. Amen."

Wednesday, August 23, 2017

Know that God is present with you and ready to converse.

"Eternal Father, you have given us the gift of eternal life through your Son, Jesus, who paid it all on the Cross. I receive your gift with thanksgiving."

Read the gospel: Matthew 20:1–16.

Jesus said, "For the kingdom of heaven is like a landowner who went out early in the morning to hire laborers for his vineyard. After agreeing with the laborers for the usual daily wage, he sent them into his vineyard. When he went out about nine o'clock, he saw others standing idle in the market-place; and he said to them, 'You also go into the vineyard, and I will pay you whatever is right.' So they went. When he went out again about noon and about three o'clock, he did the same. And about five o'clock he went out and found others standing around; and he said to them, 'Why are you standing here idle all day?' They said to him, 'Because no one has hired us.' He said to them, 'You also go into the vineyard.' When evening came, the owner of the vineyard said to his manager, 'Call the laborers and give them their pay, beginning with the last and then going to the first.' When those hired about five o'clock came, each of them received the usual daily wage. Now when the first came, they thought they would receive more; but each of them also received the usual daily wage. And when they received it, they grumbled against the landowner, saying, 'These last worked only one hour, and you have made them equal to us who have borne the burden of the day and the scorching heat.' But he replied to one of them, 'Friend, I am doing you no wrong; did you not agree with me for the usual daily wage? Take what belongs to you and go; I choose to give to this last the same as I give to you. Am I not allowed to do what I choose with what belongs to me? Or are you envious because I am generous?' So the last will be first, and the first will be last."

Notice what you think and feel as you read the gospel.

The pay they are all working for is eternal life. The last who come receive it first. The first who come receive it last. Their grumbling is human, but the Lord's generosity is divine. Behold the boundless mercy of God.

Pray as you are led for yourself and others.

"Lord, I repent of all complaining and grumbling. I open myself to your boundless mercy and goodness, and I pray for others who need to receive your mercy . . ." (Continue in your own words.)

Listen to Jesus.

Life is what I offer you, dear friend. You have it now and, following me, you will extend your life into eternity with God. Do the work I have given you to do, and you will inherit the kingdom of God. What else is Jesus saying to you?

Ask God to show you how to live today.

"Let me work today unto the Lord. I offer you all my thoughts, words, and deeds—all my joy and all my suffering. Let everything I do serve you, Jesus. Amen."

Thursday, August 24, 2017
Saint Bartholomew, Apostle

Know that God is present with you and ready to converse.

"I come into your presence today, Lord God of hosts. I am blessed by your Holy Spirit teaching me by your Word."

Read the gospel: John 1:45–51.

Philip found Nathanael and said to him, "We have found him about whom Moses in the law and also the prophets wrote, Jesus son of Joseph from Nazareth." Nathanael said to him, "Can anything good come out of Nazareth?" Philip said to him, "Come and see." When Jesus saw Nathanael coming towards him, he said of him, "Here is truly an Israelite in whom there is no deceit!" Nathanael asked him, "Where did you come to know me?" Jesus answered, "I saw you under the fig tree before Philip called you." Nathanael replied, "Rabbi, you are the Son of God! You are the King of Israel!" Jesus answered, "Do you believe because I told you that I saw you under the fig tree? You will see greater things than these." And he said to him, "Very truly, I tell you, you will see heaven opened and the angels of God ascending and descending upon the Son of Man."

Notice what you think and feel as you read the gospel.

Nathanael is a good man, but he is skeptical about Jesus being the great prophet Moses and the prophets foretold. After all, Jesus is from Nazareth. When Jesus sees him approaching, he calls him a man without deceit. Nathanael, still skeptical, asks Jesus how he could know that. That's when Jesus tells Nathanael that he saw him under the fig tree even before Philip called him. Nathanael immediately believes that Jesus is the Son of God.

Pray as you are led for yourself and others.

"Glorious Lord and King, I long to see you as you are. I praise you and thank you for all your love and mercy to me and those you have given me . . ." (Continue in your own words.)

Listen to Jesus.

You shall see me and know me as I am, beloved disciple. Set your heart on heaven. What else is Jesus saying to you?

Ask God to show you how to live today.

"Keep the kingdom of heaven front and center in my mind, Lord, that I may realize my work here is meaningful and good. I thank you for your goodness. Amen."

Friday, August 25, 2017

Know that God is present with you and ready to converse.

"Sweep away all my confusion and distraction, Lord, as I listen to you."

Read the gospel: Matthew 22:34–40.

When the Pharisees heard that Jesus had silenced the Sadducees, they gathered together, and one of them, a lawyer, asked him a question to test him. "Teacher, which commandment in the law is the greatest?" He said to him, 'You shall love the Lord your God with all your heart, and with all your soul, and with all your mind.' This is the greatest and first commandment. And a second is like it: 'You shall love your neighbor as yourself.' On these two commandments hang all the law and the prophets."

Notice what you think and feel as you read the gospel.

The lawyer of the Pharisees tests Jesus with the question about the greatest commandment. Jesus gives him two greatest commandments—to love God and to love others—for all of the rest of the laws and the prophets hang on those two commandments of love.

Pray as you are led for yourself and others.

"Seeking to obey you, I give all my heart, my soul, and my mind to God. Increase my love for God and my neighbor. I pray for . . ." (Continue in your own words.)

Listen to Jesus.

Your love for God and others can grow infinitely. You are right, child, to aspire to God's perfect love. This is the joy of living, to increase in the knowledge and love of God. Come often in prayer. What else is Jesus saying to you?

Ask God to show you how to live today.

"Teach me to pray, Lord, for I am eager to know you, love you, and please you more and more. How may I return your love? Amen."

Saturday, August 26, 2017

Know that God is present with you and ready to converse.

"Most High Lord of Heaven and Earth, I bow before you. Instruct me by your Word."

Read the gospel: Matthew 23:1–12.

Then Jesus said to the crowds and to his disciples, "The scribes and the Pharisees sit on Moses' seat; therefore, do whatever they teach you and follow it; but do not do as they do, for they do not practice what they teach. They tie up heavy burdens, hard to bear, and lay them on the shoulders of others; but they themselves are unwilling to lift a finger to move them. They do all their deeds to be seen by others; for they make their phylacteries broad and their fringes long. They love to have the place of honor at banquets and the best seats in the synagogues, and to be greeted with respect in the market-places, and to have people call them rabbi. But you are not to be called rabbi, for you have one teacher, and you are all students. And call no one your father on earth, for you have one Father—the one in heaven. Nor are you to be called instructors, for you have one instructor, the Messiah. The greatest among you will be your servant. All who exalt themselves will be humbled, and all who humble themselves will be exalted."

Notice what you think and feel as you read the gospel.

Jesus speaks against religious hypocrisy, for the hypocrites put earthly honors ahead of pleasing God. Jesus urges humility of his disciples, saying that the greatest is the servant. He himself humbled himself to serve and save sinners.

Pray as you are led for yourself and others.

"I exalt you, Lord, for loving us so much you came among us as a man and opened our way to God and eternal life. You alone are my Father and Instructor. I offer myself to serve . . ." (Continue in your own words.)

Listen to Jesus.

I see your heart, my beloved. I thank you for loving me. I give you power to follow me. What else is Jesus saying to you?

Ask God to show you how to live today.

"Thank you for being with me, loving and leading me all day long. I have so much to learn about being your servant. Stay near me, Lord. Amen."

Sunday, August 27, 2017
Twenty-First Sunday in Ordinary Time

Know that God is present with you and ready to converse.

Following Jesus is not easy. Jesus asks us to convert completely, to turn away from all that is not God and follow him in loving service of others. Following Jesus is serious business. He teaches by his Word and by his own actions the cost of discipleship. He also teaches that the rewards are great, both here and hereafter.

"Lord Jesus Christ, I long to follow you, to know God the Father, Son, and Holy Spirit. I open myself now to your Word."

Read the gospel: Matthew 16:13–20.

Now when Jesus came into the district of Caesarea Philippi, he asked his disciples, "Who do people say that the Son of Man is?" And they said, "Some say John the Baptist, but others Elijah, and still others Jeremiah or one of the prophets." He said to them, "But who do you say that I am?" Simon Peter answered, "You are the Messiah, the Son of the living God." And Jesus answered him, "Blessed are you, Simon son of Jonah! For flesh and blood has not revealed this to you, but my Father in heaven. And I tell you, you are Peter, and on this rock I will build my church, and the gates of Hades will not prevail against it. I will give you the keys of the kingdom of heaven, and whatever you bind on earth will be bound in heaven, and whatever you loose on earth will be loosed in heaven." Then he sternly ordered the disciples not to tell anyone that he was the Messiah.

Notice what you think and feel as you read the gospel.

Jesus wants people to know that he is the Messiah, the Son of the living God. Those who believe in him are blessed, like Peter, on whom he builds his church and gives the keys of the kingdom. Why does he then command his disciples to tell no one that he is the Messiah? He knows what he is doing.

Pray as you are led for yourself and others.

"Lord, thank you for your Church, for it is your Body here on earth. It will continue for all time, for you are with us to the end. I pray for the leaders of your Church . . ." (Continue in your own words.)

Listen to Jesus.

Your prayers have power to do good and to strengthen the hands of those who serve my people. Thank you, dear disciple. There are some things I ask you to do. What else is Jesus saying to you?

Ask God to show you how to live today.

"Son of the living God, be near me now. Son of the living God, be near me always. In you I place all my trust. Amen."

Monday, August 28, 2017

Know that God is present with you and ready to converse.

"Judge of all, search my heart today and teach me by your Word."

Read the gospel: Matthew 23:13–22.

Jesus said, "But woe to you, scribes and Pharisees, hypocrites! For you lock people out of the kingdom of heaven. For you do not go in yourselves, and when others are going in, you stop them. Woe to you, scribes and Pharisees, hypocrites! For you cross sea and land to make a single convert, and you make the new convert twice as much a child of hell as yourselves.

"Woe to you, blind guides, who say, 'Whoever swears by the sanctuary is bound by nothing, but whoever swears by the gold of the sanctuary is bound by the oath.' You blind fools! For which is greater, the gold or the sanctuary that has made the gold sacred? And you say, 'Whoever swears by the altar is bound by nothing, but whoever swears by the gift that is on the altar is bound by the oath.' How blind you are! For which is greater, the gift or the altar that makes the gift sacred? So whoever swears by the altar, swears by it and by everything on it; and whoever swears by the sanctuary, swears by it and by the one who dwells in it; and whoever swears by heaven, swears by the throne of God and by the one who is seated upon it."

Notice what you think and feel as you read the gospel.

Jesus is angry at hypocritical religious leaders, for they lock people out of the kingdom of heaven by establishing foolish, unnecessary rules.

Pray as you are led for yourself and others.

"Lord, make me 100 percent true to you and correct any falseness within me, especially hypocrisy that hurts others. I pray also for wisdom and integrity among religious leaders . . ." (Continue in your own words.)

Listen to Jesus.

Fear the lie, especially when it is your own, my child. Seek truth and walk in it.
I am the Truth. What else is Jesus saying to you?

Ask God to show you how to live today.

"Let no lie come from me today, Lord. Let your healing truth go with me always. Amen."

Tuesday, August 29, 2017
Martyrdom of Saint John the Baptist

Know that God is present with you and ready to converse.

"Almighty God, your Word reveals the human heart, even in its blindness, madness, and violence. Deliver us from evil."

Read the gospel: Mark 6:17–29.

Herod himself had sent men who arrested John, bound him, and put him in prison on account of Herodias, his brother Philip's wife, because Herod had married her. For John had been telling Herod, "It is not lawful for you to have your brother's wife." And Herodias had a grudge against him, and wanted to kill him. But she could not, for Herod feared John, knowing that he was a righteous and holy man, and he protected him. When he heard him, he was greatly perplexed; and yet he liked to listen to him. But an opportunity came when Herod on his birthday gave a banquet for his courtiers and officers and for the leaders of Galilee. When his daughter Herodias came in and danced, she pleased Herod and his guests; and the king said to the girl, "Ask me for whatever you wish, and I will give it." And he solemnly swore to her, "Whatever you ask me, I will give you, even half of my kingdom." She went out and said to her mother, "What should I ask for?" She replied, "The head of John the baptizer." Immediately she rushed back to the king and requested, "I want you to give me at once the head of John the Baptist on a platter." The king was deeply grieved; yet out of regard for his oaths and for the guests, he did not want to refuse her. Immediately the king sent a soldier of the guard with orders to bring John's head. He went and beheaded him in the prison, brought his head on a platter, and gave it to the girl.

Then the girl gave it to her mother. When his disciples heard about it, they came and took his body, and laid it in a tomb.

Notice what you think and feel as you read the gospel.

John the Baptist had called out Herod for marrying his brother's wife. Herodias gets revenge, manipulating Herod into beheading John. The scene is rife with drinking, foolish oaths, and, we must presume, lewd dancing. John's head is brought in on a platter. Even this horrible death could not tarnish the righteousness or dignity of the prophet.

Pray as you are led for yourself and others.

"Lord, let me never by surprised by evil in the world. Help me to walk trusting your goodness and love, come what may. You have overcome the world . . ." (Continue in your own words.)

Listen to Jesus.

Walk in light, my beloved, for the darkness is wide. I have made a way for you. What else is Jesus saying to you?

Ask God to show you how to live today.

"I will have no part with the wicked, Lord. Give me your grace. Amen."

Wednesday, August 30, 2017

Know that God is present with you and ready to converse.

"Lord, you came to defeat evil on earth, and your work continues until you establish your everlasting kingdom among us. Work in me by your Word today."

Read the gospel: Matthew 23:27–32.

Jesus said, "Woe to you, scribes and Pharisees, hypocrites! For you are like whitewashed tombs, which on the outside look beautiful, but inside they are full of the bones of the dead and of all kinds of filth. So you also on the outside look righteous to others, but inside you are full of hypocrisy and lawlessness.

"Woe to you, scribes and Pharisees, hypocrites! For you build the tombs of the prophets and decorate the graves of the righteous, and you say, 'If we had lived in the days of our ancestors, we would not have taken part with them in shedding the blood of the prophets.' Thus you testify against yourselves that you are descendants of those who murdered the prophets. Fill up, then, the measure of your ancestors."

Notice what you think and feel as you read the gospel.

Jesus condemns religious hypocrites, pointing out how they seek to justify themselves by putting themselves above their ancestors who killed the prophets. Jesus exposes them and pronounces woe upon them.

Pray as you are led for yourself and others.

"Woe is me, Lord, if I pretend to be holy. Save me from that. I pray for all who are prone to religious hypocrisy . . ." (Continue in your own words.)

Listen to Jesus.

Hypocrisy is sewn into human nature, my child, but by my grace it can be overcome. Look carefully at your behavior, especially things you do for the sake of appearance. What else is Jesus saying to you?

Ask God to show you how to live today.

"Let me be ready to receive your light, Lord, which exposes any falseness or phoniness in me so that by your grace I may be cleansed. Thank you, Savior. Amen."

Thursday, August 31, 2017

Know that God is present with you and ready to converse.

"Lord, let me awaken now to you. You are already here with me. I ask for your blessing as I give myself to your Word."

Read the gospel: Matthew 24:42–51.

Jesus said, "Keep awake therefore, for you do not know on what day your Lord is coming. But understand this: if the owner of the house had known in what part of the night the thief was coming, he would have stayed awake and would not have let his house be broken into. Therefore you also must be ready, for the Son of Man is coming at an unexpected hour.

"Who then is the faithful and wise slave, whom his master has put in charge of his household, to give the other slaves their allowance of food at the proper time? Blessed is that slave whom his master will find at work when he arrives. Truly I tell you, he will put that one in charge of all his possessions. But if that wicked slave says to himself, 'My master is delayed,' and he begins to beat his fellow-slaves, and eats and drinks with drunkards, the master of that slave will come on a day when he does not expect him and at an hour that he does not know. He will cut him in pieces and put him with the hypocrites, where there will be weeping and gnashing of teeth."

Notice what you think and feel as you read the gospel.

Jesus exhorts us to watch and wait for his coming, for he will come unexpectedly. The faithful slave manages the household well while his master is gone. Tired of waiting, the unfaithful slave neglects his duties. The master will come and reward the faithful and punish the unfaithful.

Pray as you are led for yourself and others.

"Lord, let me be faithful to you, to others, to my work. I pray for your help especially in these areas and with these people . . ." (Continue in your own words.)

Listen to Jesus.

Do a small thing well for me today, dear servant. That thing you have done will make it easier to do another small thing well. Fill up your time doing small things well. I will love you and reward you. What else is Jesus saying to you?

Ask God to show you how to live today.

"Let me receive your words to me today with utmost seriousness. Let me do some small thing to please you. Amen."

Friday, September 1, 2017

Know that God is present with you and ready to converse.

"Lord, you sometimes speak solemnly to your disciples, for you know the dangers. Let your Word protect me from whatever may endanger my soul."

Read the gospel: Matthew 25:1–13.

Jesus said, "Then the kingdom of heaven will be like this. Ten brides-maids took their lamps and went to meet the bridegroom. Five of them were foolish, and five were wise. When the foolish took their lamps, they took no oil with them; but the wise took flasks of oil with their lamps. As the bridegroom was delayed, all of them became drowsy and slept. But at midnight there was a shout, 'Look! Here is the bridegroom! Come out to meet him.' Then all those bridesmaids got up and trimmed their lamps. The foolish said to the wise, 'Give us some of your oil, for our lamps are going out.' But the wise replied, 'No! there will not be enough for you and for us; you had better go to the dealers and buy some for yourselves.' And while they went to buy it, the bridegroom came, and those who were ready went with him into the wedding banquet; and the door was shut. Later the other bridesmaids came also, saying, 'Lord, lord, open to us.' But he replied, 'Truly I tell you, I do not know you.' Keep awake therefore, for you know neither the day nor the hour."

Notice what you think and feel as you read the gospel.

Jesus urges vigilance among those who are waiting for his return. Like the five wise bridesmaids, we should keep our lamps filled with oil. What is this oil? Readiness, even though the wait is long. What Jesus says to the foolish bridesmaids is very telling: "I do not know you."

Pray as you are led for yourself and others.

"Jesus, I am here today with you to love you and know you more and more; I want to be ready. I pray for myself and those you have given me . . ." (Continue in your own words.)

Listen to Jesus.

To keep your lamp filled, pray. Pray until you know my peace and love. Then nothing can keep us apart. What else is Jesus saying to you?

Ask God to show you how to live today.

"I offer you all that I have, all that I do, and all that I am today. Use me as you will. I give you glory, Lord. Amen."

Saturday, September 2, 2017

Know that God is present with you and ready to converse.

"You came to teach me the way to eternal life, Lord. You are here to teach me now. Let me have ears to hear."

Read the gospel: Matthew 25:14–30.

Jesus said, "For it is as if a man, going on a journey, summoned his slaves and entrusted his property to them; to one he gave five talents, to another two, to another one, to each according to his ability. Then he went away. The one who had received the five talents went off at once and traded with them, and made five more talents. In the same way, the one who had the two talents made two more talents. But the one who had received the one talent went off and dug a hole in the ground and hid his master's money. After a long time the master of those slaves came and settled accounts with them. Then the one who had received the five talents came forward, bringing five more talents, saying, 'Master, you handed over to me five talents; see, I have made five more talents.' His master said to him, 'Well done, good and trustworthy slave; you have been trustworthy in a few things, I will put you in charge of many things; enter into the joy of your master.' And the one with the two talents also came forward, saying, 'Master, you handed over to me two talents; see, I have made two more talents.' His master said to him, 'Well done, good and trustworthy slave; you have been trustworthy in a few things, I will put you in charge of many things; enter into the joy of your master.' Then the one who had received the one talent also came forward, saying, 'Master, I knew that you were a harsh man, reaping where you did not sow, and gathering where you did not scatter seed; so I was afraid, and I went and hid your talent in the ground. Here you have what is yours.' But his master replied, 'You wicked and lazy slave! You knew, did you, that I reap where I did not sow, and gather where I did not scatter? Then you ought to have invested my money with the bankers, and on my return I would have received what was my own with interest. So take the talent from him, and give it to the one with the ten talents. For to all those who have, more will be given, and they will have an abundance; but from those who have nothing, even what they have will be taken away. As for this worthless slave, throw him into the outer darkness, where there will be weeping and gnashing of teeth.'"

Notice what you think and feel as you read the gospel.

The Master is preparing his disciples for their work after he is gone. When he returns, he expects they will have made something of what he has given them and will reward each one proportionately. The one who hides his talent for fear of the Master is punished.

Pray as you are led for yourself and others.

"Master, help me to serve you with love and not fear. Cast out all fear in me. I pray also for others who serve you . . ." (Continue in your own words.)

Listen to Jesus.

I give you the will and the grace to serve my people, beloved disciple. Come to me daily and tell me what you need. I love you. What else is Jesus saying to you?

Ask God to show you how to live today.

"I love you, too, dear Lord. Let me do one thing today—one of many things—that please you and glorify you. Lead me, Lord. Amen."

Sunday, September 3, 2017
Twenty-Second Sunday in Ordinary Time

Know that God is present with you and ready to converse.

God promises to be with us though we walk through the valley of the shadow of death, so we need not fear. But, being human, we do fear. We worry. We doubt. God gives us the Holy Spirit and the healing Word to keep us on course. God gives us faith, hope, and love. Without those three, we have nothing.

"Lord, I welcome you today. Sometimes I struggle in my faith and my prayers. Give me your Spirit that I may pray well today."

Read the gospel: Matthew 16:21–27.

From that time on, Jesus began to show his disciples that he must go to Jerusalem and undergo great suffering at the hands of the elders and chief priests and scribes, and be killed, and on the third day be raised. And Peter took him aside and began to rebuke him, saying, "God forbid it, Lord! This must never happen to you." But he turned and said to Peter, "Get behind me, Satan! You are a stumbling-block to me; for you are setting your mind not on divine things but on human things."

Then Jesus told his disciples, "If any want to become my followers, let them deny themselves and take up their cross and follow me. For those who want to save their life will lose it, and those who lose their life for my sake will find it. For what will it profit them if they gain the whole world but forfeit their life? Or what will they give in return for their life?

"For the Son of Man is to come with his angels in the glory of his Father, and then he will repay everyone for what has been done."

Notice what you think and feel as you read the gospel.

Peter means well in rebuking Jesus for speaking of his passion and death, but Jesus calls him a stumbling block because Peter sees things as a human does, not as God does. Not only must Jesus carry the cross to his death so must we, for we follow him.

Pray as you are led for yourself and others.

"Jesus, you ask from me for what you gave: everything. I offer to you my life today and always. It is yours to use as you will . . ." (Continue in your own words.)

Listen to Jesus.

I will give you grace to persevere in all I ask you to do, my dear servant. I will turn your sorrow to joy. I am abiding in you and will never leave you. What else is Jesus saying to you?

Ask God to show you how to live today.

"What is my cross today, Jesus? Do not allow me to look past it but instead by your grace to pick it up and carry it, following you. Let your kingdom come soon, my God. Amen."

Monday, September 4, 2017

Know that God is present with you and ready to converse.

"Lord, I receive you here and now and your Spirit to heal me and teach me. You are the Word of the Father."

Read the gospel: Luke 4:16–30.

When Jesus came to Nazareth, where he had been brought up, he went to the synagogue on the sabbath day, as was his custom. He stood up to read, and the scroll of the prophet Isaiah was given to him. He unrolled the scroll and found the place where it was written:

> "The Spirit of the Lord is upon me,
> because he has anointed me
> to bring good news to the poor.
> He has sent me to proclaim release to the captives
> and recovery of sight to the blind,
> to let the oppressed go free,
> to proclaim the year of the Lord's favor."

And he rolled up the scroll, gave it back to the attendant, and sat down. The eyes of all in the synagogue were fixed on him. Then he began to say to them, "Today this scripture has been fulfilled in your hearing." All spoke well of him and were amazed at the gracious words that came from his mouth. They said, "Is not this Joseph's son?" He said to them, "Doubtless you will quote to me this proverb, 'Doctor, cure yourself'! And you will say, 'Do here also in your home town the things that we have heard you did at Capernaum.'" And he said, "Truly I tell you, no prophet is accepted in the prophet's home town. But the truth is, there were many widows in Israel in the time of Elijah, when the heaven was shut up for three years and six months, and there was a severe famine over all the land; yet Elijah was sent to none of them except to a widow at Zarephath in Sidon. There were also many lepers in Israel in the time of the prophet Elisha, and none of them was cleansed except Naaman the Syrian." When they heard this, all in the synagogue were filled with rage. They got up, drove him out of the town, and led him to the brow of the hill on which their town was built, so that they might hurl him off the cliff. But he passed through the midst of them and went on his way.

Notice what you think and feel as you read the gospel.

Using scripture, Jesus proclaims himself the Messiah in his hometown synagogue, and the people are outraged. They think they know exactly who he is: Joseph's son. They believe they should throw him off a cliff for blasphemy, but his time is not yet. Later he would be killed by others accusing him of making himself God's equal.

Pray as you are led for yourself and others.

"Son of God, your coming among us is a great marvel, difficult to comprehend. Help me to believe in you more and more. I pray also for the faith of others whom you have given me . . ." (Continue in your own words.)

Listen to Jesus.

Beloved disciple, I understand you. I know everything about you and love you dearly. Seek to know me, and your faith will be strong. What else is Jesus saying to you?

Ask God to show you how to live today.

"Interrupt me today, Jesus, with moments of awareness of you knowing me, loving me, and helping me serve and do your bidding. Amen."

Tuesday, September 5, 2017

Know that God is present with you and ready to converse.

"Maker of heaven and earth, you rule over all, yet you have made me free to hear your Word. I choose to do so now."

Read the gospel: Luke 4:31–37.

Jesus went down to Capernaum, a city in Galilee, and was teaching them on the sabbath. They were astounded at his teaching, because he spoke with authority. In the synagogue there was a man who had the spirit of an unclean demon, and he cried out with a loud voice, "Let us alone! What have you to do with us, Jesus of Nazareth? Have you come to destroy us? I know who you are, the Holy One of God." But Jesus rebuked him, saying, "Be silent, and come out of him!" When the demon had thrown him down before them, he came out of him without having done him any harm. They were all amazed and kept saying to one another, "What kind of utterance is this? For with authority and power he commands the unclean spirits, and out they come!" And a report about him began to reach every place in the region.

Notice what you think and feel as you read the gospel.

Jesus shows his authority over demons, casting one of them out by his word of command. People are astounded by his power. Who is this that even the demon calls him the Holy One of God?

Pray as you are led for yourself and others.

"Let your Word and your words to me cast out all darkness and uncleanness from my spirit, Lord Jesus. I pray that your goodness may powerfully help and heal all those you have given me . . ." (Continue in your own words.)

Listen to Jesus.

My Father has made me king of heaven and earth and given me all power. I choose to show mercy, to let the hearts of people turn to me. I will save them from sin and death. What else is Jesus saying to you?

Ask God to show you how to live today.

"Let your power work through me today, Jesus. Give me the right words to show love and mercy. Let my actions follow my words. Amen."

Wednesday, September 6, 2017

Know that God is present with you and ready to converse.

"Jesus, you did only the will of your Father on earth. Let your spirit of obedience fill me as I seek you in your Word."

Read the gospel: Luke 4:38–44.

After leaving the synagogue Jesus entered Simon's house. Now Simon's mother-in-law was suffering from a high fever, and they asked him about her. Then he stood over her and rebuked the fever, and it left her. Immediately she got up and began to serve them.

As the sun was setting, all those who had any who were sick with various kinds of diseases brought them to him; and he laid his hands on each of them and cured them. Demons also came out of many, shouting, "You are the Son of God!" But he rebuked them and would not allow them to speak, because they knew that he was the Messiah.

At daybreak he departed and went into a deserted place. And the crowds were looking for him; and when they reached him, they wanted to prevent him from leaving them. But he said to them, "I must proclaim the good news of the kingdom of God to the other cities also; for I was sent for this purpose." So he continued proclaiming the message in the synagogues of Judea.

Notice what you think and feel as you read the gospel.

Jesus is thronged day and night with people needing healing. When he heals Peter's mother, she gets up to serve them. At daybreak he goes off alone, but the crowds find him and want to prevent him from leaving. But Jesus says he must go proclaim the Good News in other cities for this is why the Father sent him.

Pray as you are led for yourself and others.

"Jesus, you served with very little rest. You must have found strength in your time with your Father. Let me find strength in my time with you . . ." (Continue in your own words.)

Listen to Jesus.

You may rest in me, beloved disciple. I am in your rest, and I am in your work. What else is Jesus saying to you?

Ask God to show you how to live today.

"You are good, dear Lord. I praise you for your goodness. Let it spread through all the earth and glorify God. I offer myself for your purposes. Amen."

Thursday, September 7, 2017

Know that God is present with you and ready to converse.

"Lord of all the earth, you gather your people to yourself. I am among them, looking to you for light."

Read the gospel: Luke 5:1–11.

Once while Jesus was standing beside the lake of Gennesaret, and the crowd was pressing in on him to hear the word of God, he saw two boats there at the shore of the lake; the fishermen had gone out of them and were washing their nets. He got into one of the boats, the one belonging to Simon, and asked him to put out a little way from the shore. Then he sat down and taught the crowds from the boat. When he had finished speaking, he said to Simon, "Put out into the deep water and let down your nets for a catch." Simon answered, "Master, we have worked all night long but have caught nothing. Yet if you say so, I will let down the nets." When they had done this, they caught so many fish that their nets were beginning to break. So they signaled to their partners in the other boat to come and help them. And they came and filled both boats, so that they began to sink. But when Simon Peter saw it, he fell down at Jesus' knees, saying, "Go away from me, Lord, for I am a sinful man!" For he and all who were with him were amazed at the catch of fish that they had taken; and so also were James and John, sons of Zebedee, who were partners with Simon. Then Jesus said to Simon, "Do not be afraid; from now on you will be catching people." When they had brought their boats to shore, they left everything and followed him.

Notice what you think and feel as you read the gospel.

When the disciples follow Jesus' directions and catch many fish, Peter's response is to fall down before Jesus and beg him to leave him, for he is a sinful man. He must have understood in that moment that Jesus was indeed the Son of God, almighty, holy, and altogether without sin.

Pray as you are led for yourself and others.

"Send your Spirit, Lord, that I and those you have given me may truly know who you are and worship you . . ." (Continue in your own words.)

Listen to Jesus.

I want you to know me as I know you, to love me as I love you. This is the joy of the kingdom of heaven. What else is Jesus saying to you?

Ask God to show you how to live today.

"Whatever I do today, Lord, let it be motivated by love. Let your loving words and actions flow through me to others. Amen."

Friday, September 8, 2017
Nativity of the Blessed Virgin Mary

Know that God is present with you and ready to converse.

"God, you are Lord of all the peoples of the earth, and you accomplish your purposes through us. Be with me now and work in me by your Word."

Read the gospel: Matthew 1:1–16, 18–23.

An account of the genealogy of Jesus the Messiah, the son of David, the son of Abraham.

Abraham was the father of Isaac, and Isaac the father of Jacob, and Jacob the father of Judah and his brothers, and Judah the father of Perez and Zerah by Tamar, and Perez the father of Hezron, and Hezron the father of Aram, and Aram the father of Aminadab, and Aminadab the father of Nahshon, and Nahshon the father of Salmon, and Salmon the father of Boaz by Rahab, and Boaz the father of Obed by Ruth, and Obed the father of Jesse, and Jesse the father of King David.

And David was the father of Solomon by the wife of Uriah, and Solomon the father of Rehoboam, and Rehoboam the father of Abijah, and Abijah the father of Asaph, and Asaph the father of Jehoshaphat, and Jehoshaphat the father of Joram, and Joram the father of Uzziah, and Uzziah the father of Jotham, and Jotham the father of Ahaz, and Ahaz the father of Hezekiah, and Hezekiah the father of Manasseh, and Manasseh the father of Amos, and Amos the father of Josiah, and Josiah the father of Jechoniah and his brothers, at the time of the deportation to Babylon.

And after the deportation to Babylon: Jechoniah was the father of Salathiel, and Salathiel the father of Zerubbabel, and Zerubbabel the father of Abiud, and Abiud the father of Eliakim, and Eliakim the father of Azor, and Azor the father of Zadok, and Zadok the father of Achim, and Achim the father of Eliud, and Eliud the father of Eleazar, and Eleazar the father of Matthan, and Matthan the father of Jacob, and Jacob the father of Joseph the husband of Mary, of whom Jesus was born, who is called the Messiah. . . .

Now the birth of Jesus the Messiah took place in this way. When his mother Mary had been engaged to Joseph, but before they lived together, she was found to be with child from the Holy Spirit. Her husband Joseph, being a righteous man and unwilling to expose her to public disgrace, planned to dismiss her quietly. But just when he had resolved to do this, an angel of the Lord appeared to him in a dream and said, "Joseph, son of David, do not be afraid to take Mary as your wife, for the child conceived in her is from the Holy Spirit. She will bear a son, and you are to name him Jesus, for he will save his people from their sins." All this took place to fulfill what had been spoken by the Lord through the prophet:

> "Look, the virgin shall conceive and bear a son,
>   and they shall name him Emmanuel,"

which means, "God is with us."

Notice what you think and feel as you read the gospel.

This genealogy is full of familiar and unfamiliar figures of the Old Testament, up until the conception of Jesus by the Holy Spirit in the womb of Mary. The Lord tells Joseph in a dream that her son will be called "God is with us." Joseph must have been amazed, but he also must have believed God. Somehow this child, Jesus, would save his people from their sins.

Pray as you are led for yourself and others.

"Lord, give me the faith of Joseph. Let me believe God for the salvation of those you have given me. . ." (Continue in your own words.)

Listen to Jesus.

I was born of the Holy Spirit to reconcile people with God. You, too, are born of the Spirit. I ask you to serve others in the power of God. What else is Jesus saying to you?

Ask God to show you how to live today.

"Lord, I offer you all I am today so that you may animate me by your Spirit. I am at your service. Thank you for this assignment. Amen."

Saturday, September 9, 2017

Know that God is present with you and ready to converse.

"Almighty Father, Son, and Holy Spirit, your nature is to love. I choose to receive you now. Let your Word free me to love."

Read the gospel: Luke 6:1–5.

One sabbath while Jesus was going through the cornfields, his disciples plucked some heads of grain, rubbed them in their hands, and ate them. But some of the Pharisees said, "Why are you doing what is not lawful on the sabbath?" Jesus answered, "Have you not read what David did when he and his companions were hungry? He entered the house of God and took and ate the bread of the Presence, which it is not lawful for any but the priests to eat, and gave some to his companions?" Then he said to them, "The Son of Man is lord of the sabbath."

Notice what you think and feel as you read the gospel.

The Pharisees quibble with Jesus about Sabbath law. Jesus refutes them with scripture and then by asserting that he is Lord of the Sabbath.

Pray as you are led for yourself and others.

"Lord, let everything I do be done in you, for you, and through you, for you are Lord of all. I pray for all those who begrudge your goodness and the goodness of those who serve you . . ." (Continue in your own words.)

Listen to Jesus.

Every day is new, beloved, when you follow me. When you face a decision, come to me. Are you facing a decision now? What else is Jesus saying to you?

Ask God to show you how to live today.

"Lord, I lay down my freedom before you and ask only that I may serve you as you will. Yet you respond by multiplying my freedom. Lead me to do acts of love. Amen."

Sunday, September 10, 2017
Twenty-Third Sunday in Ordinary Time

Know that God is present with you and ready to converse.

We always want to make our lives better, safer, and more pleasant. This is natural. At the same time we have a supernatural power within—the Holy Spirit—who seeks to lead us into the kingdom of heaven. Jesus opened the way for us. His way is the way of the cross. He challenges us to take up our cross and follow him. God give us grace to do so.

"Lord, you are among those who follow you. I open myself to your Word."

Read the gospel: Matthew 18:15–20.

Jesus said, "If another member of the church sins against you, go and point out the fault when the two of you are alone. If the member listens to you, you have regained that one. But if you are not listened to, take one or two others along with you, so that every word may be confirmed by the evidence of two or three witnesses. If the member refuses to listen to them, tell it to the church; and if the offender refuses to listen even to the church, let such a one be to you as a Gentile and a tax-collector. Truly I tell you, whatever you bind on earth will be bound in heaven, and whatever you loose on earth will be loosed in heaven. Again, truly I tell you, if two of you agree on earth about anything you ask, it will be done for you by my Father in heaven. For where two or three are gathered in my name, I am there among them."

Notice what you think and feel as you read the gospel.

Jesus gives practical advice about healing divisions among his followers. His Church has power to bind and to loose on earth and in heaven, for he is here among us.

Pray as you are led for yourself and others.

"Lord, as your Spirit is present with me, it is present even more in your Church, which is your Body. What would you have me do today? Let me begin by praying for all those who feed your sheep and your lambs . . ." (Continue in your own words.)

Listen to Jesus.

God is at work in little things as well as great, dear servant. Attend closely to little things, and great things will come out of them. What else is Jesus saying to you?

Ask God to show you how to live today.

"Give me small things to do today, Lord. Let God be glorified in the small things I do. Thank you for giving my life holy purpose. Amen."

Monday, September 11, 2017

Know that God is present with you and ready to converse.

"Father in heaven, you gave us Jesus so that we can know and love you. Let your Word help me to do that now."

Read the gospel: Luke 6:6–11.

On another sabbath Jesus entered the synagogue and taught, and there was a man there whose right hand was withered. The scribes and the Pharisees watched him to see whether he would cure on the sabbath, so that they might find an accusation against him. Even though he knew what they were thinking, he said to the man who had the withered hand, "Come and stand here." He got up and stood there. Then Jesus said to them, "I ask you, is it lawful to do good or to do harm on the sabbath, to save life or to destroy it?" After looking around at all of them, he said to him, "Stretch out your hand." He did so, and his hand was restored. But they were filled with fury and discussed with one another what they might do to Jesus.

Notice what you think and feel as you read the gospel.

Jesus defies the Pharisees to their faces as he heals the man with the withered hand in the synagogue on the Sabbath. He knows what they are thinking, but he heals the man anyway, infuriating the Pharisees. What will they do to him?

Pray as you are led for yourself and others.

"Lord, you were fearless. You knew where all this was leading, yet you persevered in doing good. I ask you for that same Spirit. Let all those who do the works of God be fearless, come what may . . ." (Continue in your own words.)

Listen to Jesus.

Nothing can ultimately hurt you, child. Even your sufferings have power when you unite them with my sufferings. You are already walking in the kingdom of heaven. What else is Jesus saying to you?

Ask God to show you how to live today.

"I do suffer, Lord. I resolve not to complain but to offer my pain to you for the good of someone else who is suffering. I remember that what I do for them I do for you. I praise you for your glorious ways, O God. Amen."

Tuesday, September 12, 2017

Know that God is present with you and ready to converse.

"You are waiting for me here, my God. Thank you for calling me and choosing me for your own."

Read the gospel: Luke 6:12–19.

Now during those days Jesus went out to the mountain to pray; and he spent the night in prayer to God. And when day came, he called his disciples and chose twelve of them, whom he also named apostles: Simon, whom he named Peter, and his brother Andrew, and James, and John, and Philip, and Bartholomew, and Matthew, and Thomas, and James son of Alphaeus, and Simon, who was called the Zealot, and Judas son of James, and Judas Iscariot, who became a traitor.

He came down with them and stood on a level place, with a great crowd of his disciples and a great multitude of people from all Judea, Jerusalem, and the coast of Tyre and Sidon. They had come to hear him and to be healed of their diseases; and those who were troubled with unclean spirits were cured. And all in the crowd were trying to touch him, for power came out from him and healed all of them.

Notice what you think and feel as you read the gospel.

Jesus spends the night in prayer to God. What was it like for him to pray? He must have delighted in the loving communion of Father, Son, and Holy Spirit. The love of the Trinity is pure mystery. Jesus brings that mystery of God's love down to earth.

Pray as you are led for yourself and others.

"Jesus, you call people to your work. I pray that many answer your call and come to you for forgiveness and healing . . ." (Continue in your own words.)

Listen to Jesus.

By my Spirit, I continue to do the works of God among people. Be filled with my Spirit and join us in this holy work, my child. What else is Jesus saying to you?

Ask God to show you how to live today.

"Today let me walk closely in the light and power of your Spirit, Lord. When I step off the path, set me straight. I love you, Jesus. Amen."

Wednesday, September 13, 2017

Know that God is present with you and ready to converse.

"Lord, your ways are high above our ways. Help me to understand you by your Word."

Read the gospel: Luke 6:20–26.

Then Jesus looked up at his disciples and said:

> "Blessed are you who are poor,
> > for yours is the kingdom of God.
> "Blessed are you who are hungry now,
> > for you will be filled.
> "Blessed are you who weep now,
> > for you will laugh.

"Blessed are you when people hate you, and when they exclude you, revile you, and defame you on account of the Son of Man. Rejoice on that day and leap for joy, for surely your reward is great in heaven; for that is what their ancestors did to the prophets.

"But woe to you who are rich,
  for you have received your consolation.
"Woe to you who are full now,
  for you will be hungry.
"Woe to you who are laughing now,
  for you will mourn and weep.

  "Woe to you when all speak well of you, for that is what their ancestors did to the false prophets."

Notice what you think and feel as you read the gospel.

Jesus defines blessedness and woe opposite to what we would naturally think. Poverty, hunger, sorrow, and rejection—these will lead to rejoicing. Earthly comforts will lead to grief. Our suffering has redemptive power, meriting reward in heaven.

Pray as you are led for yourself and others.

"Jesus, you came from heaven and knew you were going to heaven, so you saw this life in a heavenly way. Give us that vision . . ." (Continue in your own words.)

Listen to Jesus.

I am with you in all your suffering, beloved. Your sufferings will be turned to joy, so endure them now with patience and hope. What else is Jesus saying to you?

Ask God to show you how to live today.

"Help me to get my mind off my own troubles and do something to relieve the troubles of someone else. I want to live that way, Blessed Lord. Amen."

Thursday, September 14, 2017
Exaltation of the Holy Cross

Know that God is present with you and ready to converse.

"Heavenly King, you came down from heaven to show us the love of God. You are here with me to do the same. Alleluia."

Read the gospel: John 3:13–17.

Jesus said, "No one has ascended into heaven except the one who descended from heaven, the Son of Man. And just as Moses lifted up the serpent in the wilderness, so must the Son of Man be lifted up, that whoever believes in him may have eternal life.

"For God so loved the world that he gave his only Son, so that everyone who believes in him may not perish but may have eternal life.

"Indeed, God did not send the Son into the world to condemn the world, but in order that the world might be saved through him."

Notice what you think and feel as you read the gospel.

Jesus compares his coming crucifixion with the lifting up of the serpent in the wilderness as God commanded Moses for the healing of the people. So the Son of Man must be lifted up, that whoever believes in him has eternal life. This is the love of God.

Pray as you are led for yourself and others.

"I honor your Cross, Lord, the mysterious symbol and sign of God's great love for fallen humanity. Let others who have never known that come to understand it today, that they, too, may have eternal life . . ." (Continue in your own words.)

Listen to Jesus.

I am blessed by those who understand and embrace my cross. Look to the life to come, beloved, but know, too, that I walk with you today. What else is Jesus saying to you?

Ask God to show you how to live today.

"Let me be mindful of your cross and understand what it means for my life, today, tomorrow, and always. I take up my cross and follow you. Amen."

Friday, September 15, 2017
Our Lady of Sorrows

Know that God is present with you and ready to converse.

"Father in heaven, save us, for they have crucified the Lord."

Read the gospel: John 19:25–27.

Meanwhile, standing near the cross of Jesus were his mother, and his mother's sister, Mary the wife of Clopas, and Mary Magdalene. When Jesus saw his mother and the disciple whom he loved standing beside her, he said to his mother, "Woman, here is your son." Then he said to the disciple, "Here is your mother." And from that hour the disciple took her into his own home.

Notice what you think and feel as you read the gospel.

What sorrow would a mother feel standing before her crucified son? Mary's sorrows must have been infinite in that moment. Out of love for her and for John, Jesus gives him to her as a son to care for her. Then he gives his Mother to John to care for him.

Pray as you are led for yourself and others.

"I, too, am a beloved child of God. I take Jesus' Mother as my own. Mother, I am touched by your sorrow . . ." (Continue in your own words.)

Listen to Jesus.

You see how love triumphs, beloved? I transform evil into good, sorrow into joy. What else is Jesus saying to you?

Ask God to show you how to live today.

"Give me your compassion for the suffering, Lord. Let me not fear their suffering, but do what I can to console them and relieve their suffering. Amen."

Saturday, September 16, 2017

Know that God is present with you and ready to converse.

"I call upon you, Lord, for I know I need you. You are always here for me. Thank you for your Word."

Read the gospel: Luke 6:43–49.

Jesus said, "No good tree bears bad fruit, nor again does a bad tree bear good fruit; for each tree is known by its own fruit. Figs are not gathered from thorns, nor are grapes picked from a bramble bush. The good person out of the good treasure of the heart produces good, and the evil person out of evil treasure produces evil; for it is out of the abundance of the heart that the mouth speaks.

"Why do you call me 'Lord, Lord,' and do not do what I tell you? I will show you what someone is like who comes to me, hears my words, and acts on them. That one is like a man building a house, who dug deeply and laid the foundation on rock; when a flood arose, the river burst against that house but could not shake it, because it had been well built. But the one who hears and does not act is like a man who built a house on the ground without a foundation. When the river burst against it, immediately it fell, and great was the ruin of that house."

Notice what you think and feel as you read the gospel.

Jesus knows that some receive his message superficially, passively. He seeks a heart relationship. He seeks obedience. He asks us to build our spiritual house on a rock, upon him. Those who do bear fruit.

Pray as you are led for yourself and others.

"Lord, I am one of those who say 'Lord, Lord' but am slow to obey, slow to give you my whole heart. I hear, but I do not act as I should. I offer myself to you anew today. Help me give my all . . ." (Continue in your own words.)

Listen to Jesus.

Every day is a gift to you. Every day I ask you to give your day to me. You may not see it, but the day you give to me bears fruit for your good and for the good of those I have given you. What else is Jesus saying to you?

Ask God to show you how to live today.

"Lord, shake me out of complacency. Come into my heart that I may truly know you and speak out of the abundance you provide. What do you want me to do today? Amen."

Sunday, September 17, 2017
Twenty-Fourth Sunday in Ordinary Time

Know that God is present with you and ready to converse.

Jesus, our Savior, spoke in many ways trying to get his message through to people. His amazing Good News was that God is, that God is Love, and that God gives eternal life to all who come to him. The Son of God would reveal God's love by being disbelieved, rejected, tortured, and killed. Mysteriously, through that sacrifice he restores us to God.

"Lord, I long to hear your Good News in the depth of my heart, in the bottom of my soul. Speak to me."

Read the gospel: Matthew 18:21–35.

Then Peter came and said to Jesus, "Lord, if another member of the church sins against me, how often should I forgive? As many as seven times?" Jesus said to him, "Not seven times, but, I tell you, seventy-seven times.

"For this reason the kingdom of heaven may be compared to a king who wished to settle accounts with his slaves. When he began the reckoning, one who owed him ten thousand talents was brought to him; and, as he could not pay, his lord ordered him to be sold, together with his wife and children and all his possessions, and payment to be made. So the slave fell on his knees before him, saying, 'Have patience with me, and I will pay you everything.' And out of pity for him, the lord of that slave released him and forgave him the debt. But that same slave, as he went out, came upon one of his fellow-slaves who owed him a hundred denarii; and seizing him by the throat, he said, 'Pay what you owe.' Then his fellow-slave fell down and pleaded with him, 'Have patience with me, and I will pay you.' But he refused; then he went and threw him into prison until he should pay the debt. When his fellow-slaves saw what had happened, they were greatly distressed, and they went and reported to their lord all that had taken place. Then his lord summoned him and said to him, 'You wicked slave! I forgave you all that debt because you pleaded with me. Should you not have had mercy on your fellow-slave, as I had mercy on you?' And in anger his lord handed him over to be tortured until he should pay his entire debt. So my heavenly Father will also do to every one of you, if you do not forgive your brother or sister from your heart."

Notice what you think and feel as you read the gospel.

Jesus teaches about forgiveness. If we want God's forgiveness, we must forgive. Again and again we must forgive. And this is just, for we are children of God, who is infinite mercy.

Pray as you are led for yourself and others.

"God, thank you for forgiving me my many sins: past, present, and future. Let me see others with your eyes of mercy. I pray for . . ." (Continue in your own words.)

Listen to Jesus.

From the heart; forgive your brother or sister from your heart. Can you do that? Can you do that even if they do not ask for forgiveness? Come to me, and I will show you how. What else is Jesus saying to you?

Ask God to show you how to live today.

"You must help me, Lord. I wish to set aside all my grudges, anger, coldness, and resentment against others. Take them all at once from my heart, or take them one by one. I come to you for salvation. Amen."

Monday, September 18, 2017

Know that God is present with you and ready to converse.
"Lord, you exist far off in a heaven of love, yet you count me worthy to be in your presence. Glory to you, Almighty."

Read the gospel: Luke 7:1–10.
After Jesus had finished all his sayings in the hearing of the people, he entered Capernaum. A centurion there had a slave whom he valued highly, and who was ill and close to death. When he heard about Jesus, he sent some Jewish elders to him, asking him to come and heal his slave. When they came to Jesus, they appealed to him earnestly, saying, "He is worthy of having you do this for him, for he loves our people, and it is he who built our synagogue for us." And Jesus went with them, but when he was not far from the house, the centurion sent friends to say to him, "Lord, do not trouble yourself, for I am not worthy to have you come under my roof; therefore I did not presume to come to you. But only speak the word, and let my servant be healed. For I also am a man set under authority, with soldiers under me; and I say to one, 'Go,' and he goes, and to another, 'Come,' and he comes, and to my slave, 'Do this,' and the slave does it." When Jesus heard this he was amazed at him, and turning to the crowd that followed him, he said, "I tell you, not even in Israel have I found such faith." When those who had been sent returned to the house, they found the slave in good health.

Notice what you think and feel as you read the gospel.
Jesus loves the faith of the centurion, and he heals his slave from a distance, just as the centurion asks. The centurion understands chain of command. He understands power. His acknowledgement of his own unworthiness somehow makes him worthy.

Pray as you are led for yourself and others.
"Lord, I am not worthy of you, but only speak the word and those I pray for will be helped and healed . . ." (Continue in your own words.)

Listen to Jesus.
It is good for you to pray with faith in me, beloved. Without faith, how can you know me? With faith, you live and move in the power of God. What else is Jesus saying to you?

Ask God to show you how to live today.

"Help me find a way to please you with my faith today, Jesus. I want to please you, and I want to help others in need. Thank you. Amen."

Tuesday, September 19, 2017

Know that God is present with you and ready to converse.

"God, you know me thoroughly. You know my need for you. I am ready for your touch."

Read the gospel: Luke 7:11–17.

Soon afterwards Jesus went to a town called Nain, and his disciples and a large crowd went with him. As he approached the gate of the town, a man who had died was being carried out. He was his mother's only son, and she was a widow; and with her was a large crowd from the town. When the Lord saw her, he had compassion for her and said to her, "Do not weep." Then he came forward and touched the bier, and the bearers stood still. And he said, "Young man, I say to you, rise!" The dead man sat up and began to speak, and Jesus gave him to his mother. Fear seized all of them; and they glorified God, saying, "A great prophet has risen among us!" and "God has looked favorably on his people!" This word about him spread throughout Judea and all the surrounding country.

Notice what you think and feel as you read the gospel.

Jesus raises a young man from the dead out of compassion for his mother, a widow, for this was her only son. The crowd is seized with fear and glorifies God.

Pray as you are led for yourself and others.

"Lord, you have compassion even on those who do not ask you. Today I ask you for nothing, but I give myself to you in love. I give you all those who do not ask for anything . . ." (Continue in your own words.)

Listen to Jesus.

Dearly beloved disciple, I want to spend this time with you. This is your time to experience heaven, to taste the wine of the kingdom. I give you my blessing. What else is Jesus saying to you?

Ask God to show you how to live today.

"Do not depart from me, Jesus. Be my companion throughout this day and night. I love you. Amen."

Wednesday, September 20, 2017

Know that God is present with you and ready to converse.

"Wisdom of the Father, I cast aside all my own understanding and intelligence so that I can gain the highest knowledge, the knowledge of God."

Read the gospel: Luke 7:31–35.

Jesus said, "To what then will I compare the people of this generation, and what are they like? They are like children sitting in the market-place and calling to one another,

> 'We played the flute for you, and you did not dance;
>   we wailed, and you did not weep.'

For John the Baptist has come eating no bread and drinking no wine, and you say, 'He has a demon'; the Son of Man has come eating and drinking, and you say, 'Look, a glutton and a drunkard, a friend of tax-collectors and sinners!' Nevertheless, wisdom is vindicated by all her children."

Notice what you think and feel as you read the gospel.

Jesus understands that people are never satisfied. They place themselves above even the ways of God, who out of love for them seeks them by every possible means. People criticize God.

Pray as you are led for yourself and others.

"Lord, I have complained against you, too, not trusting you with all the events and circumstances of my life, not understanding how much you love me within and through these events and circumstances. Forgive me. Let me trust you, for you alone are the lover of my soul . . ." (Continue in your own words.)

Listen to Jesus.

You are my child. I impart to you wisdom higher and deeper than all earthly knowledge. The wisdom is this: God is Love and God is yours. What else is Jesus saying to you?

Ask God to show you how to live today.

"Lord, alert me to any complaint that rises from my heart today, especially any complaint about you. By your grace, transform that complaint to trust in you and praise. I am yours today. Amen."

Thursday, September 21, 2017
Saint Matthew, Apostle and Evangelist

Know that God is present with you and ready to converse.
"Lord, you come to me where I am. You call me. I follow you."

Read the gospel: Matthew 9:9–13.
As Jesus was walking along, he saw a man called Matthew sitting at the tax booth; and he said to him, "Follow me." And he got up and followed him.

  And as he sat at dinner in the house, many tax-collectors and sinners came and were sitting with him and his disciples. When the Pharisees saw this, they said to his disciples, "Why does your teacher eat with tax-collectors and sinners?" But when he heard this, he said, "Those who are well have no need of a physician, but those who are sick. Go and learn what this means, 'I desire mercy, not sacrifice.' For I have come to call not the righteous but sinners."

Notice what you think and feel as you read the gospel.
It is impossible for Jesus to please the Pharisees no matter what he does. Jesus knows this, but he doesn't stop educating them in the true ways of God. God desires mercy from them and humble admission of their sinfulness, not sacrifice, not criticism, not superiority.

Pray as you are led for yourself and others.
"You desire mercy, not sacrifice, Lord. What does that mean for me? I am a sinner. Have mercy on me and upon all those you have given me . . ." (Continue in your own words.)

Listen to Jesus.
As I called Matthew, I call you, my friend. I know you and love you with all my heart. Do you love me? What else is Jesus saying to you?

Ask God to show you how to live today.
"I am overwhelmed by your love for me, Lord. Give me ways to share it with others. Make me an instrument of your love. Amen."

Friday, September 22, 2017

Know that God is present with you and ready to converse.
"Lord, you came to save sinners. You have come to save me today. I need you."

Read the gospel: Luke 8:1–3.
Soon afterwards Jesus went on through cities and villages, proclaiming and bringing the good news of the kingdom of God. The twelve were with him, as well as some women who had been cured of evil spirits and infirmities: Mary, called Magdalene, from whom seven demons had gone out, and Joanna, the wife of Herod's steward Chuza, and Susanna, and many others, who provided for them out of their resources.

Notice what you think and feel as you read the gospel.
Besides the twelve male disciples, many women followed Jesus. They were grateful to him for freeing them from evil spirits and infirmities. They seem to have been practical women of some means, for they provide for Jesus and his other disciples.

Pray as you are led for yourself and others.
"How strange this throng of disciples must have appeared as they visited the cities and villages! Lord, help me to be open to everyone who wants to follow you, knowing that your love and grace is for everyone."

Listen to Jesus.
Those who follow me are free. You are free from sin and death. You are free from the judgment of others. You are free in me. What else is Jesus saying to you?

Ask God to show you how to live today.
"Let me exercise my freedom from the judgment of others, Lord, following you without reservation or shame. For you have done great things for me. Glory be to the Father, the Son, and the Holy Spirit. Amen."

Saturday, September 23, 2017

Know that God is present with you and ready to converse.
"Jesus, I come to you to learn the ways of God and the kingdom of God. Let me perceive and understand."

Read the gospel: Luke 8:4–15.

When a great crowd gathered and people from town after town came to Jesus, he said in a parable: "A sower went out to sow his seed; and as he sowed, some fell on the path and was trampled on, and the birds of the air ate it up. Some fell on the rock; and as it grew up, it withered for lack of moisture. Some fell among thorns, and the thorns grew with it and choked it. Some fell into good soil, and when it grew, it produced a hundredfold." As he said this, he called out, "Let anyone with ears to hear listen!"

Then his disciples asked him what this parable meant. He said, "To you it has been given to know the secrets of the kingdom of God; but to others I speak in parables, so that

'looking they may not perceive,
and listening they may not understand.'

"Now the parable is this: The seed is the word of God. The ones on the path are those who have heard; then the devil comes and takes away the word from their hearts, so that they may not believe and be saved. The ones on the rock are those who, when they hear the word, receive it with joy. But these have no root; they believe only for a while and in a time of testing fall away. As for what fell among the thorns, these are the ones who hear; but as they go on their way, they are choked by the cares and riches and pleasures of life, and their fruit does not mature. But as for that in the good soil, these are the ones who, when they hear the word, hold it fast in an honest and good heart, and bear fruit with patient endurance."

Notice what you think and feel as you read the gospel.

Those who bear fruit hold fast to the Word of God in an honest and good heart. They bear fruit through patient endurance.

Pray as you are led for yourself and others.

"I have a sinner's heart, Lord. How can I receive your words with an honest and good heart? How can I endure in patience? Only by your grace . . ." (Continue in your own words.)

Listen to Jesus.

Have you seen others fall away from faith? Beloved disciple, pray for those who have lost faith in God. What else is Jesus saying to you?

Ask God to show you how to live today.

"Is there anything I can do today, Lord? I offer myself to serve those who have lost faith in God. If they cannot believe, let them at least hope in you. Amen."

Sunday, September 24, 2017
Twenty-Fifth Sunday in Ordinary Time

Know that God is present with you and ready to converse.

From the beginning, people have come to God from every nation, every people, and every age. In their hearts, people have always known that they were made to know and love God, and God has always sought those who will worship God in spirit and in truth. God is merciful and good, Lord of all the earth.

"Lord, I place myself at the end of the line, for I come to you now behind all those who came to you before. But I am with you now to worship you in spirit and in truth."

Read the gospel: Matthew 20:1–16a.

Jesus said, "For the kingdom of heaven is like a landowner who went out early in the morning to hire laborers for his vineyard. After agreeing with the laborers for the usual daily wage, he sent them into his vineyard. When he went out about nine o'clock, he saw others standing idle in the market-place; and he said to them, 'You also go into the vineyard, and I will pay you whatever is right.' So they went. When he went out again about noon and about three o'clock, he did the same. And about five o'clock he went out and found others standing around; and he said to them, 'Why are you standing here idle all day?' They said to him, 'Because no one has hired us.' He said to them, 'You also go into the vineyard.' When evening came, the owner of the vineyard said to his manager, 'Call the laborers and give them their pay, beginning with the last and then going to the first.' When those hired about five o'clock came, each of them received the usual daily wage. Now when the first came, they thought they would receive more; but each of them also received the usual daily wage. And when they received it, they grumbled against the landowner, saying, 'These last worked only one hour, and you have made them equal to us who have borne the burden of the day and the scorching heat.' But he replied to one of them, 'Friend, I am doing you no wrong; did you not agree with me for the usual daily wage? Take what belongs to you and go; I choose to give to this last the same as I give to you. Am I not allowed to do what I choose with what belongs to me? Or are you envious because I am generous?' So the last will be first, and the first will be last."

Notice what you think and feel as you read the gospel.

Speaking of the kingdom of heaven, Jesus concludes that the last will be first, and the first last. Does it make a difference who and when as long as they enter the kingdom? To enter is the great thing, the only thing to be desired. What difference does it make whether you work all day or just for the last hour? God is just, merciful, and generous.

Pray as you are led for yourself and others.

"Lord, it is beautiful that you continue to call people to your kingdom. You pour out your mercy early and late. I pray for those who have served you long . . ." (Continue in your own words.)

Listen to Jesus.

I came to call people to the kingdom of heaven, an eternity of peace, love, and joy in God. This is the nature of God. You are invited, my beloved. Enter into the joy of God. What else is Jesus saying to you?

Ask God to show you how to live today.

"Lord, I willingly take up my work today. I work to enter your kingdom, a blessing I cannot earn and cannot deserve except through you. I praise you for your generosity, my Savior and King. Amen."

Monday, September 25, 2017

Know that God is present with you and ready to converse.

"Lord, I am here with you to listen. Let me truly hear you in your Word."

Read the gospel: Luke 8:16–18.

Jesus said, "No one after lighting a lamp hides it under a jar, or puts it under a bed, but puts it on a lampstand, so that those who enter may see the light. For nothing is hidden that will not be disclosed, nor is anything secret that will not become known and come to light. Then pay attention to how you listen; for to those who have, more will be given; and from those who do not have, even what they seem to have will be taken away."

Notice what you think and feel as you read the gospel.

We may think things are secret or hidden, but nothing will remain secret or hidden. All will come to light. So Jesus says to listen well and receive. Those who have will receive more.

Pray as you are led for yourself and others.

"I pray for those who seem to have, Lord, those who are in danger of having what they seem to have taken away. I pray they will listen carefully to you . . ." (Continue in your own words.)

Listen to Jesus.

God is light, and there is no shadow or darkness in God. That is where you want to be, dear disciple. Let the light into your soul. Do not fear it. What else is Jesus saying to you?

Ask God to show you how to live today.

"Teach me to walk in the light, Lord. I will fear no evil because you are with me. Thank you. Amen."

Tuesday, September 26, 2017

Know that God is present with you and ready to converse.

"Lord, you are present in your Word. I come to hear it."

Read the gospel: Luke 8: 19–21.

Then Jesus' mother and his brothers came to him, but they could not reach him because of the crowd. And he was told, "Your mother and your brothers are standing outside, wanting to see you." But he said to them, "My mother and my brothers are those who hear the word of God and do it."

Notice what you think and feel as you read the gospel.

Jesus restructures family relationships, calling those who hear and do God's will the true members of his family. In so doing, he emphasizes the only important thing, obeying God. He is ready to show brotherly favor to all who do God's will.

Pray as you are led for yourself and others.

"Lord, I have heard you and now seek to do your will. I pray to know it today . . ." (Continue in your own words.)

Listen to Jesus.

I am with you, child. I place before you the work I ask you to do. When you do these things, I help you. Rejoice in me, your master, your helper, and your brother. What else is Jesus saying to you?

Ask God to show you how to live today.

"I understand a few things, Jesus. I understand that I can do nothing without you. Thank you for your care. Show me how you can use me. Amen."

Wednesday, September 27, 2017

Know that God is present with you and ready to converse.

"You seek my attention, Lord. I praise you for your faithful love. Let me please you today."

Read the gospel: Luke 9:1–6.

Then Jesus called the twelve together and gave them power and authority over all demons and to cure diseases, and he sent them out to proclaim the kingdom of God and to heal. He said to them, "Take nothing for your journey, no staff, nor bag, nor bread, nor money—not even an extra tunic. Whatever house you enter, stay there, and leave from there. Wherever they do not welcome you, as you are leaving that town shake the dust off your feet as a testimony against them." They departed and went through the villages, bringing the good news and curing diseases everywhere.

Notice what you think and feel as you read the gospel.

Jesus puts his disciples to work, giving them authority and power to proclaim the kingdom and to heal. He asks them to trust God for everything and to just do the work and move on, regardless of what happens.

Pray as you are led for yourself and others.

"Let me throw myself into your service, Lord. Do you want me to do the good works that you did? Give me power to do them and then send me . . ." (Continue in your own words.)

Listen to Jesus.

I do give you power, servant. I set before you the things that you can do for others. To please me, please them. What else is Jesus saying to you?

Ask God to show you how to live today.

"Help me to transform my desire to please you into concrete action. That is the power I ask of you today. I am grateful, Lord. Amen."

Thursday, September 28, 2017

Know that God is present with you and ready to converse.

"Who can know you, Lord, except you reveal yourself? Would you show yourself to me? I long to know you."

Read the gospel: Luke 9:7–9.

Now Herod the ruler heard about all that had taken place, and he was perplexed, because it was said by some that John had been raised from the dead, by some that Elijah had appeared, and by others that one of the ancient prophets had arisen. Herod said, "John I beheaded; but who is this about whom I hear such things?" And he tried to see him.

Notice what you think and feel as you read the gospel.

Hearing about Jesus, Herod is perplexed, despite his power and his actions to control things. Why does he want to see Jesus?

Pray as you are led for yourself and others.

"Lord, I pray for the powerful. You give power to do good and to do evil. I pray that those in power do good . . ." (Continue in your own words.)

Listen to Jesus.

All power is mine. The power of this world comes to nothing. I give you my power to do my will, dear servant. Our good work shall endure. What else is Jesus saying to you?

Ask God to show you how to live today.

"I will not seek earthly power, Lord. I serve by your grace and power. Amen."

Friday, September 29, 2017
Saints Michael, Gabriel, and Raphael, Archangels

Know that God is present with you and ready to converse.

"Lord, your creation sings your praise and glorifies you. Let me join in the song."

Read the gospel: John 1:47–51.

When Jesus saw Nathanael coming towards him, he said of him, "Here is truly an Israelite in whom there is no deceit!" Nathanael asked him, "Where did you come to know me?" Jesus answered, "I saw you under the fig tree before Philip called you." Nathanael replied, "Rabbi, you are the Son of God! You are the King of Israel!" Jesus answered, "Do you believe because I told you that I saw you under the fig tree? You will see greater things than these." And he said to him, "Very truly, I tell you, you will see heaven opened and the angels of God ascending and descending upon the Son of Man."

Notice what you think and feel as you read the gospel.

Who are these angels ascending and descending upon the Lord? When will we see heaven open to reveal this? Jesus speaks "very truly," and Nathanael believes that he is the Son of God.

Pray as you are led for yourself and others.

"You are worthy of all worship, Jesus Christ. May I join the angels in honoring you?" (Continue in your own words.)

Listen to Jesus.

I receive your praise, beloved. My Father is pleased with me. We are pleased with you and thank you for your love. What else is Jesus saying to you?

Ask God to show you how to live today.

"Let my heart and my lips praise you all day long, for you are King above all. You are the glorious Lamb of God, worthy of all glory. Amen."

Saturday, September 30, 2017

Know that God is present with you and ready to converse.

"You are high, my God, and I am low. How can I understand you? Yet you are speaking to me in your Word."

Read the gospel: Luke 9:43b–45.

And all were astounded at the greatness of God.

While everyone was amazed at all that he was doing, he said to his disciples, "Let these words sink into your ears: The Son of Man is going to be betrayed into human hands." But they did not understand this saying; its meaning was concealed from them, so that they could not perceive it. And they were afraid to ask him about this saying.

Notice what you think and feel as you read the gospel.

In the midst of his mighty works of healing, Jesus injects a dose of reality. He predicts his betrayal, but his disciples do not understand, and they are afraid to ask him to explain himself.

Pray as you are led for yourself and others.

"Lord, keep me grounded in reality, in your truth. Let your words sink into my ears. I pray for others, too, that they may understand your words . . ." (Continue in your own words.)

Listen to Jesus.

You follow me in the way of the cross, beloved. Do so willingly and without fear, for I go before you, and I am with you to the end. This way is life. What else is Jesus saying to you?

Ask God to show you how to live today.

"Give me courage to accept your truth, my God. Let me persevere on my way into your kingdom. Amen."

Sunday, October 1, 2017
Twenty-Sixth Sunday in Ordinary Time

Know that God is present with you and ready to converse.

Jesus Christ, the Son of God, challenges us as he challenged those who heard him. He spoke of his Father who sent him. He asked people to believe in God, to believe in God's Son, and to follow him. Who else but the Lord could speak so boldly?

"Jesus, you are the Son of God and you speak to me. Help me to respond as you would have me respond."

Read the gospel: Matthew 21:28–32.

Jesus said, "What do you think? A man had two sons; he went to the first and said, 'Son, go and work in the vineyard today.' He answered, 'I will not'; but later he changed his mind and went. The father went to the second and said the same; and he answered, 'I go, sir'; but he did not go. Which of the two did the will of his father?" They said, "The first." Jesus said to them, "Truly I tell you, the tax-collectors and the prostitutes are going into the kingdom of God ahead of you. For John came to you in the way of righteousness and you did not believe him, but the tax-collectors and the prostitutes believed him; and even after you saw it, you did not change your minds and believe him."

Notice what you think and feel as you read the gospel.

Jesus illustrates that obedience is not a matter of words but of action. Sinners are entering the kingdom of God ahead of those who stand by trusting in their own righteousness. Sinners may come late, but they hear the call and come to God.

Pray as you are led for yourself and others.

"Thank you for saving sinners, Lord. I pray for all those who do not know that they need you, particularly . . ." (Continue in your own words.)

Listen to Jesus.

I will that every person come to me, believe in me, and go with me into the kingdom of God. Tell people of my love, dear friend. What else is Jesus saying to you?

Ask God to show you how to live today.

"Lord, I am saying 'I go, sir.' Let it not be lip-service. Let me be the one who actually goes to work in the vineyard. I rejoice that you have given me this work. Amen."

Monday, October 2, 2017
The Guardian Angels

Know that God is present with you and ready to converse.

"Lord of Hosts, how many love you and serve you throughout the universe and in heaven? Here I am, Lord, use me."

Read the gospel: Matthew 18:1–5, 10.

At that time the disciples came to Jesus and asked, "Who is the greatest in the kingdom of heaven?" He called a child, whom he put among them, and said, "Truly I tell you, unless you change and become like children, you will never enter the kingdom of heaven. Whoever becomes humble like this child is the greatest in the kingdom of heaven. Whoever welcomes one such child in my name welcomes me. . . .

"Take care that you do not despise one of these little ones; for, I tell you, in heaven their angels continually see the face of my Father in heaven."

Notice what you think and feel as you read the gospel.

Jesus asks his followers to become humble like children. Those shall be greatest in his kingdom, for even though they are humble, the children have angels in heaven.

Pray as you are led for yourself and others.

"Lord, set your guard of angels around me and all those you have given me, especially the children . . ." (Continue in your own words.)

Listen to Jesus.

Come to me, child. I care for you and those for whom you pray. You are all mine, for you have given them to me with yourself. What else is Jesus saying to you?

Ask God to show you how to live today.

"You ask me to change, Lord, to become like a child. Show me what I need to change in my life, in myself, and give me power to do it. I seek to do your will. Amen."

Tuesday, October 3, 2017

Know that God is present with you and ready to converse.

"Lord, you give your love and mercy unmerited. I am grateful for that because I do not deserve your blessings. I open myself to your Word now."

Read the gospel: Luke 9:51–56.

When the days drew near for him to be taken up, Jesus set his face to go to Jerusalem. And he sent messengers ahead of him. On their way they entered a village of the Samaritans to make ready for him; but they did not receive him, because his face was set towards Jerusalem. When his disciples James and John saw it, they said, "Lord, do you want us to command fire to come down from heaven and consume them?" But he turned and rebuked them. Then they went on to another village.

Notice what you think and feel as you read the gospel.

Humble and compassionate, Jesus simply goes on his way when the Samaritan village does not receive him. He is not angry at them, but he rebukes James and John for suggesting commanding fire from heaven to consume them.

Pray as you are led for yourself and others.

"Be in me Spirit of Jesus Christ, and I will resent no one, even those who have hurt me. I pray for them . . ." (Continue in your own words.)

Listen to Jesus.

My virtues belong to you, beloved. Exercise them and grow strong. What else is Jesus saying to you?

Ask God to show you how to live today.

"Lord, your face is set for Jerusalem. Let me walk with you today. Amen."

Wednesday, October 4, 2017

Know that God is present with you and ready to converse.

"You made me to love you, Father. You are already with me loving me."

Read the gospel: Luke 9:57–62.

As they were going along the road, someone said to Jesus, "I will follow you wherever you go." And Jesus said to him, "Foxes have holes, and birds of the air have nests; but the Son of Man has nowhere to lay his head." To another he said, "Follow me." But he said, "Lord, first let me go and bury my father." But Jesus said to him, "Let the dead bury their own dead; but as for you, go and proclaim the kingdom of God." Another said, "I will follow you, Lord; but let me first say farewell to those at my home." Jesus said to him, "No one who puts a hand to the plough and looks back is fit for the kingdom of God."

Notice what you think and feel as you read the gospel.

Jesus responds to the excuses of those who hold back from following him in that moment. His call demands a decision and a continuing commitment. Don't look back.

Pray as you are led for yourself and others.

"Lord, I have decided to follow you. Let me do so now without reservation, and give me the grace of perseverance to the end. I pray also for those you have given me . . ." (Continue in your own words.)

Listen to Jesus.

We are together in this, beloved. I have called you and chosen you to persevere. It is your part to come to me and persist in your calling. My way is blessed. I give you my blessing now. What else is Jesus saying to you?

Ask God to show you how to live today.

"Lord, I am afraid that I may fail you on the way, that my faith will waver, that I may fall. I trust you but not myself. Help me persevere. Amen."

Thursday, October 5, 2017

Know that God is present with you and ready to converse.

"Lord, I get distracted and overwhelmed sometimes. Wake me up to your presence in my life and in your Word."

Read the gospel: Luke 10:1-12.

After this the Lord appointed seventy others and sent them on ahead of him in pairs to every town and place where he himself intended to go. He said to them, "The harvest is plentiful, but the laborers are few; therefore ask the Lord of the harvest to send out laborers into his harvest. Go on your way. See, I am sending you out like lambs into the midst of wolves. Carry no purse, no bag, no sandals; and greet no one on the road. Whatever house you enter, first say, 'Peace to this house!' And if anyone is there who shares in peace, your peace will rest on that person; but if not, it will return to you. Remain in the same house, eating and drinking whatever they provide, for the laborer deserves to be paid. Do not move about from house to house. Whenever you enter a town and its people welcome you, eat what is set before you; cure the sick who are there, and say to them, 'The kingdom of God has come near to you.' But whenever you enter a town and they do not welcome you, go out into its streets and say, 'Even the dust of your town that clings to our feet, we wipe off in protest against you. Yet know this: the kingdom of God has come near.' I tell you, on that day it will be more tolerable for Sodom than for that town."

Notice what you think and feel as you read the gospel.

Jesus makes the work of the kingdom seem pretty simple. Just heal the sick and announce that the kingdom of God is near. Some will accept; some will not. Move on.

Pray as you are led for yourself and others.

"The unharvested fields are vast, Lord. Send laborers to bring in the harvest. I offer you myself . . ." (Continue in your own words.)

Listen to Jesus.

Where you go, I follow, beloved. Do what you can do and leave the rest for me. What else is Jesus saying to you?

Ask God to show you how to live today.

"Give me wisdom and grace to do your work well, Lord. Thank you for working alongside of me. Amen."

Friday, October 6, 2017

Know that God is present with you and ready to converse.

"My God, I am listening to you. Open my ears to your voice."

Read the gospel: Luke 10:13–16.

Jesus said, "Woe to you, Chorazin! Woe to you, Bethsaida! For if the deeds of power done in you had been done in Tyre and Sidon, they would have repented long ago, sitting in sackcloth and ashes. But at the judgement it will be more tolerable for Tyre and Sidon than for you. And you, Capernaum, will you be exalted to heaven? No, you will be brought down to Hades.

"Whoever listens to you listens to me, and whoever rejects you rejects me, and whoever rejects me rejects the one who sent me."

Notice what you think and feel as you read the gospel.

Jesus pronounces woe upon the towns that reject him. He is among them doing mighty deeds, and they still refuse to repent. He tells his disciples that they are speaking for and as him. Those who hear them, hear Jesus.

Pray as you are led for yourself and others.

"Let me hear your voice in others, Lord. And let me speak of your kingdom as you would. I pray for all who bear your message and your name ..." (Continue in your own words.)

Listen to Jesus.

The Gospel of the kingdom is yours to proclaim, beloved disciple. When you speak of it, speak from the heart to the heart of those who hear you. Some will hear you now. Some will hear you later. What else is Jesus saying to you?

Ask God to show you how to live today.

"Let me speak with your love, Jesus, Master. I do not wish to dishonor your good name. Amen."

Saturday, October 7, 2017

Know that God is present with you and ready to converse.

"Lord of heaven and earth, I thank you. I am happy to be with you again."

Read the gospel: Luke 10:17–24.

The seventy returned with joy, saying, "Lord, in your name even the demons submit to us!" Jesus said to them, "I watched Satan fall from heaven like a flash of lightning. See, I have given you authority to tread on snakes and scorpions, and over all the power of the enemy; and nothing will hurt you. Nevertheless, do not rejoice at this, that the spirits submit to you, but rejoice that your names are written in heaven."

At that same hour Jesus rejoiced in the Holy Spirit and said, "I thank you, Father, Lord of heaven and earth, because you have hidden these things from the wise and the intelligent and have revealed them to infants; yes, Father, for such was your gracious will. All things have been handed over to me by my Father; and no one knows who the Son is except the Father, or who the Father is except the Son and anyone to whom the Son chooses to reveal him."

Then turning to the disciples, Jesus said to them privately, "Blessed are the eyes that see what you see! For I tell you that many prophets and kings desired to see what you see, but did not see it, and to hear what you hear, but did not hear it."

Notice what you think and feel as you read the gospel.

When the disciples rejoice over the power Jesus has given them, Jesus says that what's really worth rejoicing about is that their names are written in heaven. Then he rejoices and thanks his Father that he reveals his truths to infants, not to the intelligent. Only the Father can reveal the Son to someone; only the Son can reveal the Father. Knowing God is the ultimate blessing.

Pray as you are led for yourself and others.

"Let me know you more and more, Lord: Father, Son, and Holy Spirit. I rejoice in you and pray that many, many come to know you as you are . . ." (Continue in your own words.)

Listen to Jesus.

This is what matters, beloved. God desires souls who love God as God loves them. This is the time of mercy. Come to the Son and love the Father. What else is Jesus saying to you?

Ask God to show you how to live today.

"Lord, I come. Thank you for your words and your grace. Amen."

Sunday, October 8, 2017
Twenty-Seventh Sunday in Ordinary Time

Know that God is present with you and ready to converse.

Jesus Christ came among us to reveal to us his Father, who is Love. He and the Father are one in the unity of the Holy Spirit. When we encounter God, we enter into the kingdom of heaven, a community of love and eternal life. We start where we are, but we have a way to go.

"Jesus, I enter your kingdom today as I follow you into the Word of God."

Read the gospel: Matthew 21:33–43.

Jesus said, "Listen to another parable. There was a landowner who planted a vineyard, put a fence around it, dug a wine press in it, and built a watch-tower. Then he leased it to tenants and went to another country. When the harvest time had come, he sent his slaves to the tenants to collect his produce. But the tenants seized his slaves and beat one, killed another, and stoned another. Again he sent other slaves, more than the first; and they treated them in the same way. Finally he sent his son to them, saying, 'They will respect my son.' But when the tenants saw the son, they said to themselves, 'This is the heir; come, let us kill him and get his inheritance.' So they seized him, threw him out of the vineyard, and killed him. Now when the owner of the vineyard comes, what will he do to those tenants?" They said to him, "He will put those wretches to a miserable death, and lease the vineyard to other tenants who will give him the produce at the harvest time."

Jesus said to them, "Have you never read in the scriptures:

'The stone that the builders rejected
　　has become the cornerstone;
this was the Lord's doing,
　　and it is amazing in our eyes'?

Therefore I tell you, the kingdom of God will be taken away from you and given to a people that produces the fruits of the kingdom."

Notice what you think and feel as you read the gospel.

In this prophetic parable, Jesus knows exactly what he is talking about. He tells the history of the Jewish prophets who were often rejected by the people they sought to save and turn back to God. What will the owner of the vineyard do when they reject and kill his son? He lets them answer that question. Did they know they were condemning themselves? Yet the killed Son, now risen, has become the cornerstone.

Pray as you are led for yourself and others.
"Lord, in your death and resurrection you reveal the mercy of God. Let the mercy of God cover all the earth. Turn the hearts of people to you . . ." (Continue in your own words.)

Listen to Jesus.
Some reject mercy for they will not repent. Do not be like them, my beloved. Do you have a need for my mercy? What else is Jesus saying to you?

Ask God to show you how to live today.
"Help me to show mercy to others, Savior, for I have received the mercy of God. Amen."

Monday, October 9, 2017

Know that God is present with you and ready to converse.
"The love of God surrounds me here. I taste eternal life."

Read the gospel: Luke 10:25–37.
Just then a lawyer stood up to test Jesus. "Teacher," he said, "what must I do to inherit eternal life?" He said to him, "What is written in the law? What do you read there?" He answered, "You shall love the Lord your God with all your heart, and with all your soul, and with all your strength, and with all your mind; and your neighbor as yourself." And he said to him, "You have given the right answer; do this, and you will live."

But wanting to justify himself, he asked Jesus, "And who is my neighbor?" Jesus replied, "A man was going down from Jerusalem to Jericho, and fell into the hands of robbers, who stripped him, beat him, and went away, leaving him half dead. Now by chance a priest was going down that road; and when he saw him, he passed by on the other side. So likewise a Levite, when he came to the place and saw him, passed by on the other side. But a Samaritan while travelling came near him; and when he saw him, he was moved with pity. He went to him and bandaged his wounds, having poured oil and wine on them. Then he put him on his own animal, brought him to an inn, and took care of him. The next day he took out two denarii, gave them to the innkeeper, and said, 'Take care of him; and when I come back, I will repay you whatever more you spend.' Which of these three, do you think, was a neighbor to the man who fell into the hands of the robbers?" He said, "The one who showed him mercy." Jesus said to him, "Go and do likewise."

Notice what you think and feel as you read the gospel.

The lawyer answers his own question correctly: love God, love your neighbor, and you will inherit eternal life. The parable identifies who our neighbor is: everyone. Who may receive eternal life? Everyone who shows mercy to neighbor—in this case, the Samaritan, not the priest or the Levite who profess to keep the commandments. Jesus commands us to "go and do likewise" and show mercy to our neighbors.

Pray as you are led for yourself and others.

"I know some who suffer, Lord. I pray for them now as you lead me . . ." (Continue in your own words.)

Listen to Jesus.

I hear your prayers, my friend. Are there ways you can show mercy to any of those you have prayed for? What else is Jesus saying to you?

Ask God to show you how to live today.

"You will help me find ways to love my neighbor, Teacher. Let my heart be moved with pity as I stop to help whoever is in need. For I long to inherit eternal life. Amen."

Tuesday, October 10, 2017

Know that God is present with you and ready to converse.

"When I am overwhelmed, calm me and simplify my life with your presence. Be with me now, Lord."

Read the gospel: Luke 10:38–42.

Now as they went on their way, he entered a certain village, where a woman named Martha welcomed him into her home. She had a sister named Mary, who sat at the Lord's feet and listened to what he was saying. But Martha was distracted by her many tasks; so she came to him and asked, "Lord, do you not care that my sister has left me to do all the work by myself? Tell her then to help me." But the Lord answered her, "Martha, Martha, you are worried and distracted by many things;

there is need of only one thing. Mary has chosen the better part, which will not be taken away from her."

Notice what you think and feel as you read the gospel.

Martha is being a good hostess as people visit her house to hear Jesus. Martha's sister, Mary, is one of them. Martha points out to Jesus that her sister isn't helping her. Jesus gently puts the situation in perspective for Martha. The better part is to sit at Jesus' feet and listen to him.

Pray as you are led for yourself and others.

"You are present, Lord, so I am listening now. I love to hear you. Then let me serve others . . ." (Continue in your own words.)

Listen to Jesus.

Prayer is spending time with God, sharing your whole heart, soul, and mind. Out of that comes service and the best results. What else is Jesus saying to you?

Ask God to show you how to live today.

"Jesus, I offer you my day of service as a prayer of thanks for all those you have given me. Thank you for staying by me today. Amen."

Wednesday, October 11, 2017

Know that God is present with you and ready to converse.

"I turn to you today, my God, and ask you to lead me in prayer, for I need you to teach me."

Read the gospel: Luke 11:1–4.

Jesus was praying in a certain place, and after he had finished, one of his disciples said to him, "Lord, teach us to pray, as John taught his disciples." He said to them, "When you pray, say:

> Father, hallowed be your name.
>> Your kingdom come.
>> Give us each day our daily bread.
>> And forgive us our sins,
>>> for we ourselves forgive everyone indebted to us.
>> And do not bring us to the time of trial."

Notice what you think and feel as you read the gospel.

Luke records this shorter prayer that begins by praising the Father, and immediately asks for the coming of the kingdom of God. The prayer ends differently from the one Matthew records, asking God not to bring us to the time of trial. To what does this refer?

Pray as you are led for yourself and others.

"I fear I will fail in trial. If I must undergo trial, Lord, as you yourself did, give me grace to accept it and to do your will. I can do it in your strength. I pray for all who are undergoing trials . . ." (Continue in your own words.)

Listen to Jesus.

All are tested by trials, but trials are in the nature of things, not brought on by God. Often they are brought on by oneself. You learn obedience by trials. What else is Jesus saying to you?

Ask God to show you how to live today.

"Lord, I abandon myself to your providence. You know what is best for me. You love me. I trust you. Amen."

Thursday, October 12, 2017

Know that God is present with you and ready to converse.

"I desire closeness with God, dear Lord. Enfold me in yourself."

Read the gospel: Luke 11:5–13.

And Jesus said to them, "Suppose one of you has a friend, and you go to him at midnight and say to him, 'Friend, lend me three loaves of bread; for a friend of mine has arrived, and I have nothing to set before him.' And he answers from within, 'Do not bother me; the door has already been locked, and my children are with me in bed; I cannot get up and give you anything.' I tell you, even though he will not get up and give him anything because he is his friend, at least because of his persistence he will get up and give him whatever he needs.

"So I say to you, Ask, and it will be given to you; search, and you will find; knock, and the door will be opened for you. For everyone who asks receives, and everyone who searches finds, and for everyone who knocks, the door will be opened. Is there anyone among you who, if your child asks for a fish, will give a snake instead of a fish? Or if the child asks for an egg, will give a scorpion? If you then, who are evil, know how to give good gifts to your children, how much more will the heavenly Father give the Holy Spirit to those who ask him!"

Notice what you think and feel as you read the gospel.

Jesus tells his disciples to persist in asking, searching, and knocking, saying that God will give what we ask. God wants to give us the Holy Spirit, the best gift of all.

Pray as you are led for yourself and others.

"You put desire for you in my heart, Lord. Let this hunger grow not just in me but in all those you have given me . . ." (Continue in your own words.)

Listen to Jesus.

I will satisfy your hunger for God, beloved disciple. God hears your prayers and is filling you with the fullness of God. What else is Jesus saying to you?

Ask God to show you how to live today.

"By your grace, my God, I will walk in your Spirit today, doing small acts of love whenever I can. Glory to you, O Lord. Amen."

Friday, October 13, 2017

Know that God is present with you and ready to converse.

"Lord, you come to me as invisible Spirit to teach me about Jesus and his way. You give me the Word of God."

Read the gospel: Luke 11:15–26.

But some of the crowd said, "He casts out demons by Beelzebul, the ruler of the demons." Others, to test him, kept demanding from him a sign from heaven. But he knew what they were thinking and said to them, "Every kingdom divided against itself becomes a desert, and house falls on house. If Satan also is divided against himself, how will his kingdom stand?—for you say that I cast out the demons by Beelzebul. Now if I cast out the demons by Beelzebul, by whom do your exorcists cast them out? Therefore they will be your judges. But if it is by the finger of God that I cast out the demons, then the kingdom of God has come to you. When a strong man, fully armed, guards his castle, his property is safe. But when one stronger than he attacks him and overpowers him, he takes away his armor in which he trusted and divides his plunder. Whoever is not with me is against me, and whoever does not gather with me scatters.

"When the unclean spirit has gone out of a person, it wanders through waterless regions looking for a resting-place, but not finding any, it says, 'I will return to my house from which I came.' When it comes, it finds it swept and put in order. Then it goes and brings seven other spirits more evil than itself, and they enter and live there; and the last state of that person is worse than the first."

Notice what you think and feel as you read the gospel.

In response to being accused of being in league with the devil, Jesus speaks about the nature of evil spirits as they work in the world. He has power over them for he is the Lord of all. He can cast them out, but the unclean spirit can return to the person in whom it once was and, with other spirits, make it even worse for the person.

Pray as you are led for yourself and others.

"Lord, protect me and those I love from all the powers of evil, for there is spiritual warfare going on. Place your Holy Spirit upon us so that no evil can remain in us . . ." (Continue in your own words.)

Listen to Jesus.

There is a struggle between light and darkness, good and evil, in the world and in every person's soul. I have power, and I give you power to resist and defeat evil. Be careful and stay nearby, my child. What else is Jesus saying to you?

Ask God to show you how to live today.

"By your power I am enemy to all the evil I encounter. Give me wisdom to do what I should do in opposing it, and let God be victorious. Amen."

Saturday, October 14, 2017

Know that God is present with you and ready to converse.

"Blessed Lord, I welcome you. Let me hear your Word in the deepest regions of my soul."

Read the gospel: Luke 11:27–28.

While Jesus was saying this, a woman in the crowd raised her voice and said to him, "Blessed is the womb that bore you and the breasts that nursed you!" But he said, "Blessed rather are those who hear the word of God and obey it!"

Notice what you think and feel as you read the gospel.

A woman in the crowd raises her voice in praise of Jesus' mother, calling her blessed. Jesus turns her blessing back upon the whole crowd by proclaiming that the true blessed are those who hear and obey the Word of God.

Pray as you are led for yourself and others.

"I seek to obey your Word, dear Savior, for I want your blessedness for me and for those you have given me . . ." (Continue in your own words.)

Listen to Jesus.

You are one of the holy family, with all the saints of all time. We love you and watch over you as you journey through this world. We will welcome you into the kingdom, beloved disciple. What else is Jesus saying to you?

Ask God to show you how to live today.

"You are wonderful to me, my God. If I should face some difficulty or sorrow today, remind me of your goodness to me and your promises. Glory be to the Father, the Son, and the Holy Spirit. Amen."

Sunday, October 15, 2017
Twenty-Eighth Sunday in Ordinary Time

Know that God is present with you and ready to converse.

Jesus Christ is not a person to take for granted. He is the Lord, risen in the power of God as King of all the earth. In the end he will judge every person, our thoughts, words, and deeds. The Word of God reminds us of the high stakes of faith and obedience to God.

"Lord, stir up my soul to attend to you now, for you have the words of eternal life."

Read the gospel: Matthew 22:1-14.

Once more Jesus spoke to them in parables, saying: "The kingdom of heaven may be compared to a king who gave a wedding banquet for his son. He sent his slaves to call those who had been invited to the wedding banquet, but they would not come. Again he sent other slaves, saying, 'Tell those who have been invited: Look, I have prepared my dinner, my oxen and my fat calves have been slaughtered, and everything is ready; come to the wedding banquet.' But they made light of it and went away, one to his farm, another to his business, while the rest seized his slaves, maltreated them, and killed them. The king was enraged. He sent his troops, destroyed those murderers, and burned their city. Then he said to his slaves, 'The wedding is ready, but those invited were not worthy. Go therefore into the main streets, and invite everyone you find to the wedding banquet.' Those slaves went out into the streets and gathered all whom they found, both good and bad; so the wedding hall was filled with guests.

"But when the king came in to see the guests, he noticed a man there who was not wearing a wedding robe, and he said to him, 'Friend, how did you get in here without a wedding robe?' And he was speechless. Then the king said to the attendants, 'Bind him hand and foot, and throw him into the outer darkness, where there will be weeping and gnashing of teeth.' For many are called, but few are chosen."

Notice what you think and feel as you read the gospel.

Jesus compares the kingdom of heaven to a wedding banquet to which the invited guests do not come. They decide they have better things to do. They even mistreat the king's slaves, killing them. Enraged, the king has his banquet hall filled with anyone and everyone they can find, good and bad. He casts out the man who was not wearing a wedding garment—for while many are called, few are chosen.

Pray as you are led for yourself and others.

"I know many people who are far from you, Lord, and do not seem to want you in their lives. I pray for them. Send your Holy Spirit and revive in their hearts a desire for you . . ." (Continue in your own words.)

Listen to Jesus.

People are free to come to me. Many do. Many do not. Many more will. I continue to call. What else is Jesus saying to you?

Ask God to show you how to live today.

"Lord, what can I do? Send me out to invite guests to your wedding banquet. Give me the words. Amen."

Monday, October 16, 2017

Know that God is present with you and ready to converse.

"You are here, Lord. Cut through my darkness with the light of your Word."

Read the gospel: Luke 11:29–32.

When the crowds were increasing, Jesus began to say, "This generation is an evil generation; it asks for a sign, but no sign will be given to it except the sign of Jonah. For just as Jonah became a sign to the people of Nineveh, so the Son of Man will be to this generation. The queen of the South will rise at the judgement with the people of this generation and condemn them, because she came from the ends of the earth to listen to the wisdom of Solomon, and see, something greater than Solomon is here! The people of Nineveh will rise up at the judgement with this generation and condemn it, because they repented at the proclamation of Jonah, and see, something greater than Jonah is here!"

Notice what you think and feel as you read the gospel.

Jesus condemns those who ask him for signs. He has performed many mighty works as well as spoken with authority about his Father and the kingdom of heaven, and yet they still want a sign. The only sign they will get is the sign of Jonah, Jesus says, for Jonah was three days in the belly of a fish. When he appeared in Nineveh, the people repented. At the judgment they will rise and condemn this generation for refusing to repent despite the warnings of the Son of God.

Pray as you are led for yourself and others.

"Lord, give me true repentance for my sins. I pray for those you have given me, that they will come to you seeking your forgiveness . . ." (Continue in your own words.)

Listen to Jesus.

Every generation is the same, beloved. My heart longs for them to come to me and to know the blessedness of God. Would you share my longing? What else is Jesus saying to you?

Ask God to show you how to live today.

"Lord, you work in many ways behind the scenes, often in ways I cannot see at the time. Let me see and understand how I can help. Your kingdom come and your will be done on earth. Amen."

Tuesday, October 17, 2017

Know that God is present with you and ready to converse.

"I am a sinner, Lord, but you are here with me to save me by your Word."

Read the gospel: Luke 11:37–41.

While Jesus was speaking, a Pharisee invited him to dine with him; so he went in and took his place at the table. The Pharisee was amazed to see that he did not first wash before dinner. Then the Lord said to him, "Now you Pharisees clean the outside of the cup and of the dish, but inside you are full of greed and wickedness. You fools! Did not the one who made the outside make the inside also? So give for alms those things that are within; and see, everything will be clean for you."

Notice what you think and feel as you read the gospel.

Jesus asks for inner cleanness, not a show of outer cleanness. He says that the Pharisees are full of greed and wickedness. "Give for alms," he says, "those things that are within; and see, everything will be clean for you."

Pray as you are led for yourself and others.

"Lord, I seek to abandon my own greed and wickedness so that I will be clean in your sight. Cleanse me, Lord, and make clean the hearts of all those you have given me . . ." (Continue in your own words.)

Listen to Jesus.

You are clean, my beloved. I wash you in the water of my Word and put my Holy Spirit within you. Let us walk together. What else is Jesus saying to you?

Ask God to show you how to live today.

"I rejoice in you, my God. All things are possible for you, mighty Savior of the world. Let me do what you want me to do today. Amen."

Wednesday, October 18, 2017
Saint Luke, Evangelist

Know that God is present with you and ready to converse.

"The peace of God is yours, Jesus. Let me breathe it in now with your Word."

Read the gospel: Luke 10:1–9.

After this the Lord appointed seventy others and sent them on ahead of him in pairs to every town and place where he himself intended to go. He said to them, "The harvest is plentiful, but the laborers are few; therefore ask the Lord of the harvest to send out laborers into his harvest. Go on your way. See, I am sending you out like lambs into the midst of wolves. Carry no purse, no bag, no sandals; and greet no one on the road. Whatever house you enter, first say, 'Peace to this house!' And if anyone is there who shares in peace, your peace will rest on that person; but if not, it will return to you. Remain in the same house, eating and drinking whatever they provide, for the laborer deserves to be paid. Do not move about from house to house. Whenever you enter a town and its people welcome you, eat what is set before you; cure the sick who are there, and say to them, 'The kingdom of God has come near to you.'"

Notice what you think and feel as you read the gospel.

Jesus asks his disciples to work to bring people into the kingdom of God and to pray that God sends even more people to do this great work. He gives them power to heal the sick and words to say to them: "The kingdom of God has come near to you."

Pray as you are led for yourself and others.

"The kingdom, the power, and the glory are yours, O Lord. I pray for those who speak your words and for those who hear them, that all may come into your blessed kingdom . . ." (Continue in your own words.)

Listen to Jesus.

Let us stay close, you and I, for I want to go with you. We must work together for the coming of the kingdom. What else is Jesus saying to you?

Ask God to show you how to live today.

"I know you ask us to do good things for others, Lord. I offer myself to do good today. Thank you for being near me. Amen."

Thursday, October 19, 2017

Know that God is present with you and ready to converse.

"You are holy, O Lord, and the fountain of all holiness, present with me now as I turn to your Word."

Read the gospel: Luke 11:47-54.

Jesus said, "Woe to you! For you build the tombs of the prophets whom your ancestors killed. So you are witnesses and approve of the deeds of your ancestors; for they killed them, and you build their tombs. Therefore also the Wisdom of God said, 'I will send them prophets and apostles, some of whom they will kill and persecute,' so that this generation may be charged with the blood of all the prophets shed since the foundation of the world, from the blood of Abel to the blood of Zechariah, who perished between the altar and the sanctuary. Yes, I tell you, it will be charged against this generation. Woe to you lawyers! For you have taken away the key of knowledge; you did not enter yourselves, and you hindered those who were entering."

When he went outside, the scribes and the Pharisees began to be very hostile towards him and to cross-examine him about many things, lying in wait for him, to catch him in something he might say.

Notice what you think and feel as you read the gospel.

Jesus opposes the scribes and Pharisees, accusing them of killing God's prophets as their ancestors did. He condemns the lawyers for taking away the "key of knowledge," not entering themselves and hindering others from entering. The scribes and Pharisees become very hostile and lie in wait to trap him in his words.

Pray as you are led for yourself and others.

"Jesus, no one can trap you in your words. You are the Word of God and speak only truth. I pray for those who are hostile toward you, that they may see your truth and goodness . . ." (Continue in your own words.)

Listen to Jesus.

My Word rings forth throughout the earth and captures hearts and minds. Let those who have ears to hear, hear. What else is Jesus saying to you?

Ask God to show you how to live today.

"Let your words remain in me today as I do what you have given me to do. Make holy the works of my hands, dear Lord. Amen."

Friday, October 20, 2017

Know that God is present with you and ready to converse.

"Teacher, Friend, Savior, I come before you with an open, humble heart."

Read the gospel: Luke 12:1–7.

Meanwhile, when the crowd gathered in thousands, so that they trampled on one another, Jesus began to speak first to his disciples, "Beware of the yeast of the Pharisees, that is, their hypocrisy. Nothing is covered up that will not be uncovered, and nothing secret that will not become known. Therefore whatever you have said in the dark will be heard in the light, and what you have whispered behind closed doors will be proclaimed from the housetops.

"I tell you, my friends, do not fear those who kill the body, and after that can do nothing more. But I will warn you whom to fear: fear him who, after he has killed, has authority to cast into hell. Yes, I tell you, fear him! Are not five sparrows sold for two pennies? Yet not one of them is forgotten in God's sight. But even the hairs of your head are all counted. Do not be afraid; you are of more value than many sparrows."

Notice what you think and feel as you read the gospel.

Jesus first tells his disciples not to be hypocrites for, in the end, all things will be known. Then he tells them to fear no one, not even those who can kill them. We have great value in God's eyes. We can trust God.

Pray as you are led for yourself and others.

"I pray for the conversion of hypocrites and for courage and comfort for those who are persecuted. I think of these . . ." (Continue in your own words.)

Listen to Jesus.

Keep your heart open, child, and I will fill it with my love for others. It is my love that gives you power to do good. What else is Jesus saying to you?

Ask God to show you how to live today.

"I receive your love, Lord. Lead me on my way to love and serve others. Amen."

Saturday, October 21, 2017

Know that God is present with you and ready to converse.

"Holy Spirit, you are present in the Word of God to teach us about Jesus Christ. Be present within me so that I may receive him as my Lord."

Read the gospel: Luke 12:8–12.

Jesus said, "And I tell you, everyone who acknowledges me before others, the Son of Man also will acknowledge before the angels of God; but whoever denies me before others will be denied before the angels of God. And everyone who speaks a word against the Son of Man will be forgiven; but whoever blasphemes against the Holy Spirit will not be forgiven. When they bring you before the synagogues, the rulers, and the authorities, do not worry about how you are to defend yourselves or what you are to say; for the Holy Spirit will teach you at that very hour what you ought to say."

Notice what you think and feel as you read the gospel.

Jesus asks that we acknowledge him before others and not deny him. When others oppose you, don't worry about defending yourself, for the Holy Spirit will show you what to say in that hour.

Pray as you are led for yourself and others.

"Lord, give me your Spirit without measure so that I can serve you and others fearlessly and well . . ." (Continue in your own words.)

Listen to Jesus.

I love you, child, and I thank you for turning to me. Know that no matter how others treat you because of me, I will be with you always. What else is Jesus saying to you?

Ask God to show you how to live today.

"Jesus, I want to know God and love God more and more, in part so I can speak confidently when others question my faith. Tell me how to do that today and tomorrow and always. I praise you for your great glory. Amen."

Sunday, October 22, 2017
Twenty-Ninth Sunday in Ordinary Time

Know that God is present with you and ready to converse.

Jesus Christ is Alpha and Omega, the beloved Son of the Father, the Lamb of God, risen King, and Judge of all. He is with his Church to the end of the age. He brings us victory.

"Let us come into his presence to adore him."

Read the gospel: Matthew 22:15–21.

Then the Pharisees went and plotted to entrap Jesus in what he said. So they sent their disciples to him, along with the Herodians, saying, "Teacher, we know that you are sincere, and teach the way of God in accordance with truth, and show deference to no one; for you do not regard people with partiality. Tell us, then, what you think. Is it lawful to pay taxes to the emperor, or not?" But Jesus, aware of their malice, said, "Why are you putting me to the test, you hypocrites? Show me the coin used for the tax." And they brought him a denarius. Then he said to them, "Whose head is this, and whose title?" They answered, "The emperor's." Then he said to them, "Give therefore to the emperor the things that are the emperor's, and to God the things that are God's."

Notice what you think and feel as you read the gospel.

They try, but the Pharisees and Herodians cannot trap Jesus. He calls them on their hypocrisy and malice. Then he answers their question: give to the emperor what is the emperor's and to God what is God's.

Pray as you are led for yourself and others.

"All I have is yours, my God, so I give it all to you. I also give to you now those you have given to me . . ." (Continue in your own words.)

Listen to Jesus.

I ask those who follow me to abandon themselves into my care. As you do this, you will know me more and more and enjoy the good things of the kingdom of heaven. What else is Jesus saying to you?

Ask God to show you how to live today.

"Thank you for your constant care for me, Lord. Let me in turn care for someone else you love. Amen."

Monday, October 23, 2017

Know that God is present with you and ready to converse.

"God, your Word contains the riches of God: truth, beauty, light, and wisdom. Your Spirit speaks through your Word. Let it speak to me."

Read the gospel: Luke 12:13–21.

Someone in the crowd said to Jesus, "Teacher, tell my brother to divide the family inheritance with me." But he said to him, "Friend, who set me to be a judge or arbitrator over you?" And he said to them, "Take care! Be on your guard against all kinds of greed; for one's life does not consist in the abundance of possessions." Then he told them a parable: "The land of a rich man produced abundantly. And he thought to himself, 'What should I do, for I have no place to store my crops?' Then he said, 'I will do this: I will pull down my barns and build larger ones, and there I will store all my grain and my goods. And I will say to my soul, 'Soul, you have ample goods laid up for many years; relax, eat, drink, be merry.' But God said to him, 'You fool! This very night your life is being demanded of you. And the things you have prepared, whose will they be?' So it is with those who store up treasures for themselves but are not rich towards God."

Notice what you think and feel as you read the gospel.

Jesus teaches that life does not consist in the abundance of possessions. The soul outlives any material things we may possess, and then what will we have? We need to be rich in the things of God, for those we may carry into God's blessed kingdom.

Pray as you are led for yourself and others.

"It is hard not to be covetous of earthly riches, Lord, but by your Spirit we can hold all things lightly and be generous with those in need. Let me give with true generosity today . . ." (Continue in your own words.)

Listen to Jesus.

I work in you to purify your heart, to sanctify your motives. This is the work of my Spirit within you. Beloved disciple, give yourself to God's work within you. What else is Jesus saying to you?

Ask God to show you how to live today.

"I bow before you, Lord God of Hosts. Light my way today as I walk into the kingdom of heaven, focusing on the riches of your kingdom and not those of this earth. Amen."

Tuesday, October 24, 2017

Know that God is present with you and ready to converse.

"You are everywhere, Lord, fully present throughout the universe and in heaven. You bless me by being here with me now as I turn to your Word."

Read the gospel: Luke 12:35–38.

Jesus said, "Be dressed for action and have your lamps lit; be like those who are waiting for their master to return from the wedding banquet, so that they may open the door for him as soon as he comes and knocks. Blessed are those slaves whom the master finds alert when he comes; truly I tell you, he will fasten his belt and have them sit down to eat, and he will come and serve them. If he comes during the middle of the night, or near dawn, and finds them so, blessed are those slaves."

Notice what you think and feel as you read the gospel.

Jesus tells his followers to be ready for his return so we can open the door to him. What will he do? He will have us sit down to eat, and he himself will serve us.

Pray as you are led for yourself and others.

"Jesus, you are so good. Let me not grow weary of waiting for you but expect you always. I pray that all the earth will be ready to receive you . . ." (Continue in your own words.)

Listen to Jesus.

I came to serve people and to give myself for them. This is the love I ask of you, for you are mine. What else is Jesus saying to you?

Ask God to show you how to live today.

"Give me the Spirit of the vigilant servant, Lord, to do your work with patience and perseverance. Amen."

Wednesday, October 25, 2017

Know that God is present with you and ready to converse.

"Lord, you condescend to speak to us. Let me hear and obey your Word."

Read the gospel: Luke 12:39–48.

Jesus said, "But know this: if the owner of the house had known at what hour the thief was coming, he would not have let his house be broken into. You also must be ready, for the Son of Man is coming at an unexpected hour."

Peter said, "Lord, are you telling this parable for us or for everyone?" And the Lord said, "Who then is the faithful and prudent manager whom his master will put in charge of his slaves, to give them their allowance of food at the proper time? Blessed is that slave whom his master will find at work when he arrives. Truly I tell you, he will put that one in charge of all his possessions. But if that slave says to himself, 'My master is delayed in coming,' and if he begins to beat the other slaves, men and women, and to eat and drink and get drunk, the master of that slave will come on a day when he does not expect him and at an hour that he does not know, and will cut him in pieces, and put him with the unfaithful. That slave who knew what his master wanted, but did not prepare himself or do what was wanted, will receive a severe beating. But one who did not know and did what deserved a beating will receive a light beating. From everyone to whom much has been given, much will be required; and from one to whom much has been entrusted, even more will be demanded."

Notice what you think and feel as you read the gospel.

Jesus says he will return at an unexpected hour. Blessed is that slave whom the master will find at work when he comes. The lazy, abusive slave will be punished. Much is expected from those to whom much is given.

Pray as you are led for yourself and others.

"Let my faith become a long and fruitful faithfulness, Lord, for you have given me much. I pray for those I serve . . ." (Continue in your own words.)

Listen to Jesus.

Do not be afraid, beloved disciple, friend, and servant. I am with you now and I will be with you always. God is faithful. What else is Jesus saying to you?

Ask God to show you how to live today.

"How may I serve today, Lord? Give me ways to please you. Amen."

Thursday, October 26, 2017

Know that God is present with you and ready to converse.

"You are Lord of all the earth, Almighty God. Open my understanding to walk in your way."

Read the gospel: Luke 12:49–53.

Jesus said, "I came to bring fire to the earth, and how I wish it were already kindled! I have a baptism with which to be baptized, and what stress I am under until it is completed! Do you think that I have come to bring peace to the earth? No, I tell you, but rather division! From now on, five in one household will be divided, three against two and two against three; they will be divided: father against son and son against father, mother against daughter and daughter against mother, mother-in-law against her daughter-in-law and daughter-in-law against mother-in-law."

Notice what you think and feel as you read the gospel.

Jesus knows he brings fire, stress, and division to the earth. He speaks of the division he will bring even to families as some follow and some reject him.

Pray as you are led for yourself and others.

"I pray for the unity of peoples and especially of families throughout the earth, torn apart by religious differences. Let us be one in God. I pray for those in my own family . . ." (Continue in your own words.)

Listen to Jesus.

I know you suffer as I suffer, wanting peace and love to reign over all. That day is coming, beloved. In the meantime, there are things to do. What else is Jesus saying to you?

Ask God to show you how to live today.

"I offer myself to you today to serve. Thank you for this privilege. Amen."

Friday, October 27, 2017

Know that God is present with you and ready to converse.

"You come to me in Word and in Spirit, my God. Help me to interpret and apply your Word."

Read the gospel: Luke 12:54–59.

Jesus also said to the crowds, "When you see a cloud rising in the west, you immediately say, 'It is going to rain'; and so it happens. And when you see the south wind blowing, you say, 'There will be scorching heat'; and it happens. You hypocrites! You know how to interpret the appearance of earth and sky, but why do you not know how to interpret the present time?

"And why do you not judge for yourselves what is right? Thus, when you go with your accuser before a magistrate, on the way make an effort to settle the case, or you may be dragged before the judge, and the judge hand you over to the officer, and the officer throw you in prison. I tell you, you will never get out until you have paid the very last penny."

Notice what you think and feel as you read the gospel.

Jesus wants us to put our affairs in order as we await the coming of the kingdom. He urges us to settle disputes quickly. We have it in us to know what is right.

Pray as you are led for yourself and others.

"Lord, I pray for those who accuse me or dispute with me. Let me forgive them from my heart and seek to settle with them on the way . . ." (Continue in your own words.)

Listen to Jesus.

Take care that the things and the struggles of this life do not distract you from the goal of heaven. Come to me and I will show you the treasures of heaven. What else is Jesus saying to you?

Ask God to show you how to live today.

"Help me not to engage in pointless disputes with others, Lord. Put a guard on my lips until I can speak a word of peace in season. Amen."

Saturday, October 28, 2017
Saints Simon and Jude, Apostles

Know that God is present with you and ready to converse.

"Lord, you have called me to yourself. You wish to speak to me by your Word. Glory to you, O Lord."

Read the gospel: Luke 6:12–16.

Now during those days Jesus went out to the mountain to pray; and he spent the night in prayer to God. And when day came, he called his disciples and chose twelve of them, whom he also named apostles: Simon, whom he named Peter, and his brother Andrew, and James, and John, and Philip, and Bartholomew, and Matthew, and Thomas, and James son of Alphaeus, and Simon, who was called the Zealot, and Judas son of James, and Judas Iscariot, who became a traitor.

Notice what you think and feel as you read the gospel.

Clearly, Jesus set the twelve apostles in a separate category from the rest of his followers. He prayed to his Father and chose those twelve to be his inner circle. How different they were from one another. They seem simple and ordinary, yet they would carry on after him. And one of them would betray him.

Pray as you are led for yourself and others.

"Your purposes are inscrutable, Lord. I accept whatever you have given me, the people and circumstances of my life, and I thank you for them . . ." (Continue in your own words.)

Listen to Jesus.

I like to use ordinary things for the glory of my Father. I like using you, my beloved. In me you are great. What else is Jesus saying to you?

Ask God to show you how to live today.

"Simple acts of love—let me do them. Inspire me today, dear Lord. Amen."

Sunday, October 29, 2017
Thirtieth Sunday in Ordinary Time

Know that God is present with you and ready to converse.

If we had a little faith in God, would that change things in our lives? Jesus thought so. The religious people of his own day often put him to the test, hoping to catch him in some error. For many in the crowd believed he was the Messiah, more than a prophet, but God-with-us.

"Jesus, you promised to be present with each believer. You are the Word of God with me now. Let me receive you with faith."

Read the gospel: Matthew 22:34–40.

When the Pharisees heard that Jesus had silenced the Sadducees, they gathered together, and one of them, a lawyer, asked him a question to test him. "Teacher, which commandment in the law is the greatest?" He said to him, "'You shall love the Lord your God with all your heart, and with all your soul, and with all your mind.' This is the greatest and first commandment. And a second is like it: 'You shall love your neighbor as yourself.' On these two commandments hang all the law and the prophets."

Notice what you think and feel as you read the gospel.

Jesus makes obedience to God simple: love God and love your neighbor. He asks us to love with all our might and in every way. That's all.

Pray as you are led for yourself and others.

"Lord, my love falls short. Put your love within me. I pray now for those you have asked me to love . . ." (Continue in your own words.)

Listen to Jesus.

Love is of God, child. Those who love know God and please God. Organize your life around love. What else is Jesus saying to you?

Ask God to show you how to live today.

"I offer myself to you today, Lord of Love. Teach me how to walk in simple love. Even this is possible for me, for you are in me, Jesus. Amen."

Monday, October 30, 2017

Know that God is present with you and ready to converse.

"Lord, move in me to wash me and heal me. Only say the Word and I shall be healed."

Read the gospel: Luke 13:10–17.

Now Jesus was teaching in one of the synagogues on the sabbath. And just then there appeared a woman with a spirit that had crippled her for eighteen years. She was bent over and was quite unable to stand up straight. When Jesus saw her, he called her over and said, "Woman, you are set free from your ailment." When he laid his hands on her, immediately she stood up straight and began praising God. But the leader of the synagogue, indignant because Jesus had cured on the sabbath, kept saying to the crowd, "There are six days on which work ought to be done; come on those days and be cured, and not on the sabbath day." But the Lord answered him and said, "You hypocrites! Does not each of you on the sabbath untie his ox or his donkey from the manger, and lead it away to give it water? And ought not this woman, a daughter of Abraham whom Satan bound for eighteen long years, be set free from this bondage on the sabbath day?" When he said this, all his opponents were put to shame; and the entire crowd was rejoicing at all the wonderful things that he was doing.

Notice what you think and feel as you read the gospel.

Jesus heals a woman who had suffered a long time. It was the Sabbath, so the leader of the synagogue was indignant, saying it is wrong to heal or be healed on the Sabbath. Jesus points out that a person is of more consequence than a donkey or an ox which one leads away to give it water even on the Sabbath. The crowd rejoices.

Pray as you are led for yourself and others.

"Lord, you know what I need. I reach out to you, asking you to do with me as you see fit. I pray also for others . . ." (Continue in your own words.)

Listen to Jesus.

I see into your heart and soul, beloved, and I find faith. Would you like me to increase your faith? What else is Jesus saying to you?

Ask God to show you how to live today.

"Let my faith in you light my way, Lord. I want to do something extraordinary because you are with me. Amen."

Tuesday, October 31, 2017

Know that God is present with you and ready to converse.

"Wherever you are, Lord, mercy and truth abounds. You grant peace to troubled souls. I turn to you now, my God."

Read the gospel: Luke 13:18–21.

Jesus said therefore, "What is the kingdom of God like? And to what should I compare it? It is like a mustard seed that someone took and sowed in the garden; it grew and became a tree, and the birds of the air made nests in its branches."

And again he said, "To what should I compare the kingdom of God? It is like yeast that a woman took and mixed in with three measures of flour until all of it was leavened."

Notice what you think and feel as you read the gospel.

The kingdom of God starts small but grows large by its own energy. That energy must be the Holy Spirit. May the kingdom grow large on earth. May the kingdom grow large within us.

Pray as you are led for yourself and others.

"I pray for the coming of the kingdom of heaven. May it leaven every nation and every person that God may be glorified for God's goodness and might . . ." (Continue in your own words.)

Listen to Jesus.

You don't need to do anything, beloved disciple. I have already done everything, and the Spirit is working within you, renewing your life. What else is Jesus saying to you?

Ask God to show you how to live today.

"Then let me behave as one who lives by the life of God. Let me honor and never disgrace you, Lord Jesus Christ, for I am called by your name. Amen."

Wednesday, November 1, 2017
All Saints

Know that God is present with you and ready to converse.

"Let me receive your Word deep within, Lord, that I may know true blessedness."

Read the gospel: Matthew 5:1–12a.

When Jesus saw the crowds, he went up the mountain; and after he sat down, his disciples came to him. Then he began to speak, and taught them, saying:

"Blessed are the poor in spirit, for theirs is the kingdom of heaven.

"Blessed are those who mourn, for they will be comforted.

"Blessed are the meek, for they will inherit the earth.

"Blessed are those who hunger and thirst for righteousness, for they will be filled.

"Blessed are the merciful, for they will receive mercy.

"Blessed are the pure in heart, for they will see God.

"Blessed are the peacemakers, for they will be called children of God.

"Blessed are those who are persecuted for righteousness' sake, for theirs is the kingdom of heaven.

"Blessed are you when people revile you and persecute you and utter all kinds of evil against you falsely on my account. Rejoice and be glad, for your reward is great in heaven, for in the same way they persecuted the prophets who were before you."

Notice what you think and feel as you read the gospel.

Jesus teaches his disciples about blessedness, how to find greatest happiness and fulfillment. The poor, the suffering, the humble, the good, the merciful, the pure, the peaceable, and the persecuted—these are the ones favored with blessedness, now and forever. They will inherit the kingdom and the earth, be comforted, be satisfied with righteousness, receive mercy, see God, be called children of God, and be rewarded in heaven.

Pray as you are led for yourself and others.

"Jesus, you ask me to be better than I have ever been. I ask you to help me with this. I pray also for those you have given me . . ." (Continue in your own words.)

Listen to Jesus.

The kingdom is within you, my beloved, and it is growing. Rejoice in God. What else is Jesus saying to you?

Ask God to show you how to live today.

"By your grace I will walk today in God's blessedness. I am rich with nothing more than my love for God and my resolve to seek God in all things. Amen."

Thursday, November 2, 2017
The Commemoration of All the Faithful Departed (All Souls)

Know that God is present with you and ready to converse.

"Many have died and are with you, Lord. When I die, let me join that great company, praising you for eternity, starting now."

Read the gospel: John 6:37–40.

Jesus said, "Everything that the Father gives me will come to me, and anyone who comes to me I will never drive away; for I have come down from heaven, not to do my own will, but the will of him who sent me. And this is the will of him who sent me, that I should lose nothing of all that he has given me, but raise it up on the last day. This is indeed the will of my Father, that all who see the Son and believe in him may have eternal life; and I will raise them up on the last day."

Notice what you think and feel as you read the gospel.

Jesus says he will never drive away anyone who comes to him. The Father wills that Jesus lose no one. He will raise us up to eternal life on the last day.

Pray as you are led for yourself and others.

"Who can imagine the fulfillment of that promise? Jesus describes God as generous, mighty, and faithful. May all those you have given me come to believe in God . . ." (Continue in your own words.)

Listen to Jesus.

My Father is glorious, and he has given glory to me. You, too, live and move in the glory of God. We love you because you are ours. What else is Jesus saying to you?

Ask God to show you how to live today.

"If I am a beloved child of God, I will find ways to honor and serve God today. What shall I do? Amen."

Friday, November 3, 2017

Know that God is present with you and ready to converse.

"How wonderful you are, Lord, that you humble yourself to be among the people of the earth, to be here with me now!"

Read the gospel: Luke 14:1–6.

On one occasion when Jesus was going to the house of a leader of the Pharisees to eat a meal on the sabbath, they were watching him closely. Just then, in front of him, there was a man who had dropsy. And Jesus asked the lawyers and Pharisees, "Is it lawful to cure people on the sabbath, or not?" But they were silent. So Jesus took him and healed him, and sent him away. Then he said to them, "If one of you has a child or an ox that has fallen into a well, will you not immediately pull it out on a sabbath day?" And they could not reply to this.

Notice what you think and feel as you read the gospel.

Jesus again deals with the legalism of Sabbath work. Is it lawful to heal people on the Sabbath? Would you rescue your child (or your ox) fallen into a well on the Sabbath? It's just common sense to do good any day you can.

Pray as you are led for yourself and others.

"Keep us free of pointless rules and regimens, Lord. Let our eyes remain on you. Be our shepherd . . ." (Continue in your own words.)

Listen to Jesus.

I do not tire of loving you, dear disciple. Love is infinitely rewarding. Learn to love. Follow me. What else is Jesus saying to you?

Ask God to show you how to live today.

"I shall love as you love, blessed Lord, and I will show love in every way and at any moment I can. Thank you. Amen."

Saturday, November 4, 2017

Know that God is present with you and ready to converse.

"Here I am, Lord, your child in need of grace and wisdom. Open me to your Word."

Read the gospel: Luke 14:1, 7–11.

On one occasion when Jesus was going to the house of a leader of the Pharisees to eat a meal on the sabbath, they were watching him closely. . . .

When he noticed how the guests chose the places of honor, he told them a parable. "When you are invited by someone to a wedding banquet, do not sit down at the place of honor, in case someone more distinguished than you has been invited by your host; and the host who invited both of you may come and say to you, 'Give this person your place,' and then in disgrace you would start to take the lowest place. But when you are invited, go and sit down at the lowest place, so that when your host comes, he may say to you, 'Friend, move up higher'; then you will be honored in the presence of all who sit at the table with you. For all who exalt themselves will be humbled, and those who humble themselves will be exalted."

Notice what you think and feel as you read the gospel.

Jesus notices that people seek honor, so he advises them to humble themselves. Those who do will receive honor, the honor of the host of the wedding banquet.

Pray as you are led for yourself and others.

"Lord, teach me true humility. You humbled yourself, Son of God. Teach me humility like yours . . ." (Continue in your own words.)

Listen to Jesus.

The honor one can receive from people is brief and unfulfilling. The honor one can receive from God is forever. I love the humble. What else is Jesus saying to you?

Ask God to show you how to live today.

"How may I demonstrate humility today, Lord? How may I place myself low or last? Let humility begin in my heart. Amen."

Sunday, November 5, 2017
Thirty-First Sunday in Ordinary Time

Know that God is present with you and ready to converse.

Jesus did what people wanted him to do; he healed them, fed them, and worked many miracles. But Jesus said things people did not expect; he taught them that God was their Father, that the poor are blessed, and that many things are the opposite of what people think. Speaking the gospel truth, Jesus challenged, amazed, and puzzled all who heard him. He does so still.

"Lord, you are with me now as I open myself to your Word. I praise your name."

Read the gospel: Matthew 23:1–12.

Then Jesus said to the crowds and to his disciples, "The scribes and the Pharisees sit on Moses' seat; therefore, do whatever they teach you and follow it; but do not do as they do, for they do not practice what they teach. They tie up heavy burdens, hard to bear, and lay them on the shoulders of others; but they themselves are unwilling to lift a finger to move them. They do all their deeds to be seen by others; for they make their phylacteries broad and their fringes long. They love to have the place of honor at banquets and the best seats in the synagogues, and to be greeted with respect in the market-places, and to have people call them rabbi. But you are not to be called rabbi, for you have one teacher, and you are all students. And call no one your father on earth, for you have one Father—the one in heaven. Nor are you to be called instructors, for you have one instructor, the Messiah. The greatest among you will be your servant. All who exalt themselves will be humbled, and all who humble themselves will be exalted."

Notice what you think and feel as you read the gospel.

Jesus puts people directly in touch with God, bypassing religious leaders and teachers who are often motivated by wealth and status. Instead, he says, come to God. God is your Teacher and your Father. You have one Messiah. Serve others with humility.

Pray as you are led for yourself and others.

"Lord Jesus Christ, grant me true humility of heart and mind. I pray also for those I serve . . ." (Continue in your own words.)

Listen to Jesus.

I am very happy that you come to me to learn and be loved. I grant you what you seek, my friend. What else is Jesus saying to you?

Ask God to show you how to live today.

"I cannot see the road ahead of me, Jesus. Walk with me and light my way. Amen."

Monday, November 6, 2017

Know that God is present with you and ready to converse.

"God, you are the object of all my longing. Instruct me by your Word so that I may know you and love you more and more."

Read the gospel: Luke 14:12–14.

Jesus said also to the one who had invited him, "When you give a luncheon or a dinner, do not invite your friends or your brothers or your relatives or rich neighbors, in case they may invite you in return, and you would be repaid. But when you give a banquet, invite the poor, the crippled, the lame, and the blind. And you will be blessed, because they cannot repay you, for you will be repaid at the resurrection of the righteous."

Notice what you think and feel as you read the gospel.

Jesus turns human social gatherings upside down. Do not invite the pretty people you want to impress and who will invite you in return. Instead, invite the poor, the crippled, the blind—those people who cannot pay you back. You will be repaid at the resurrection.

Pray as you are led for yourself and others.

"Lord, I, too, have wanted to impress others. Turn my attention to caring for the poor, the hungry, the hurting. I pray for them . . ." (Continue in your own words.)

Listen to Jesus.

To serve my people is a blessing, beloved disciple, more than you can know. Look for me among them. What else is Jesus saying to you?

Ask God to show you how to live today.

"Lord, when I look past a person, redirect my line of sight. Let me see you in every person I meet. Amen."

Tuesday, November 7, 2017

Know that God is present with you and ready to converse.

"Lord, I know you are here with me; let me not take you for granted. Let your Spirit rest upon me as I ponder your Word."

Read the gospel: Luke 14:15–24.

One of the dinner guests, on hearing this, said to him, "Blessed is anyone who will eat bread in the kingdom of God!" Then Jesus said to him, "Someone gave a great dinner and invited many. At the time for the dinner he sent his slave to say to those who had been invited, 'Come; for everything is ready now.' But they all alike began to make excuses. The first said to him, 'I have bought a piece of land, and I must go out and see it; please accept my apologies.' Another said, 'I have bought five yoke of oxen, and I am going to try them out; please accept my apologies.' Another said, 'I have just been married, and therefore I cannot come.' So the slave returned and reported this to his master. Then the owner of the house became angry and said to his slave, 'Go out at once into the streets and lanes of the town and bring in the poor, the crippled, the blind, and the lame.' And the slave said, 'Sir, what you ordered has been done, and there is still room.' Then the master said to the slave, 'Go out into the roads and lanes, and compel people to come in, so that my house may be filled. For I tell you, none of those who were invited will taste my dinner.'"

Notice what you think and feel as you read the gospel.

Jesus speaks of all the excuses people give instead of coming into the kingdom of God. Because the invited guests will not come to the dinner, the master of the house sends his servants to bring in the poor, the crippled, and the blind. They will eat his dinner.

Pray as you are led for yourself and others.

"Lord, knock down all my defenses and everything that hinders me from loving and serving you completely. I place myself in your loving care. I also place in your care all those you have given me . . . ." (Continue in your own words.)

Listen to Jesus.

Have no fear of the future, dear friend, and make no excuses to not follow me. You will always find me near you, and I will help you prepare for the marriage supper of the Lamb. What else is Jesus saying to you?

Ask God to show you how to live today.

"Make me mindful of making excuses, Master, and give me courage simply to act as one who follows you. I am yours, Lord. Amen."

Wednesday, November 8, 2017

Know that God is present with you and ready to converse.

"Lord of Hosts, Creator and Savior, your servants love you and learn your virtues. Teach me."

Read the gospel: Luke 14:25–33.

Now large crowds were travelling with him; and Jesus turned and said to them, "Whoever comes to me and does not hate father and mother, wife and children, brothers and sisters, yes, and even life itself, cannot be my disciple. Whoever does not carry the cross and follow me cannot be my disciple. For which of you, intending to build a tower, does not first sit down and estimate the cost, to see whether he has enough to complete it? Otherwise, when he has laid a foundation and is not able to finish, all who see it will begin to ridicule him, saying, 'This fellow began to build and was not able to finish.' Or what king, going out to wage war against another king, will not sit down first and consider whether he is able with ten thousand to oppose the one who comes against him with twenty thousand? If he cannot, then, while the other is still far away, he sends a delegation and asks for the terms of peace. So therefore, none of you can become my disciple if you do not give up all your possessions."

Notice what you think and feel as you read the gospel.

Jesus seeks followers who are completely committed to him and his way of the cross. He exhorts us to be realistic about it, to count the cost, which includes forsaking people, possessions, and even life itself to follow him.

Pray as you are led for yourself and others.

"Lord, I am still learning to forsake all. Today I give you everything—those I love, those you have given me, all I possess, my talents, my thoughts, my words, and my deeds . . ." (Continue in your own words.)

Listen to Jesus.

I can use you, beloved disciple, and teach you to forsake all. Come with me. What else is Jesus saying to you?

Ask God to show you how to live today.

"If you lead me, Lord, I will follow. Let me venture into the unknown with holy expectations. What lies ahead? Amen."

Thursday, November 9, 2017
Dedication of the Lateran Basilica in Rome

Know that God is present with you and ready to converse.

"Our Father, heaven cannot contain you. You are Spirit, the very Spirit that raised Jesus Christ from the dead, present with me now."

Read the gospel: John 2:13–22.

The Passover of the Jews was near, and Jesus went up to Jerusalem. In the temple he found people selling cattle, sheep, and doves, and the money-changers seated at their tables. Making a whip of cords, he drove all of them out of the temple, both the sheep and the cattle. He also poured out the coins of the money-changers and overturned their tables. He told those who were selling the doves, "Take these things out of here! Stop making my Father's house a market-place!" His disciples remembered that it was written, "Zeal for your house will consume me." The Jews then said to him, "What sign can you show us for doing this?" Jesus answered them, "Destroy this temple, and in three days I will raise it up." The Jews then said, "This temple has been under construction for forty-six years, and will you raise it up in three days?" But he was speaking of the temple of his body. After he was raised from the dead, his disciples remembered that he had said this; and they believed the scripture and the word that Jesus had spoken.

Notice what you think and feel as you read the gospel.

Jesus shows anger in this passage because people are using God to make money and enrich themselves. He drives the animals out of the temple and overturns the tables, for they have made a marketplace out of his Father's house. Then he speaks of the temple of his body, how it will be raised from the dead in three days. Only later would his disciples understand.

Pray as you are led for yourself and others.

"Lord, let me serve you without greed or selfishness. I don't trust my own motives. Shine your light in me . . ." (Continue in your own words.)

Listen to Jesus.

I have many things to tell you, beloved. Come to me with the matters that weigh on your heart, all your desires, all your secrets. I will sanctify your way. What else is Jesus saying to you?

Ask God to show you how to live today.

"Risen Jesus, I surrender to you. Help me to trust you in everything, for you love me, know me, and will guide me as is best. Thank you, my God. Amen."

Friday, November 10, 2017

Know that God is present with you and ready to converse.

"Lord, write your Word in my heart. I come joyfully into your presence and receive you here."

Read the gospel: Luke 16:1–8.

Then Jesus said to the disciples, "There was a rich man who had a manager, and charges were brought to him that this man was squandering his property. So he summoned him and said to him, 'What is this that I hear about you? Give me an account of your management, because you cannot be my manager any longer.' Then the manager said to himself, 'What will I do, now that my master is taking the position away from me? I am not strong enough to dig, and I am ashamed to beg. I have decided what to do so that, when I am dismissed as manager, people may welcome me into their homes.' So, summoning his master's debtors one by one, he asked the first, 'How much do you owe my master?' He answered, 'A hundred jugs of olive oil.' He said to him, 'Take your bill, sit down quickly, and make it fifty.' Then he asked another, 'And how much do you owe?' He replied, 'A hundred containers of wheat.' He said to him, 'Take your bill and make it eighty.' And his master commended the dishonest manager because he had acted shrewdly; for the children of this age are more shrewd in dealing with their own generation than are the children of light."

Notice what you think and feel as you read the gospel.

Jesus uses this unusual parable of the dishonest manager to teach his disciples a spiritual lesson. What is he teaching? That the children of light should be as shrewd in spiritual things as the ungodly are in worldly things. As the children of light, we, too, will have to account to our Master how we have used the resources we have been given.

Pray as you are led for yourself and others.

"Lord, let your meaning and your message go deep in me. I pray for the dishonest and the wasteful, especially those in positions of authority. I pray also for those you have given me . . ." (Continue in your own words.)

Listen to Jesus.

Being a child of the light requires awareness. Take time with me to learn my ways. Be prudent. Do what you know is right. What else is Jesus saying to you?

Ask God to show you how to live today.

"Lord, let me be a serious disciple, prudent in my service of you and others. Let me bring honor to you, Father in heaven. Amen."

Saturday, November 11, 2017

Know that God is present with you and ready to converse.

"Jesus, my constant companion, I am here to encounter you by your Spirit and your Word. Lead me, Lord."

Read the gospel: Luke 16:9–15.

Jesus said, "And I tell you, make friends for yourselves by means of dishonest wealth so that when it is gone, they may welcome you into the eternal homes.

"Whoever is faithful in a very little is faithful also in much; and whoever is dishonest in a very little is dishonest also in much. If then you have not been faithful with the dishonest wealth, who will entrust to you the true riches? And if you have not been faithful with what belongs to another, who will give you what is your own? No slave can serve two masters; for a slave will either hate the one and love the other, or be devoted to the one and despise the other. You cannot serve God and wealth."

The Pharisees, who were lovers of money, heard all this, and they ridiculed him. So he said to them, "You are those who justify yourselves in the sight of others; but God knows your hearts; for what is prized by human beings is an abomination in the sight of God."

Notice what you think and feel as you read the gospel.

Ending the parable of the dishonest steward, Jesus begins by urging his hearers to manage worldly wealth wisely and generously so they may obtain the true wealth of eternal life. You cannot cheat the system and serve two masters, God and wealth. One excludes the other. It's all about our hearts. God knows our hearts.

Pray as you are led for yourself and others.

"Lord, I ask you for a single eye dedicated to seeking God and all that pleases God. Let God alone be my treasure. I pray the same for all those you have given me . . ." (Continue in your own words.)

Listen to Jesus.

I am glad that my Father has given you to me, beloved. Thank you for loving me. Know that I love you always and will never abundon you on the road. What else is Jesus saying to you?

Ask God to show you how to live today.

"If I am tempted to be dishonest in any way today, Lord, arrest me by your Spirit and let me receive your grace to resist sin. Thank you for loving me. Amen."

Sunday, November 12, 2017
Thirty-Second Sunday in Ordinary Time

Know that God is present with you and ready to converse.

How strange and wonderful that Almighty God—the Trinity and the Creator—loves us. God does not need us, but God loves us. Jesus Christ reveals that love in everything he said and did. The gospels tell this story of the greatest love ever known. By the gospels, we can know the God who loves us so much.

"Lord, I accept your great gift of love and seek to know you better through your holy Word."

Read the gospel: Matthew 25:1–13.

Jesus said, "Then the kingdom of heaven will be like this. Ten brides-maids took their lamps and went to meet the bridegroom. Five of them were foolish, and five were wise. When the foolish took their lamps, they took no oil with them; but the wise took flasks of oil with their lamps. As the bridegroom was delayed, all of them became drowsy and slept. But at midnight there was a shout, 'Look! Here is the bridegroom! Come out to meet him.' Then all those bridesmaids got up and trimmed their lamps. The foolish said to the wise, 'Give us some of your oil, for our lamps are going out.' But the wise replied, 'No! there will not be enough for you and for us; you had better go to the dealers and buy some for yourselves.' And while they went to buy it, the bridegroom came, and those who were ready went with him into the wedding banquet; and the door was shut. Later the other bridesmaids came also, saying, 'Lord, lord, open to us.' But he replied, 'Truly I tell you, I do not know you.' Keep awake therefore, for you know neither the day nor the hour."

Notice what you think and feel as you read the gospel.

The master tells the foolish bridesmaids, "I do not know you." The oil they lack is knowledge of God. Keeping awake means persisting in seek-ing closeness to God. Then we will be welcomed at the wedding banquet of the bridegroom.

Pray as you are led for yourself and others.

"You are present in all things, Lord, but we do not always see you. Let me see you and know you more and more. I pray that those you have given me also see you operating in their lives . . ." (Continue in your own words.)

Listen to Jesus.

The invisible things of God are far more valuable than the things you experience with your senses. My friend, I would like to give you something of value today. What would you like? What else is Jesus saying to you?

Ask God to show you how to live today.

"Faithful Lord and Savior, keep me awake today, watching for you. Amen."

Monday, November 13, 2017

Know that God is present with you and ready to converse.

"Lord, speak plainly to your disciple for I am here to understand you and obey."

Read the gospel: Luke 17:1–6.

Jesus said to his disciples, "Occasions for stumbling are bound to come, but woe to anyone by whom they come! It would be better for you if a millstone were hung around your neck and you were thrown into the sea than for you to cause one of these little ones to stumble. Be on your guard! If another disciple sins, you must rebuke the offender, and if there is repentance, you must forgive. And if the same person sins against you seven times a day, and turns back to you seven times and says, 'I repent,' you must forgive."

The apostles said to the Lord, "Increase our faith!" The Lord replied, "If you had faith the size of a mustard seed, you could say to this mulberry tree, 'Be uprooted and planted in the sea,' and it would obey you."

Notice what you think and feel as you read the gospel.

Jesus warns his disciples to avoid being the occasion of stumbling for others. We are to be on our guard and full of forgiveness. Jesus does not talk about the power of much faith. He talks about the power of a little faith acted upon.

Pray as you are led for yourself and others.

"Lord, let me act on my little faith. Let me accomplish through prayer and action great things for those you have given me . . ." (Continue in your own words.)

Listen to Jesus.

My way of love always involves others, dear disciple. Love the others in your life and widen the circle of love. Let your love go deeper than before. Act on it. What else is Jesus saying to you?

Ask God to show you how to live today.

"Lord, make me an instrument of your love. Give me occasions to support, lift up, and help others. Amen."

Tuesday, November 14, 2017

Know that God is present with you and ready to converse.
"Lord, I welcome you into my heart. What word have you for me today?"

Read the gospel: Luke 17:7–10.
Jesus said, "Who among you would say to your slave who has just come in from ploughing or tending sheep in the field, 'Come here at once and take your place at the table'? Would you not rather say to him, 'Prepare supper for me, put on your apron and serve me while I eat and drink; later you may eat and drink'? Do you thank the slave for doing what was commanded? So you also, when you have done all that you were ordered to do, say, 'We are worthless slaves; we have done only what we ought to have done!'"

Notice what you think and feel as you read the gospel.
These words of Jesus strip us of all pride in our accomplishments. Our assignment and our job is simply to serve. If we have done that, we have done only what we ought to do. What's the merit in that?

Pray as you are led for yourself and others.
"Lord, you teach faithful service in humility. Let me serve you and others humbly. I pray for . . ." (Continue in your own words.)

Listen to Jesus.
I love the humble, beloved, and give to them my greatest blessings. Learn humility. Follow me. What else is Jesus saying to you?

Ask God to show you how to live today.
"Nothing I do for you today is my doing alone. You work in me and through me. I give you all the glory and thank you for letting me do anything for you. Amen."

Wednesday, November 15, 2017

Know that God is present with you and ready to converse.
"Merciful God, show me your glory, your power by your Word."

Read the gospel: Luke 17:11–19.
On the way to Jerusalem Jesus was going through the region between Samaria and Galilee. As he entered a village, ten lepers approached him.

Keeping their distance, they called out, saying, "Jesus, Master, have mercy on us!" When he saw them, he said to them, "Go and show yourselves to the priests." And as they went, they were made clean. Then one of them, when he saw that he was healed, turned back, praising God with a loud voice. He prostrated himself at Jesus' feet and thanked him. And he was a Samaritan. Then Jesus asked, "Were not ten made clean? But the other nine, where are they? Was none of them found to return and give praise to God except this foreigner?" Then he said to him, "Get up and go on your way; your faith has made you well."

Notice what you think and feel as you read the gospel.

Jesus shows mercy to the ten lepers, healing them. One of them returns and throws himself on his face to thank Jesus. Jesus asks about the other nine. Aren't they grateful for their healing?

Pray as you are led for yourself and others.

"Lord, you give me everything. I thank you for all you have given me . . ." (Continue in your own words.)

Listen to Jesus.

You are a jewel in my sight, beloved. I love to shower you with favors. Thank you for taking time with me. What else is Jesus saying to you?

Ask God to show you how to live today.

"What ways can I act today to show gratitude to you and to others? Prompt me, Lord, with praise and thanksgiving, for I am your own. Amen."

Thursday, November 16, 2017

Know that God is present with you and ready to converse.

"Lord, gather me into your kingdom. I seek you in your Word."

Read the gospel: Luke 17:20–25.

Once Jesus was asked by the Pharisees when the kingdom of God was coming, and he answered, "The kingdom of God is not coming with things that can be observed; nor will they say, 'Look, here it is!' or 'There it is!' For, in fact, the kingdom of God is among you."

Then he said to the disciples, "The days are coming when you will long to see one of the days of the Son of Man, and you will not see it. They will say to you, 'Look there!' or 'Look here!' Do not go, do not set off in pursuit. For as the lightning flashes and lights up the sky from one side to the other, so will the Son of Man be in his day. But first he must endure much suffering and be rejected by this generation."

Notice what you think and feel as you read the gospel.

Jesus says the coming of the kingdom is not observable. It is not here or there. It is present now among us. Others will claim it is here or there, but we shouldn't fall for it. Jesus, rejected in this world by those he came to save, will return like a flash of lightning, visible to all.

Pray as you are led for yourself and others.

"I long to see you, Jesus. Come quickly, Lord. Prepare me and those you have given me for your glorious return . . ." (Continue in your own words.)

Listen to Jesus.

In the meantime, servant, occupy your time in the work of the kingdom of God. It is pleasant work for it is my work and the work of our Father. It is the work of love. What else is Jesus saying to you?

Ask God to show you how to live today.

"Give me that work, Lord, and let me rejoice in doing it with you by my side. Thank you. Amen."

Friday, November 17, 2017

Know that God is present with you and ready to converse.

"Lord, you are mystery and you speak of mysteries to me. Help me to understand what you would have me understand."

Read the gospel: Luke 17:26–37.

Jesus said, "Just as it was in the days of Noah, so too it will be in the days of the Son of Man. They were eating and drinking, and marrying and being given in marriage, until the day Noah entered the ark, and the flood came and destroyed all of them. Likewise, just as it was in the days of Lot: they were eating and drinking, buying and selling, planting and building, but on the day that Lot left Sodom, it rained fire and sulphur from heaven and destroyed all of them—it will be like that on the day that the Son of Man is revealed. On that day, anyone on the housetop who has belongings in the house must not come down to take them away; and likewise anyone in the field must not turn back. Remember

Lot's wife. Those who try to make their life secure will lose it, but those who lose their life will keep it. I tell you, on that night there will be two in one bed; one will be taken and the other left. There will be two women grinding meal together; one will be taken and the other left." Then they asked him, "Where, Lord?" He said to them, "Where the corpse is, there the vultures will gather."

Notice what you think and feel as you read the gospel.

It will be business as usual the day the Lord returns. When he does, it will be too late to prepare or get away. Those who try to save their lives will lose them; those who lose their lives will save them. When? Where? How?

Pray as you are led for yourself and others.

"I give you my life, my Jesus. Do with it what you will. I offer you this day not for myself but for the good of those you have given me . . ." (Continue in your own words.)

Listen to Jesus.

I gave my life for love of others, beloved. That is the only way to live. Come enter into my life, child. What else is Jesus saying to you?

Ask God to show you how to live today.

"Let your mysteries swirl around me today, Lord. Let me serve you unafraid, for you are my faithful friend. Glory be to the Father, to the Son, and to the Holy Spirit. Amen."

Saturday, November 18, 2017
Dedication of the Basilica of Saints Peter and Paul, Apostles

Know that God is present with you and ready to converse.

"Jesus, do you have a word for me today? Refresh me in your Spirit."

Read the gospel: Matthew 14:22–33.

Immediately Jesus made the disciples get into the boat and go on ahead to the other side, while he dismissed the crowds. And after he had dismissed the crowds, he went up the mountain by himself to pray. When evening came, he was there alone, but by this time the boat, battered by the waves, was far from the land, for the wind was against them. And early in the morning he came walking towards them on the lake. But when the disciples saw him walking on the lake, they were terrified, saying, "It is a ghost!" And they cried out in fear. But immediately Jesus spoke to them and said, "Take heart, it is I; do not be afraid."

Peter answered him, "Lord, if it is you, command me to come to you on the water." He said, "Come." So Peter got out of the boat, started walking on the water, and came towards Jesus. But when he noticed the strong wind, he became frightened, and beginning to sink, he cried out, "Lord, save me!" Jesus immediately reached out his hand and caught him, saying to him, "You of little faith, why did you doubt?" When they got into the boat, the wind ceased. And those in the boat worshipped him, saying, "Truly you are the Son of God."

Notice what you think and feel as you read the gospel.

Peter doubts Jesus even while he is walking on the water toward him. Safe in the boat, Peter and all the disciples worship Jesus as the Son of God.

Pray as you are led for yourself and others.

"Lord, why do I doubt? Because, like Peter, I am flesh and blood. Help me to walk to you by faith, not doubting, though the storm mounts. I pray also for faith for those you have given me. Jesus, save us . . ." (Continue in your own words.)

Listen to Jesus.

I am with you, beloved. Because you are mine, I am your Savior in all your circumstances. Look to God in prayer. Look to me. What else is Jesus saying to you?

Ask God to show you how to live today.

"When I start to sink down in doubt today, my Jesus, show me your hand stretched out toward me. Let me come to you. Amen."

Sunday, November 19
Thirty-Third Sunday in Ordinary Time

Know that God is present with you and ready to converse.

Jesus Christ taught a spiritual way, but his way involves being in a world that opposes us as it opposed him. What does Jesus ask of us? Love for God and others. That love expresses itself in faithful and courageous service to God and others.

"Lord, I am not worthy that you should enter under my roof, yet you are here with me, glorious in your holy Word."

Read the gospel: Matthew 25:14–30.

Jesus said, "For it is as if a man, going on a journey, summoned his slaves and entrusted his property to them; to one he gave five talents, to another two, to another one, to each according to his ability. Then he went away. The one who had received the five talents went off at once and traded with them, and made five more talents. In the same way, the one who had the two talents made two more talents. But the one who had received the one talent went off and dug a hole in the ground and hid his master's money. After a long time the master of those slaves came and settled accounts with them. Then the one who had received the five talents came forward, bringing five more talents, saying, 'Master, you handed over to me five talents; see, I have made five talents.' His master said to him, 'Well done, good and trustworthy slave; you have been trustworthy in a few things, I will put you in charge of many things; enter into the joy of your master.' And the one with the two talents also came forward, saying, 'Master, you handed over to me two talents; see, I have made two more talents.' His master said to him, 'Well done, good and trustworthy slave; you have been trustworthy in a few things, I will put you in charge of many things; enter into the joy of your master.' Then the one who had received the one talent also came forward, saying, 'Master, I knew that you were a harsh man, reaping where you did not sow, and gathering where you did not scatter seed; so I was afraid, and I went and hid your talent in the ground. Here you have what is yours.' But his master replied, 'You wicked and lazy slave! You knew, did you, that I reap where I did not sow, and gather where I did not scatter? Then you ought to have invested my money with the bankers, and on my return I would have received what was my own with interest. So take the talent from him, and give it to the one with the ten talents. For to all those who have, more will be given, and they will have an abundance; but from those who have nothing, even what they have will be taken away. As for this worthless slave, throw him into the outer darkness, where there will be weeping and gnashing of teeth.'"

Notice what you think and feel as you read the gospel.

In this parable, the master commends the faithful servants, "well done, good and trustworthy slave" for they have invested his resources and made more of them. He invites them to enter into his joy. Why did the slave with one talent fail the master?

Pray as you are led for yourself and others.

"Lord, I am just a person. Help me to make the most of the gifts you have given me, even if it is just a single gift. Let me understand your spiritual economics, so that I and all those you have given me can enter into the joy of the Lord . . ." (Continue in your own words.)

Listen to Jesus.

Faith, not fear, will prosper you, beloved. Believe in God's goodness and generosity and imitate God. What else is Jesus saying to you?

Ask God to show you how to live today.

"Lord, if I am being stingy, correct me today. If I am fearful, correct me. I offer myself to you, Good Shepherd. Amen."

Monday, November 20, 2017

Know that God is present with you and ready to converse.

"Son of David, have mercy on me. Do not pass me by."

Read the gospel: Luke 18:35–43.

As Jesus approached Jericho, a blind man was sitting by the roadside begging. When he heard a crowd going by, he asked what was happening. They told him, "Jesus of Nazareth is passing by." Then he shouted, "Jesus, Son of David, have mercy on me!" Those who were in front sternly ordered him to be quiet; but he shouted even more loudly, "Son of David, have mercy on me!" Jesus stood still and ordered the man to be brought to him; and when he came near, he asked him, "What do you want me to do for you?" He said, "Lord, let me see again." Jesus said to him, "Receive your sight; your faith has saved you." Immediately he regained his sight and followed him, glorifying God; and all the people, when they saw it, praised God.

Notice what you think and feel as you read the gospel.

The blind man shouts to Jesus because he believes Jesus can heal him. When Jesus heals him, everyone glorifies God.

Pray as you are led for yourself and others.

"God, give me persistent faith like the blind man, for I want to follow you and glorify you in my life. I entrust to you all these people . . ." (Continue in your own words.)

Listen to Jesus.

I will give you whatever you desire, whatever is good for you. Give yourself to me, and I will give myself to you, beloved. What else is Jesus saying to you?

Ask God to show you how to live today.

"You are glorious, loving God. How may I persevere in loving and praising you today? Amen."

Tuesday, November 21, 2017

Know that God is present with you and ready to converse.

"Jesus, you are always aware of whoever wants you. You have stopped here for me this moment. Thank you, Jesus."

Read the gospel: Luke 19:1–10.

Jesus entered Jericho and was passing through it. A man was there named Zacchaeus; he was a chief tax-collector and was rich. He was trying to see who Jesus was, but on account of the crowd he could not, because he was short in stature. So he ran ahead and climbed a sycamore tree to see him, because he was going to pass that way. When Jesus came to the place, he looked up and said to him, "Zacchaeus, hurry and come down; for I must stay at your house today." So he hurried down and was happy to welcome him. All who saw it began to grumble and said, "He has gone to be the guest of one who is a sinner." Zacchaeus stood there and said to the Lord, "Look, half of my possessions, Lord, I will give to the poor; and if I have defrauded anyone of anything, I will pay back four times as much." Then Jesus said to him, "Today salvation has come to this house, because he too is a son of Abraham. For the Son of Man came to seek out and to save the lost."

Notice what you think and feel as you read the gospel.

Zacchaeus, a sinner, desires to see Jesus, and Jesus changes his life. Jesus sought him and saved him. Zacchaeus promises to make full amends for his sins.

Pray as you are led for yourself and others.

"Lord, I, too, wish to make amends for my sins. Lead me in doing so, and let it be on behalf of those you have given me . . ." (Continue in your own words.)

Listen to Jesus.

Whatever you give to another in my name, I will return sevenfold. I will load you with blessings because you are my child, my beloved, my friend, my disciple. What else is Jesus saying to you?

Ask God to show you how to live today.

"Let me remember my resolve to make amends for my sins today. By your grace, I will do it. Thank you, Savior. Amen."

Wednesday, November 22, 2017

Know that God is present with you and ready to converse.

"Lord, you dwell in awesome majesty and come to me with awesome love. You are holy. I will listen to your voice now, your Word."

Read the gospel: Luke 19:11–28.

As the people were listening to this, Jesus went on to tell a parable, because he was near Jerusalem, and because they supposed that the kingdom of God was to appear immediately. So he said, "A nobleman went to a distant country to get royal power for himself and then return. He summoned ten of his slaves, and gave them ten pounds, and said to them, 'Do business with these until I come back.' But the citizens of his country hated him and sent a delegation after him, saying, 'We do not want this man to rule over us.' When he returned, having received royal power, he ordered these slaves, to whom he had given the money, to be summoned so that he might find out what they had gained by trading. The first came forward and said, 'Lord, your pound has made ten more pounds.' He said to him, 'Well done, good slave! Because you have been trustworthy in a very small thing, take charge of ten cities.' Then the second came, saying, 'Lord, your pound has made five pounds.' He said to him, 'And you, rule over five cities.' Then the other came, saying, 'Lord, here is your pound. I wrapped it up in a piece of cloth, for I was afraid of you, because you are a harsh man; you take what you did not deposit, and reap what you did not sow.' He said to him, 'I will judge you by your own words, you wicked slave! You knew, did you, that I was a harsh man, taking what I did not deposit and reaping what I did not sow? Why then did you not put my money into the bank? Then when I returned, I could have collected it with interest.' He said to the bystanders, 'Take the pound from him and give it to the one who has ten pounds.' (And they said to him, 'Lord, he has ten pounds!') 'I tell you, to all those who have, more will be given; but from those who have nothing, even what they have will be taken away. But as for these enemies of mine who did not want me to be king over them—bring them here and slaughter them in my presence.'"

After he had said this, he went on ahead, going up to Jerusalem.

Notice what you think and feel as you read the gospel.
Jesus judges the wicked slave by his own words. The man's excuses are his undoing. Jesus, the King, shall be the just judge of all.

Pray as you are led for yourself and others.
"Lord, I make excuses. Forgive me. Let me turn away from excuses and use the gifts you have given me for the good of others, especially those you have given me . . ." (Continue in your own words.)

Listen to Jesus.
Beloved disciple, you are right to take my words to heart. I am speaking to you because I love you and want your best both now and hereafter. What else is Jesus saying to you?

Ask God to show you how to live today.
"Call my attention to my phony excuses for not doing my best in my work for you and for others. Let me lean upon your strength to do what you have put before me today and tomorrow. Amen."

Thursday, November 23, 2017

Know that God is present with you and ready to converse.
"Lord, you are with me now. Let me recognize you in your Word and in your Spirit that I may know your peace."

Read the gospel: Luke 19:41–44.
As he came near and saw the city, Jesus wept over it, saying, "If you, even you, had only recognized on this day the things that make for peace! But now they are hidden from your eyes. Indeed, the days will come upon you, when your enemies will set up ramparts around you and surround you, and hem you in on every side. They will crush you to the ground, you and your children within you, and they will not leave within you one stone upon another; because you did not recognize the time of your visitation from God."

Notice what you think and feel as you read the gospel.

Jesus knows of the future destruction of Jerusalem. He weeps that its inhabitants do not recognize that he is God among them. That failure to recognize shall be the cause of their destruction.

Pray as you are led for yourself and others.

"Lord, you are love and mercy, yet we can be blind to you. Let me take your words deep into my heart and be converted. I pray for all those who do not recognize you . . ." (Continue in your own words.)

Listen to Jesus.

Human history is full of violence and there is reason to fear destruction in many forms. But you need not fear as long as you cling to me. Love God and you will also love and serve others. What else is Jesus saying to you?

Ask God to show you how to live today.

"Help me to be brave, trusting you for safety for myself and those I love. Let me serve in your peace, Lord. I love you. Amen."

Friday, November 24, 2017

Know that God is present with you and ready to converse.

"Shine your light upon your Word, Holy Spirit. Let it draw me in and transform me."

Read the gospel: Luke 19:45–48.

Then Jesus entered the temple and began to drive out those who were selling things there; and he said, "It is written,

> 'My house shall be a house of prayer';
>   but you have made it a den of robbers."

Every day he was teaching in the temple. The chief priests, the scribes, and the leaders of the people kept looking for a way to kill him; but they did not find anything they could do, for all the people were spellbound by what they heard.

Notice what you think and feel as you read the gospel.

Jesus teaches the people every day, and they love him. Those who oppose him, the religious leaders, cannot do anything to stop him, but they want to kill him.

Pray as you are led for yourself and others.

"Evil lies in human hearts, even in those who profess to be good and holy. Jealousy, revenge, injustice, fear, self-preservation—all these and more cause us to oppose good, to oppose the will of God . . ." (Continue in your own words.)

Listen to Jesus.

Make your house a house of prayer, my child. I want to be with you. What else is Jesus saying to you?

Ask God to show you how to live today.

"Interrupt my day, Lord, with opportunities to turn to you, to speak to you, to hear from you. Teach me to pray. Amen."

Saturday, November 25, 2017

Know that God is present with you and ready to converse.

"Teacher, you love me always. I love you, too, and I give myself to your instruction now."

Read the gospel: Luke 20:27–40.

Some Sadducees, those who say there is no resurrection, came to Jesus and asked him a question, "Teacher, Moses wrote for us that if a man's brother dies, leaving a wife but no children, the man shall marry the widow and raise up children for his brother. Now there were seven brothers; the first married, and died childless; then the second and the third married her, and so in the same way all seven died childless. Finally the woman also died. In the resurrection, therefore, whose wife will the woman be? For the seven had married her."

Jesus said to them, "Those who belong to this age marry and are given in marriage; but those who are considered worthy of a place in that age and in the resurrection from the dead neither marry nor are given in marriage. Indeed they cannot die any more, because they are like angels and are children of God, being children of the resurrection. And the fact that the dead are raised Moses himself showed, in the story about the bush, where he speaks of the Lord as the God of Abraham, the God of Isaac, and the God of Jacob. Now he is God not of the dead, but of the living; for to him all of them are alive." Then some of the scribes answered, "Teacher, you have spoken well." For they no longer dared to ask him another question.

Notice what you think and feel as you read the gospel.

The Sadducees have cooked up an impossible question, seeking to confound Jesus on the topic of the resurrection. Jesus rejects their assumptions and affirms the resurrection of the dead from scripture and from his own knowledge. We will be like angels in the age to come.

Pray as you are led for yourself and others.

"Jesus, you speak with such confidence. I believe you are the Son of God. Thank you for loving us so much. Let your truth go out to all the world . . ." (Continue in your own words.)

Listen to Jesus.

The present age is subject to time. The age to come will remain forever. Come into the kingdom now, beloved, and spend your time with me. What else is Jesus saying to you?

Ask God to show you how to live today.

"Lord, you are good. How can I express to others that they, too, are beloved of God? Help me do that, please. Amen."

Sunday, November 26, 2017
Christ the King

Know that God is present with you and ready to converse.

"Your Father has made you king of heaven and earth, Jesus Christ. You are my master, Lord. I welcome you now."

Read the gospel: Matthew 25:31–46.

Jesus said, "When the Son of Man comes in his glory, and all the angels with him, then he will sit on the throne of his glory. All the nations will be gathered before him, and he will separate people one from another as a shepherd separates the sheep from the goats, and he will put the sheep at his right hand and the goats at the left. Then the king will say to those at his right hand, 'Come, you that are blessed by my Father, inherit the kingdom prepared for you from the foundation of the world; for I was hungry and you gave me food, I was thirsty and you gave me something to drink, I was a stranger and you welcomed me, I was naked and you gave me clothing, I was sick and you took care of me, I was in prison and you visited me.' Then the righteous will answer him, 'Lord, when was it that we saw you hungry and gave you food, or thirsty and gave you something to drink? And when was it that we saw you a stranger and welcomed you, or naked and gave you clothing? And when was it that we saw you sick or in prison and visited you?' And the king will answer them, 'Truly I tell you, just as you did it to one of the least of these who are members of my family, you did it to me.' Then he will say to those at his left hand, 'You that are accursed, depart from me into the eternal fire prepared for the devil and his angels; for I was hungry and you gave me no food, I was thirsty and you gave me nothing to drink, I was a stranger and you did not welcome me, naked and you did not give me clothing, sick and in prison and you did not visit me.' Then they also will answer, 'Lord, when was it that we saw you hungry or thirsty or a stranger or naked or sick or in prison, and did not take care of you?' Then he will answer them, 'Truly I tell you, just as you did not do it to one of the least of these, you did not do it to me.' And these will go away into eternal punishment, but the righteous into eternal life."

Notice what you think and feel as you read the gospel.

Our time on earth has repercussions in eternity. Jesus says that what we do now makes all the difference for us forever. What is most important? Caring for those in need, giving them what they need. When we do this for anyone in need, we are doing it to him.

Pray as you are led for yourself and others.

"Jesus, King, you invite me into your kingdom through the lowly door of service to those in need. There are so many suffering. Let me serve them today, tomorrow, and always . . ." (Continue in your own words.)

Listen to Jesus.

I will give you opportunities to serve the poor. Beloved disciple, look for me in them. I will give you joy. What else is Jesus saying to you?

Ask God to show you how to live today.

"Lord, I have good intentions. Please help me translate them into concrete actions of service. What can I do today? Amen."

Monday, November 27, 2017

Know that God is present with you and ready to converse.

"Lord, you look upon the heart. Come into my heart and speak to me today."

Read the gospel: Luke 21:1–4.

Jesus looked up and saw rich people putting their gifts into the treasury; he also saw a poor widow put in two small copper coins. He said, "Truly I tell you, this poor widow has put in more than all of them; for all of them have contributed out of their abundance, but she out of her poverty has put in all she had to live on."

Notice what you think and feel as you read the gospel.

God sees us differently than people do. Jesus commends the poor widow for her generosity even though her gift was very small.

Pray as you are led for yourself and others.

"Jesus, give me the generous heart of the poor widow. I offer all I have and am to you. I offer myself for the good of all those you have given me . . ." (Continue in your own words.)

Listen to Jesus.

The gifts God loves are spiritual, for God is Spirit. Ask God for good things—faith, hope, love, wisdom, peace, and perseverance. Those gifts will manifest themselves in your actions. What else is Jesus saying to you?

Ask God to show you how to live today.

"Jesus, lead me to little acts of love today. Let me please you as the poor widow did. Amen."

Tuesday, November 28, 2017

Know that God is present with you and ready to converse.

"Eternal God, Creator, you come to me in time and love me for eternity."

Read the gospel: Luke 21:5–11.

When some were speaking about the temple, how it was adorned with beautiful stones and gifts dedicated to God, Jesus said, "As for these things that you see, the days will come when not one stone will be left upon another; all will be thrown down."

They asked him, "Teacher, when will this be, and what will be the sign that this is about to take place?" And he said, "Beware that you are not led astray; for many will come in my name and say, 'I am he!' and, 'The time is near!' Do not go after them.

"When you hear of wars and insurrections, do not be terrified; for these things must take place first, but the end will not follow immediately." Then he said to them, "Nation will rise against nation, and kingdom against kingdom; there will be great earthquakes, and in various places famines and plagues; and there will be dreadful portents and great signs from heaven."

Notice what you think and feel as you read the gospel.

Jesus has the long view. The things of this world, even great things like the temple in Jerusalem, will not remain. The end is coming, and it will be violent. We should not be fooled by reports of his coming or afraid of these events.

Pray as you are led for yourself and others.

"Lord, you will bring this age to an end in your own good time. Give me grace to persevere in hope and peace. I pray for those you have given me, asking for grace for them . . ." (Continue in your own words.)

Listen to Jesus.

When you appear before God in the kingdom of heaven, we will show you what a great difference your prayers have made in the lives of those the Father, Holy Spirit, and I have given you. Pray with confidence, beloved disciple. What else is Jesus saying to you?

Ask God to show you how to live today.

"Lord, thank you for allowing me to serve in your kingdom. What can I do today? Who needs my prayers? Who needs an act of kindness? Please show them to me. Amen."

Wednesday, November 29, 2017

Know that God is present with you and ready to converse.

"Jesus, your name is Wisdom. I rejoice in your presence, Lord. I rejoice in your Word."

Read the gospel: Luke 21:12–19.

Jesus said, "But before all this occurs, they will arrest you and persecute you; they will hand you over to synagogues and prisons, and you will be brought before kings and governors because of my name. This will give you an opportunity to testify. So make up your minds not to prepare your defense in advance; for I will give you words and a wisdom that none of your opponents will be able to withstand or contradict. You will be betrayed even by parents and brothers, by relatives and friends; and

they will put some of you to death. You will be hated by all because of
my name. But not a hair of your head will perish. By your endurance
you will gain your souls."

Notice what you think and feel as you read the gospel.

Jesus prepares us for the terrible times to come before the end. These
things will happen and have already begun to happen. But not a hair of
your head will perish, he says. We will gain our souls through enduring
this.

Pray as you are led for yourself and others.

"Lord, with you I can do and endure anything, for this world and life
are just the door to eternal life with you. I pray for the souls of those you
have given me . . ." (Continue in your own words.)

Listen to Jesus.

*Pray for those who are being persecuted, beloved. Pray that they know that I
am with them and thank them for their witness. They will receive glory in the
kingdom of my Father.* What else is Jesus saying to you?

Ask God to show you how to live today.

"Lord, I offer myself to you, even for persecution, because I am yours.
Give me the grace to gladly suffer in your name. Amen."

Thursday, November 30, 2017
Saint Andrew, Apostle

Know that God is present with you and ready to converse.

"Lord, you seek and find those you have chosen. You have found me
today. I praise you."

Read the gospel: Matthew 4:18–22.

As Jesus walked by the Sea of Galilee, he saw two brothers, Simon, who
is called Peter, and Andrew his brother, casting a net into the lake—for
they were fishermen. And he said to them, "Follow me, and I will make
you fish for people." Immediately they left their nets and followed him.
As he went from there, he saw two other brothers, James son of Zebedee
and his brother John, in the boat with their father Zebedee, mending
their nets, and he called them. Immediately they left the boat and their
father, and followed him.

Notice what you think and feel as you read the gospel.
Here Jesus calls his chief disciples, some of the apostles. They are fishermen. He has another job for them, he says, to fish for people. They leave their work, their nets, and their father to follow him.

Pray as you are led for yourself and others.
"Lord, give me that pure, unquestioning commitment in response to your call. I choose to follow you. Let this choice bear good fruit for all those you have given me . . ." (Continue in your own words.)

Listen to Jesus.
We are workers, my child. You do my work, and I do yours. This is the way to redeem the time. Lose yourself in loving and serving others, and find me. What else is Jesus saying to you?

Ask God to show you how to live today.
"Lord, I am grateful to you for simplifying my life with your presence. Stay with me all day as I work your will. Let me do what matters to you. Amen."

Friday, December 1, 2017

Know that God is present with you and ready to converse.
"You are near to me, living Word of God. I embrace you."

Read the gospel: Luke 21:29–33.
Then Jesus told them a parable: "Look at the fig tree and all the trees; as soon as they sprout leaves you can see for yourselves and know that summer is already near. So also, when you see these things taking place, you know that the kingdom of God is near. Truly I tell you, this generation will not pass away until all things have taken place. Heaven and earth will pass away, but my words will not pass away."

Notice what you think and feel as you read the gospel.
Do we see the leaves of the fig tree sprouting? How near to us is the coming of the kingdom of God? Jesus says all things will pass away except his words.

Pray as you are led for yourself and others.

"Glory to you, Lord Jesus Christ. All things are under your command. I place myself under your command, and I give you, too, all those you have given to me . . ." (Continue in your own words.)

Listen to Jesus.

Peace to you, beloved. Remain in my peace. What else is Jesus saying to you?

Ask God to show you how to live today.

"Lord, let me be an instrument of your peace today. Amen."

Saturday, December 2, 2017

Know that God is present with you and ready to converse.

"Wake me up, Lord, and make me alert to the Spirit of God now with me. Help me to pray."

Read the gospel: Luke 21:34–36.

Jesus said, "Be on guard so that your hearts are not weighed down with dissipation and drunkenness and the worries of this life, and that day does not catch you unexpectedly, like a trap. For it will come upon all who live on the face of the whole earth. Be alert at all times, praying that you may have the strength to escape all these things that will take place, and to stand before the Son of Man."

Notice what you think and feel as you read the gospel.

Jesus warns us against dissipation, drunkenness, and worry. These things will distract us from the day of the Lord, the last day. He tells us to be alert and pray that we may be able to stand before the Son of Man.

Pray as you are led for yourself and others.

"Lord, I am not worthy to stand before you. Wash me of my sins and make me pleasing to you. Let me avoid all things that weigh me down. Let me walk closely with you to the end . . ." (Continue in your own words.)

Listen to Jesus.

I will be with you to the end, dear disciple. I know you, and you are getting to know me. There is no end to our friendship. What else is Jesus saying to you?

Ask God to show you how to live today.

"In you, Lord, let me make a difference today. Give me ideas, give me strength, give me words, and move me to do good things. Amen."

Please Take Our Survey!
Now that you've finished reading *Sacred Reading: The 2017 Guide to Daily Prayer*, please go to **avemariapress.com/feedback** to take a brief survey about your experience. Ave Maria Press and the Apostleship of Prayer appreciate your feedback.

The Apostleship of Prayer is an international Jesuit prayer ministry that reaches more than 35 million members worldwide through its popular website, apostleshipofprayer.org, and through talks, conferences, publications, and retreats. Known as "the pope's worldwide prayer network," the Apostleship's mission is to encourage Christians to make a daily offering of themselves to the Lord in union with the Sacred Heart of Jesus.

Douglas Leonard is executive director of the Apostleship of Prayer in the United States, where he has served since 2006. He earned a bachelor's degree in English in 1976, a master's degree in English in 1977, and a PhD in English in 1981, all from the University of Wisconsin-Madison. Leonard also has served in higher education, professional development, publishing, and instructional design as an executive, writer, editor, educator, and consultant.

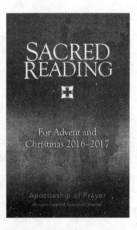